A Time to Every Purpose

"The use of planetary hours is one of the oldest techniques in Astrology, but they have been too little used by modern astrologers. Planetary hours are so clearly of value in understanding the quality of each moment of time that we all really need to look at them again. Maria Kay Simms' book is just the practical guide to their use that is needed to stimulate interest in this most ancient technique. And in her book she does this in ways that modern users can readily understand and appreciate."

—Robert Hand
Author of *Planets in Transit; Planets in Composite; Planets in Youth; Essays on Astrology;* and *Night and Day*

"Astrology is a very complicated system, and difficult to learn. Ms. Simms has extracted one component necessary for proper ritual, explained the theory behind it, and most importantly, provided a means for correct usage. This extends the value of astrology by making it more accessible to practitioners who do not wish to make astrology their specialty."

—J. Lee Lehman, Ph.D.
Horary and Electional Astrologer, Martial Artist, and Herbalist
Winner of the 1995 Marc Edmund Jones Award

"Maria Kay Simms has a rare gift for taking a complicated topic and distilling the most essential data for the reader. Whether you are a professional astrologer, a practicing Wiccan, or someone who wants to improve your timing in life, *A Time for Magick* has valuable information for you.

Whatever you want—love, health, wealth, happiness—is more likely to be achieved if you make the right moves at the right times. *A Time for Magick* shows you how to do that—quickly and easily."

—Maritha Pottenger
Author of *Complete Horoscope Interpretation* and *Planets on the Move*

"Many people don't realize, or have ignored, the powerful impact timing can have when performing magick. Maria Kay Simms, an expert in both magick and astrology, has helped reestablish the important link between magick and the planets in a way that is easy to understand and relevant to the twenty-first century. She also forges a new path by examining the meaning of the planetary hour at birth. *A Time for Magick* enables us to tap into sources of incredible power for ritual work."

—Donald Michael Kraig
Author of *Modern Magic*

About the Author

Maria Kay Simms has been an astrologer for twenty-seven years and has been actively involved in Goddess spirituality for about fifteen years. In 1991, after having studied through Third Degree in a Gardnerian/Eclectic tradition of Wicca, she became High Priestess of the Circle of the Cosmic Muse. She is the author of *The Witch's Circle*, and a number of astrology books. She blends her extensive background in astrological technique with her varied and creative experience as a ritualist to provide this new book on astrological timing for magickal practice.

To Write to the Author

If you wish to contact the author or would like more information about this book, please write to the author in care of Llewellyn Worldwide and we will forward your request. Both the author and publisher appreciate hearing from you and learning of your enjoyment of this book and how it has helped you. Llewellyn Worldwide cannot guarantee that every letter written to the author can be answered, but all will be forwarded. Please write to:

Maria Kay Simms
℅ Llewellyn Worldwide
P.O. Box 64383, Dept. 1-56718-622-X
St. Paul, MN 55164-0383, U.S.A.
Please enclose a self-addressed stamped envelope for reply,
or $1.00 to cover costs. If outside U.S.A., enclose
international postal reply coupon.

Many of Llewellyn's authors have websites with additional information and resources. For more information, please visit our website at http://www.llewellyn.com.

XI
XII
I

A
TIME
— FOR —
MAGICK

X
II

IX
III

VIII
IV

Planetary Hours
for Meditations, Rituals & Spells

MARIA KAY SIMMS

VII
V

2001
Llewellyn Publications
St. Paul, Minnesota 55164-0383, U.S.A.

VI

First Edition
First Printing, 2001

Book design by Donna Burch
Black-and-white cover art © by Kathleen Edwards
Color application by Lynne Menturweck
Cover design by Anne Marie Garrison
Editing by Andrea Neff

Coordinate and time correction data derived from ACS Mini-Atlas, courtesy of Astro Communications Services, Inc. Used by permission of the publisher.

A special thanks to Melissa Mierva for helping proofread the planetary hour tables.

Many thanks to Hollie Kilroy for producing the spiral illustration in chapter 4 and the timing illustrations in chapter 5.

Library of Congress Cataloging-in-Publication Data
Simms, Maria Kay, 1940—
    A time for magick : planetary hours for meditations, rituals & spells / Maria Kay Simms.— 1st ed.
       p. cm.
    Includes bibliographical references and index.
    ISBN 1-56718-622-X
      1. Astrology. 2. Magic. I. Title

    BF1729.M33 S56 2001
    133.5—dc21   00-067234

Llewellyn Publications
A Division of Llewellyn Worldwide, Ltd.
P.O. Box 64383, Dept. 1-56718-622-X
St. Paul, MN 55164-0383, U.S.A.
www.llewellyn.com

 Printed in the United States of America on recycled paper

Other Books by Maria Kay Simms

Millennium: Fears, Fantasies and Facts (coauthor)
(ACS, 1998)

Future Signs
(ACS, 1997)

The Witch's Circle
(Llewellyn, 1996)

Your Magical Child
(ACS, 1994)

Search for the Christmas Star (with Neil Michelsen)
(ACS, 1989)

Dial Detective
(ACS, 1988)

Twelve Wings of the Eagle
(ACS, 1988)

Acknowledgments

Many people contribute to the creation of any book, from the first spark of the idea to write it, through the developmental process, to the time it emerges in its final printed form.

Donald Michael Kraig deserves the credit for sparking that first idea for me! It was he who gave me the tip that Llewellyn wanted to do a revival of the long-out-of-print *Perpetual Planetary Hour Book* and encouraged me to propose it. He assisted once again with his prepublication review and endorsement. Thank you, Don!

Thanks to J. Lee Lehman, Ph.D., for early advice and manuscript review. Thanks also to Maritha Pottenger, Rob Hand, Skye Alexander, Silver RavenWolf, and Chic and Tabatha Cicero for prepublication reviews and thoughtful comments.

My thanks to countless friends, colleagues, and business associates for assisting me—even if you may not have realized I was often observing how the changing of the hours corresponded to our interactions!

For invaluable technical assistance, I am indebted to Arlene Kramer for Sundial; to Lois Rodden and Mark McDonough for AstroDatabank; to Esoteric Technologies and Astrolabe for Solar Fire; to Mark Pottenger for showing me how I could easily find the LMT corrections necessary to update the city lists; and to ACS for the use of ACS Mini-Atlas.

Thanks to Circle of the Cosmic Muse, I have a constant stimulation of ideas for meditation and ritual. Special thanks to Joanne O'Brien for inspiring the "Becoming Mars" meditation.

Last, but most certainly not least, comes the Llewellyn staff. I appreciate the continued encouragement of Nancy Mostad during an acquisition process delayed and interrupted while I made major life changes. During the final production of this book, Andrea Neff, my editor, has been just great in her patience and understanding, as well her strong expertise. Donna Burch was especially helpful, beyond her fine book design. To each of you, and to Lynne Menturweck, Kathleen Edwards, Anne Marie Garrison, Lisa Braun, and others whose names I do not know, my most sincere thanks!

Contents

Chapter Three
Timing by the Moon   /   59

Chapter Four
The Order and Calculation of Planetary Hours   /   79

Chapter Five
Quick Timing with an Astrological Calendar   /   179

1

Astrology: Queen of Timing

One of the great benefits you can gain through astrological knowledge is the ability to choose appropriate timing. For millennia it has been observed that the lights in the cosmos have mysterious correspondences to life on Earth, and the lights have been read as signs and portents of things to come. Astrology, more than any other practice used for divination, is truly the Queen of Timing. It generally takes more than just astrology to successfully "predict" the exact nature of an event, or the nuances of personality. For that you need context (knowledge and/or experience of the environment and mundane influences on whatever you're trying to figure out), and most likely you also need a bit of intuition. But even if a psychic may (on a good day) outdo an astrologer on *what* will happen, an astrologer is likely to do a better job picking *when* something will happen. Business people, financial analysts, and politicians, among many others, have benefited from the leverage gained from astrology's help in choosing the most propitious time to gain advantage or achieve success. Magicians, too, have used astrology to choose the most appropriate times for their workings.

The extent to which the planets and stars emit causal effects to Earth (or earthlings) is arguable. We know, of course, of the tidal pull of the Moon, and of the effects of solar flares on our weather.

We suspect that other effects might exist, but it's a far stretch to prove any causal effect akin to the "influences" claimed by astrology. Still, anyone who has seriously studied astrology knows that there is something mysteriously predictable about the ways that human personality and events on Earth correspond to cosmic cycles. The key word here is *correspond* or, as Carl Jung coined it, *synchronicity*. Observation shows that these correspondences or synchronous happenings are much more than just chance coincidences. The biblical book Genesis tells us that the lights in the sky were created as *signs* for our benefit. Certainly, causal or not, they are signs that we can read and thus learn from.

I prefer to think of the cosmos—a collective word for all the lights in the sky that we see above us, such as the stars, planets, Sun and Moon, comets, asteroids, and whatever else we may see or think we see—as our mirror. It's a magickal mirror in which we can discern the faces of our gods, the depths of our souls, and the ever-changing cycles of our lives—"As above, so below." But as we continue with the words of Hermes Tristmegistus, saying, "As within, so without," we know that the true divinity is within, as is the true responsibility for our destiny and the awesome power of choice. It is up to us, to each individual, to cause that mirror to reflect the highest and the best that we can be. "As the Universe, so the soul."

I think the highest purpose of ritual or magickal work is to seek our gods, to commune with the cosmic "mirror" and the spirits of nature in order to learn more of the divinity within ourselves and reach evermore toward personal growth in its highest expression. It has been my experience that if the purpose of my ritual or magickal working is worship—communion with the divine—it doesn't matter at all what the astrological "influences" may be at that given time. Worship transcends time and space, just as we say, or imply, that it does when we cast our circles between the worlds. I've had wonderful ritual experiences during void-of-course Moons and during the most challenging of squares and oppositions—just the type of "influences" most astrologers would tell me are unfavorable.

On the other hand, when you are working for a mundane purpose, you are connecting yourself to the mundane world with its time and space, no matter what deities you may invoke in creating your magick. In such cases, it only makes sense to give yourself all the advantage you can. Knowing the time that puts you most in sync with the signs in the sky is well worth the effort, just as it would be for any important thing you might choose to put effort into, in order to assure the most successful possible outcome of your intent.

Electional Astrology

The specific branch of astrology that involves casting a chart for a time in the future when you plan to do something is called electional astrology. The idea is that if the chart is "good" (appropriately reflecting the type of event you want to precipitate) and you manage to carry out your plans and start at the elected time, you will influence whatever you've planned to transpire according to the chart. Everything has a birth time, even an idea or a question. The reverse of electional astrology is called horary astrology, which involves casting a chart for the moment a question is asked, and then reading the chart to get your answer. This method is where astrology comes the closest to divination.

There's a "hitch" to using electional techniques, however, especially if you're a beginner. The art of electional astrology is complex, involving many interrelationships of various factors in the chart, and the rules are very strict. No matter how great the election chart is, you still have to take into account what's going on in your own natal chart, as well. I am not going to even attempt to cover electional astrology in this book. Election does not deal with psychological issues or states of spiritual development that might mitigate the interpretation of a natal chart. It just seeks to plan a time when the event is most likely to be successful.

The bibliography in this book lists some electional astrology textbooks for those of you who wish to pursue serious study. I've found that most people who are more oriented toward Wicca and magick, myself included, are disinclined to involve themselves heavily in highly technical astrology. It takes too much time! I think that it comes down to whether you want to live your life in the *now*, or live it vicariously by always looking at charts of what might or might not lie ahead. I choose, most of the time, to *be present*, so I limit my use of electional astrology to the occasional really *big* event. For the most part, when I use astrology to pick the best time for something, I use the much less complicated methods that will be covered in this book.

The most complex thing I'll cover in this book will be some hints for what I call "quick and dirty" electional astrology. These are the pieces of information that you can pick up from a quick glance at an astrological calendar.

One of the most useful timing factors is the Moon, and a chapter will be devoted to Moon signs and phases. The largest technical section of this book will focus on the ancient technique of planetary hours. This book is intended to replace Llewellyn George's long-out-of-print *Improved Perpetual Planetary Hour Book*, still widely used by magicians who can latch onto a copy.

Planetary Hours

The use of planetary hours is an ancient technique that can be dated back at least to the time of classical Greece, between 400 and 300 B.C.E. Interestingly, it is a technique that has been largely ignored by modern astrologers, and I must confess that I never even considered using it until the summer of 1994, shortly after the publication of my book *Circle of the Cosmic Muse*, which has since been republished as *The Witch's Circle*. I found myself getting a number of questions from readers who were interested in more details on how they could use astrology to time magickal acts. Of course, I could tell them about using the Moon, and I could tell them to learn how to use electional astrology. It was obvious, though, that some of my questioners were not particularly interested in pursuing such an in-depth study of astrology. They just wanted fairly easy answers that would help them focus their magick in harmony with the astrological factors at any given time.

"What techniques are accessible to a nonastrologer?" I wondered. I was aware that a planetary hour system existed, but I had not taken it seriously, because it seemed so archaic and fraught with benefic and malefic (good and evil) interpretations that are out of sync with contemporary astrological thinking. I didn't know of any astrologers who used planetary hours anymore, although I'd heard of some practitioners of magick who used them regularly. If that includes you, and you are now thinking, "Where has this woman been!", I can only plead for your patience. In presuming to revive the long-out-of-print book by Llewellyn George that you probably still use and cherish, I want to be honest about my lack of long-time personal experience with planetary hours. At the same time, I believe I have something worthwhile to contribute to the contemporary use of this technique by combining my relatively newfound use of it with my much longer experience as a working astrologer.

One major point in favor of using planetary hours is that it is a lot easier and a lot less time-consuming to consult an hour table than it is to learn how to set up a good election chart. But do the hours really work? I've never been one to believe something just because someone else told me it's true. I need to develop some sense of it through my own experience. In pursuit of more information, I looked through my own personal library and that of Astro Communications Services (ACS)[1] and found barely a definition of planetary hours, let alone any demonstrations of their use, even in books published many years ago. I vaguely remembered that I'd once seen a Llewellyn book on planetary hours, but couldn't find a copy. I knew *Dell Horoscope* magazine ran planetary hour tables for each month, so I looked at an issue, but was disturbed to find that the sunrise/sunset times were quite a bit different than those given in San Diego's newspaper, and that they were also different from the tables in *The Old Farmer's Almanac*. "How can I work with this if I can't even be sure the times are right?" I thought. I went outside to look at the ocean horizon, after making sure my watch was set to the absolutely correct time. Sure enough, the Sun sank into the sea at precisely the newspaper's time for sunset.

What accounts for the differences in time between the local newspaper and various published tables? An obvious explanation is that generalized tables for only some geographical coordinates just aren't as accurate as local timing in the actual place. I was being nitpicky, as astrologers tend to be, because I realized that for some aspects of astrological work, being a few minutes off (or just a few minutes of a degree off) can make a difference in interpretation.

As I was pondering what to do next, I had a conversation with Lee Lehman, an expert horary astrologer, who told me about her work in planetary hours through the current revival of interest within the astrological community in recovering and translating ancient texts.[2] Lee said that she had found planetary hours to be very valuable in horary and in observing human behavior. I asked Lee about the discrepancies between published planetary hour tables and various published times of sunrise/sunset. She said, "Get the hours by computer. The most accurate source I've tried is CCRS." CCRS is a calculation program by Mark Pottenger that does about everything in astrology anyone ever thought of doing. ACS sells CCRS, so I immediately tried it out, and sure enough, it agreed with the newspaper's published sunrise/sunset times to the minute. "Start watching the hours," Lee told me. "Notice how the mood or the topic of discussion within a group of people changes when the planetary hour changes." I noticed. For example, in a talk I gave shortly after our conversation, I noticed that a very subdued mood and only serious questions from the audience during a Saturn hour lightened to laughter and levity as the hour changed to Jupiter.

In August of 1994, I gave a talk on astrological timing at Merry Meet, the annual Pagan festival sponsored by the Wiccan organization Covenant of the Goddess. I took along, as a handout, a draft of a little timing booklet I was in the process of writing for Starcrafts, a metaphysical bookshop run by my daughter Molly, which included planetary hours calculated by CCRS for the three days of Merry Meet. Don Kraig, author of *Modern Magick*, was present at my workshop. He told me about a computer program from the Netherlands called Merlin's Calends, which was designed especially for Pagan use and was very inexpensive. (CCRS is great if you want a full-service astrology calculation program, but may be a bit expensive if you only want to calculate planetary hours!) Don wrote to me later, telling me that he had checked the CCRS calculations against those in Merlin's Calends, and found them to be nearly identical. Since then I've discovered another easy-to-use and economical computer alternative called Sundial, a planetary hour program developed by astrologer Arlene Kramer, which can be purchased from her.[3] (Such software is really nice, if you're into computers. I can easily print out a page of planetary hours from Arlene's program, with exact latitude and longitude for wherever I want to be, and then it takes only a glance to check the current planetary hour. However, a book can be used anywhere, even if the power is out and the computer is down . . .)

Don Kraig also said that he thought my little timing booklet was very useful, and that Llewellyn would probably be interested in reissuing the out-of-print *Perpetual Planetary Hour Book* if I offered to update it. I called to inquire if Llewellyn was indeed interested, and they were. Nancy Mostad, the acquisitions manager, even found and sent me an old copy of the book. From there, unfortunately, my good intentions to write the book got seriously derailed due to several major life changes that culminated in 1997 to 1998 with my decision to sell my business, move to New Hampshire, and get married. A positive result of my not writing the book until now is that I've been at least sporadically checking planetary hours through all this, such that I can now actually tell you about them from my own experience!

I tell you this story because I think it only fair to tell you of the perspective I bring to this project. You deserve to know where I'm coming from in evaluating what I have to offer you. What experience I have with using planetary hours began in 1994. Even more importantly, though, I think you should be aware of my philosophical perspective.

Contemporary Astrology— A Changed Perspective

First of all, I speak from a perspective of modern astrology, and from opinions and beliefs formed of my own experience, which is constantly evolving. Consequently, I reserve the right to change those beliefs through future experience!

On the surface, this book is a practical one—a "how to" manual. I will show you how to read the planetary hour tables, and how to correct them so that the times are closer to the clock times in your area. I'll tell you about both old-tradition and contemporary meanings of the planets, and I'll even give you scripts for meditations and ritual spellwork for each planet.

What I won't give you are clear-cut pronouncements labeling some planets, hours, or aspects "bad" and others "good." I am very skeptical of the contemporary value of many of the old traditional "malefic" and "benefic" interpretations from the original planetary hour book. At the same time, I am impressed with the potential value of the planetary hour system, so long as you modify the old interpretations with a more contemporary understanding of planetary themes. Please understand that I am not saying Llewellyn George was wrong. He had a great depth of knowledge of his craft. His astrological interpretations worked for him, as I'm sure they work for many others who follow his teachings. I have found through my own experience that they do not work for me, at least not without some modification. Life was quite different when the original planetary hour book was written, nearly a full century ago. Our culture has become extremely complex, and we live in a time of changing paradigms. Matters that were once clear-cut have become gray areas, relative to various opinions, positions, and circumstances. Astrology has changed, too. What was once described as "malefic," I now call, at worst, "challenging."

Some of you magickal practitioners who have used planetary hours effectively, according to the old traditions, may be shaking your head in disagreement. I respect your experience, however I think we can all agree that the primary tool of any magickal practice is the mind—let's emphasize that: *the mind*! What you intend and believe, and the power with which you focus and project your intents and beliefs is what counts, far more than which hour represents which planet and what "tradition" says each planet means.

My message, then, for all readers who use this book in their magickal practice, is this. As you harm none, use this information as you will—but remember, those of you who are new to the art, please don't either think or say, "My magick has to be done at just this time or in just this way in order to work, because Maria said so right here in this book." I have often said, when teaching techniques to members of my Circle, that if I ever hear any of them say that something is true just because I said so, that I will feel I have failed them as their high priestess. I want you to think—to question, try, challenge, probe, and learn from your own experience until you discover what works for you. If through doing that you arrive at different conclusions as to how the techniques in this book work, I invite you to write and tell me about it. Learning is a lifelong process.

Underlying all that I have written here are my personal beliefs, based on my own experience to date. Here is a three-point capsule summary. In part it repeats what I've already said, but it's important to me that you understand these three points, especially, when using the material I am offering to you.

1. The planets are not causing us to do or fail to do much of anything, or at least there's no satisfactory proof that they are. Planetary events can be observed to correspond with our lives on Earth—"As above, so below"—but it also follows, "As within, so without." If it could be said that the soul mirrors its cosmic pattern, it could also be said that one's cosmic pattern is a mirror of one's soul.

2. No planet or aspect is inherently malefic or benefic, afflicted or favorable. They have themes that we can choose to express constructively or destructively, and they may reflect events and experiences through which we can grow or not grow. Common sense says that it is better to harmonize with planetary themes and express them constructively. If that doesn't always work (and it won't), it is probably because something is there for you to learn. We generally don't learn as much through ease as we do

through challenge. When you learn what the Universe is trying to teach you, you'll grow.

3. In making magick work for you, the most important element is your own belief and faith that it will, in fact, work. Faith and confidence, and therefore success, can sometimes be aided by doing things according to a prescribed ritual or at a time set down as "auspicious." In that sense, this book, or other books teaching magickal methods, can help you get started. Remember, though, that what you do is *your* creation. The magick does not work because you follow a scripted spell, or even because a certain planet "rules" the time you begin. It works because of *you*—because of the belief, faith, emotion, and mental focus you put into it. What I am providing for you are merely tools and a few suggestions. You can make up your own rituals and do just as well—maybe even better—than by following my suggestions. Use what you read here, but don't get stuck in it!

---

1. At the time, I was still CEO of Astro Communications Services, Inc. (ACS), a large, San Diego-based astrological publisher and computer service. I sold the company in 1998.

2. Thanks to the founders of "Project Hindsight," which later branched into another group called "ARHAT" (Archives for the Retrieval of Historical Astrological Texts), old astrological texts that have never before been translated into English are being researched and translated. The aim is to reclaim the true history of astrology and thereby establish its historical importance in an academic manner. The astrological community considers this project to be so important that it has given it widespread support, with a multitude of organizations and individual astrologers contributing money to support the translators and studying the work that has been, and continues to be, translated. Many small booklets of various translations have been published. When I was still the CEO of ACS, I contributed to the support of the translation projects and read a few of the booklets, but I haven't been particularly involved in the actual experimentation with the rediscovered traditional techniques other than planetary hours. Many astrologers, though, are quite excited about their results.

3. For information on obtaining computer software, please see the bibliography.

2

The Planets: Basic Meanings

 Ancient astrologers worked only with the seven "planets" that are visible to the naked eye without the use of a telescope. Although these seven bodies are collectively called "planets," two of them are not really planets. The Sun, of course, is a star, and the Moon is a satellite of the Earth. The Sun and Moon are often set apart and referred to as "the lights," but most astrology texts, for convenience, refer to all ten bodies used in classical astrology as "planets." In addition to the Sun and Moon, there are Mercury, Venus, Mars, Jupiter, and Saturn.

Three of the ten so-called "classical" planets were discovered long after ancient astrological systems, such as the use of planetary hours, came into being. These are Uranus, Neptune, and Pluto, collectively referred to as the "transpersonal planets." They are called "transpersonal" because they are visible only through a telescope and are thus considered to be less personal in their correspondence to individual human life. Speaking as one who has had the transiting (current) position of Pluto in aspect to one birth chart planet after another for about fourteen years, I think this "less personal" idea is arguable; however, this is the contemporary astrological tradition.

The movement of Uranus, Neptune, and Pluto through the signs corresponds to mass social and political changes. Their meaning for individuals is best seen through their aspects to personal planets or their movement through the houses of the birth chart. Although my primary interpretations are for the visible planets used in the planetary hour system, I think the transpersonal planets are too significant to people of our time to leave out. I will include interpretations for the transpersonal planets, and also rituals for them, later in this book.

Planetary Glyphs

It will be necessary for you to recognize the symbol glyphs for each planet in order to use the tables in this book. Here are the glyphs. You should memorize them.

Sun	☉
Moon	☽
Mercury	☿
Venus	♀
Mars	♂
Jupiter	♃
Saturn	♄
Uranus	♅
Neptune	♆
Pluto	♇

Planetary Days

Each day has a planetary ruler for which it is named. Sun-day is, of course, named for the Sun. Monday is Moon-day. Tuesday is derived from the name of Tiw, the Teutonic god of war, and it corresponds to Mars in Latin. Wednesday is Woden's day, which corresponds in Latin to Mercury. Thursday is Thor's day, corresponding to Jupiter. Friday is derived from Freya, Teutonic goddess of love, corresponding to Venus. Saturday is Saturn's day.

Obviously, an easy step to take in planning the time of your ritual or spellworking would be to choose the day of the week that best corresponds to the nature of your intent. Most anything you might want to do fits into one of the seven planetary themes.

Planetary Hours

The ancients also considered each hour of the day and night to fall under the dominion of one of the seven planets. The day started at sunrise with the hour ruled by the same planet that ruled the day. From then on, the next six hours were ruled by the six other planets in a sequence that repeated until sunrise of the next day, when the planet of the hour would again be the planet of the day. The details of the planetary hour system and its use in timing will be covered in chapter 4. For now, in this chapter on the symbolic meaning of the planets, let's start with a question that I've not yet seen covered in any other written material on planetary hours.

In What Hour Were You Born?

In his *Improved Perpetual Planetary Hour Book*, Llewellyn George says, "Saturn describes elderly persons, and those who are thin, dark and bony, and especially those of a serious, nervous or melancholy disposition." I realize that he was referring to people one might encounter during the hour of Saturn. Still, if a Saturn hour equals a Saturn-type person, how about the very crucial hour in which one first enters this world? On impulse, I decided to check and see in what hour I was born. Wouldn't you know . . . it was Saturn. Arrgh! Well, I admit to verging on being elderly, but I am most definitely not thin, dark, or bony. I'm fairly serious much of the time, but I'm not inclined to be nervous, nor do I think of myself as melancholy.

Generally, the older tradition tends to characterize the Saturn hour as being a pretty depressing choice for almost everything. So, why did I choose to be born in it, I asked? Well, I will not be discouraged! I reject those depressing interpretations! I wondered if anyone else I knew fit them any more than I do. I began checking the birthdates and birth times of various friends and family to check on the planetary hour of their births, and discovered that Saturn, in the old tradition, has a very undeserved reputation. The Saturn-born folks were not melancholy types at all—in fact, some of them were quite outgoing and even jovial. They were also hard-working, self-disciplined people who got things done.

It was a bit puzzling to me why Llewellyn George's book mentions nothing about the planetary hour of birth. The descriptions of people in his interpretations of the nature of each planetary hour are intended, it seems, to describe only people you might meet or interact with during that hour. In some cases he mentions the people described as types who would most likely respond to the "influence" of a particular hour. For Saturn, he tells us that we might "extract the most good" out of a Saturn hour if we have our Sun sign in Capricorn or have Saturn "unafflicted and well aspected in the birth horoscope." I fit neither of these categories, according to his definition of "afflicted."

The closest Llewellyn George comes to discussing planetary hours in relation to birth time is to describe how one can rectify an unknown birth time by noting the planetary hour in which a client *asks* an astrologer for a personal horoscope. He says that the planet ruling the hour of the question will also rule either "the zodiacal sign ascending at their birth, or the sign on their Midheaven." He also gives a third option: "The planet, itself, may be posited in their Ascendant," e.g., the planet of the hour is in the first house of the birth chart. He goes on to say that for this third option, one should consult an ephemeris to find the sign occupied by that planet. That sign will be the rising sign for the birth chart. He says he tested this technique many times with horoscopes for which the birth time was known, and it usually worked. I can't verify his findings one way or the other from my own experience, because I haven't kept records of the exact time people have called to ask for their charts. If any readers do have such data, I'd be interested in hearing from you.

Undaunted by the omission of planetary hour of birth in the *Improved Perpetual Planetary Hour Book*, I decided that checking more birthdates would be a good background for writing new interpretations of what to expect of things started in each planetary hour. After all, is not a birth a major beginning? And shouldn't a lesser event begun in a particular planetary hour have some interpretive similarity to the basic nature of a person who enters this world in that hour? In all other instances, the interpretations of planets carry out essentially the same theme whether in reference to personality, event, or timing, so why not planetary hours of birth, as well?

In the appendix of this book, you'll find a list of public figures with published chart data whom I included in my study of what planetary hour of birth might mean. (I also used nonpublished data of a large number of people personally known to me.) In this chapter, I've included the added insight derived from planetary hours of birth in the interpretations of each planet that follow.

In most writings that focus on planetary hours, it seems to be customary to list the planets in either the traditional order of the hours (Saturn, Jupiter, Mars, Sun, Venus, Mercury, Moon) or, as in the case of the Llewellyn George book, in reverse order, beginning with the Moon. I will deal with the whys and wherefores of the order of the planetary hours in a later chapter. The interpretations of the planets in this chapter are meant to provide you with a general understanding of planetary themes and correspondences. The information here is to be used for reference in any manner or aspect of timing where the planetary theme is emphasized, rather than for the use of the planetary hour system alone. For this reason, I am interpreting the planets in the same order you would find them listed in any general astrology book.

The Sun

In contemporary neo-Pagan groups that include members of both sexes, the Sun is primarily associated with the God. In all-female groups, more emphasis is likely to be placed on the solar aspects of the Goddess—and there have been plenty of examples of solar goddesses from various cultures. I have worked primarily with Sun God, Moon Goddess symbolism in ritual, while emphasizing that both Sun and Moon (masculine and feminine) archetypes dwell within each person and must be integrated and balanced. It is vitally important for women to access their Sun energies within, rather than projecting them onto the men in their lives, just as it is equally important for men to access their Moon energies within, rather than projecting them onto women.

Whatever gender of deity you may assign to the Sun, it must be said that the Sun is a star and the center of our solar system. All the other planets and the Moon revolve around it, and only reflect its light. They, each in their own way, add complexities to the mix that may sometimes even seem to dominate over the Sun in terms of personality and timing, but although the Sun may be shadowed, it is never completely hidden.

This dominance of the Sun and its most common association with God and man does not please my more feminist impulses, but hey, that's the way it is. One way around this would be to change astrological interpretation and recast the Sun as feminine. Well, astrology is changing, but, like the rest of the world, not that quickly. I think it is better to concentrate on the concept of both Goddess and God within, and through that realize that all the astrological archetypes have something important to teach us in regard to the integration and balance that leads us to the Oneness in Spirit that makes us whole.

The Basic Meaning of the Sun in Astrology

In contemporary astrological interpretation, your Sun shows how you like to shine. The Sun sign, its position in your birth chart, and its aspects to other planets reveal your ego needs, and a good deal about your purpose in life, which you have incarnated on Earth to fulfill. Your capacity for self-esteem and pride are shown by your Sun. As the Sun is the center of our solar system, around which all the other planets revolve, so is the Sun in your chart your vital center.

People Born in the Hour of the Sun

In looking through chart data books, most of which emphasize celebrity charts, it was at first easier to find people born in the hour of the Sun than in the hour of any other planet. Here were plenty of actors, performers, political figures, and a few unsavory "stars," including a cult leader who killed people. Later, with the help of the vast chart data available on Lois Rodden's Internet website, AstroDatabank, my opinion of the apparent Sun preponderance in celebrity charts changed (see appendix 1).

While the background of famous (or infamous) folk born in the hour of the Sun, or any other planet for that matter, was interesting, it was only marginally of help in forming opinions about personality. Celebrities have a public persona, and even biographical write-ups often don't tell us all that much about them other than the image they wish to be revealed to the public. For this reason I also checked all the chart data I had for friends and family—people I know personally. This list gave me more personal insight into how to identify traits that those born in the same planetary hour would hold in common.

In combining my celebrity list with other people I know well, I discovered that indeed they do have traits in common that fit within the general Sun archetype. Each of those born in the hour of the Sun could be described as having a natural bent toward leadership. A Sun is a star who wants to be a star, and who thrives most happily when in a starring role in life—in a position of authority, or when receiving admiration and recognition for his or her accomplishments. Sun people are somewhat more egocentric than other planetary types. Self-esteem is extra important to them. When they are feeling good about themselves, they are sunny and fun to be with. When, for whatever reason, they are feeling unappreciated or insecure, they can become unnaturally quiet, moody, and sometimes even needy, requiring lavish ego boosts from others to reassure them. It's as if a big, black cloud has settled over them.

Sun people are generous and magnanimous. When they are feeling good—when they are shining most brightly—everyone who associates with them shares in the rays. They uplift others, make opportunities available to them, and show them the light. For this reason, they often attract loyal followers who remain in their orbit, quite willing to take on the challenge of cheering them up when the clouds come in, just so they can bask in the uplifting charge they receive when the Sun becomes bright once again.

What the Sun Rules

Each of the planets is said to "rule" certain things. That simply means that the nature of the planet is considered to be most closely akin to the things it rules. By that definition, it seems a fairly obvious conclusion that the Sun rules people in charge— leaders, public figures, people of status, and people in the spot- light. Stemming from this, we can assign to the Sun dominion over any matter in which power, status, rank, dignity, honors, and influence are concerned. The Sun rules one's social status, pres- tige, pride, and prosperity. Vitality, creative abilities, confidence, will, and sense of purpose are illuminated by the Sun.

By tradition, the Sun is most associated with the positive/mas- culine polarity in astrology, and from that stems rulership over pa- ternity, the paternal instinct, and fatherhood, as well as Father God. Do not limit the Sun, though, to mean only "male." Rather, consider it to be of active, kinetic energy—outgoing and opti- mistic. The Sun is also a sustaining energy, rather than a fleeting one. Though it may occasionally be dimmed by other influences, it always shines dependably.

Other traditional correspondences for the Sun include a nature that is hot and dry. Its favored directional association in the mag- ickal circle is south—the "summerland" home to which it returns in the dead of the winter, leaving Earth's Northern Hemisphere in short, cold days and long, colder nights. Watch the sunrises each morning from the autumnal equinox until the winter solstice and you'll see this happening. Each day the Sun rises a bit more to the south. After solstice it begins rising each day a bit further east again until spring equinox, when it begins rising each day slightly more to the north. At summer solstice it rises at its extreme northern declination, giving Mother Earth's Northern Hemisphere its longest and warmest days.

The Sun's element is fire. It rules the sign of Leo, and is exalted in Aries. ("Exalted" means that it expresses powerfully and naturally in that sign.) In the sign opposite the sign that it rules, a planet is said to be "in detriment" (weakened), and in the sign opposite the sign in which it is exalted, a planet is said to be "in fall" (again, weakened in that it is not able to express quite naturally). The Sun is in detriment in Aquarius, and in fall in Libra.

The Sun's metal is gold, and its colors are bright yellow, gold, orange, and the scarlet robes of royalty. Corresponding gems are the golden topaz, amber, and diamond. Herbs include cedar, cinnamon, frankincense, orange blossom, and rosemary. Other objects ruled by the Sun are things that are valuable and things that glisten.

In health matters, the Sun rules one's general vitality, the heart, the upper spinal region, the right eye of males, and the left eye of females.

Sun Timing

Choose the hour of the Sun, or other times when the Sun is emphasized, to work for career success, improvement in social status, employment or promotion, honors, favors, or prosperity. Sun times are good for making presentations or announcements, public speaking, approaching an authority figure, or beginning a social occasion. Workings to attract business, brighten the disposition, or attract friends and supporters are favored by the hour of the Sun, or other times when the Sun is emphasized. Choose Sun times for healing rituals to improve general vitality, or to heal the areas of the body ruled by the Sun. The Sun is an excellent choice for rituals designed for spiritual development and attunement with deities, especially those associated with Sun qualities. While a Sun time may be a good choice for initiating a project, it is really because of the fact that the Sun rules the fixed sign of Leo that you choose it for building, developing, and sustaining the energy of your efforts on any goal toward which you've been working.

Since the Sun rules the astrological fifth house, it is also a good choice for matters associated with that house: success in any speculative enterprise (including gambling or investing in the stock market), creative self-expression through leisure activities or sports, success in the performing arts, greater enjoyment of life in general, or matters involving your children.

A time when the Sun is emphasized is an excellent choice for working on yourself, so do something special to improve your self-esteem, your attractiveness, your sense of inner power, or your ability to effect creative and positive change within.

The Moon

The Moon, in neo–Pagan mythology, is primarily associated with the Goddess. This has most likely been true since the beginning of humanity's attempts to reckon time. The lunar cycle of changing faces was naturally associated with the changes in the female body—as it swelled with growing life, gave birth, and returned to slimness again, or as it moved monthly (moon-thly) through the cycles of bleeding. Out of some cultures, however, came the idea of the Man in the Moon. In my mind, that old-man image just doesn't seem to fit, logically or intuitively. I've always looked up at the Full Moon and seen feminine features.

As for the changing faces of the Moon, I'll cover those and more in chapter 3, "Timing by the Moon."

The Basic Meaning of the Moon in Astrology

Astrological tradition from way back considers the Moon to rule the feminine, and the Moon in your horoscope (among other things) refers to your mother, to maternal instincts, and to nurturing qualities. So, too, is the Moon the Divine Mother. In ancient Christian art, obviously influenced by pre-Christian concepts, Mary is often seen standing upon the Moon.

Interpretations of the Moon in older astrology books, however, tend to be influenced by patriarchal ideas in regard to the feminine. In my opinion, that no longer quite works in astrology, any more than it does in other aspects of contemporary Western culture. For example, Llewellyn George's original planetary hour book characterizes the Moon hour as "negative, changeable, and unstable." It relates to people and things of "ordinary or common type and character." All power and authority are assigned to the Sun, while servitude and domesticity are assigned to the Moon.

Associating the Moon with change is appropriate. She moves much faster than any of the other planets. Associating change with negativity or instability is a judgment of opinion and perception. Change can just as easily be a positive step that increases stability. As for "ordinary and common," a prominent Moon in a horoscope often denotes a person of prominence in the public. It didn't surprise me a bit that nearly as many actors and entertainers showed up on my Moon list as on my Sun list.

The Moon shows your emotional self—how you feel. As such, it is nearly as significant as the Sun in understanding personality, for how you feel and how you express (or suppress) your feelings influences absolutely everything else in life. More than with any other body in our solar system, we can note a causal effect on Earth from the Moon. The ebb and flow of moods and temperament with the phases of the Moon are cited by many people, including law enforcement officials and health care workers, as the cause for the increased activity in their jobs at the New and Full Moons. The word "lunacy" emerged out of folk tales of intense mood changes to the point of craziness corresponding with the phases of the Moon—and in truth, that's not far off from what some women feel at certain stages of their "time of the Moon," the monthly menstrual cycle.

Astrology also counts instinct, intuition, and memory among the Moon's themes. In this sense, the Moon must be considered to correspond to a powerful aspect of the mind. In our traditional association of Mercury as the mental planet, and of intellect with logical, left-brain thought, we mustn't lose sight of the fact that the left brain is only half a brain. In recent history, the right brain has been getting some long-overdue attention, and is associated much more with lunar themes than with themes of Mercury.

People Born in the Hour of the Moon

As mentioned before, I found nearly as many actors and entertainers among the celebrities born in the hour of the Moon as in the hour of the Sun. Among personal friends and family born in the hour of the Moon, there are some strong leaders, including two who have been popular speakers and teachers. The difference, I think, has nothing to do with one's ability to perform, to be outgoing, or even to demonstrate a high level of charisma, but rather it is in the level of egocentrism involved. The Moon people I know personally are less self-conscious than the Sun people. They are more concerned with how they are being received by others than with how they appear, how they are doing, or if they are presenting well.

What I've just said may sound like splitting hairs. The difference is subtle and easier to feel than to explain. (I guess that's lunar, too!) Here's another way of putting it: Sun people, generous though they may be, are primarily concerned about the reactions of their audience in relation to themselves; Moon people are more interested in whether their audience is understanding and benefiting from what they are offering. The Moon conveys qualities of nurturing and service, even when shining fully. Moon people, even when otherwise quite extroverted, have a natural modesty that is also apparent. In a way, they tend to reflect back the sunlight in other people. They seek to bring out the best in others when they can, shining more brightly, then, in turn. They can also be responsive to other people's quieter moods, and reflect them sensitively, without feeling diminished themselves.

What the Moon Rules

Mothers, women, childbirth, and all manner of things having to do with the home are said to be ruled by the Moon—domestic work, food, the land, real estate, and any object used in cooking or cleaning. The Moon has general dominion over liquids, including any body of water, and stemming from that, the Moon rules bathing, beverages, boating, fishing, sewers, swimming, things that contain water, places that are near water . . . the possibilities are too numerous to list, but I think you get the idea. The Moon is indelibly associated with water and rules the astrological sign of Cancer, the cardinal water sign. The Moon is exalted in Taurus, in detriment in Capricorn, and in fall in Scorpio.

Since Cancer rules the fourth house of the natural zodiac, the Moon also rules this house of home, roots, and ancestors. In the west of a magickal circle, where the Sun sets, the Moon rules as the queen of the night. It follows that the Moon's nature (like west's wind) is classified as moist and cold.

The Moon's metal is silver, and its colors are silver, pale blue, or softly iridescent hues. Its gems are moonstone, of course, as well as pearl, opal, and other milky white stones. The Moon rules things that are smooth and soft. Favored flowers are those that are white, appearing clearly in the moonlight, such as white roses or star jasmine. Favored herbs include eucalyptus, jasmine, lotus, lemon balm, myrrh, and sandalwood.

Where the Sun is vital, pure energy, the Moon rules form and flow. In health matters, the Moon corresponds to the stomach and to all female organs and functions having to do with childbearing.

Mystery, intuition, prophecy, secrets, and emotions all fall under the dominion of the Moon. In mundane astrology, the Moon represents the people (the public), matters of popular interest, women's issues, and female leaders. In all things, the Moon rules fluctuation and change.

Moon Timing

Since chapter 3 is entirely devoted to timing by the Moon, I won't comment on it here, other than to say this. Your awareness of the Moon's phases and signs offers you both the easiest and the most important astrological method you can use to improve your ability to choose the most appropriate time for anything you do.

Mercury

Mythologically, we associate Mercury with the Roman god who had wings on his feet and was the fleet messenger of the gods. His forerunner was the Greek god Hermes. Though these are obviously males, Mercury is said to be androgynous by astrological tradition. I suppose that could be akin to the generic "he," since Western astrological tradition started with the Greeks. So, Mercury flies above such earthy, not-quite-clean matters like sex, and is at home in the airy, cerebral realm of the mind, where he can happily dwell on abstractions rather than feelings. For this reason, it's not all that easy to come up with really appropriate Goddess correspondences, should we want to shake up that "he" connotation. Probably the closest correspondence would be Athena, goddess of wisdom, who managed to avoid both the messiness and the warm, fuzzy feelings of a normal birth by springing full-grown out of the head of her father, Zeus.

Ptolemy, the Greek astrologer/astronomer (they were one and the same back then) who invented much of what is still very basic astrological tradition, assigned planetary rulers to the signs of the zodiac rather arbitrarily. The Sun and Moon were given dominion over Leo and Cancer, the two signs that were then at the zenith in the warmest part of the year. He then assigned the other planets to each adjacent sign from either direction according to standard planetary order. That is how Mercury came to be the ruler of both Gemini and Virgo. Gemini remains a good fit, but Virgo—that, in my opinion, was never more than an unfortunate patriarchal artifact. The only goddess of the constellations, the lady of the harvest, was, by the dubious virtue of being ruled by androgynous, airy, and rational Mercury, consigned to a fate as a chaste, subservient virgin—barren and obsessively picky and prudish—rather than the independent, earthy, and sensual virgin standing triumphantly upon the crescent Moon, as she was meant to be. Oh well, so much for my little tirade! Obviously, I am one of those astrologers who would like to see a new ruler for Virgo. Some have suggested the asteroid Ceres. I definitely think the image of Ceres or Demeter would be a more appropriate association.

The Basic Meaning of Mercury in Astrology

Mercury represents how you think and how you communicate your thoughts. It symbolizes the mind and the intellect. For Mercury, the mind is pure intellect, and that means left-brained, logical, rational, and abstract thinking. Being the closest planet to the Sun, Mercury is never more than 28° from the Sun in a horoscope. Considered to be the messenger of the Sun (God), Mercury either consciously communicates the Sun's theme in exactly the Sun's style, when in the same sign, or by adding a different nuance of interpretation to the message, if in either of the two signs adjacent to the Sun.

Like the god with wings on his feet, Mercury travels quickly, symbolizing adaptability, flexibility, or a scattered indecisiveness. Mercury is knowledge, but not necessarily wisdom, which requires more than abstractions and the gathering of information. The direction Mercury will take in a horoscope depends a great deal on the aspects it makes to other planets. In that sense, too, Mercury is very much a messenger of the gods—and those gods include the likes of Loki, the trickster.

People Born in the Hour of Mercury

Of the celebrities who were born in the hour of Mercury, I still found a smattering of actors and entertainers (as I did in all the planetary hours), but here there were more people who have been associated notably with ideas, ideologies, and the communication of ideas. Whether that would change if I continued with a much larger sample, I do not know, but this is certainly the way things went within the random checks I did. It turned out that fewer of my personal charts were in Mercury than in the other planetary hours, which surprised me a bit, since my personal group included quite a few who are in Mercury-type occupations—and most of them were not born under Mercury!

Here, judging from both the celebrity and personal charts on my list, Mercury people are likely to be strongly identified with a particular philosophy or ideology. Often through this identification, and through their ability to articulate their message, they are quite influential on the thoughts of others. Several have a gift for writing (but then so do others on my list born in other planetary hours). Some on my personal list are people who, though they seem serious at first impression, have an easy sense of humor and are wonderful storytellers.

What Mercury Rules

Mercury's rulership of conscious thought, logic, reason, the intellect, speaking, writing, teaching, studying, memorizing, and motion have already been suggested above. From all that stems such things as schools, books, newspapers, magazines, writing tools, mail, authors, editors, or other workers and tools associated with publishing offices and with other kinds of offices, too, as well as office equipment (including computers), secretaries, salespeople, advertising, and contracts. Motion includes all forms of short-distance travel—cars, buses, trains, directional signs and traffic, and also the fluent hand gestures that often accompany speaking.

Mercury rules Gemini and Virgo, as previously stated. This dual rulership means that Mercury is in detriment in Sagittarius and Pisces. Some authorities like to call Virgo the exaltation and Pisces the fall, but it is probably more common to see Mercury listed as being exalted in Aquarius and in fall in Leo. Mercury also rules the natural houses of Gemini and Virgo, the third house and sixth house, respectively. Third-house matters include (besides many things already mentioned) neighbors, siblings, and all matters of the immediate environment (neighborhood). The sixth house includes small animals (pets), coworkers, employees, servants, and matters of health, hygiene, and nutrition. In health matters, Mercury has dominion over the hands, the nervous system, the thyroid, and the organs of speech. Stress, nervous headaches and other nervous disorders, thyroid problems, respiratory colds or infections, and memory loss are all Mercury health issues.

Mercury's element is air, and its color is yellow for the east, thus taking on the aura of the Sun to which it is eternally bound. Its temperature is cool, but it is considered to be both dry and moist. Quicksilver and lodestones have been associated with Mercury, as well as agates, adventurine, and fluorite. Mercury herbs include lavender, marjoram, peppermint, and lemon verbena.

Mercury Timing

Llewellyn George, true to his time, advised using the hour of the Moon only for such things that were then defined as "women's work," or were of a "common" character, or perhaps for trips over water or for changing things, the Moon being "unstable." Some other things that a modern astrologer might list among positive attributes of the Moon, he advised be done in the hour of Mercury, as Mercury "tends to increase intuition, imagination . . ." I agree with the moderns on this, and say that your meditations and intuitive workings are better assigned to the Moon. I agree, however, with most other things Llewellyn George advised for Mercury.

Generally, times when Mercury is emphasized should favor your efforts at mental alertness, good speech, effective communication, correspondence, accounting, studying, reading, and most anything else having to do with education, business, advertising, publishing—all things of an intellectual nature. Sign papers, send off significant mail, resolve your computer problems, fix something, buy or sell, make that phone call, run an important errand, book tickets for a trip, or choose the time to begin your travel. Plan magickal workings for this time if your primary intent involves any of these Mercury topics. Since Mercury is adaptable, this time is also good for adjusting to minor changes.

There's a caveat: Mercury can be a trickster. Use your intuition on this and, if you know enough about your personal astrology to look at your current cycles and daily transits, be aware of those, too. If you are feeling (note: *feeling*) down in the dumps or mentally fogged, don't trust Mercury. Also, be wary during periods of Mercury retrograde. During such times, of course, you will often need to go ahead and do Mercury-type things, but you are well advised to double-check your work—or the fine print in someone else's work. Use the Mercury hour when you are feeling upbeat, or at least mentally clear. If it's your feelings that are clearly dominant at the time, choosing the hour of Mercury to act won't necessarily do the trick—at least not in the way you may have intended. It might be better to do a little Moon-time meditation and sort out those feelings, and then, if you must take action, perhaps choose a congenial time like the hour of Jupiter or Venus.

Venus

Venus is named for the Roman goddess of love who was the successor to Aphrodite of the Greeks, and whose Nordic counterpart Freya gave her name to Friday, the day that Venus rules. There is absolutely no debate on the gender association of this planet. She is definitely, emphatically *she*. Indeed, the symbol glyph for this planet is universally recognized as a symbol of the feminine. Easily visible to earthlings, Venus is seen as the brightest morning or evening star. When she appears in the evening sky, she is invariably the one to whom millions gaze as they say, "Star light, star bright, first star I see tonight. I wish I may, I wish I might, have the wish I wish tonight." That little verse, in itself, is a key to her meaning. Venus is the archetype of desire and of the magnetic attraction that is her power. Her love is boundless, and she delights in all the sensations of the material world.

Of course, Venus is not a star at all, but a planet—the planet that orbits between the Earth and Sun, in the closest *relationship* to our planet Earth—another important key to her meaning. Because Venus is the next planet out from the Sun after Mercury, she, too, is always fairly close in degree to the Sun, never more than two signs away.

The Basic Meaning of Venus in Astrology

The position of Venus in your birth chart shows how you love—the way you like to express affection, your style in attracting others, and what you need to receive in the expression of affection, appreciation, and love from others. Venus is desire—she shows what you enjoy, how you respond to beauty, and what makes you feel comfortable. Venus describes what you want and what you value in life, both of an intangible and a more tangible nature. In the latter sense, her themes are associated with matters of finance and of possessions. This lady can have a bit of a mercenary streak along with all that charm! Being comfortable has quite a bit to do with feeling secure.

Orbiting as she does in the closest relationship to Earth of all the other planets, Venus shows us how to relate to each other. Her themes in the horoscope show our style of relating—what we want and need from our close associations with others, how we handle intimacy, what turns us on or off sexually, and what kinds of people or relationship situations we attract.

Venus in the horoscope also describes our sense of aesthetics, what we appreciate and find beautiful. She shows our potential talent and interest in developing skill in artistic fields. Peace, so essential to the harmonious relationships, sense of equilibrium, and comfort Venus craves, is another major theme of our planetary goddess of love.

People Born in the Hour of Venus

After I compiled my random list of celebrities who were born in the hour of this planet so strongly associated with love and peace, I was quite surprised to find several notable examples of people who are well-known to have stirred up war, or at least major controversy! Interesting. Not one on this list has a major reputation as a peace maker, unless you allow the idea that often the act of making war may be the only way you can see to bring about the particular type of peace you desire. Some of those on the celebrity list have no association with war. Their fame is entirely based on the ability to entertain or to bring beauty into the world, and often in the process, to enlighten others.

When I looked at my second Venus list, derived from people I know personally, I found one mild-mannered soul who usually avoids controversy, preferring peace and comfort. Again, though, I found that most of my examples had some association with fighting! This group includes a military commander, a competitor in martial arts, and others who have been involved in various political or legal scraps, or in activism that has included being in the middle of acrimonious controversy. All of them, however, are people who much prefer harmony, peace, and comfort in their lives. Still, studying the birth hours has caused me to muse on whether choosing the hour of Venus for timing can really be counted upon as being as benign an influence as the old references tell us.

Judging from my compiled list of births, plus the general themes of Venus, it seems that those born in the hour of Venus have in common a strong sense of what they need to have balance and harmony in their lives. If it isn't there, these people are willing to fight for it, in no uncertain terms. They need a sense of equilibrium and comfort to feel secure and at peace within themselves. Without this, they are restless and agitated. The Venus-born definitely know how to relate to others when they want to—many of them have a good deal of charm and charisma. Leaders among them attract and inspire loyal followers. Often there's a flair for diplomacy, and all of them most likely would prefer to negotiate rather than fight, if possible. If negotiation fails, though, watch out! None of my lists revealed greater numbers of strong competitors than this one.

In a small minority of cases (notably demonstrated by Hitler on the celebrity list), the Venus born may even go insanely overboard, to extremes of non-Venusian behavior, in an attempt to create the perfect world of balance, comfort, and beauty that they visualize. In the majority of cases, the Venus born will work to create an environment of beauty and balance through creating art, entertainment, humor, peace, and harmony in the most positive sense. Few of them, though, will back off from a fight if they consider it necessary to restore peace.

What Venus Rules

Venus rules love, peace, harmony, balance, relationships, social affairs, diplomacy, comfort, art, desire, values, attraction, and many other synonyms for these that we could name. Venus rules the signs of Taurus and Libra, the natural signs of the second house and the seventh house, respectively. From Taurus and the second house come the emphasis on sensuality, intimacy, comfort, values, security, and finance. The elemental correspondence of Venus here is earth and all the material delights of touch, sight, sound, taste, and scent that go with it. From Libra and the seventh house come the emphasis on relationships, social interaction, diplomacy, tact, charm, refinement, fairness, harmony, proportion, and, when necessary, competition. The elemental correspondence of Venus here is air and all the intellectual needs and judgments that go with it.

Venus is in detriment in Scorpio and Aries. She is exalted in Pisces and in fall in Virgo. (The fall is, in my opinion, another archaic interpretation from ancient astrology. I don't understand how Virgo, goddess of the constellations, holding the grains of the harvest, could be thought to be somehow expressed badly or out of character when she shows the earthy sensuality of Venus.)

Objects ruled by Venus include jewelry and ornaments, fine apparel, things that are polished and reflective, things of luxury and pleasure, flowers, pictures, and anything that is valued for its beauty. Venus also signifies those who are closely associated with such things: artists, craftspeople, designers, entertainers, interior decorators—all professions connected with the arts, or with women and their adornment. Ambassadors, diplomats, and other workers for peace are also ruled by Venus.

The flavor of Venus is sweet, and her colors are tints such as sky blue, pale green, lemon, and rose. Venus likes gemstones such as emerald and sapphire, as well as semiprecious stones, such as rose quartz, turquoise, and malachite. Her metal is copper, and her favored herbs include balm of Gilead, catnip, geranium, mugwort, myrtle, rose, thyme, and yarrow. Venus rules the throat, the kidneys, the lower back, and the skin, or sense of touch.

Venus Timing

Times when Venus is emphasized are traditionally considered to be good choices for meeting new people, for giving parties or going to parties, for courtship, and for marriage—and also, of course, for love spells. Other traditionally favored Venusian activities include asking for a favor, making a social call, visiting a friend, buying articles of adornment, and buying luxury items. This could also be the right time to initiate a financial investment.

Using the additional insight of hour-of-Venus births, Venus should favor your initiation of a reconciliation with someone from whom you've been estranged, or for the successful mediation of a matter of dispute among your associates. Don't count on always achieving quick resolution within the hour, though. Hang in there—the restoration of balance might be a challenge that takes a little longer. Venus timing may enhance any ability you possess to be a catalyst for positive change in your relationships, through magnetism and attraction (earth) plus the power of reason (air), but the initiation of this is not always comfortable. Still, someone has to make the first move—why not you?

Use the Venus hour for meditation and magickal workings to increase balance in your life, to achieve calm after stress, or to heal the areas of the body Venus rules. Workings for peace of any kind are most appropriate during the times ruled by Venus.

Create Venus-timed spells to bring more love into your life, but be forewarned against directing such spells toward any specific person. Not only is this potentially against the free will of the other person, but it may boomerang on you according to the old adage "Be careful what you wish for—you may be so unfortunate as to receive it." All too often, those who long romantically for the seemingly unattainable object of their affection, once having won love, discover to their chagrin that the prince (or princess) turned out to be a frog, or worse! It is by far best to do your magick for love such that you effect creative change within yourself—that you become more loving, more attractive, wiser in your manner of relating, and worthy of happiness. As you create these things within yourself, a person who is truly right for you will surely respond.

Mars

Mars, the red planet, is the Earth's next neighbor outward from the Sun. As Venus is unequivocally Goddess, Mars, mythologically, is most definitely portrayed as the God, and a god of war at that. His symbol glyph is a universal symbol for masculine energy, well-known among many people who otherwise know little or nothing about astrology. Despite all that, the concept of the Amazon is reemerging rather strongly these days. Although my Venus "research" into planetary hour of birth demonstrated a warlike side of Venus, I'd still be inclined to characterize Xena, warrior princess, as more of a Mars archetype. Venus will try diplomacy, persuasion, and magnetic charm first; Mars is blunt and direct—raw energy—the energy of action.

The Basic Meaning of Mars in Astrology

Mars has often been considered the astrological symbol for sexuality, but he is not the sensual, magnetic attraction of Venus. His form of sex (taken out of context from the softening influence of Venus) demands surrender and seeks gratification, perhaps even dominance. Concern for the equal satisfaction of his partner is not necessarily paramount. In truth, then, sexuality is astrologically symbolized by the combination of Venus and Mars, rather than being the province of either of them alone. A lesson of those ruled by Mars is to learn the wisdom of sharing resources and pleasures with a partner. Mars, by his basic nature, looks out for number one. Being first also means that Mars is associated with initiating, pioneering activity.

Mars, in your horoscope, shows how you act—how you express your assertive energy and personal power. The position and aspects of Mars help an astrologer understand your sense of personal identity and how you stick up for yourself, or fail to do so. Here is shown the manner in which you go out and get what your Venus shows you desire in life. The principle here is action—make that Action, with a capital *A*. Depending on the sign and aspects of your Mars, your way of acting could possibly be procrastination or trying to get around a task the easy way, but nevertheless, action is the issue. Stemming from this, Mars themes are closely related to the work we do in the world, to our style of working, and to our level of competitiveness.

People Born in the Hour of Mars

My lists of birth charts for both celebrities and personal friends or family born in the hour of Mars contain notably fewer people whom I would call outright fighters than does the Venus list. The Mars lists contain plenty of people whom I consider to be strongly competitive, in whatever their chosen fields. Quite a few others, though, are not known for anything having to do with fighting. Their careers are varied, including quite a number of people you'd more easily associate with some other planet than Mars. There are those whose work is primarily associated with the mind, and others who are noted entertainers. A few have notable problems with highly dysfunctional energy. Four people turned up on the Mars list whose notoriety stems from brutal murders or assassination. What could these Mars people have in common?

In general, those people on the Mars list whom I know personally express their energy quite directly and openly. They know what they want and they go after it. You know "where they're coming from"—there's no mystery about it. If you ask, they'll tell you. I know quite a few of them to be keenly competitive. They are not afraid of breaking new turf, even though considerable risk may be involved. One chart on my list is for a business, rather than a person, and that business is a known pioneer in its field. In other cases, my hour-of-Mars births include people whose energy, in my observation, is at least mildly dysfunctional, and in some cases is sorely suppressed. Three of these people have chosen to work in menial jobs far below the potential of their talents. In each case, it seems that an original professional goal or dream proved not to be as expected. Rather than readjust and go for another goal, these people work at jobs that pay the rent and provide basic necessities, and essentially live their lives through avocational interests that are unconventional. In two of the cases, their unconventionality is hidden from family and all but like-minded friends. In another example, the frustrated energy of behaving conventionally, while hiding the true passion from family and other key people, may have turned inward, for this person, who is highly talented in a field that is out of the mainstream, also suffers from chronic health problems.

In two other personal examples, these people abandoned their original leadership-oriented goals, both in highly trained, Mars-oriented military positions in favor of redirected goals that still involve leadership, but in unconventional, nonmainstream areas. In one case, the actual job, as well as the avocational leadership, stem from owning and operating an occult supply business; in the other case, the job-for-income is in a skilled managerial position, but the leadership and primary interest is in being a coven leader.

Putting all this together, I would describe those born in the hour of Mars as being naturally direct, forceful, and competitive. When they are successful in their chosen goals, they have no problem sticking up for their rights or expressing how they think things should be. When success evades them, though, they do not seem to handle frustration very well. If they can't be first and foremost, or if they otherwise become disappointed in the goal they originally chose, they may withdraw or turn inward, sometimes seeking recognition among those whom the mainstream world may consider to be unconventional or eccentric. At their best, these people are dynamic individualists, hard-driving, confident, direct in expression, and often entrepreneurial.

What Mars Rules

Mars rules action, energy, assertion, ambition, competition, challenge, war, assault, anger, impulse, initiative, courage, conflict, and passion. It rules things, people, or events associated with these such as the military, patriotism, weapons of war, knives, scissors, cuts, surgeons, butchers, accidents, injuries, arguments, armor, fire, stoves, arson, firemen, furnaces, engineers, carpenters, steel workers, athletes, dangerous occupations, explosives, crime, criminals, police, lust, contests, and heroes. Mars rules Aries and Scorpio, signs of the first and eighth houses, respectively. From Aries and the first house comes the emphasis on that which is assertive, impulsive, and initiating, as well as the elemental correspondence with fire. From Scorpio and the eighth house comes the emphasis on passion, raw sexuality, and also an association with various matters, things, people, and places that might be associated with death. In modern astrology, Scorpio and the eighth house are usually said to be ruled by Pluto, but the ancient ruler, Mars, is used in the planetary hour system. Mars is best kept in mind as a coruler in other matters of astrological interpretation, as well.

Mars is in detriment in Libra and Taurus, is exalted in Capricorn, and is in fall in Cancer. His color is red, and stone correspondences include diamond, bloodstone, garnet, and red jasper. Mars is hot and dry, his metals are iron and steel, and his tastes are acid, sharp, and astringent. Herbs include allspice, basil, dragon's blood, hops, pennyroyal, pine, and wormwood. In matters of health and the body, Mars rules headaches, fevers, bites or stings, itching in general, burns, contagious disease, high blood pressure, hemorrhage, hysterical outburst, afflictions of the sex organs, inflammatory conditions, and surgery.

Mars Timing

According to Llewellyn George and other older sources, Mars and Saturn are malefic planets. Their hours are to be considered unfortunate for all people and for all things unless they have Mars or Saturn as their "planetary ruler" (ruler of their Sun sign), or as their Significator (ruler of the sign rising at time of birth), and unafflicted . . ." Such people "will find these hours favorable, taken in connection with affairs ruled by those planets; subject to the provision that there is a good aspect to the planet on that day."

Obviously, if all these warnings are to be followed, nobody can safely choose the hour of Mars for timing, unless they have their Sun or Ascendant in Aries or Scorpio and are able to read an astrological calendar well enough to know whether there are favorable aspects to Mars at the time. I don't agree that it should be that limiting. Admittedly, I have Sun in Scorpio, but I have worked with very challenging Mars aspects on occasion with successful outcomes.

In an earlier part of his planetary hour book, Llewellyn George says that Mars is a good hour for dealings connected with Mars people (engineers, contractors, machinists, barbers, police, dentists, surgeons, etc.) and "in lines related to medicine, pharmacy, assaying, construction and mechanical affairs generally." He recommends doing "things requiring great muscular exertion in the Mars hours; also attend to those matters that require boldness, courage, nerve, and active enterprise."

I'd say that if you are by nature impulsive, or if you are very angry or stressed, caution is called for in choosing the Mars hour. On the other hand, if you have your feelings in check, and your intent and the situation call for bolstering up your courage to take an action you know you should take, Mars could be your best choice, with one caveat. It would be well worth your while to learn to recognize and avoid, by reading that astrological calendar, the days in which Mars is in challenging aspect to another planet. There are Mars hours every day, so it shouldn't be hard to find a day in which the Mars aspects are also cooperative. In this regard, I think Llewellyn George and I may be fairly well in agreement. Choose the Mars day and hour, with favorable Mars aspects, for positive magick that is appropriate to positive Mars themes, such as winning honorably in competition, building courage, taking initiative, or sticking up for yourself in a challenge—but always be very sure to add the tag "and it bring harm to none, according to the free will of all." For curing negative Mars issues, though, it would be better to choose a planetary theme of a modifying nature. For example, to resolve a conflict, choose Venus for peace. To soothe Mars' fires (or fevers), you might choose a cool planet such as the Moon.

Jupiter

Jupiter is the Roman equivalent of Zeus—the god king of the Olympians, the chief of all the deities, god of thunder and of the sky. We can also learn something about Jupiter from other words that are derived from its name. "Jove" means to gleam or shine. The expression "by Jove" exclaims one's astonishment. "Jovial" describes a genial person who is full of hearty, playful, good humor. That seems to come from the idea that, astrologically, people born under the "influence" of Jupiter are joyful—and why wouldn't they be, if they could take after this mythological character who pretty much got his own way on everything. Jupiter is the largest of the planets in our solar system, which probably explains why it was named for the chief of the gods.

The Basic Meaning of Jupiter in Astrology

From the bigness of Jupiter is derived the concept of expansion and growth. Jupiter symbolizes how you grow. This planet is associated with Lady Luck, but its primary benevolence is not at all through luck, but rather through the growth you achieve in life through spirit, education, honest and just behavior, broadness of vision, and openness to new ideas. Jupiter relates to idealism, reason, dignity, generosity, harmony of feeling and thought, wisdom (as contrasted with mere knowledge), philosophical views, sound judgment, and common sense. Jupiter has a touch of grandeur, of course. At best, Jupiterian people embody all these positive things, as well as being optimistic, enthusiastic, good-natured, and perhaps more than a little dramatic. With Jupiter overdone or distorted, they can be braggarts, extravagant, overindulgent, hypocritical, or downright lazy. Too much of a good thing can be, well, just too much. Too much ease can make one complacent; too much confidence can result in the "pride that goeth before the fall." The primary mistake most people make in regarding Jupiter, especially the transits of Jupiter they see coming up in their charts, is to expect more than is delivered. Jupiter has been considered the "great benefic" from the time of the ancients, but this is usually not the kind of luck that falls in your lap. Rather it is the growth in wisdom, creativity, vision, judgment, and Spirit that comes with an openness for constantly learning from life, and from regarding everything as an opportunity for learning and further growth.

People Born in the Hour of Jupiter

My list of celebrities born in the hour of Jupiter is an interesting mix of people. There are several entertainment personalities with charisma and flair, but others are known primarily for their ideas and ideals, or in the case of the renowned twins Ann Landers and "Dear Abby," for their wisdom and common sense. There's the proper Emily Post, the ultimate Queen Elizabeth II, and former President Clinton, the charismatic and lucky politician who seems to have great difficulty learning from his mistakes. Then we also have a gangster, an assassin, and the guru who led his flock to mass suicide in anticipation of being saved by an alien ship hidden behind comet Hale-Bopp. Tying this group together is hardly easy. My personal group shows quite a variety of personalities as well. One thing that ties all of them together, though, is a very strong interest in spiritual paths. One is a devout Christian, two are Wiccans with backgrounds in other religions, another is an astrologer whose work has a spiritual emphasis, and one is my daughter who has studied extensively and traveled far in pursuit of her studies in comparative religion and in why people believe as they do. All of them have a certain charismatic attractiveness about them, or at least that is how I regard them. One senses the wisdom of the "old soul," but also a great openness to continued learning.

What Jupiter Rules

Jupiter rules optimism, wisdom, judgment, idealism, expansion, growth, generosity, grandeur, and temperance. As the ruler of Sagittarius and the ninth house, Jupiter rules religion, education (particularly higher education), philosophy, legal affairs, the law, justice, sports of a noncompetitive nature, enthusiasm, inspiration, and that which is far away—long-distance travel, foreign countries, and foreign people and their customs. Generosity relates to philanthropy, charity, or any benevolent enterprise. The principle of expansion corresponds to business and material things, so Jupiter rules bankers, brokers, businesses, affluence, and increase. The "luck" connotation relates to winning prizes. Wisdom relates to publishing and writing. Jupiter people are lawyers, judges, professors, clergy, doctors (medical and any Ph.D.), dignitaries, foreign diplomats, journalists, writers, publishers, merchants, ceremonial magicians, rich people, overweight people, boastful people, prizewinners, and royalty. Objects derived from all this include gavels, legal briefs, books, paper, ritual tools, ritual robes, regalia, medals, and trophies. From the Sagittarius centaur we get Jupiter as ruler of such things as horses, saddles, archery, and archery equipment.

Jupiter is in detriment in Gemini, exalted in Cancer, and in fall in Capricorn. Its element is fire, its stones are amethyst and turquoise, its metal is tin, and its colors are royal purple and deep blue. Herbs include cloves, juniper berry, sage, witch grass, and wood betony. In medical correspondence, Jupiter rules the liver, hips, thighs, pituitary gland, and growth. Overdoing it in general can be a medical problem, and abnormal growth can correspond to diseases such as cancer. Jupiter is traditionally classified as warm and moist, with a flavor that is fragrant but bland.

Jupiter Timing

Jupiter, in planetary hour tradition, is considered to be the most favorable hour of all, and good for just about anything. "All important affairs should be launched in this benign Jovian hour," says Llewellyn George. Jupiter should be chosen for opening a business, buying and selling, seeking favors, healing—you name it. All things positive. I would add this caveat, though. Jupiter is given to excess. If you are prone to excess or overindulgence, Jupiter is probably not your best choice to attempt to overcome such problems. Try Saturn instead! Jupiter timing is good for any intent that seeks improvement of the mind and spirit, or for that which seeks benefit, whether material or intangible. Enterprises or projects begun in the Jupiter hour, or with aspects of Jupiter (even some of the challenging ones), are more likely to be successful. For example, Sun–Jupiter aspects are considered to be excellent for a business chart, even the square or opposition. Later on in the business, though, a Sun–Jupiter aspect could mean expansion—or it could mean unwise, hasty overexpansion. Overindulgence of any kind can be an issue when Jupiter is involved. Many people, including myself, have noticed that trying to lose weight during a Jupiter transit to one's natal Sun or Moon is a major struggle, like trying to swim upstream against a strong current!

Jupiter, being grand and loving ceremony, would be good for almost any elaborate ritual of high magick, and it would also be fun for dramatic or ecstatic circle dancing! The Jupiter hour should generally be favorable for any kind of new beginning, for charging an enterprise, or for charging your own self-confidence to succeed. Prosperity spells are appropriate, as are preparations for such things as winning honorable competitions, speculation, increasing freedom, starting off on a trip—all, of course, with harm to none and according to the free will of all.

Saturn

Saturn is the Roman equivalent of Chronos, father of time. Although the familiar mythological figure of Father Time is male, Saturn is the ruler of a feminine sign, so let's also consider Anna Perrina, Grandmother of Time. However we personify it, however, time is limiting. It binds us to the physical world and our limited life span within it—to schedules, routines, obligations, and other boundaries that limit and contain. Going back to that Father Time image, we often also see the Grim Reaper blended into the image of that old guy with the scythe. Saturn can be scary, but only when you are trying to evade its call. When you understand its message, you'll find it an enormous help in accomplishing your goals in life. Saturn's themes are about being grounded, as in "ground and center," and about learning to deal with the realities of living in the physical world and in a physical body.

The Basic Meaning of Saturn in Astrology

Saturn is the opposite of Jupiter—Jupiter is expansion, and Saturn is contraction. Saturn limits and demands that we play within the rules, but to think of it only that way is unnecessarily self-limiting. It is much more constructive to think of Saturn as the building of structure. Saturn is that which is concrete, real, and solid. Saturn is physical manifestation. With responsibility and discipline, we build the structures for our life that will allow our goals and dreams to manifest. Saturn in your birth chart describes how you deal with responsibility, rules, limitations—with reality. Success with Saturn requires a thoughtful, serious attitude, patience, perseverance, self-discipline, and organization. It doesn't sound like much fun, I know, but Saturn goes a long way in providing the environment through which the joy of life can be expressed minus such nagging mundane concerns as whether there will be a next meal or shelter from a storm.

Saturn is the creative faculty that is concrete, ordered, organized, and practical. Through Saturn, thoughts truly become things. Saturn is cautious, conservative, traditional, patient, and prudent, with a strong sense of justice and fairness. Emotions are controlled; the will is focused. Where Jupiter is the optimist, Saturn tends to be the pessimist. On the downside, a Saturnine image could be the fearful, defensive, narrow-minded stick-in-the-mud. On the upside, think of the stable, realistic authority with the wisdom of experience of one who has seen it all—the Sage or Crone.

People Born in the Hour of Saturn

This brings me right back to the earlier part of this chapter to my discovery that I was born in the hour of Saturn. I said that on finding several other friends also born in Saturn hours, I could identify a common denominator of hard-working, self-disciplined people who get things done.

My Saturn celebrities comprise quite a variety or people, as did the other planetary hours. No standout number of similar occupations emerged. This certainly was not a list of melancholy types, with the likes of Lenny Bruce, Carol Channing, and Robin Williams included. One can only speculate on whether these people fit a common Saturnine theme or not. There are people of strong accomplishment on every list, and there's often a considerable difference between public persona and the private person.

There is no question, though, that the majority of my Saturn-born personal examples are hard-working types, most of them with managerial qualities. One particular person would not seem so on the surface, being one who does not work at a mundane job and could be characterized as a dropout from society. Still, even this person is seldom ever idle. He works constantly for charities or for friends, making considerable contributions in his own unique way. Another on this list is known for being a good comedian, but behind that facade is a highly disciplined performer.

I think that some of the things I've often said about myself might also be fair to say about many others in this group, so here goes. My life is my work is my life. I don't really separate the work I do to generate income from the work I do for my family, within volunteer organizations, for friends, within a magickal circle, or just for myself. Everything I do is "my work"—a way of walking my path in life. I like to work. Some things can be a little tedious at times, but mostly I feel good through my accomplishments and I enjoy what I do. I feel very fortunate that I have managed to find ways to make a living doing things I like to do. Sometimes I feel overly busy and think it would be nice to just take some time off from everything. But even if I sit and contemplate nature, I am working. Some of my best ideas come that way.

What Saturn Rules

Saturn rules responsibility, discipline, tradition, reality, and manifestation. It rules the sign of Capricorn and the tenth house, and is also the ancient ruler of Aquarius and the eleventh house. That means Saturn is in detriment in Cancer and Leo. It is exalted in Libra and in fall in Aries.

From Capricorn and the tenth house come themes of authority, status, and reputation. Here is where one lives up to the world's expectations, plays according to the rules of the game, and plays to win—to accomplish, to "climb the highest mountain." From Aquarius and the eleventh house come concern for the welfare of the group, the reform and improvement of society, and the manifestation of one's hopes and wishes. Both images, in their own way, insist on justice, and the exaltation of Saturn in Libra again emphasizes the aspect of fair play. Saturn is less comfortable within the self-oriented themes of Leo and Aries, and its cold practicality and concern for matters of the larger world are not at home in emotional and home-centered Cancer.

Saturn rules businesses, government, the land, commodities taken from the land, people who work the land, people who build, bridges, buildings, walls, architects, archeologists, coroners, and gravediggers. It also rules authority figures, fathers in particular, rules and the letter of the law, the elderly, teachers, those who deal with matters of death, and common laborers. Some common things ruled by Saturn include pottery, farm and garden equipment, glue, gloves, hardware, ice, ice cream (now that's not so serious!), ink, junk, purses, raincoats, refrigerators, rocks, salt, sculpture, snakes, snow, and, in general, things that are heavy and dull (not shiny).

Saturn is of the earth element—solid, stable, with boundaries that contain and seek to control the waters of emotion, the winds of change, and the fires of untamed passion. It is cold and dry, and its colors are black and brown. Saturn's stones include all that are black—hematite, jet, black tourmaline, Apache tears, and onyx. Some references also cite deep red stones such as garnet or ruby. The metal is lead, and herbs or vegetation include patchouli, rue, cypress, hemlock, holly, and hemp. In body, health, and healing work, Saturn is associated with chronic ailments, arthritis, and depression. Saturn rules the skin, hair, teeth, knees, bones, spleen, and sense of hearing.

Saturn Timing

As the primary malefic planet, along with Mars, Saturn is not recommended for much of anything according to the older books. Those who have Saturn well aspected in their horoscopes are supposed to be able to use Saturn successfully for timing on days in which there are favorable transiting aspects to Saturn. "Favorable" generally meant only trine or sextile in the old days. In modern astrology, the natures of the two planets combined is usually considered more important. Squares and oppositions are not to be considered "bad," but rather as active "action" aspects, as contrasted with the passive trines and sextiles. With the conjunction, it's definitely the nature of how the themes of the two planets combine that matters.

While Llewellyn George warns sternly against the Saturn hour in one place in his book, in another place he recommends it to increase "systematizing, organizing, and also for constructive and executive ability." He says the hours of Saturn "tend to produce a thoughtful, serious, conservative, prudent, sober, contemplative, and diplomatic state of mind."

I find Saturn to be a good hour for meditation and contemplation. For one reason, I often find I feel sleepy then, and need that kind of respite. Many times I've hit a moment in the day when all of a sudden I just feel tired. If I'm working at my computer, my eyes want to close. If the planetary hour list is handy, I've looked and often found that time has just shifted into the hour of Saturn. When I first began studying planetary hours and asked Lee Lehman for some assistance, she said, "Observe when you're in a group gathering or meeting, how the energy often drops when the Saturn hour begins." I did, and she's right. It often happens. I once observed a large conclave where the group engaged in a lot of talk and expressed feelings, but didn't come to any resolution during the Moon hour. The Saturn hour began, and they buckled down to business, came to a consensus, and got things done. At almost the moment of the change to the Jupiter hour, they happily made a decision to break for lunch. How interesting.

I don't avoid the Saturn hour, by any means. Many times I have used it to plow through tedious work and it becomes very productive. If that tired feeling hits me, though, I find that it's best not to fight it. Instead I take time to either meditate or just rest, and find that this is a great way to restore my energy.

I am inclined to avoid deliberately initiating an activity or important contact during the Saturn hour, unless my intent and purpose is definitely of a Saturn theme. That's a good general rule for the use of Saturn timing for magick, as well. Choose Saturn for rituals of banishing, for breaking an unwanted habit, or for binding yourself to a disciplined structure in order to accomplish a goal. If you want to develop self-discipline, get organized, lose weight, accept a responsibility, become more grounded, or, in general, turn thoughts into things, Saturn can be a "benefic" for your purpose. Saturn is your friend when you respect and honor its message.

Uranus

Uranus stands out with eccentricity from the other planets in our solar system. Instead of rotating normally on its axis like all the others, it rolls around sidewise. It figures—Uranus just can't be expected to follow expected norms. This planet, discovered in 1781, would never have been discovered without a telescope, and it represented quite a shock to the world. For thousands of years prior to this discovery, all planetary systems and related symbologies (like the days of the week or the chakras) had been based on the well-known Seven.

Imagine what upsets this caused! No wonder Uranus was associated with revolutionary activity. Uranus was around at the time of the American Revolution, the French Revolution, and the beginning of the Industrial Revolution. Old ideas were getting a major shaking up everywhere.

Uranus was named for the ancient Greek god of the heavens who was both the son and husband of Gaia. Their children included the twelve Titans. Eventually, one of them, Chronos, the forerunner of Saturn, assisted an angry Gaia in castrating Uranus and consequently usurping his throne. The genitals of Uranus, cast into the sea, changed into the white foam from which Aphrodite was born.

It is interesting that whoever named this first of the transpersonal planets also broke with the tradition of naming planets after Roman gods, and instead went back to the early Greeks; yet the next two to be named, Neptune and Pluto, returned to the Roman pantheon.

The Basic Meaning of Uranus in Astrology

True to the circumstances of its discovery, Uranus represents the breaking of boundaries. Saturn represents the rules, and Uranus disdains them. Revolutionary, independent, original, and eccentric, Uranus in your horoscope shows your freedom urges and how you develop and express your individuality. With Uranus you transcend the norm, stand out from the crowd, and stick up for your right to be who you are. Such change and challenge can be scary, but resisting a strong call of Uranus through its transits or directions—digging in your heels and refusing to change—is most likely to elicit only the stress, tension, and upsets that are the downside manifestations of this planet. Surprise, sudden opportunity, and excitement—or upheaval, upset, and shock. Whether provoked by you or through an external event to which you must react, the choice is yours. Predicting the events or outcome of a Uranus passage is unlikely. Expect the unexpected, one could say. If this unpredictable planet's themes were truly predictable, it just wouldn't be Uranus.

What Uranus Rules

The previously Saturnine sign of Aquarius got a major reimaging after the discovery of Uranus. The new planet was named the ruler of Aquarius, and, ever since then, Aquarians have congratulated themselves on being "ahead of their time" and children of the "New Age" (even when they are being just as stubborn and intractable as this fixed sign can be!). Saturn and Uranus are contrary energies. If the Aquarian nature sometimes seems to be fraught with inner conflict, it may be a reflection of the contradictory quality of its dual sign rulerships. For this reason, merely reverting to the hour of Saturn for Uranian themes doesn't make much sense. Uranus is considered to be the "higher octave" of Mercury. Despite its corulership of Virgo, Mercury is primarily associated with the element or air, and Uranus is also an air planet. The hour of Mercury is your best choice for most purposes of a Uranian theme. As an airy planet, Uranus is intellectual rather than emotional. Indeed, like its Aquarian sign, it can be quite emotionally detached—more at home with abstractions than with feelings. The natural house is the eleventh house, and from that we add the themes of humanitarian concern for the welfare of the group, or working for causes, ideas, and goals with peers, or with group reform.

Uranus is an airy planet? But what about the Aquarian *Water-bearer*? I've heard quite a number of nonastrologers or even entry-level students call Aquarius a water sign because of that symbol. Think of the waves being poured out from the celestial water-bearer as air waves or waves of light. The fish of Pisces are bound together, swimming in the womb of Earth. Eventually (not nearly as soon as most people think), the Aquarian Goddess (yes, more and more often the waterbearer is being portrayed as *she*) will pour out her urn and set the fish free—free to roam the stars and experience different worlds and different zodiacs. Unimaginable boundaries will be broken then!

Uranus rules upheaval, revolution, reform, eccentricity, upset, sudden change, surprise, independence, insubordination, lawlessness, and the unexpected. Some assorted Uranian things include airplanes, ambulances, automobiles, batteries, bombs, bullets, inventions, detours, earthquakes, electricity, divorces, explosives, lights, hearing aids, hurricanes, tornadoes, microphones, movies, radio, television, telephones, machines, photography, trains, watches, and x-rays. Computers are usually said to be Uranian, but they also get listed under Mercury. I think the computer, itself, is very much a product of Virgo and Mercury, but the Internet, with all its weirdness and breaking of boundaries—that is Uranus. Uranian-ruled people include adventurers, aviators, astronauts, astrologers, broadcasters, cartoonists, clairvoyants, electricians, geniuses, hippies, hobos, inventors, magicians, nonconformists, outlaws, Pagans, photographers, psychiatrists, reformers, strangers, usurpers, and zealots.

Uranus is in detriment in Leo. It is exalted in Scorpio (the sign of transformation and regeneration) and in fall in Taurus. Uranus has been classified as being cold and moist, and its assigned colors are mixed—streaks, plaids, and checks. The color most associated with Aquarius, though, is electric blue, so for greater simplicity, you can use the brightest blue you can find. Appropriate stones are lapis lazuli, amber, and lodestones. Uranian metal rulerships are radium and uranium—or everything radioactive and magnetic. I have not found herbal assignments for the transpersonal planets. For Uranus, choose from those that correspond to Mercury. In health and body matters, Uranus rules the ankles, the parathyroid gland, and the aura. It is also associated with the nervous system and blood circulation. Uranus relates to accidents, especially injuries to the ankles and feet. I ruefully remember one broken ankle that resulted from tripping over my own feet at an overworked time when I was trying to ignore the fact that I had said out loud to the Universe, "I really need a break." Later, I noted that it was also at the time of a transit to my natal Uranus. Be careful what you say to the Universe. She may take you literally!

Uranus Timing

Uranus spends approximately seven years transiting each sign, reflecting noticeable generational changes in social issues associated with the sign through which it is moving. The changes of Uranus passages are most likely, at least in part, behind the familiar adage of the "seven-year itch." Transits (current positions of the planets in comparison to your birth chart planets) from each of the three transpersonal planets can remain in aspect to a birth planet for months and sometimes years. For this reason, learning about their themes and cycles will assist you in understanding the significant challenges in your life that may well underlie your choices for the types of magick you'll be wanting to do at the time. This is also true of the transiting cycles of the slowest moving of the seven ancient planets, Saturn.

Generally, I would recommend the day and hour of Mercury for Uranus rituals or magick, or the days when the Moon is in Aquarius. If you know your own birth chart well, you might also work with times relating to the sign of your natal Uranus, or of transiting Uranus, and the times relating to your traditional (Sun through Saturn) planets that Uranus aspects. You could also accentuate the energy of Uranus in your ritual plans by scanning an astrological calendar for days when appropriate aspects of Uranus are listed.

Since Uranus has to do with breaking away from the norm, which is most likely to mean banishing something old to make way for the new, the Last Quarter or Balsamic Moon phases are appropriate timing. If you have made your break and are ready to charge forward, choose New Moon phases (see chapter 3).

Uranus magickal themes could include breaking old unwanted habits, gaining freedom, achieving independence, increasing creativity, adapting to change, initiating reform, working for a humanitarian goal, building group energy and group mind, aura cleansing or healing, sending a beacon or magnetic attraction, or seeking inspiration from the gods.

Neptune

Neptune, the next planet in order out from the Sun, is named for the Roman counterpart to the Greek god Poseidon, lord of the sea. His familiar symbol, the trident, makes the planetary glyph for Neptune easy to recognize. This god has been characterized in mythology as a jealous god, grumpy and quarrelsome. He doesn't fit the astrological themes for his namesake planet much at all. What we know of Neptune comes much more, it seems, from the sign it was given to rule following its discovery in 1846. That choice must have been made by some grumpy old man who thought no further than "Pisces = fish = water. Let's give it to Neptune."

Poor Pisces, the feminine, visionary, spiritual sign of our age, brought in by a myth about Mary, very slightly renamed from an earlier pre–Christian goddess of the sea, who gave birth to the God-man known as Jesus (a name possibly derived from Zeus). Always misunderstood is she, and badly distorted in interpretation—both the Goddess and the sign. She may yet come into her full flowering before this age is past.

Neptune the planetary archetype is really no more of a traditionalist than Uranus. If I could reimage astrology and bring the astronomers into line, I'd dump grumpy old Neptune, break with

Roman tradition completely, and pick a goddess name for this planet. If not Mary, perhaps Yemanja? Or how about Isis, with an ankh for a glyph? Dream on . . . and that, in part, is what Neptune is about: dreams—beautiful, visionary dreams.

The Basic Meaning of Neptune in Astrology

Neptune is the antithesis of Saturn's insistence on reality. Neptune is anything but realistic. Some astrological interpretations seem to focus mostly on the negative, speaking of confusion, lethargy, nebulousness, illusion, deception, delusion, impressionability, and indecisiveness. Higher qualities of Neptune include compassion, idealism, imagination, and universal love. My favorite keyword is escape, because, in a way, this says it all. The means by which we escape from reality are very wide-ranging, from the depths of substance abuse to the heights of spiritual vision. In between are the victims, codependent martyrs, and daydreamers who visualize castles in the air but never seem to actually build them. At a higher level are the artists—poets, writers, painters, sculptors, and musicians—who lift our spirits, inspire our imaginations, and touch our souls. Then there are the athletes, such as dancers and figure skaters, who create fantasy in motion, as well as the philanthropists, healers, spiritual leaders, and mystical visionaries. With Neptune, the ego is set aside for the development of a higher level of awareness. Call it the quest for beauty, love, the infinite, the sublime, for transcendence, or for Oneness with whatever or whoever is seen as the Divine.

What Neptune Rules

Neptune rules the sign of Pisces (although the ancient planet Jupiter must not be forgotten as a coruler), so it is in detriment in Virgo—and it is easy to see how Neptune might be uncomfortable in this oh-so-practical sign. Neptune is exalted in compassionate Cancer, and is in fall in that other most practical sign of Capricorn. Neptune is considered to be the higher octave of Venus, planet of the goddess of love. Its element is, of course, water. It's natural home is the twelfth house, the house traditionally associated with self-undoing, solitude, karma, restriction, and the deep psychological cobwebs of our minds that we tend to hide even from ourselves.

Neptune is deception and illusion, and therefore represents liars, charlatans, and all those who are able to use such arts for constructive purposes, as well—actors and other performers, stage magicians, and, in some cases, trial lawyers. All things liquid are Neptunian, as well as all things that blur the mind and cause loss of consciousness, whether used for good or abused—drugs, narcotics, alcohol, and anesthetics. Neptune rules chemicals and also chemical engineers and chemists. Other themes come from artists and all arts of fantasy, psychism and psychics, all manner of psychic experiences, spiritual initiation and powers, spiritual counselors, spiritualism and séances, and idealists and idealism (but not the practical kind!). Neptune also rules the navy, navigators, and all things nautical. A potpourri of other correspondences includes aliases, alibis, alms, angels, assassins, asylums, bathing, bloating, bribery, butterflies, camouflage, clouds, coffee, comas, conspiracies, crystal balls, dissolution, dreams, enchantment, espionage, fairies, fakes, fictitious names, floods, fog, genius (artistic), glamour, glass, gullibility, hypochondria, hysteria, imitation, imprisonment, infidelity, instability, kundalini, leaks, lutes, magick, makeup, mazes, music, mystery, nudity, obscurity, oil, opticians, paint, persecution, poison, puzzles, retirement, reverence, romance, scandal, secrets, sleep, sorcery, suffering, thieves, tobacco, vacillation, and weirdness.

Neptune's colors are lavender, sea green, mauve, and opalescent hues. Its flavor is seductive, and its favored stones are coral, jade, aquamarine, or ivory. It is characterized as warm and moist, and its metal is platinum. Neptune rules the pineal gland, psychic centers, and, through Pisces, the feet and the lymphatic system. Health issues could involve glandular imbalances, energy depletion, water retention, hypochondria, or addictions. Neptune also relates to psychic healing.

Neptune Timing

Neptune's themes are even more generational than Uranus' themes—it spends about thirteen years in each sign. If transiting Neptune is aspecting an important planet or sector of your birth chart, you are likely to be experiencing very noticeable Neptunian themes in your life. Watching your astrological calendar for the times when Neptune aspects are in focus might be your best first step in deciding when a corresponding activity might be most beneficial—or best avoided. If you are feeling tired or confused, it is best not to fight it by engaging in mundane activities. Try to escape, even for a little while, to commune with nature, especially near water, for restored perspective. Regular meditation and yoga are also excellent practices.

When Neptune is dominant, avoid actions or rituals that are ego-centered or self-serving. Neptune denies the ego. Success in working with Neptune comes by transcending the ego—art for art's sake, altruism, meditation, or the seeking of Oneness. Healing rituals are most appropriate. Divination should yield profound results, so long as your intent is truly divine. Meditative rituals that seek to reveal a mystery, interpret a dream, cleanse and open the chakras, or improve visualization capabilities are all good choices. I do *not* recommend the use of any mind-altering drugs. You do not need them to do any of these things and are far better off without them. They may seem like a shortcut, but remember that Neptune is illusion and fraught with self-deception. In short, you can really mess up your head. It isn't worth it! If you really think you need special preparation for deep ritual or trancework, try the time-honored method of fasting. Abstain from heavy foods like meat and from all even mildly addictive substances like nicotine or caffeine for at least several days prior to your chosen time, and then precede your meditation or magickal ritual with a ritual bath.

For Neptune theme workings, use the planetary days and hours of either Venus or Jupiter, depending on which one seems most suitable for your theme and style (review their correspondences). The Moon in Pisces or the exaltation sign of Cancer are good; or Scorpio, the other water sign, could also be an appropriate choice, especially if the theme of your ritual has to do with revealing mystery or seeking inner transformation. Since an aspect of the Full Moon is the seeking of illumination, working at the Full Moon seems particularly fitting, although divinatory rituals should also work very well in the dark of the Moon prior to the New Moon.

Pluto

Pluto is the outermost known planet in our solar system, although its extremely elliptical orbit sometimes takes it inside the orbit of Neptune. This was true of the past twenty years (February 1979 to February 1999), but it won't happen again for over 200 more years. Discovered in 1930, and quite small in size compared to the other planets, Pluto has been threatened by some astronomers with demotion to a planetoid, but its archetypal impact packs such a strong wallop (well-known to anyone who has experienced a Pluto transit to a highly significant birth chart position) that astrologers can just smile knowingly and say "planet *plus*."

Pluto takes its name from the Roman lord of the Underworld, whose predecessor was the Greek god Hades (just in case the name Pluto might tend to trigger thoughts of that Disney dog instead of the dark lord that he is). Again, if I could reimage astrology and bring a bit more balance to its pantheon, I would change the name of this planetary ruler of the feminine sign of Scorpio to Hecate. Some Pluto themes may sound scary, but remember, here is also awesome power. In the darkness, the seeds of rebirth are germinated. From death comes life, transformed, renewed, and rising grandly out of the ashes of destruction. The phoenix, which is the primary symbol of Scorpio, most clearly epitomizes the transformative power of Plutonian energy.

The Basic Meaning of Pluto in Astrology

Pluto has been widely associated with power, but when it expresses in dominance issues, power struggles, or fear of power, it is dysfunctional and missing the point. Pluto's power is to be found within, and its purpose is the ruthless soul-searching for that inner truth that is both comfortable with power and the easy expression of it, and at the same time lets go of any need or desire to control external events or other people. The goal is mastery of the inner self, the awareness of one's purpose and destiny in life, and the will to walk that path, while at the same time harboring a secret smile at the frailty of our fleeting moment on this Earth in the vastness of time. Pluto is both death and rebirth. It is intensity, the drive for transformation, the process of learning to know when it is time to let go, and how to share intimacy and resources without the need to control. Pluto confronts the darkness within and the death of change, learns to laugh at them rather than fear them, and is transformed.

What Pluto Rules

After Pluto was discovered, it seems quite natural that, given its name alone, it was assigned to be the ruler of Scorpio and the eighth house, both of which were already associated with themes of death and rebirth. Pluto is considered to be the higher octave of Mars, the same planet that is the traditional ruler of Scorpio. Both planetary symbols represent powerful energy. The primary difference is that the energy of Mars is expressed outwardly—externalized, while the energy of Pluto is internalized, intensely inward and magnetic. In this, Pluto fits with the feminine symbolism of the sign it rules. Masculine energy thrusts outward directly. In *The Witch's Circle*, I described it as being kinetic. Feminine energy, I described as being magnetic. It draws inward, spiraling. This is more akin to the intensity and controlled repression of Pluto's power. Which is more powerful? Think about it.

Pluto is in detriment in Taurus, which I suppose is a sign that is a bit too interested in comfort to relish dealing with Pluto's churning emotions. Pluto is exalted in Mars-ruled Aries and in fall in Libra. A potpourri of keywords for what Pluto rules (some of them derived from the eighth house that Pluto also rules) includes abyss, annihilation, atomic energy, autopsy, brimstone, brothels, cesspools, chasms, organized crime, collective unconscious, compulsion, corruption, debauchery, demons, detectives, dictators, disasters, enigmas, espionage, garbage, germination, Hades, havoc, insurance, legacies, lynchings, masochism, masses, mass media, metamorphosis, mobs, mob psychology, mortality, nihilism, nuclear fission, oblivion, orgasm, outrage, passion, petroleum, pollution, power, pornography, procreation, prostitution, psychoanalysis, purging, recycling, reincarnation, rejuvenation, repression, satire, scavengers, secrets, sexuality, snakes, sorcery, submarines, subversion, taxation, terrorists, transcendence, transmutation, treachery, underworld, undertakers, vice, villains, vindictiveness, waste, wars (global), and wreckers.

This list, shall we say, is not without its challenges! Anyone who has been through a strong Pluto passage will confirm that this planetary theme demands intense self-examination that probes and confronts the darkness within, and the fears, and perhaps even the absurdity of ego, in an intense search for truth and a higher meaning for one's life. One surrenders control over that which is outside the self and, achieving a higher level of self-mastery, emerges rejuvenated and reborn—like the phoenix.

I could not find a classification reference for Pluto, because most of the earlier books that dealt with this type of thing are too old. They hadn't yet come to terms with Pluto. Let's call it hot (for seething passion and Hades) and moist (for the water sign it rules). Fire and water make steam, and that fits, too. Or boiling oil, perhaps? Read lightness in my tone, here. I've just been through about fourteen years of constant Pluto transits, all either by conjunction or opposition. Pluto taught me a lot, and I've also learned to laugh at it a little. Stones ruled by Pluto are beryl, obsidian, and lava rock. Most references list topaz as the Scorpio birthstone, so that would fit, too. The favored color is deep red or burgundy. The metal correspondence is plutonium and tungsten. Parts of the body are the pancreas, the metabolism, the organs of elimination, and from

Scorpio, the sexual organs. Diseases or disorders of any of these could be potential health issues. Recuperative powers are strong.

Pluto Timing

The Moon in Scorpio, times when Pluto symbolism is activated in your chart, or times when your astrological calendar shows aspects involving Pluto are all appropriate choices for spell or ritual work that focuses on Pluto themes. It is important in mundane activities, though, to be aware of yourself and your own reactions. When Pluto is strongly in focus, confrontational or power struggle issues are more likely to surface around you. If you should find yourself being drawn into such a situation, recognize that egos may be on the line. Your ability to understand your own ego will serve you well in creating a win-win solution, or at least in knowing when to let go. At the same time, it is not good to suppress strong feelings, for when you do that, you tend to attract (project) confrontation. Take a deep breath, tap into the power that dwells within you, and express yourself constructively. Claiming your own power to be the best you can be does not require dominance. Be creative—seek win-win solutions. Pluto favors your efforts in taking steps forward toward necessary major changes.

For the use of planetary days or hours in working with Pluto's themes, the obvious choice is Mars. The energy of Mars is outward and direct, though. This would not seem to fit all the more inwardly directed possibilities for Pluto rituals. For those, I suggest the Moon. For banishing and cleansing rituals or for meditations, choose the dark of the Moon. Use the nocturnal hours, in any case. Sex magick is a rather obvious association with Pluto, as is any spellwork that seeks to probe within fearlessly for transformative change. Past-life regression work, rebirthing rituals, initiations, and psychic healings also correspond to Pluto symbolism. Another possibility is drumming or dancing to the point of trance, a form of surrender to the unseen forces.

3

Timing by the Moon

Timing by the Moon is the oldest form of timing known to humanity. Prehistoric bones with markings cut in correspondence to the lunar cycles are proof of that. Ancient people looked at the Moon in her constantly changing faces, saw that her cycle coincided with the cycle of women, and the Moon became Goddess. As she showed her varied faces, the people wove myths and planned activities according to her recurring phases. Despite the Moon's changeable nature, her changes were predictable in that she added an element of stability to their lives and the ability to plan ahead.

As time went on, it was observed that the Moon traveled across the night sky against a backdrop of the constellations in a manner that revealed a much more slowly moving pattern, such that not only the months but also a full year of her cycles became predictable. Now, in addition to the much more slowly changing lengthening or shortening of the days seen from the Sun's yearly cycle, the onset of seasonal changes might also be predicted by the constellational pattern to be seen during the darker phases of the Moon.

What Is Your Sign?

Although this chapter is about Moon signs and phases and how you can use them in choosing appropriate times, it occurs to me that I first ought to clear up just what a "sign" is. While some readers may take that for granted, others may have read the considerable number of published opinions about tropical versus sidereal astrology by various Pagan authors, some of whom say, without really explaining why, that the sidereal signs should be used because they match better with the constellations, which have shifted with the change of the ages. I use the tropical signs, but I do not expect you to agree with that just because I say so, or disagree just because someone else says so. Whatever you use is fine with me, but I do think one's choice should be factually informed. Astrologers well-schooled in differing systems all seem to make their systems work quite well. What I'll do right now is explain to you exactly what a sign is, why there is not one but three systems called the "zodiac, " why none of these systems are either "right" or "wrong," just different, and, last but not least, why I prefer the tropical signs.

A Brief History of the Zodiac

The system of zodiacal signs primarily used by Western astrologers is called the *tropical zodiac*. This means that just about every Sun sign or popular horoscope column, most magazine articles, the majority of books published in this country and Europe, and your Llewellyn annuals are all based on the tropical zodiac. Eastern astrologers and some Western astrologers use the *sidereal zodiac*. When you read those newspaper "starwatches" written by astronomers, you can bet they are using the *constellational zodiac*. Yes, it's confusing. Blame the Greeks.

Back in the time of classical Greece, a new method of identifying the positions of the planets was devised. Previously, the most popular method had been the Babylonian system, which used as its reference points the axis of the fixed stars Aldebaran (the bull's eye of Taurus) and Antares (the heart of the Scorpion), which were almost exactly opposite each other across that great zodiac circle in the cosmos. This places the Babylonian system in the category of sidereal astrology, because "sidereal" means star, and this system uses fixed stars as its reference points. From the Aldebaran-Antares axis, equal sectors of the circle marked the signs, into which planetary positions could be identified. (When I say "circle" in this context, I refer to the arc across the southern sky against which the Moon and planets can be seen moving slowly against the backdrop of zodiacal constellations in a yearly cycle. This is the ecliptic, the orbital path of the Earth around the Sun—the same path that we on Earth see as the planets moving around us. Viewpoint is relative. We *are* the center of our Universe—we even have Einstein to cite on that!

In the heyday of the Babylonian zodiac, Aldebaran was seen to lead the zodiac train . . .

> *Can you bring out the signs of the zodiac in their season*
> *or guide Aldebaran and its train?*
> —Job 38:32[1]

Taurus was considered to be the first sign of the zodiac, Cardinal East. The four fixed signs, Taurus, Leo, Scorpio, and Aquarius, were considered to be the four corners of the world. The significance of the ancient signs can still be seen in church statuary (though most have forgotten the origin), and the Ox, the Lion, the Eagle, and the Man are still important symbols in some schools of ritual magick.

Now come the Greeks. They decided to make the equinoxes and solstices the reference points for the zodiac. An equinox is the intersection of the ecliptic with the equator (see figure 1). The two great circles are tilted at different angles. The solstices are the points at which they are farthest apart. The vernal equinox is the point at which the Sun's apparent path around the Earth (as seen from the viewpoint of earthlings) crosses the ecliptic moving north.

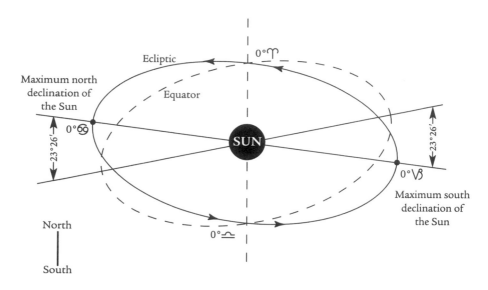

Figure 1. The Equinoxes and Solstices.

The vernal equinox was chosen as the fiducial point (zero point) of the zodiac circle. At that time, the sky patterns had slowly shifted, due to the precession of the equinoxes. The constellation that could at the time be seen approximately beyond the first sector of the ecliptic from the vernal equinox was Aries, so Aries became the first sign and the new Cardinal East point (cardinal Ascendant to astrologers). Zero degrees of Aries became the first degree of the zodiac. The other sectors, called signs, were assigned the constellations that lay approximately within each successive 30° demarcation.

Unfortunately, even though the constellations conveniently provided much more colorful names and symbols for the signs than Sign 1, Sign 2, etc., ever could have, the sky, most inconveniently, kept slowly shifting. Hipparchus, of the classical Greek time period, has been proven to have known this, but alas, like most humans he had little foresight for what might happen a couple of thousand years after his time. Unfortunately for later generations of astrologers who have to explain all this, precessional motion has now caused the constellations (for the most part) to now be offset nearly one sign sector backward from where they were when the Greeks chose to use their names for the signs. This is much to the delight of some astronomers who just love to use this as an excuse to jibe that astrologers don't even know where their signs are. Most of us do, but these great defenders of reason know quite well (bless them) that many in the general public will believe their misinformation anyway.

Precession is a very, very slowly moving offset of the equinoctial points against the backdrop of the constellations. Simply put, it's been said to be due to a slight wobble of the Earth's axis, comparable to the movement of a child's top. Because of this, the vernal point slowly moves backward against all the zodiac constellations over about a period of about 26,000 years. This is what forms the Great Ages. If we were to divide the ages equally, like the sign sectors on the ecliptic are divided, each age would be around 2,000 years long, but that's tantamount to forgetting that it's really about the *offset* of equinoctial points and constellations—*not* about dividing a time circle into equal sectors. If you consider the actual offset, we are still in the Age of Pisces, an age that began at around the same time as when the Greeks were creating all this confusion. The vernal equinox point now coincides with the nose of the west fish in the Pisces constellation, between 4° and 3° from the tip. It will actually wobble its way past the last star in Pisces and into the constellation of Aquarius at around A.D. 2700–2800. (Sorry about that, those of you who are expecting the Age of Aquarius to be here any time soon.)[2]

Sidereal zodiac systems attempt to compensate for the confusion of the Greeks' tropical zodiac versus the constellational zodiac by moving the vernal point to reference a fixed star that will put the signs more clearly in line with the constellations for which the signs are named. Not all agree on just where the reference point should be which is why there are multiple sidereal systems (not very different from each other, however), rather than just one system. Once the beginning point of Aries is set, though, the signs follow along the ecliptic in 30° equal sectors. So, its signs may match up with the constellations better than the signs of the tropical zodiac do, but they still don't match.

The actual constellations vary in size from about 18° to 46° in arc, some overlap, there are gaps in between others, and there are even a couple of nonzodiac constellations that partially intrude on the ecliptic. Are you perhaps an Ophichus or a Cetus? Then what fun! Despite the intrusions, the astronomers, in some mysterious nontechnical adherence to the symbols of ancient tradition, still consider the zodiac to be numbered twelve and will sometimes call the vernal point "zero Aries," but they generally ignore the astrological signs (except to make fun of them). They show (in their starwatch newspaper columns) diagrams of the planet's places according to where they can be seen against the actual stars of the constellations, zodiac or not.

So, as I said, use whatever system of signs you like. As for me, being a Witch has given me yet another reason to like the tropical zodiac best (other than the fact that it's the system in which I was first trained, and that it has always worked well for me as an astrologer). Why? Because the tropical zodiac, marked out by the equinox, solstice, and cross-quarter points, clearly and unequivocally marks out the seasonal Sabbats that I celebrate! The seasonally inspired interpretations of the sign archetypes add a dimension that both complements and enriches the mythologies of the Wheel of the Year. Plus, the Full Moon's change from sign to sign, always in opposition to the sign of the Sun, gives me endless theme variations to work with in creating Full Moon rituals. (Find examples of astrologically inspired rituals for all the Sabbat and Full Moons in *The Witch's Circle*.)

The Moon and the Astrological Signs

The Moon moves very quickly through the signs of the zodiac, changing signs about every third day, and going through all the signs in less than a month. A keyword knowledge of astrological sign symbolism can aid you in selecting a day when the theme of your ritual is in harmony with the theme of the Moon's sign. In this way you can increase the success of your magick by being in the flow and in sync with the all-powerful tidal pull of the Moon Goddess. If you look around, you'll often see subtle signs that the moods of people in general are responding to the current sign of the Moon.

One of the best ways to know what sign the Moon is in is to purchase an annual astrological calendar and keep it where you can easily consult it at a glance. Exact times are given for when the Moon changes signs, and when the Moon makes each aspect to a planet. (Be sure you take note of the time zone for which your calendar is calculated, so you can adjust the time if you live in a different zone. You add an hour as you go east. So, 9:00 A.M. Pacific Standard Time is 10:00 A.M. Mountain Standard Time, 11:00 A.M. Central Standard Time, and 12:00 P.M. Eastern Standard Time. The astrological calendars recommended in the appendix of this book also tell you when daylight saving time begins and ends.

The following are basic keyword meanings for each of the signs, with a few suggested themes for ritual or magickal workings for each one. As for the workings suggested with each sign, these are not to be considered as the *only* appropriate times for such activities, but rather as suggestions for an appropriate "fit." Some workings would fit nearly as well with other signs, usually within those signs of the same elemental nature.

Keywords for the Astrological Signs

Aries

Element: Fire.

Quality of Action: Cardinal, initiating.

Polarity: Positive, masculine.

Color: Red.

Planetary Ruler: Mars.

Keywords: Initiative, new beginnings, instinct, impulse, adventure, courage, pioneering, self-identity, forceful, direct, energetic, aggressive.

Aries Magickal Themes: To honor the warrior goddesses or gods, to call upon Mars energy within, to celebrate pioneering spirit, to create adventure in your life, to learn to live in the *now*, to start a project, to initiate any change, to build courage, to become more assertive, to resolve to start an exercise program, to take a risk, and to charge any new beginning.

Taurus

Element: Earth.
Quality of Action: Fixed.
Polarity: Negative, feminine.
Colors: Pastels—blue, pink, and green.
Planetary Ruler: Venus.
Keywords: Stable, practical, sensual, possessive, needs security, persistent, patient, stubborn, protective, calm, wants comfort, holds on.
Taurus Magickal Themes: To honor or call upon the energies of Venus (or Aphrodite or a corresponding goddess within), to worship the Mother in the abundance of her green plant growth, to attract wealth, to create prosperity (however prosperity is defined to you), to increase sensuality, to relax, to become more grounded, to create protection, to increase patience, to persist in any goal, and to become calm when stressed.

Gemini

Element: Air.
Quality of Action: Mutable, adaptable.
Polarity: Masculine, positive.
Color: Yellow.
Planetary Ruler: Mercury.
Keywords: Adaptability, flexibility, restlessness, communicative, versatile, logical, curious, spontaneous, intellectual, two sides to every question, changeable.
Gemini Magickal Themes: To honor or call upon the energies of Mercury, Hermes, Athena, Minerva, or other deities associated with the mind and communication, to improve your ability to communicate, to solve a puzzle, to prepare for a speech or test, to send a message, to increase logic, to charge an educational pro-

ject, to learn a new skill, to come to a decision, and to adjust to change.

Cancer

Element: Water.

Quality of Action: Cardinal, initiating.

Polarity: Negative, feminine.

Colors: Silver, soft pastels.

Planetary Ruler: The Moon.

Keywords: Emotional, sensitive, protective, moody, nurturing, sentimental, easily hurt, security oriented, sympathetic, empathic, instinctual, vulnerable.

Cancer Magickal Themes: To honor or call upon the energies of any of the Moon goddesses, to honor or call upon the energies of the Mother Goddess, to cleanse the home, to bless the home, to ward the home, to improve one's homelife, to increase fertility, to protect or shield children, to understand one's emotions, to replace fear or hurt feelings with love, to buy or sell real estate, and to handle emotional matters well.

Leo

Element: Fire.

Quality of Action: Fixed.

Polarity: Positive, masculine.

Colors: Gold, yellow-orange.

Planetary Ruler: The Sun.

Keywords: Creative, risk-taking, charismatic—in the spotlight, egocentric, needs applause, fun-loving, generous, proud, honest, exciting, magnanimous.

Leo Magickal Themes: To honor or call upon the energies of any Sun god or goddess, to increase or inspire creativity, to charge one's ability to give a good performance, to increase self-esteem, to access the inner child, to set a beacon for a new lover or for a new child, to excel in a sports competition, to win at speculation, and to express joy of life—just for fun!

Virgo

Element: Earth.

Quality of Action: Mutable.

Polarity: Negative, feminine.

Colors: Brown, russet, moss green.

Planetary Ruler: Mercury (or the asteroid Ceres).

Keywords: Efficient, pragmatic, attentive to detail, discreet, modest, precise, worker or workaholic, health-conscious, service-oriented, likes to fix things, earthy.

Virgo Magickal Themes: To honor Ceres, Demeter, any gods or goddesses of the grain and harvest, Lugh as maker of tools, or the virgin goddesses, to improve working conditions, to improve relationships with coworkers, to become more organized, grounding, healing, to heal the Earth, to charge one's intent to diet, for successful work on a ritual tool, and to charge the harvest.

Libra

Element: Air.

Quality of Action: Cardinal, initiating.

Polarity: Masculine, positive.

Colors: Sky blue, rose.

Planetary Ruler: Venus.

Keywords: Cooperative, fair, diplomatic, fence-sitting, need to balance, competitive or compromising, aesthetically inclined, charming, needs peace and to relate.

Libra Magickal Themes: To honor or call upon the energies of goddesses or gods of love and marriage, to seek balance within, to come to a decision, to achieve compromise in a dispute, to bring about peace, to achieve harmony with a partner, to charge an artistic endeavor, to bring about fairness and justice, to set a beacon for a mate or partner, and to compete with honor.

Scorpio

Element: Water.

Quality of Action: Fixed.

Polarity: Negative, feminine.

Colors: Wine red, deep blues, or greens.

Planetary Ruler: Ancient ruler—Mars; modern ruler—Pluto.

Keywords: Intense, penetrating, powerful, resourceful, compulsive, jealous, secretive, controls/manipulates or lets go/eliminates, mysterious, inscrutable, shrewd.

Scorpio Magickal Themes: To honor or call upon the Dark Goddess or Dark Lord, to confront and understand one's dark side, to achieve self-mastery and inner transformation, to reveal a mystery, to discover a secret, to eliminate a bad habit, raising energy through sex magick, rebirthing rituals, workings that deal with or assist in healing after grief or a death, to receive a loan, and to improve any issue of fairness in sharing with a partner.

Sagittarius

Element: Fire.

Quality of Action: Mutable, adaptable.

Polarity: Positive, masculine.

Color: Purple.

Planetary Ruler: Jupiter.

Keywords: Optimistic, enthusiastic, idealistic, extravagant, has faith (may be dogmatic about beliefs), inspired, confident, freedom-loving, goal-oriented.

Sagittarius Magickal Themes: To honor or call upon the energies of such deities as Diana of the hunt or Epona, to build confidence, to express one's ideals, to seek faith or inspiration from spirit, to work with any matter of higher education, to charge a long-distance trip, for success in publishing, for success in a legal matter, and to achieve greater freedom.

Capricorn

Element: Earth.

Quality of Action: Cardinal, initiating.

Polarity: Negative, feminine.

Colors: Dark brown, deep blue, black.

Planetary Ruler: Saturn.

Keywords: Responsible, formal, traditional, authoritative, career/ business-oriented, pragmatic, serious (with dry humor), pessimistic, disciplined, organized.

Capricorn Magickal Themes: A good time for formal, highly structured ritual work according to traditional forms. Work to seek career gains, to attract business, to overcome negativity, to deal with authorities, to increase one's ability for disciplined work, to accept responsibility, to heal a damaged reputation, to gain status, to protect the Earth, for grounding, and for wise leadership.

Aquarius

Element: Air.

Quality of Action: Fixed.

Polarity: Masculine, positive.

Color: Electric blue.

Planetary Ruler: Ancient ruler—Saturn; modern ruler—Uranus.

Keywords: Eccentric, rebellious, independent, innovative, objective, emotionally detached, future-oriented, revolutionary, group consciousness, humanitarian.

Aquarius Magickal Themes: To invoke gods and goddesses of air, to seek universal truths, spellwork for the enlightenment, reform, or welfare of the masses, to charge acts of political activism, to increase personal independence, to express individuality, to achieve greater freedom, to achieve cohesion in one's group, to create thought-forms, and to break boundaries.

Pisces

Element: Water.

Quality of Action: Mutable, adaptable.

Polarity: Negative, feminine.

Colors: Sea green, lavender.

Planetary Ruler: Ancient ruler—Jupiter; modern ruler—Neptune.

Keywords: Compassionate, mystical, sensitive, spiritual, dreamy, confused, intuitive, impressionable, empathic, escapist, indecisive, imaginative, visionary.

Pisces Magickal Themes: To induce deep communion with deity, to seek answers for any question through deep meditation, through divination tools, or through scrying in water, to interpret your dreams, to induce dreams, for past-life regression, for aura reading, for chakra healing, for spiritual healing, for vision quests, for cleansing rituals, ritual bathing, and trance work.

Lunar Phases

There are eight phases of the Moon all clearly observable by looking at the sky. The days for the New Moon, First Quarter Moon, Full Moon, and Last Quarter Moon are shown on many calendars. The exact times they occur are shown on astrological calendars. Generally, calendars do not show the other four phases, the cross quarters, although visually, the approximate times of these can also be clearly seen in the sky. These phases are the Crescent Moon (midway between the New Moon and First Quarter Moon), the Gibbous Moon (midway between the First Quarter Moon and Full Moon), the Disseminating Moon (midway between the Full Moon and Last Quarter Moon) and the Balsamic Moon (midway between the Last Quarter Moon and New Moon). The Crescent Moon is often confused with the New Moon. At the New Moon, the night sky is dark, except for the stars—the Moon is conjunct the Sun, and therefore cannot be seen because she is "up" in the daytime and is lost from our sight within the Sun's much brighter rays.

The cross-quarter phases, according to the great astrological philosopher Dane Rudhyar, are the points of greatest momentum and critical release of energy. In *The Witch's Circle*, I pointed out this fact in connection with the designation of the four cross-quarter points in the eight phases of the Wheel of the Year as the Greater Sabbats. Since the monthly lunar phases change so quickly, a choice of magickal workings appropriate to the four phases shown on your calendar will often be close enough. Still, it is useful to know the subtle shadings of theme that can apply to the cross-quarter phases, as well. Each phase lasts approximately three and one-half days.

The most important general rule to keep in mind is that from the New Moon until the Full Moon, the Moon is *waxing* (increasing) in light. Energy is building, and your rituals should be planned accordingly. From the Full Moon until the night sky is dark again in anticipation of the New Moon, the Moon is *waning* (decreasing in light). This is the time to finish things up, wind down, and then prepare to let go in anticipation of beginning anew.

The Waxing Moon Period

For half of the lunar month, when the Moon is increasing in light, energy is building, and you can effectively build your own energy toward any intended accomplishment or fulfillment.

● **The New Moon** is a time of new beginnings, but at the time the New Moon occurs, the night sky is dark, and there is no visual reference as to the exact conjunction of the Moon with the Sun. Because of this, you should consult an astrological calendar to make sure the New Moon has occurred, for the symbolism of the waning "dark Moon," just *before* the New Moon, is quite different. Work at the New Moon (exactly on or just after the time of conjunction) when you wish to focus your intent on beginnings or on taking initiative. The New Moon phase of any eightfold lunar cycle is the time that symbolizes the spontaneity of acting on impulse or instinct, however, rather than through studied planning. This is not to say you shouldn't plan to do a "new beginning" ritual at the next New Moon. It is a suggestion that perhaps you should let the mood and inspiration of the moment determine exactly how you will work. It might be better to go out in the dark of the night, be it pleasantly warm or even in a storm, and look around for a sign, a symbol, or a natural tool that catches your eye, rather than having a carefully planned structure. Move freely and spontaneously as you cast a circle around you. Call upon the Maiden to dance out of chaos and bring you a message that will assist you in focusing on your new beginning. The New Moon is a good time to visualize your intent, to set your resolve, or to take action on something you know you should do—perhaps to plant seeds that symbolize your intent, to send out a psychic beacon to attract love, or better yet, to cause the love you feel within you to increase and flow out to the world around you.

☽ **The Crescent Moon** brings the visible sign of the lovely sliver of the Maiden Moon, appearing in the night sky not long after sunset. The waxing crescent is bright on the right side as you look at her, with the "horns" pointing toward the left, and often tilted more or less up. At the exact Crescent phase, she has moved 45° ahead of the Sun in the zodiac, allowing her light to become visible after the Sun's strong rays have faded below the horizon. The Crescent phase symbolizes just that theme—first visible light. This is the time when that which was initiated at the New Moon may begin to show visible results. Bring new light into a project you've begun, shed light on a puzzle, see a situation more clearly, take steps to make yourself more attractive, work to firm up a decision you've made, and accept the challenge to persist—especially if any signs of lethargy are evident! Work to shield yourself from whatever influences tempt you away from pursuing your resolved plan.

◑ **The First Quarter Moon** is visible as the Moon half-light, half-dark. This is a point of balance and equilibrium, after which the light increases. The Moon is making her waxing square aspect to the Sun. Dane Rudhyar called the First Quarter phase the "crisis of action." This is a time when you must forge ahead decisively. Assess the progress you have made since the New Moon. If necessary, you might work to symbolically sweep away or break the bonds of anything from the past—your own lethargy or lack of will or the sounds of naysayers in your environment—and fortify your will to move forward with confidence and faith. Charge your courage, charge your assertiveness, if need be. Make decisions. Take action! Continue to work to build energy toward fulfillment of your goals.

○ **The Gibbous Moon,** when the Moon is bright, but not yet full—a bit flat or dented on the left side, as you look at her—is the 135° aspect of the Moon moving past the Sun, known as the sesquare or tri-octile. Like the youthful God chasing the Maiden at Beltane, full of life, feeling all grown up but not yet aware of the consequences that will loom after he finally gets what he thinks he wants, the Gibbous phase symbolizes growth with confidence, even though the results are not yet known. Here you should focus your energy on charging whatever activities are necessary to build your skill, gain increased knowledge, spark creativity, or do whatever you need to do to make your wishes come true. This is definitely *not* the time to read charts or read cards, or whatever you do, to try to find out what will happen in the future. Read them only if they can give you intuitive insight into what you will *make* happen! Do rituals that will charge and build your energy—dance, drum, create joy, and keep focused on your goals.

○ **The Full Moon.** The magickal time of the bright Full Moon, sending light that creates elfin shadows on the land, is a time of fulfillment, and perhaps your ritual might be a celebration of something achieved. But this is also a time to seek illumination—insight into what the true purpose might be for the goals you have achieved in life and for what you have and who you are, and how you might share any and all of these things with others. This is the time when our Lady Moon reflects the full light of the Sun, but positions herself directly opposite him in the zodiac, showing the "other side"—there *always* is one, you know. Whatever the Sun "says" or shows, the Moon makes the message objective, demonstrating the other half that makes the message whole. The Moon is the Sun's opposite, and also his complement.

At this optimum time for all magick, it is important to seek balance within, and harmony with the elements and with the inner feminine and masculine, Goddess and God. In this you partake in the illumination that is the necessary part of receiving the full benefit of this phase. With no illumination within, success is hollow and unsatisfying, for once a goal is achieved—once you have climbed to the top of a mountain—where next must you go? There is nothing constant in life but change. What is up, must come down. What has fully culminated in light, must begin to wane. The wheel keeps turning. Without illumination, one may hold to the mundane and fear the future. With it, one knows that all phases are of equal importance in the cycle of life, and one can live fully in the *now*, savoring each moment.

The sign of the Full Moon will be given on any astrological calendar or in an ephemeris. While all forms of magick are favored at the Full Moon, perhaps a ritual theme for the achievement of inner balance might be found by meditating on the complementary opposite signs of the Sun and Moon. Full rituals for each are given in *The Witch's Circle*, but here, for example, are some key themes.

Full Moon Themes
of Balancing Polarities for Each Sign

Full Moon in Aries (Sun in Libra)—Balance assertiveness with compromise.

Full Moon in Taurus (Sun in Scorpio)—Balance saving with eliminating; balance holding on with letting go.

Full Moon in Gemini (Sun in Sagittarius)—Balance logic and reason with inspiration and faith.

Full Moon in Cancer (Sun in Capricorn)—Balance home and family life with career life.

Full Moon in Leo (Sun in Aquarius)—Balance your own individual expression with peer pressure.

Full Moon is in Virgo (Sun in Pisces)—Balance a practical approach with following your dreams.

Full Moon in Libra (Sun in Aries)—Balance the harmony of your relationships with your personal desires.

Full Moon in Scorpio (Sun in Taurus)—Balance inner self-mastery with mastery over material things.

Full Moon in Sagittarius (Sun in Gemini)—Balance idealism with facts.

Full Moon in Capricorn (Sun in Cancer)—Balance your responsibilities with your emotional needs.

Full Moon in Aquarius (Sun in Leo)—Balance the goals of your family, coworkers, or any other group to which you belong with your own ego needs.

Full Moon in Pisces (Sun in Virgo)—Balance the needs of your Spirit with the demands of reality.

Look to the sign correspondences previously given, for both the Full Moon and current sign of the Sun, for additional ideas.

The Waning Moon Period

From the time of the Full Moon until the New Moon occurs again, light/energy gradually decreases. This is a time for sharing, giving thanks, bringing things to completion, and letting go of that which is finished or that which you desire to eliminate from your life. While rituals devoted to any of these themes are appropriate during the entire waning period, the intermediate phases each have a distinct theme.

◯ **The Disseminating Moon** is when the Moon, which has been round and full, now appears somewhat flattened or dented on the right side—the opposite side from which the dent appeared at the Gibbous phase. The symbolic themes of this phase are sharing, communication, maturity, and wisdom. Having received illumination and balance at the Full Moon, one must now give back to the Universe what one has learned. Meditations and rituals of thanksgiving, as well as of continued assimilation of Full Moon balancing insights, are appropriate. Focus on workings that will offer insight into giving back what you have received. Charge activities of teaching, speaking, or writing—anything that allows you to share knowledge or experience that might benefit others. This is also the time to work toward bringing projects to completion. Assess your progress and what still needs to be done, and then charge your energy and will to do it.

◑ **The Last Quarter Moon** is the waning square of the Moon to the Sun—half-light, half-dark, but now the darkness will soon increase and overtake the light. Dane Rudhyar called this phase the "crisis of consciousness." This is a good time to offer a special candle meditation of thanks for what you have received, but also to meditate on what a future goal might be. At this phase, the energy turns inward to a more contemplative mode. Outwardly, you may be doing your work and going about your life, quite as usual, but inwardly you may be thinking, "Is this all there is? Isn't there something more?" Divination for insight at this time may aid in focusing your thoughts on new possibilities. Use whatever methods you like best within a magickal circle. Work not to foretell the future, for the future is largely up to you. Work for ideas, insight, and direction. Work for thanksgiving, and for greater attunement with the divine that dwells within you.

☽ **The Balsamic Moon** is the Crone's Moon. Now the Moon is but a sliver again, this time bright on the left side with horns pointing toward the right. You'll probably have to get up very early in the morning to see her toward the eastern end of the ecliptic arc, in the hours before sunrise. At the exact beginning of this phase, she has 45° more to travel through the zodiac before once again conjoining with the Sun. The ancients saw her as going into the Underworld to bring the Sun to rebirth. During this last three and one-half days of the waning crescent, you are at the optimum time for rituals of banishing and letting go. Work to eliminate whatever habits, doubts, or fears are holding you back from achieving what you want in life. If you grieve or are holding on to something or someone that you know in your heart you should release, draw on your own inner strength and the infinite power of Spirit to end it and let go with love. This would be a good time to firm your resolve to do things such as quitting smoking, losing weight, or anything else that involves banishing or decrease. This is a most powerful phase for magick.

Lest you think that this sounds too negative, think again. I was once standing in my daughter Molly's Starcrafts store in San Diego when a customer asked about obtaining supplies for a prosperity ritual. She expressed her wish to do something that very night, but was restless because she would have to wait for the New Moon, which was still a couple days ahead. She thought one could only work for something positive during the waxing Moon. I suggested that one could work for just about any purpose at any time, but the intent is best tailored to the cosmic mirror of the time. I asked her if she could identify some of the reasons within herself or her circumstances that made her feel less prosperous than she'd like. Could she let go of them, in order to create space for change? Together we planned a ritual to eliminate poverty consciousness.

Death is only change. Letting go creates room for something new to come in. For every door that closes, another will open. Within every ending, there lies the seed of a bright new beginning. Banishing rituals are especially effective at any time from the beginning of the balsamic period through the dark Moon period, until the actual astronomical onset of the New Moon. As said before, since the sky is still dark at the New Moon, you should consult an astrological calendar or ephemeris to find out exactly when the New Moon occurs.

---

1. See Job 38:32 New English Bible.

2. A much more thorough background on the changing of the ages can be found in chapter 2, "A New Age Is Emerging—But What Is It?", of my book *The Witch's Circle* (St. Paul, Minn.: Llewellyn Publications, 1996).

4

The Order and Calculation of Planetary Hours

The twenty-four hour day is a modern notion. The ancients considered their "day" to begin at sunrise and end at sunset. Hours were reckoned as divisions of the diurnal day (daylight) or of the nocturnal night (sunset to sunrise). Day and night both had twelve hours each, but the twelve hours were not neatly divided into sixty-minute sections. The planetary hour system clearly reflects the reality that in the summer, daytime hours are longer than nighttime hours, while in the winter, daytime hours become shorter and nighttime hours become longer.

The first planetary hour of a day is ruled by the same planet that rules that day, e.g., the first hour of Sunday is ruled by the Sun. The sequential order of the planets that rule the hours is an ancient Chaldean order based on the speed of the planets, slowest to fastest: Saturn, Jupiter, Mars, Sun, Venus, Mercury, Moon. The length of each diurnal hour is essentially the length of time between sunrise and sunset divided by twelve.

At sunset, the nocturnal hours begin, with their length determined by figuring the time between sunset and sunrise and dividing by twelve. The first hour after sunset is the next in sequence after the last hour before sunset. The sequence continues on in the same order until sunrise on the next day, when you will find yourself on exactly the "right" planet to begin that day—the one that rules that day.

In this system, days (as named divisions of the week) do not begin and end at midnight. They begin at sunrise and continue until the following sunrise. Sunday lasts from sunrise on Sunday until sunrise on Monday. In your various Llewellyn annuals, you'll find a table like this.

Planetary Sunrise and Sunset Hours

Sunrise

Hour	Sun	Mon	Tue	Wed	Thu	Fri	Sat
1	☉	☽	♂	☿	♃	♀	♄
2	♀	♄	☉	☽	♂	☿	♃
3	☿	♃	♀	♄	☉	☽	♂
4	☽	♂	☿	♃	♀	♄	☉
5	♄	☉	☽	♂	☿	♃	♀
6	♃	♀	♄	☉	☽	♂	☽
7	♂	☿	♃	♀	♄	☉	☿
8	☉	☽	♂	☿	♃	♀	♄
9	♀	♄	☉	☽	♂	☿	♃
10	☿	♃	♀	♄	☉	☽	♂
11	☽	♂	☿	♃	♀	♄	☉
12	♄	☉	☽	♂	☿	♃	♀

Sunset

Hour	Sun	Mon	Tue	Wed	Thu	Fri	Sat
1	♃	♀	♄	☉	☽	♂	☽
2	♂	☿	♃	♀	♄	☉	☿
3	☉	☽	♂	☿	♃	♀	♄
4	♀	♄	☉	☽	♂	☿	♃
5	☿	♃	♀	♄	☉	☽	♂
6	☽	♂	☿	♃	♀	♄	☉
7	♄	☉	☽	♂	☿	♃	♀
8	♃	♀	♄	☉	☽	♂	☽
9	♂	☿	♃	♀	♄	☉	☿
10	☉	☽	♂	☿	♃	♀	♄
11	♀	♄	☉	☽	♂	☿	♃
12	☿	♃	♀	♄	☉	☽	♂

☉ Sun, ☽ Moon, ♂ Mars, ☿ Mercury, ♃ Jupiter, ♀ Venus, ♄ Saturn

The elegance by which the sequence of hours that begins Sunday winds up at the hour before sunrise on Monday with Mercury, so that hour number one at sunrise will neatly be the Moon, is more easily seen in this spiral illustration. I first saw a spiral similar to this in Lee Lehman's horary astrology course booklet, and asked her for permission to repeat the idea. Lee told me that the spiral design is very old and appears in public domain sources.

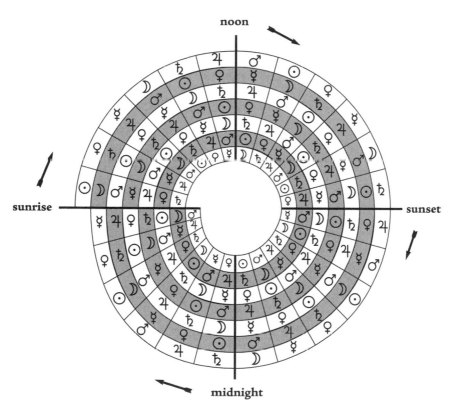

Figure 2. Spiral Illustration of Sequence of Planetary Hours.

Local mean times of sunrise and sunset change slightly each day, and vary with the latitude. If you know the right times for your latitude, you can, of course, figure this out fairly well for yourself. *The Old Farmer's Almanac* lists sunrise and sunset Eastern Standard Times for every day of the year, plus the exact length of the total diurnal (daylight) period. A sunrise/sunset list also appears in Llewellyn's *Daily Planetary Guide*. Your local newspaper publishes exact sunrise and sunset times, though with only one day's advance notice. *Dell Horoscope*, a monthly popular astrology magazine, publishes planetary hours every month, though I found that their sunrise times differ somewhat from those in *The Old Farmer's Almanac*. The perpetual planetary hour tables in this book are quite a bit easier to use than generalized tables and yield more accurate results—but I must say, the easiest way to use planetary hours on a frequent basis is with computer software that corrects precisely for your own latitude and time zone on any date you choose. Still, computers can be down or the power out at just the time you need information, so it's never good to be overly dependent on electronic assistance. Don't forget how to look at the sky!

Calculating Planetary Hours by Hand

Before giving you instructions for using the perpetual planetary hour tables in this book, I'll first show you how to figure the planetary hours by a "quick and dirty" method. This is a fairly easy way to get a less-than-precise, but workable, knowledge of the hours. Say you don't have any reference that tells you even the sunrise or sunset times, and you can't find this book, and your computer is down. In that case, find a flat horizon place to look at the sky. I tested this in San Diego, where I could judge the time the sun sank into the sea against published sunset hours. That was right on. If you live where flat horizons are few and far between, I suggest you test visible sunrise with the published times in your local newspaper for several days to see just how far off you are, and then you can compensate for the discrepancy. Here are the basic steps.

1. Memorize the planetary order according to speed, slowest to fastest: Saturn, Jupiter, Mars, Sun, Venus, Mercury, Moon. Memorize which day goes with which planet: Sun-day, Moon-day, Tuesday-Tiw/Mars, Wednesday-Woden/Mercury, Thursday-Thor/Jupiter, Friday-Freya/Venus, and Saturday-Saturn.

2. Go somewhere outdoors where you can see the horizon at sunrise and sunset.

3. Clock sunrise and sunset times as closely as you can, according to your own local time, and do this for several days. Repeat as the seasons change. You will find that as the year advances from winter to the summer solstice, sunrise is just a minute or two earlier each day, and sunset a minute or two later. After the summer solstice, the reverse is true. Right at spring and the fall equinox, the days and nights will be the same length. Once you have clocked sunrise and sunset for several days, you'll know about how much to adjust each day, and can therefore make a good guess even on the days when the sky is too clouded to see the Sun rise or set.

4. Start with the planetary ruler of the day, and assign it to the first diurnal hour to begin at sunrise. Make a vertical list of twelve planets, beginning with the day ruler and continuing according to the order you've memorized. When you've listed all seven planets, start again with the day ruler. When you've assigned all twelve diurnal hours, move to your nocturnal list, and continue in the same order, e.g., if your diurnal hours ended with Mars, your first nocturnal hour is the Sun. Yes, I know you have the table in this book, but what if you don't have a book handy? It's essential to memorize the order!

5. Figure the total number of hours and minutes between sunrise and sunset. Divide your total by twelve, and add one equal division to sunrise, another to this result, and so on. Each equal division represents one diurnal hour. Write down a list of what time each diurnal hour begins.

One important note: When you're calculating time by hand, you have to treat the hours and minutes separately. Add or subtract the minutes. Whatever the result, if it is over sixty, that is one hour. Move it over to the hour column. To work with hours and minutes, it is sometimes easier to change it all into minutes. For example, 5 hours and 30 minutes is 5 x 60 = 300 + 30, or 330 minutes. With that, you can do the math without having to move hours. For other operations, I find it faster to deal with the hours and minutes, so I'll demonstrate that, too.

The following is a typical diurnal planetary hours list, using a computer list time for my location, Kensington, NH (latitude 42 N 44), on the left. To the right of it is my hand calculation of the planetary hours using very simple math. (I am math-phobic—if I can do this, you can, too!) As you can see, the hand calculations are never more than a minute off. In this example, I ended up with exactly the same sunset time as the computer list.

Diurnal Planetary Hours

Wednesday, May 12

Kensington, NH, latitude 42 N 44 (Eastern Standard Time)

	Computer		Hand Calculations
Mercury	5:30 A.M.	sunrise	5:30 A.M.
Moon	6:42 A.M.		6:42 A.M.
Saturn	7:53 A.M.		7:54 A.M.
Jupiter	9:05 A.M.		9:06 A.M.
Mars	10:17 A.M.		10:17 A.M.
Sun	11:29 A.M.		11:28 A.M.
Venus	12:41 P.M.		12:40 P.M.
Mercury	1:52 P.M.		1:52 P.M.

Moon	3:04 P.M.		3:04 P.M.
Saturn	4:16 P.M.		4:15 P.M.
Jupiter	5:28 P.M.		5:27 P.M.
Mars	6:39 P.M.		6:39 P.M.
Jupiter	7:51 P.M.	sunset	7:51 P.M.

Here's the math.

12:00	(noon)
+ 7:51	(12 + 7:51 P.M. changes time to 24-hour format)
= 19:51	(total hours of clock day to 7:51 P.M.)
– 5:30	(subtract sunrise time)
= 14:21	(or 14 hours 21 minutes: total amount of diurnal planetary hours and minutes)

It's easy to see here that 14:21 hours means that every one of the 12 diurnal planetary hours will be at least 1 clock hour long. Now you've got 2 extra hours (14 – 12 = 2) plus 21 extra minutes. Convert this to minutes: 2 x 60 minutes = 120 + 21 = 141 minutes. Divide 141 by 12 and you get about 11¾ minutes. (A hand calculator would say 11.75.) So, one diurnal hour = 1 hour 11¾ minutes.

We could handle that extra ¾ of a minute by rounding up to 12 minutes for 3 hours and then just using 11 minutes every fourth hour: 5:30 + 1 hour 12 minutes = 6:42; 6:42 + 1 hour 12 minutes = 7:54; 7:54 + 1 hour 12 minutes = 8:66 (move the 60 minutes to the 8 to make 9) or 9:06; 9:06 + 1 hour 11 minutes = 10:17, and so on. I was a minute off here and there, but still ended up with 7:51 for sunset, the same as the computer sunset time. Not bad!

6. To find the number of nocturnal planetary hours, subtract the number of diurnal planetary hours from the total 24 hours of a day.

24:00	(total hours in a clock day)
–14:21	(total number of diurnal hours)
9:39	(total of 9 hours and 39 minutes of nocturnal hours)

Convert this to minutes: 9 x 60 minutes = 540 minutes. Add the 39 minutes and you have 579 minutes. Divide that by 12 and you get 48¼ minutes for each nocturnal hour. (A hand calculator would say 4.16) Another fraction! Though we've observed that the night gets a minute or so shorter every day this time of year, we probably don't have to be that picky. Let's just round down to 48 minutes and see how we come out. As you can see from the table below, the hand calculations matched the computer right up to the next sunrise, when the computer time is one minute less. So the computer compensated for the fraction and the decreasing light. That's close enough for the scratch pad method, and not so "dirty" after all (but not as "quick" as the computer, either!).

Nocturnal Planetary Hours

Wednesday, May 12

Kensington, NH, latitude 42 N 44 (Eastern Standard Time)

	Computer		Hand Calculations
Sun	7:51 P.M.	sunset, May 12	7:51 P.M.
Venus	8:39 P.M.		8:39 P.M.
Mercury	9:28 P.M.		9:27 P.M.
Moon	10:16 P.M.		10:16 P.M.
Saturn	11:04 P.M.		11:04 P.M.
Jupiter	11:52 P.M.		11:52 P.M.
Mars	12:41 A.M.	May 13	12:40 A.M.
Sun	1:29 A.M.		1:29 A.M.
Venus	2:17 A.M.		2:17 A.M.
Mercury	3:05 A.M.		3:05 A.M.
Moon	3:53 A.M.		3:53 A.M.
Saturn	4:42 A.M.		4:42 A.M.
Jupiter	5:29 A.M.	sunrise, May 13	5:30 A.M.

If you have a computer program that calculates planetary hours, or study the planetary hour tables year to year, you'll find that the daily incremental changes follow a predictable pattern. Even so, I recommend looking at the sky whenever possible—sunrises and sunsets are good for the soul!

A problem with relying on either perpetual planetary hour tables based on sunrise/sunset times for latitudes other than your own, or looking at the sky at anything other than a very flat horizon, is that your times for the beginning of each planetary hour will not be absolutely precise. The planetary hour tables are not perfect (although much better than almanac listings) unless you are right on the button of one of the rounded-off latitudes given and adjust according to the proper correction of clock time for your city. For this reason, it is always best not to work too close to the beginning or ending of a particular planetary hour if it's really important to you to be within the time that a particular planet rules.

Unless you're working with a precisely calculated computer printout, I'd recommend waiting about ten minutes into the planetary hour you've selected to begin your working—and certainly don't start any closer than that to the end of it. It is probably for the best, anyway, to be fully into the swing of your chosen planetary energy at the time you act.

Calculating Planetary Hours with Perpetual Planetary Hour Tables

In the next section of this book, you will find tables from which you can find the correct, or at least very close to the correct, beginning of each planetary hour for any year in any location. Each table covers about one week out of each month. Latitudes are rounded off in whole degrees, every 2° from 27° to 55°. The title lines at the top of the tables are for northern latitude locations, but notice that at the bottom of each table is a line showing an alternative month and dates for which the table can be used for southern latitude locations.

Following the planetary hour tables you will find an extensive list of cities, each with the time correction you would need to make for accuracy. This is because the planetary hour tables are not set according to the time on your clock. Clocks are set according to a standard time zone, such as Eastern Standard Time, Central Standard Time, British Summer Time, and so on. These standardized times are not the same as the true local Sun time (called Local Mean Time, or for short, LMT) for your exact location, so accurate astrological computations require time adjustments. The planetary hour tables are set for LMT, and that is why you will need to make a time correction for most cities in order to use the tables.

Why is this? Because clock times are set according to a central longitude within each time zone. Every degree of longitude requires a four-minute correction from standard time to LMT, either added (+) or subtracted (–) depending on whether the city is east or west of the center of the zone. For example, the central time zone in the United States is set according to 90° west longitude. Chicago, Illinois, is at 87 W 40, to the *east* of the 90th longitude, so you must *add* 9 minutes to your clock time to get LMT. Council Bluffs, Iowa, is at 95 W 55, to the *west* of the 90th longitude, so you must *subtract* 23 minutes to get LMT.

Frankly, I found the extensive and detailed rules about time corrections and coordinates in the old Llewellyn George book to be somewhat confusing. So I've decided that rather than give you a list of standard all-purpose rules, it will be more useful to walk you through four practical demonstrations of how to use the tables. You'll find two exercises for each of the two most typical approaches one might take.

There is one "rule" of time, covered in the examples to follow, that needs to be set apart and emblazoned in your memory, because these tables deal only with the difference between LMT and *standard* time for the time zones of the listed cities.

Rule: Spring forward, fall back.

That is, when changing from standard time to daylight saving time, add an hour. When changing from daylight saving time back to standard time, subtract an hour.

If the time on your clock happens to reflect daylight saving time, British Summer Time, or any of the other artificial arrangements used by governments to make the daylight hours more convenient, it is up to you to know when those time changes take place for your location. Make the appropriate adjustment to standard time, when necessary, in order to use these tables accurately.

Approach A

When do the hours of Venus (or any planet) occur today? Then, after you've looked up your planetary hour and the LMT time it begins in the planetary hour tables, what time will this be on your clock?

Example 1

Let's first look for an hour of Venus that occurs during daytime business hours in my home city of Kensington, NH, on January 26, 2001, which is a Friday.

1. Look up New Hampshire in the city list (page 160). Kensington isn't there. Pick the closest city that is listed. If you're not sure, pick the one with the closest latitude to your city. If you don't know the latitude of your city, you can find it on a map. I am picking Exeter, which has a +16 time correction, and I will round off the latitude to 43°. The latitude of Exeter is 42.59; that of Kensington is 42.44.

2. Look for the planetary hour table that includes January 26. It is on page 98, which is the table for January 24 to 31. In the center of the table where all the astrological glyphs are located, run your finger down the Friday col-

umn (head "F") until you find the Venus glyphs. Bypass the sunrise Venus—that's too early. Stop at the next one. Now look to your right to the latitude column for 43°. Note the time: 1:01. So, at 1:01 P.M. LMT, the Venus hour begins. It continues until the Mercury hour begins at 1:49 P.M.

3. Now, change the LMT times given for your planetary hour into your clock time. What time on your clock corresponds to 1:01 P.M. and 1:49 P.M.? The time correction is +16, but that is for adding to your clock time to get LMT. Here we have to subtract in order to convert LMT back to your standard clock time. So, subtract 16 minutes from 1:01 P.M., and you get 12:45 P.M. Subtract 16 minutes from 1:49 P.M. and you get 1:33 P.M. This means that according to your clock, the Venus hour begins at 12:45 P.M. and is over at 1:33 P.M.

Example 2

Let's look for the hour of the Sun during the evening of the Leo Moon day in Leo's month of August. In 2001, that happens to be on Saturday, August 18. Our location is St. Paul, MN.

1. Look in the city list for Minnesota (pages 156–157). St. Paul has a –12 correction, at latitude 44.58. We'll round that off to 45°.

2. Turn to the planetary hour table for August 16 to 23 (page 125). Run your finger down the "Sa" (Saturday) column past the daytime hours until you come to the first Sun glyph in the evening. Hold your place and look to the right to find the time under the Lat. 45° column. The Sun hour begins at 11:15 P.M. and goes until the Venus hour begins at 12:05 A.M.

3. Now, convert the LMT times given in the table to your clock time. The –12 time correction for St. Paul means

that its standard time is 12 minutes faster than LMT. So, in this case, we must add 12 minutes to what we see in the tables to get Central Standard Time (CST).

But . . . there is now an additional wrinkle. This is August. Daylight saving time is in effect. Remember the old adage "Spring forward, fall back?" Once you get to standard time, you must then "spring forward" and add one full hour in order to find the Central Daylight Time that corresponds to the LMT Sun hour in the tables. Your results should show that the Sun hour begins at 12:27 A.M. CDT and runs until the Venus hour begins at 1:17 A.M. CDT.

Approach B

What planetary hour is in effect at exactly 2:00 P.M. (or any time) on my clock?

Example 3

Let's pretend that on Thursday, July 12, you've been asked to schedule an appointment at 2:00 P.M. in Leucadia, CA, and you want to know what planetary hour that is before you agree to the meeting.

1. Figure out the LMT equivalent of your 2:00 P.M. clock time in Leucadia, CA. Turn to the city list for California (pages 145–147). Leucadia is not on the list, but you know that it is close to Oceanside, so use that. Oceanside is a +10 time correction. (Also note that it is latitude 33.12, which most closely rounds off to 33°—you'll need that information soon.) First of all, remember that your clock is set for daylight saving time. "Spring forward, fall back." So 2:00 P.M. is 1:00 P.M. in standard time. Add the 10 minute time correction and you have 1:10 P.M.

2. Look at the planetary hour table that includes July 12. The table for July 8 to 15 is on page 120. Run your finger

down the daytime hours under Lat. 33° until you come to the closest time you can find that is just before 1:10. It is 12:05. Run your finger across horizontally until you are in the glyph column under "Th." There you will find the glyph for Saturn (♄). The next time down from 12:05 is 1:16. This means that the Saturn hour will still be in effect at 1:10 LMT, although it's very close to the change to the Jupiter hour, which starts at 1:16 LMT (2:06 PDT).

Mmm . . . Unless the topic of your appointment really works well within a Saturn theme, you could consider either being fashionably late or suggesting a slightly later appointment time. About 2:30 P.M. would do nicely—well into the Jupiter hour, but not too close to the end of it.

Example 4

Let's look for the planetary hour at 3:00 A.M. on November 18 in Kilauea, HI, which falls on Sunday in 2001. (Hey, if I happened to be in Hawaii at the time of my solar return, I'd think of something more creative to do at 3:00 A.M. than to sleep through it!)

1. Look at the city list for Hawaii (pages 149–150). Kilauea is a –38 correction at latitude 22.13. That means the standard clock time of 3:00 A.M. must be changed to 38 minutes less, or 2:22 LMT.

2. Look in the planetary hour table for November 18, which is on page 137 for November 15 to 22. Look under Lat. 23°. . . ahh, another problem.

   The latitudes only go as low as 27°. With latitudes rounded off at every 2°, that would mean we have to go two steps lower. Scan all the way down the Lat. 27° column, into the nocturnal hours, and look at the pattern across the entire horizontal line of latitudes. There's no more than a two-minute difference from one latitude column to the next. Decreasing the 1:56 and 3:02 times given under Lat. 27° would give us a range of time for our target planetary hour of 1:52 A.M. to 2:58 A.M. Our time of 2:22 A.M. is within this hour.

3. Look across your horizontal line of latitudes to the glyph columns and find the planet that comes under the "Sa" column for Saturday.

Whoa! Saturday? Yes, I did say that November 18 falls on a Sunday on my calendar . . . *but* this is a time before sunrise. In the planetary hour system, a day begins at sunrise, rather than at midnight, as our calendar system dictates. November 18 may be a Sunday on our calendar, but according to the rules for planetary hours, 3:00 A.M. on Sunday is definitely before sunrise and therefore still belongs to the nocturnal hours of Saturday. Therefore, the planetary hour for 3:00 A.M. at standard time for Hawaii on Sunday, November 18, is the Moon.

Let's see how our results stack up with a computer. For my computer check, I used Arlene Kramer's Sundial software (see bibliography and resource list) and the exact latitude and longitude for the cities in the examples, whether they appear in this book's city lists or not. The software lists the planetary hours according to the clock time of the city in neat little columns for each day. Admittedly, this is a much easier way to check planetary hours. I run off a printout for several weeks at a time from Sundial and keep that list handy to use at a glance. Still, even if you have software, it is worthwhile to know how to look up the planetary hours from the tables.

Example 1: Sundial has the Venus hour beginning at 12:44 P.M. and the Mercury hour beginning at 1:32 P.M. This is only one minute different from our hand calculations.

Example 2: Sundial has the Sun hour beginning at 12:24 A.M., and the Venus hour at 1:16 A.M. Here our table calculations are three minutes off for the beginning of the Sun hour, but only one minute off for the end of it.

Example 3: Sundial, like our table calculation, shows 2:00 P.M. PDT to be within the Saturn hour, but very close to the end of it. The Jupiter hour starts at 2:04 P.M. PDT, only two minutes off from the table calculation. Though the example exercise didn't necessitate translating the beginning of the Saturn hour back into PDT, according to Sundial it is 12:55 P.M.

Example 4: Sundial agrees with our tables calculation that 3:00 A.M. Hawaiian Standard Time falls within the hour of the Moon. The Moon hour is listed under Saturday, November 17, as beginning at 2:33 A.M., while the hour of Saturn that follows begins at 3:39 A.M. If we take the LMT time range for the Moon hour and add back the 38-minute time corrections, we get 2:34 A.M. to 3:36 A.M., just one minute off for the beginning of the hour and three minutes off for the end of the hour.

The bottom line is that the computer results and the table calculations are not a perfect match, but they are very close.

In his *Improved Perpetual Planetary Hour Book*, Llewellyn George said, "When choosing a certain planetary hour for any important affair, allow about fifteen minutes of the hour to elapse before commencing operations, and then the affair will be safely started under the desired influence. The strongest or most important part of a planetary hour is approximately the center."

In the precomputer days of hand calculations, fifteen minutes was a fair safety net. Considering that none of our table-versus-computer examples were any more than three minutes off, and it's probably safe to cut things a little closer than that. Still, I won't dispute Llewellyn George's wisdom that the strongest part of a planetary hour is its center. If your math is a little off, the center of the hour is also definitely the safest!

Perpetual Planetary Hour Tables

JANUARY 1st to 7th, ANY YEAR, in North Latitude

♄ Saturn; ♃ Jupiter; ♂ Mars; ☉ Sun; ♀ Venus; ☿ Mercury; ☽ Moon.

Day Hours; Sunrise to Sunset. Mean Time.

Lat. 27°	Lat. 29°	Lat. 31°	Lat. 33°	Lat. 35°	Lat. 37°	Lat. 39°	Lat. 41°	Su	M	Tu	W	Th	F	Sa	Lat. 43°	Lat. 45°	Lat. 47°	Lat. 49°	Lat. 51°	Lat. 53°	Lat. 55°
6.50	6.54	6.58	7.03	7.08	7.14	7.19	7.25	☉	☽	♂	☿	♃	♀	♄	7.32	7.38	7.46	7.55	8.04	8.14	8.26
7.42	7.46	7.49	7.53	7.57	8.02	8.06	8.11	♀	♄	☉	☽	♂	☿	♃	8.17	8.22	8.29	8.36	8.44	8.52	9.02
8.35	8.37	8.40	8.43	8.47	8.51	8.54	8.58	☿	♃	♀	♄	☉	☽	♂	9.03	9.07	9.12	9.18	9.24	9.31	9.39
9.27	9.29	9.31	9.33	9.36	9.39	9.41	9.44	☽	♂	☿	♃	♀	♄	☉	9.48	9.51	9.55	9.59	10.04	10.09	10.15
10.19	10.20	10.21	10.23	10.25	10.27	10.28	10.31	♄	☉	☽	♂	☿	♃	♀	10.33	10.35	10.38	10.41	10.44	10.47	10.51
11.11	11.12	11.13	11.13	11.14	11.16	11.17	11.17	♃	♀	♄	☉	☽	♂	☿	11.18	11.19	11.21	11.22	11.24	11.25	11.28
12.04	12.04	12.04	12.04	12.04	12.04	12.04	12.04	♂	☿	♃	♀	♄	☉	☽	12.04	12.04	12.04	12.04	12.04	12.04	12.04
12.56	12.55	12.54	12.54	12.53	12.52	12.52	12.50	☉	☽	♂	☿	♃	♀	♄	12.49	12.48	12.46	12.45	12.43	12.42	12.40
1.48	1.47	1.45	1.44	1.42	1.41	1.40	1.37	♀	♄	☉	☽	♂	☿	♃	1.34	1.32	1.29	1.26	1.23	1.20	1.17
2.40	2.38	2.36	2.33	2.31	2.29	2.27	2.23	☿	♃	♀	♄	☉	☽	♂	2.20	2.17	2.12	2.09	2.03	1.58	1.53
3.33	3.30	3.27	3.24	3.21	3.17	3.14	3.10	☽	♂	☿	♃	♀	♄	☉	3.05	3.01	2.55	2.50	2.43	2.37	2.29
4.24	4.22	4.18	4.14	4.09	4.06	4.02	3.56	♄	☉	☽	♂	☿	♃	♀	3.50	3.45	3.38	3.32	3.23	3.15	3.06
Night Hours; Sunset to Sunrise.																					
5.17	5.13	5.09	5.04	4.59	4.54	4.48	4.42	♃	♀	♄	☉	☽	♂	☿	4.35	4.29	4.21	4.12	4.03	3.53	3.42
6.25	6.21	6.18	6.14	6.10	6.06	6.01	5.56	♂	☿	♃	♀	♄	☉	☽	5.50	5.45	5.38	5.31	5.23	5.15	5.06
7.33	7.30	7.27	7.24	7.21	7.17	7.13	7.09	☉	☽	♂	☿	♃	♀	♄	7.05	7.01	6.55	6.49	6.43	6.37	6.29
8.40	8.38	8.36	8.34	8.31	8.29	8.26	8.23	♀	♄	☉	☽	♂	☿	♃	8.19	8.16	8.12	8.08	8.03	7.58	7.53
9.48	9.47	9.45	9.44	9.42	9.41	9.38	9.36	☿	♃	♀	♄	☉	☽	♂	9.34	9.32	9.29	9.26	9.23	9.20	9.17
10.56	10.55	10.54	10.54	10.53	10.52	10.51	10.50	☽	♂	☿	♃	♀	♄	☉	10.49	10.48	10.46	10.45	10.43	10.42	10.40
12.04	12.04	12.04	12.04	12.04	12.04	12.04	12.04	♄	☉	☽	♂	☿	♃	♀	12.04	12.04	12.04	12.04	12.04	12.04	12.04
1.11	1.12	1.13	1.13	1.14	1.16	1.16	1.17	♃	♀	♄	☉	☽	♂	☿	1.18	1.19	1.22	1.22	1.24	1.25	1.28
2.19	2.20	2.22	2.23	2.25	2.27	2.29	2.31	♂	☿	♃	♀	♄	☉	☽	2.33	2.35	2.39	2.42	2.44	2.47	2.51
3.27	3.29	3.31	3.33	3.36	3.39	3.41	3.44	☉	☽	♂	☿	♃	♀	♄	3.48	3.50	3.56	4.00	4.04	4.09	4.15
4.35	4.37	4.40	4.43	4.47	4.51	4.55	4.58	♀	♄	☉	☽	♂	☿	♃	5.03	5.06	5.13	5.19	5.24	5.31	5.39
5.42	5.46	5.49	5.53	5.57	6.02	6.07	6.11	☿	♃	♀	♄	☉	☽	♂	6.17	6.22	6.29	6.37	6.44	6.52	7.02

JULY 1st to 7th, ANY YEAR, in South Latitude

JANUARY 8th to 15th, ANY YEAR, in North Latitude

♄ Saturn; ♃ Jupiter; ♂ Mars; ☉ Sun; ♀ Venus; ☿ Mercury; ☽ Moon.

Day Hours; Sunrise to Sunset. Mean Time.

Lat. 27°	Lat. 29°	Lat. 31°	Lat. 33°	Lat. 35°	Lat. 37°	Lat. 39°	Lat. 41°	Su	M	Tu	W	Th	F	Sa	Lat. 43°	Lat. 45°	Lat. 47°	Lat. 49°	Lat. 51°	Lat. 53°	Lat. 55°
6.51	6.55	6.59	7.04	7.09	7.14	7.19	7.25	☉	☽	♂	☿	♃	♀	♄	7.32	7.38	7.46	7.53	8.03	8.12	8.23
7.44	7.47	7.50	7.55	7.59	8.02	8.07	8.12	♀	♄	☉	☽	♂	☿	♃	8.18	8.23	8.30	8.35	8.44	8.51	9.00
8.36	8.39	8.42	8.45	8.48	8.52	8.55	8.59	☿	♃	♀	♄	☉	☽	♂	9.04	9.08	9.13	9.18	9.24	9.30	9.38
9.29	9.31	9.33	9.36	9.38	9.41	9.43	9.46	☽	♂	☿	♃	♀	♄	☉	9.50	9.53	9.57	10.00	10.05	10.10	10.15
10.22	10.23	10.24	10.26	10.28	10.29	10.31	10.33	♄	☉	☽	♂	☿	♃	♀	10.35	10.37	10.40	10.42	10.46	10.49	10.52
11.14	11.15	11.16	11.17	11.17	11.18	11.19	11.20	♃	♀	♄	☉	☽	♂	☿	11.21	11.22	11.24	11.24	11.26	11.28	11.30
12.07	12.07	12.07	12.07	12.07	12.07	12.07	12.07	♂	☿	♃	♀	♄	☉	☽	12.07	12.07	12.07	12.07	12.07	12.07	12.07
1.00	12.59	12.58	12.58	12.57	12.56	12.55	12.54	☉	☽	♂	☿	♃	♀	♄	12.53	12.52	12.51	12.49	12.48	12.46	12.44
1.52	1.51	1.50	1.48	1.46	1.45	1.43	1.41	♀	♄	☉	☽	♂	☿	♃	1.39	1.37	1.34	1.31	1.28	1.25	1.22
2.45	2.43	2.41	2.39	2.36	2.34	2.31	2.28	☿	♃	♀	♄	☉	☽	♂	2.25	2.22	2.18	2.13	2.09	2.05	1.59
3.38	3.35	3.32	3.29	3.26	3.22	3.19	3.15	☽	♂	☿	♃	♀	♄	☉	3.10	3.06	3.01	2.56	2.50	2.44	2.36
4.30	4.27	4.24	4.20	4.15	4.11	4.07	4.02	♄	☉	☽	♂	☿	♃	♀	3.56	3.51	3.45	3.38	3.30	3.23	3.14

Night Hours; Sunset to Sunrise.

Lat. 27°	Lat. 29°	Lat. 31°	Lat. 33°	Lat. 35°	Lat. 37°	Lat. 39°	Lat. 41°	Su	M	Tu	W	Th	F	Sa	Lat. 43°	Lat. 45°	Lat. 47°	Lat. 49°	Lat. 51°	Lat. 53°	Lat. 55°
5.23	5.19	5.15	5.10	5.05	5.00	4.55	4.49	♃	♀	♄	☉	☽	♂	☿	4.42	4.36	4.28	4.20	4.11	4.02	3.51
6.30	6.27	6.24	6.20	6.15	6.11	6.07	6.02	♂	☿	♃	♀	♄	☉	☽	5.56	5.51	5.44	5.38	5.30	5.23	5.14
7.38	7.35	7.32	7.29	7.26	7.22	7.19	7.15	☉	☽	♂	☿	♃	♀	♄	7.10	7.06	7.01	6.56	6.50	6.44	6.36
8.45	8.43	8.41	8.39	8.36	8.34	8.31	8.28	♀	♄	☉	☽	♂	☿	♃	8.24	8.21	8.17	8.13	8.09	8.04	7.59
9.52	9.51	9.50	9.48	9.46	9.45	9.43	9.41	☿	♃	♀	♄	☉	☽	♂	9.38	9.36	9.34	9.31	9.28	9.25	9.21
11.00	10.59	10.58	10.58	10.57	10.56	10.55	10.54	☽	♂	☿	♃	♀	♄	☉	10.52	10.51	10.50	10.49	10.47	10.46	10.44
12.07	12.07	12.07	12.07	12.07	12.07	12.07	12.07	♄	☉	☽	♂	☿	♃	♀	12.07	12.07	12.07	12.07	12.07	12.07	12.07
1.14	1.15	1.16	1.17	1.17	1.18	1.19	1.20	♃	♀	♄	☉	☽	♂	☿	1.21	1.22	1.23	1.24	1.26	1.27	1.29
2.22	2.23	2.24	2.26	2.28	2.29	2.31	2.33	♂	☿	♃	♀	♄	☉	☽	2.35	2.37	2.39	2.42	2.45	2.48	2.52
3.29	3.31	3.33	3.36	3.38	3.41	3.43	3.46	☉	☽	♂	☿	♃	♀	♄	3.49	3.52	3.56	4.00	4.04	4.09	4.14
4.36	4.39	4.42	4.45	4.48	4.52	4.55	4.59	♀	♄	☉	☽	♂	☿	♃	5.03	5.07	5.12	5.18	5.24	5.30	5.37
5.44	5.47	5.50	5.55	5.59	6.03	6.07	6.12	☿	♃	♀	♄	☉	☽	♂	6.17	6.22	6.29	6.35	6.43	6.50	6.59

JULY 8th to 15th, ANY YEAR, in South Latitude

JANUARY 16th to 23rd, ANY YEAR, in North Latitude

♄ Saturn; ♃ Jupiter; ♂ Mars; ⊙ Sun; ♀ Venus; ☿ Mercury; ☽ Moon.

Day Hours; Sunrise to Sunset. Mean Time.

Lat. 27°	Lat. 29°	Lat. 31°	Lat. 33°	Lat. 35°	Lat. 37°	Lat. 39°	Lat. 41°	Su	M	Tu	W	Th	F	Sa	Lat. 43°	Lat. 45°	Lat. 47°	Lat. 49°	Lat. 51°	Lat. 53°	Lat. 55°
6.51	6.55	6.59	7.04	7.08	7.12	7.17	7.23	⊙	☽	♂	☿	♃	♀	♄	7.29	7.35	7.42	7.49	7.57	8.06	8.16
7.44	7.48	7.51	7.55	7.58	8.02	8.06	8.11	♀	♄	⊙	☽	♂	☿	♃	8.16	8.21	8.27	8.33	8.39	8.47	8.55
8.37	8.40	8.43	8.46	8.49	8.51	8.55	8.59	☿	♃	♀	♄	⊙	☽	♂	9.03	9.07	9.11	9.16	9.21	9.27	9.34
9.31	9.33	9.35	9.37	9.39	9.41	9.43	9.47	☽	♂	☿	♃	♀	♄	⊙	9.50	9.53	9.56	10.00	10.04	10.08	10.13
10.24	10.25	10.26	10.28	10.29	10.30	10.32	10.34	♄	⊙	☽	♂	☿	♃	♀	10.36	10.38	10.41	10.43	10.46	10.49	10.52
11.17	11.18	11.18	11.19	11.20	11.20	11.21	11.22	♃	♀	♄	⊙	☽	♂	☿	11.23	11.24	11.25	11.27	11.28	11.29	11.31
12.10	12.10	12.10	12.10	12.10	12.10	12.10	12.10	♂	☿	♃	♀	♄	⊙	☽	12.10	12.10	12.10	12.10	12.10	12.10	12.10
1.03	1.03	1.02	1.01	1.00	12.59	12.58	12.58	⊙	☽	♂	☿	♃	♀	♄	12.57	12.56	12.55	12.54	12.52	12.51	12.49
1.56	1.55	1.54	1.52	1.51	1.49	1.47	1.46	♀	♄	⊙	☽	♂	☿	♃	1.44	1.42	1.39	1.37	1.34	1.31	1.28
2.50	2.48	2.46	2.43	2.41	2.38	2.36	2.34	☿	♃	♀	♄	⊙	☽	♂	2.31	2.28	2.24	2.21	2.17	2.12	2.07
3.43	3.40	3.37	3.34	3.31	3.28	3.25	3.21	☽	♂	☿	♃	♀	♄	⊙	3.17	3.13	3.09	3.04	2.59	2.53	2.46
4.36	4.33	4.29	4.25	4.22	4.17	4.13	4.09	♄	⊙	☽	♂	☿	♃	♀	4.04	3.59	3.53	3.48	3.41	3.33	3.25

Night Hours; Sunset to Sunrise.

Lat. 27°	Lat. 29°	Lat. 31°	Lat. 33°	Lat. 35°	Lat. 37°	Lat. 39°	Lat. 41°	Su	M	Tu	W	Th	F	Sa	Lat. 43°	Lat. 45°	Lat. 47°	Lat. 49°	Lat. 51°	Lat. 53°	Lat. 55°
5.29	5.25	5.21	5.16	5.12	5.07	5.02	4.57	♃	♀	♄	⊙	☽	♂	☿	4.51	4.45	4.38	4.31	4.23	4.14	4.04
6.36	6.33	6.29	6.25	6.22	6.17	6.13	6.09	♂	☿	♃	♀	♄	⊙	☽	6.04	5.59	5.53	5.47	5.41	5.33	5.25
7.43	7.40	7.37	7.34	7.31	7.28	7.25	7.21	⊙	☽	♂	☿	♃	♀	♄	7.17	7.13	7.09	7.04	6.59	6.53	6.46
8.50	8.48	8.46	8.43	8.41	8.38	8.36	8.34	♀	♄	⊙	☽	♂	☿	♃	8.30	8.27	8.24	8.20	8.16	8.12	8.07
9.56	9.56	9.54	9.52	9.51	9.49	9.47	9.46	☿	♃	♀	♄	⊙	☽	♂	9.43	9.41	9.39	9.37	9.34	9.31	9.28
11.03	11.03	11.02	11.01	11.00	10.59	10.59	10.58	☽	♂	☿	♃	♀	♄	⊙	10.56	10.55	10.54	10.53	10.52	10.50	10.49
12.10	12.10	12.10	12.10	12.10	12.10	12.10	12.10	♄	⊙	☽	♂	☿	♃	♀	12.10	12.10	12.10	12.10	12.10	12.10	12.10
1.17	1.18	1.18	1.19	1.20	1.20	1.21	1.22	♃	♀	♄	⊙	☽	♂	☿	1.23	1.24	1.25	1.26	1.27	1.29	1.30
2.24	2.25	2.26	2.28	2.29	2.30	2.32	2.34	♂	☿	♃	♀	♄	⊙	☽	2.36	2.38	2.40	2.42	2.45	2.48	2.51
3.31	3.33	3.35	3.37	3.39	3.41	3.43	3.47	⊙	☽	♂	☿	♃	♀	♄	3.49	3.52	3.55	3.59	4.03	4.07	4.12
4.37	4.40	4.43	4.46	4.49	4.51	4.55	4.59	♀	♄	⊙	☽	♂	☿	♃	5.02	5.06	5.11	5.15	5.21	5.27	5.33
5.44	5.48	5.51	5.55	5.58	6.02	6.06	6.11	☿	♃	♀	♄	⊙	☽	♂	6.15	6.20	6.26	6.32	6.38	6.46	6.54

JULY 16th to 23rd, ANY YEAR, in South Latitude

JANUARY 24th to 31st, ANY YEAR, in North Latitude

♄ Saturn; ♃ Jupiter; ♂ Mars; ☉ Sun; ♀ Venus; ☿ Mercury; ☽ Moon.

Day Hours; Sunrise to Sunset. Mean Time.

Lat. 27°	Lat. 29°	Lat. 31°	Lat. 33°	Lat. 35°	Lat. 37°	Lat. 39°	Lat. 41°	Su	M	Tu	W	Th	F	Sa	Lat. 43°	Lat. 45°	Lat. 47°	Lat. 49°	Lat. 51°	Lat. 53°	Lat. 55°
6.50	6.53	6.57	7.01	7.05	7.09	7.14	7.19	☉	☽	♂	☿	♃	♀	♄	7.24	7.29	7.35	7.42	7.49	7.57	8.06
7.44	7.46	7.50	7.53	7.56	8.00	8.04	8.08	♀	♄	☉	☽	♂	☿	♃	8.12	8.16	8.21	8.27	8.33	8.40	8.47
8.38	8.40	8.42	8.45	8.48	8.50	8.54	8.57	☿	♃	♀	♄	☉	☽	♂	9.00	9.04	9.08	9.12	9.17	9.22	9.28
9.31	9.33	9.35	9.37	9.39	9.41	9.44	9.46	☽	♂	☿	♃	♀	♄	☉	9.49	9.51	9.54	9.57	10.01	10.03	10.09
10.25	10.26	10.27	10.29	10.30	10.31	10.33	10.35	♄	☉	☽	♂	☿	♃	♀	10.37	10.38	10.40	10.42	10.45	10.47	10.50
11.19	11.19	11.20	11.21	11.21	11.22	11.23	11.24	♃	♀	♄	☉	☽	♂	☿	11.25	11.25	11.26	11.27	11.28	11.30	11.31
12.13	12.13	12.13	12.13	12.13	12.13	12.13	12.13	♂	☿	♃	♀	♄	☉	☽	12.13	12.13	12.13	12.13	12.13	12.13	12.13
1.06	1.06	1.05	1.04	1.04	1.03	1.03	1.02	☉	☽	♂	☿	♃	♀	♄	1.01	1.00	12.59	12.58	12.56	12.55	12.54
2.00	1.59	1.58	1.56	1.55	1.54	1.53	1.51	♀	♄	☉	☽	♂	☿	♃	1.49	1.47	1.45	1.43	1.40	1.38	1.35
2.54	2.52	2.50	2.48	2.46	2.44	2.43	2.40	☿	♃	♀	♄	☉	☽	♂	2.38	2.34	2.31	2.28	2.24	2.20	2.16
3.48	3.46	3.43	3.40	3.38	3.35	3.32	3.29	☽	♂	☿	♃	♀	♄	☉	3.26	3.22	3.18	3.13	3.08	3.03	2.57
4.41	4.39	4.35	4.32	4.29	4.25	4.22	4.18	♄	☉	☽	♂	☿	♃	♀	4.14	4.09	4.04	3.58	3.52	3.45	3.38

Night Hours; Sunset to Sunrise.

Lat. 27°	Lat. 29°	Lat. 31°	Lat. 33°	Lat. 35°	Lat. 37°	Lat. 39°	Lat. 41°	Su	M	Tu	W	Th	F	Sa	Lat. 43°	Lat. 45°	Lat. 47°	Lat. 49°	Lat. 51°	Lat. 53°	Lat. 55°
5.35	5.32	5.28	5.24	5.20	5.16	5.12	5.07	♃	♀	♄	☉	☽	♂	☿	5.02	4.56	4.50	4.43	4.36	4.28	4.19
6.41	6.39	6.35	6.32	6.29	6.25	6.22	6.18	♂	☿	♃	♀	♄	☉	☽	6.14	6.09	6.04	5.58	5.52	5.45	5.38
7.48	7.46	7.43	7.40	7.38	7.35	7.32	7.29	☉	☽	♂	☿	♃	♀	♄	7.26	7.22	7.18	7.13	7.08	7.03	6.57
8.54	8.52	8.50	8.48	8.46	8.44	8.42	8.40	♀	♄	☉	☽	♂	☿	♃	8.37	8.34	8.31	8.28	8.24	8.20	8.16
10.00	9.59	9.58	9.56	9.55	9.54	9.52	9.51	☿	♃	♀	♄	☉	☽	♂	9.49	9.47	9.45	9.43	9.40	9.37	9.35
11.06	11.06	11.05	11.04	11.04	11.03	11.02	11.02	☽	♂	☿	♃	♀	♄	☉	11.01	11.00	10.59	10.58	10.56	10.54	10.54
12.13	12.13	12.13	12.13	12.13	12.13	12.13	12.13	♄	☉	☽	♂	☿	♃	♀	12.13	12.13	12.13	12.13	12.13	12.13	12.13
1.19	1.19	1.20	1.21	1.21	1.22	1.23	1.23	♃	♀	♄	☉	☽	♂	☿	1.24	1.25	1.26	1.27	1.29	1.30	1.31
2.25	2.26	2.27	2.29	2.30	2.31	2.33	2.34	♂	☿	♃	♀	♄	☉	☽	2.36	2.38	2.40	2.42	2.45	2.47	2.50
3.31	3.33	3.35	3.37	3.39	3.41	3.43	3.45	☉	☽	♂	☿	♃	♀	♄	3.48	3.51	3.54	3.57	4.01	4.04	4.09
4.38	4.40	4.42	4.45	4.48	4.50	4.53	4.56	♀	♄	☉	☽	♂	☿	♃	5.00	5.04	5.08	5.12	5.17	5.22	5.28
5.44	5.46	5.50	5.53	5.56	6.00	6.03	6.07	☿	♃	♀	♄	☉	☽	♂	6.11	6.16	6.21	6.27	6.33	6.39	6.47

JULY 24th to 31st, ANY YEAR, in South Latitude

FEBRUARY 1st to 7th, ANY YEAR, in North Latitude

♄ Saturn; ♃ Jupiter; ♂ Mars; ⊙ Sun; ♀ Venus; ☿ Mercury; ☽ Moon.

Day Hours; Sunrise to Sunset. Mean Time.

Lat. 27°	Lat. 29°	Lat. 31°	Lat. 33°	Lat. 35°	Lat. 37°	Lat. 39°	Lat. 41°	Su	M	Tu	W	Th	F	Sa	Lat. 43°	Lat. 45°	Lat. 47°	Lat. 49°	Lat. 51°	Lat. 53°	Lat. 55°
6.46	6.49	6.52	6.55	6.59	7.03	7.07	7.11	⊙	☽	♂	☿	♃	♀	♄	7.16	7.21	7.27	7.32	7.38	7.45	7.52
7.41	7.43	7.46	7.48	7.51	7.55	7.58	8.01	♀	♄	⊙	☽	♂	☿	♃	8.06	8.10	8.15	8.19	8.24	8.30	8.36
8.35	8.37	8.39	8.41	8.44	8.47	8.49	8.52	☿	♃	♀	♄	⊙	☽	♂	8.55	8.59	9.03	9.06	9.10	9.15	9.19
9.30	9.31	9.33	9.34	9.36	9.38	9.40	9.42	☽	♂	☿	♃	♀	♄	⊙	9.45	9.48	9.51	9.53	9.56	10.00	10.03
10.24	10.25	10.26	10.27	10.29	10.30	10.31	10.33	♄	⊙	☽	♂	☿	♃	♀	10.34	10.36	10.38	10.40	10.42	10.44	10.47
11.19	11.19	11.20	11.20	11.21	11.22	11.22	11.23	♃	♀	♄	⊙	☽	♂	☿	11.24	11.25	11.27	11.27	11.28	11.29	11.30
12.14	12.14	12.14	12.14	12.14	12.14	12.14	12.14	♂	☿	♃	♀	♄	⊙	☽	12.14	12.14	12.14	12.14	12.14	12.14	12.14
1.08	1.08	1.07	1.07	1.06	1.05	1.05	1.04	⊙	☽	♂	☿	♃	♀	♄	1.03	1.03	1.02	1.01	1.00	12.59	12.58
2.03	2.02	2.01	2.00	1.58	1.57	1.56	1.54	♀	♄	⊙	☽	♂	☿	♃	1.53	1.52	1.50	1.48	1.46	1.44	1.41
2.57	2.56	2.54	2.53	2.51	2.49	2.47	2.45	☿	♃	♀	♄	⊙	☽	♂	2.42	2.41	2.37	2.35	2.32	2.29	2.25
3.52	3.50	3.48	3.46	3.43	3.41	3.38	3.35	☽	♂	☿	♃	♀	♄	⊙	3.32	3.29	3.25	3.23	3.18	3.13	3.09
4.46	4.44	4.41	4.39	4.36	4.32	4.29	4.26	♄	⊙	☽	♂	☿	♃	♀	4.21	4.18	4.13	4.10	4.04	3.58	3.52

Night Hours; Sunset to Sunrise.

Lat. 27°	Lat. 29°	Lat. 31°	Lat. 33°	Lat. 35°	Lat. 37°	Lat. 39°	Lat. 41°	Su	M	Tu	W	Th	F	Sa	Lat. 43°	Lat. 45°	Lat. 47°	Lat. 49°	Lat. 51°	Lat. 53°	Lat. 55°
5.41	5.38	5.35	5.32	5.28	5.24	5.20	5.16	♃	♀	♄	⊙	☽	♂	☿	5.11	5.07	5.02	4.57	4.50	4.43	4.36
6.46	6.44	6.41	6.39	6.36	6.32	6.29	6.26	♂	☿	♃	♀	♄	⊙	☽	6.21	6.18	6.14	6.10	6.04	5.58	5.52
7.52	7.50	7.48	7.46	7.43	7.41	7.38	7.35	⊙	☽	♂	☿	♃	♀	♄	7.32	7.29	7.26	7.23	7.18	7.13	7.09
8.57	8.56	8.54	8.53	8.51	8.49	8.47	8.45	♀	♄	⊙	☽	♂	☿	♃	8.42	8.40	8.38	8.35	8.32	8.28	8.25
10.03	10.02	10.01	10.00	9.58	9.57	9.55	9.54	☿	♃	♀	♄	⊙	☽	♂	9.53	9.51	9.50	9.48	9.46	9.43	9.41
11.08	11.08	11.07	11.07	11.06	11.06	11.05	11.04	☽	♂	☿	♃	♀	♄	⊙	11.03	11.02	11.02	11.01	11.00	10.58	10.57
12.14	12.14	12.14	12.14	12.14	12.14	12.14	12.14	♄	⊙	☽	♂	☿	♃	♀	12.14	12.14	12.14	12.14	12.14	12.14	12.14
1.19	1.19	1.20	1.20	1.21	1.22	1.23	1.23	♃	♀	♄	⊙	☽	♂	☿	1.24	1.25	1.25	1.26	1.27	1.29	1.30
2.24	2.25	2.26	2.27	2.29	2.30	2.32	2.33	♂	☿	♃	♀	♄	⊙	☽	2.34	2.36	2.39	2.39	2.41	2.44	2.46
3.30	3.31	3.33	3.34	3.36	3.38	3.41	3.43	⊙	☽	♂	☿	♃	♀	♄	3.45	3.45	3.49	3.52	3.55	3.59	4.02
4.35	4.37	4.39	4.41	4.44	4.46	4.49	4.52	♀	♄	⊙	☽	♂	☿	♃	4.55	4.58	5.01	5.05	5.09	5.14	5.19
5.41	5.43	5.46	5.48	5.51	5.54	5.58	6.01	☿	♃	♀	♄	⊙	☽	♂	6.06	6.09	6.13	6.17	6.23	6.29	6.35

AUGUST 1st to 7th, ANY YEAR, in South Latitude

FEBRUARY 8th to 14th, ANY YEAR, in North Latitude

♄ Saturn; ♃ Jupiter; ♂ Mars; ☉ Sun; ♀ Venus; ☿ Mercury; ☽ Moon.

Day Hours; Sunrise to Sunset. Mean Time.

Lat. 27°	Lat. 29°	Lat. 31°	Lat. 33°	Lat. 35°	Lat. 37°	Lat. 39°	Lat. 41°	Su	M	Tu	W	Th	F	Sa	Lat. 43°	Lat. 45°	Lat. 47°	Lat. 49°	Lat. 51°	Lat. 53°	Lat. 55°
6.42	6.45	6.48	6.51	6.54	6.57	7.00	7.04	☉	☽	♂	☿	♃	♀	♄	7.08	7.12	7.17	7.22	7.27	7.33	7.39
7.37	7.40	7.42	7.45	7.47	7.50	7.52	7.56	♀	♄	☉	☽	♂	☿	♃	7.59	8.02	8.07	8.11	8.15	8.20	8.25
8.33	8.35	8.37	8.39	8.41	8.43	8.45	8.48	☿	♃	♀	♄	☉	☽	♂	8.50	8.53	8.56	9.00	9.03	9.07	9.11
9.28	9.30	9.31	9.33	9.34	9.36	9.37	9.39	☽	♂	☿	♃	♀	♄	☉	9.41	9.43	9.46	9.48	9.51	9.54	9.57
10.23	10.24	10.26	10.27	10.28	10.29	10.30	10.31	♄	☉	☽	♂	☿	♃	♀	10.32	10.34	10.35	10.37	10.39	10.41	10.43
11.19	11.19	11.20	11.21	11.21	11.22	11.22	11.23	♃	♀	♄	☉	☽	♂	☿	11.23	11.24	11.25	11.26	11.27	11.28	11.29
12.14	12.14	12.14	12.15	12.15	12.15	12.15	12.15	♂	☿	♃	♀	♄	☉	☽	12.15	12.15	12.15	12.15	12.15	12.15	12.15
1.09	1.09	1.09	1.08	1.08	1.07	1.07	1.06	☉	☽	♂	☿	♃	♀	♄	1.06	1.05	1.04	1.03	1.02	1.02	1.01
2.05	2.03	2.03	2.02	2.01	2.00	1.59	1.58	♀	♄	☉	☽	♂	☿	♃	1.57	1.55	1.54	1.52	1.50	1.49	1.47
3.00	2.59	2.58	2.56	2.55	2.53	2.52	2.50	☿	♃	♀	♄	☉	☽	♂	2.48	2.46	2.43	2.41	2.38	2.36	2.33
3.55	3.53	3.52	3.50	3.48	3.46	3.44	3.42	☽	♂	☿	♃	♀	♄	☉	3.39	3.36	3.33	3.30	3.26	3.23	3.19
4.51	4.48	4.47	4.44	4.42	4.39	4.37	4.33	♄	☉	☽	♂	☿	♃	♀	4.30	4.27	4.22	4.18	4.14	4.10	4.05

Night Hours; Sunset to Sunrise.

Lat. 27°	Lat. 29°	Lat. 31°	Lat. 33°	Lat. 35°	Lat. 37°	Lat. 39°	Lat. 41°	Su	M	Tu	W	Th	F	Sa	Lat. 43°	Lat. 45°	Lat. 47°	Lat. 49°	Lat. 51°	Lat. 53°	Lat. 55°
5.46	5.43	5.41	5.38	5.35	5.32	5.29	5.25	♃	♀	♄	☉	☽	♂	☿	5.21	5.17	5.12	5.07	5.02	4.57	4.51
6.51	6.48	6.47	6.44	6.42	6.39	6.37	6.33	♂	☿	♃	♀	♄	☉	☽	6.30	6.26	6.22	6.18	6.14	6.10	6.05
7.55	7.53	7.52	7.50	7.48	7.46	7.44	7.41	☉	☽	♂	☿	♃	♀	♄	7.39	7.36	7.33	7.29	7.26	7.23	7.19
9.00	8.59	8.58	8.56	8.55	8.53	8.52	8.50	♀	♄	☉	☽	♂	☿	♃	8.47	8.45	8.43	8.41	8.38	8.36	8.33
10.05	10.04	10.03	10.02	10.01	10.00	9.59	9.58	☿	♃	♀	♄	☉	☽	♂	9.56	9.55	9.53	9.52	9.50	9.48	9.46
11.09	11.09	11.09	11.08	11.08	11.07	11.07	11.06	☽	♂	☿	♃	♀	♄	☉	11.05	11.04	11.03	11.02	11.02	11.01	11.00
12.14	12.14	12.14	12.14	12.14	12.14	12.14	12.14	♄	☉	☽	♂	☿	♃	♀	12.14	12.14	12.14	12.14	12.14	12.14	12.14
1.19	1.19	1.20	1.20	1.21	1.21	1.22	1.22	♃	♀	♄	☉	☽	♂	☿	1.22	1.23	1.24	1.25	1.26	1.27	1.28
2.23	2.24	2.25	2.26	2.27	2.28	2.29	2.30	♂	☿	♃	♀	♄	☉	☽	2.31	2.32	2.34	2.36	2.38	2.40	2.42
3.28	3.30	3.31	3.32	3.34	3.35	3.37	3.39	☉	☽	♂	☿	♃	♀	♄	3.40	3.42	3.44	3.47	3.50	3.52	3.56
4.33	4.35	4.36	4.38	4.40	4.42	4.44	4.47	♀	♄	☉	☽	♂	☿	♃	4.49	4.51	4.55	4.58	5.02	5.05	5.09
5.37	5.40	5.42	5.44	5.47	5.49	5.52	5.55	☿	♃	♀	♄	☉	☽	♂	5.57	6.01	6.05	6.09	6.14	6.18	6.23

AUGUST 8th to 14th, ANY YEAR, in South Latitude

FEBRUARY 15th to 21st, ANY YEAR, in North Latitude

♄ Saturn; ♃ Jupiter; ♂ Mars; ⊙ Sun; ♀ Venus; ☿ Mercury; ☽ Moon.

Day Hours; Sunrise to Sunset. Mean Time.

Lat. 27°	Lat. 29°	Lat. 31°	Lat. 33°	Lat. 35°	Lat. 37°	Lat. 39°	Lat. 41°	Su	M	Tu	W	Th	F	Sa	Lat. 43°	Lat. 45°	Lat. 47°	Lat. 49°	Lat. 51°	Lat. 53°	Lat. 55°
6.38	6.40	6.42	6.45	6.47	6.50	6.53	6.56	⊙	☽	♂	☿	♃	♀	♄	6.59	7.02	7.06	7.10	7.14	7.19	7.24
7.34	7.36	7.37	7.40	7.42	7.44	7.47	7.49	♀	♄	⊙	☽	♂	☿	♃	7.52	7.54	7.57	8.01	8.04	8.08	8.12
8.30	8.32	8.33	8.35	8.36	8.38	8.40	8.42	☿	♃	♀	♄	⊙	☽	♂	8.44	8.46	8.49	8.52	8.54	8.58	9.01
9.26	9.27	9.28	9.30	9.31	9.32	9.34	9.35	☽	♂	☿	♃	♀	♄	⊙	9.37	9.38	9.40	9.43	9.44	9.47	9.49
10.22	10.23	10.24	10.25	10.25	10.26	10.27	10.28	♄	⊙	☽	♂	☿	♃	♀	10.29	10.30	10.32	10.33	10.34	10.36	10.38
11.18	11.19	11.19	11.20	11.20	11.20	11.21	11.21	♃	♀	♄	⊙	☽	♂	☿	11.22	11.22	11.23	11.24	11.24	11.25	11.26
12.15	12.15	12.15	12.15	12.15	12.15	12.15	12.15	♂	☿	♃	♀	♄	⊙	☽	12.15	12.15	12.15	12.15	12.15	12.15	12.15
1.11	1.10	1.10	1.09	1.09	1.09	1.08	1.08	⊙	☽	♂	☿	♃	♀	♄	1.07	1.07	1.06	1.06	1.05	1.04	1.03
2.07	2.06	2.05	2.04	2.04	2.03	2.02	2.01	♀	♄	⊙	☽	♂	☿	♃	2.00	1.59	1.57	1.57	1.55	1.53	1.51
3.03	3.03	3.01	2.59	2.58	2.57	2.55	2.54	☿	♃	♀	♄	⊙	☽	♂	2.52	2.51	2.49	2.48	2.45	2.42	2.40
3.59	3.57	3.56	3.54	3.53	3.51	3.49	3.47	☽	♂	☿	♃	♀	♄	⊙	3.45	3.43	3.40	3.38	3.35	3.32	3.28
4.55	4.53	4.52	4.49	4.47	4.45	4.42	4.40	♄	⊙	☽	♂	☿	♃	♀	4.37	4.35	4.32	4.29	4.25	4.21	4.17

Night Hours; Sunset to Sunrise.

Lat. 27°	Lat. 29°	Lat. 31°	Lat. 33°	Lat. 35°	Lat. 37°	Lat. 39°	Lat. 41°	Su	M	Tu	W	Th	F	Sa	Lat. 43°	Lat. 45°	Lat. 47°	Lat. 49°	Lat. 51°	Lat. 53°	Lat. 55°
5.51	5.49	5.47	5.44	5.42	5.39	5.36	5.33	♃	♀	♄	⊙	☽	♂	☿	5.30	5.27	5.23	5.20	5.15	5.10	5.05
6.55	6.53	6.51	6.49	6.47	6.45	6.42	6.40	♂	☿	♃	♀	♄	⊙	☽	6.37	6.35	6.31	6.29	6.25	6.21	6.16
7.59	7.57	7.56	7.54	7.53	7.51	7.49	7.46	⊙	☽	♂	☿	♃	♀	♄	7.45	7.43	7.40	7.38	7.35	7.31	7.28
9.03	9.02	9.01	8.59	8.58	8.57	8.55	8.53	♀	♄	⊙	☽	♂	☿	♃	8.52	8.50	8.48	8.47	8.44	8.42	8.39
10.06	10.06	10.05	10.04	10.03	10.02	10.01	10.00	☿	♃	♀	♄	⊙	☽	♂	9.59	9.58	9.57	9.56	9.54	9.52	9.51
11.11	11.10	11.10	11.09	11.09	11.08	11.08	11.07	☽	♂	☿	♃	♀	♄	⊙	11.06	11.06	11.05	11.05	11.04	11.03	11.02
12.15	12.15	12.14	12.14	12.14	12.14	12.14	12.14	♄	⊙	☽	♂	☿	♃	♀	12.14	12.14	12.14	12.14	12.14	12.14	12.14
1.18	1.19	1.19	1.19	1.19	1.20	1.20	1.20	♃	♀	♄	⊙	☽	♂	☿	1.21	1.21	1.22	1.23	1.23	1.24	1.25
2.23	2.23	2.23	2.24	2.25	2.26	2.26	2.27	♂	☿	♃	♀	♄	⊙	☽	2.28	2.29	2.30	2.32	2.33	2.35	2.36
3.27	3.27	3.28	3.29	3.30	3.32	3.33	3.34	⊙	☽	♂	☿	♃	♀	♄	3.35	3.37	3.39	3.41	3.44	3.45	3.48
4.30	4.32	4.32	4.34	4.35	4.37	4.39	4.41	♀	♄	⊙	☽	♂	☿	♃	4.43	4.45	4.47	4.50	4.53	4.56	4.59
5.34	5.36	5.37	5.39	5.41	5.43	5.46	5.48	☿	♃	♀	♄	⊙	☽	♂	5.50	5.52	5.56	5.59	6.02	6.06	6.11

AUGUST 15th to 21st, ANY YEAR, in South Latitude

FEBRUARY 22nd to 28th or 29th, ANY YEAR, in North Latitude

♄ Saturn; ♃ Jupiter; ♂ Mars; ☉ Sun; ♀ Venus; ☿ Mercury; ☽ Moon.

Day Hours; Sunrise to Sunset. Mean Time.

Lat. 27°	Lat. 29°	Lat. 31°	Lat. 33°	Lat. 35°	Lat. 37°	Lat. 39°	Lat. 41°	Su	M	Tu	W	Th	F	Sa	Lat. 43°	Lat. 45°	Lat. 47°	Lat. 49°	Lat. 51°	Lat. 53°	Lat. 55°
6.31	6.33	6.35	6.37	6.39	6.41	6.43	6.46	☉	☽	♂	☿	♃	♀	♄	6.48	6.51	6.54	6.57	7.01	7.04	7.08
7.28	7.30	7.32	7.33	7.35	7.37	7.38	7.41	♀	♄	☉	☽	♂	☿	♃	7.42	7.45	7.47	7.50	7.53	7.56	7.59
8.25	8.27	8.28	8.29	8.31	8.32	8.33	8.35	☿	♃	♀	♄	☉	☽	♂	8.37	8.39	8.41	8.43	8.45	8.47	8.50
9.22	9.24	9.25	9.26	9.27	9.28	9.28	9.30	☽	♂	☿	♃	♀	♄	☉	9.31	9.33	9.34	9.36	9.38	9.39	9.41
10.19	10.20	10.21	10.22	10.22	10.23	10.23	10.25	♄	☉	☽	♂	☿	♃	♀	10.25	10.26	10.27	10.28	10.30	10.31	10.32
11.16	11.17	11.18	11.17	11.18	11.19	11.18	11.19	♃	♀	♄	☉	☽	♂	☿	11.19	11.20	11.21	11.21	11.20	11.22	11.23
12.14	12.14	12.14	12.14	12.14	12.14	12.14	12.14	♂	☿	♃	♀	♄	☉	☽	12.14	12.14	12.14	12.14	12.14	12.14	12.14
1.11	1.11	1.11	1.10	1.10	1.10	1.09	1.09	☉	☽	♂	☿	♃	♀	♄	1.08	1.08	1.07	1.07	1.07	1.06	1.05
2.08	2.08	2.07	2.06	2.06	2.05	2.04	2.03	♀	♄	☉	☽	♂	☿	♃	2.02	2.02	2.01	2.00	1.59	1.57	1.56
3.05	3.05	3.04	3.03	3.02	3.01	2.59	2.58	☿	♃	♀	♄	☉	☽	♂	2.56	2.56	2.54	2.53	2.51	2.49	2.47
4.02	4.01	4.00	3.59	3.57	3.56	3.54	3.53	☽	♂	☿	♃	♀	♄	☉	3.50	3.49	3.47	3.45	3.44	3.41	3.38
4.59	4.58	4.57	4.55	4.53	4.52	4.49	4.47	♄	☉	☽	♂	☿	♃	♀	4.45	4.43	4.41	4.38	4.36	4.32	4.29

Night Hours; Sunset to Sunrise.

Lat. 27°	Lat. 29°	Lat. 31°	Lat. 33°	Lat. 35°	Lat. 37°	Lat. 39°	Lat. 41°	Su	M	Tu	W	Th	F	Sa	Lat. 43°	Lat. 45°	Lat. 47°	Lat. 49°	Lat. 51°	Lat. 53°	Lat. 55°
5.56	5.55	5.53	5.51	5.49	5.47	5.44	5.42	♃	♀	♄	☉	☽	♂	☿	5.39	5.37	5.34	5.31	5.28	5.24	5.20
6.59	6.58	6.56	6.55	6.53	6.51	6.49	6.47	♂	☿	♃	♀	♄	☉	☽	6.45	6.43	6.41	6.38	6.36	6.32	6.29
8.02	8.01	8.00	7.58	7.58	7.56	7.54	7.52	☉	☽	♂	☿	♃	♀	♄	7.50	7.49	7.47	7.45	7.43	7.40	7.38
9.05	9.04	9.03	9.02	9.01	9.00	8.59	8.58	♀	♄	☉	☽	♂	☿	♃	8.56	8.55	8.54	8.52	8.51	8.49	8.47
10.08	10.07	10.07	10.06	10.05	10.04	10.03	10.03	☿	♃	♀	♄	☉	☽	♂	10.02	10.01	10.00	9.59	9.58	9.56	9.55
11.11	11.10	11.10	11.09	11.09	11.09	11.08	11.08	☽	♂	☿	♃	♀	♄	☉	11.07	11.07	11.07	11.06	11.06	11.05	11.04
12.14	12.14	12.14	12.14	12.13	12.13	12.13	12.13	♄	☉	☽	♂	☿	♃	♀	12.13	12.13	12.13	12.13	12.13	12.13	12.13
1.16	1.17	1.17	1.18	1.18	1.18	1.18	1.18	♃	♀	♄	☉	☽	♂	☿	1.19	1.19	1.20	1.20	1.21	1.21	1.22
2.19	2.20	2.20	2.21	2.21	2.22	2.23	2.23	♂	☿	♃	♀	♄	☉	☽	2.24	2.25	2.26	2.27	2.29	2.29	2.31
3.22	3.23	3.24	3.25	3.25	3.26	3.28	3.29	☉	☽	♂	☿	♃	♀	♄	3.30	3.31	3.33	3.34	3.36	3.38	3.40
4.25	4.26	4.27	4.29	4.29	4.30	4.32	4.34	♀	♄	☉	☽	♂	☿	♃	4.36	4.37	4.39	4.41	4.44	4.46	4.48
5.28	5.29	5.31	5.32	5.33	5.35	5.37	5.39	☿	♃	♀	♄	☉	☽	♂	5.41	5.43	5.46	5.48	5.51	5.54	5.57

AUGUST 22nd to 31st, ANY YEAR, in South Latitude

MARCH 1st to 7th, ANY YEAR, in North Latitude

♄ Saturn; ♃ Jupiter; ♂ Mars; ☉ Sun; ♀ Venus; ☿ Mercury; ☽ Moon.

Day Hours; Sunrise to Sunset. Mean Time.

Lat. 27°	Lat. 29°	Lat. 31°	Lat. 33°	Lat. 35°	Lat. 37°	Lat. 39°	Lat. 41°	Su	M	Tu	W	Th	F	Sa	Lat. 43°	Lat. 45°	Lat. 47°	Lat. 49°	Lat. 51°	Lat. 53°	Lat. 55°
6.25	6.26	6.28	6.29	6.30	6.32	6.33	6.35	☉	☽	♂	☿	♃	♀	♄	6.37	6.39	6.41	6.44	6.46	6.49	6.52
7.23	7.24	7.26	7.26	7.27	7.29	7.30	7.31	♀	♄	☉	☽	♂	☿	♃	7.33	7.35	7.36	7.38	7.41	7.43	7.46
8.21	8.22	8.23	8.24	8.24	8.26	8.26	8.28	☿	♃	♀	♄	☉	☽	♂	8.29	8.30	8.32	8.34	8.35	8.37	8.39
9.19	9.20	9.21	9.21	9.21	9.22	9.23	9.24	☽	♂	☿	♃	♀	♄	☉	9.25	9.26	9.27	9.29	9.30	9.31	9.33
10.17	10.17	10.18	10.18	10.18	10.19	10.19	10.20	♄	☉	☽	♂	☿	♃	♀	10.21	10.22	10.22	10.23	10.24	10.25	10.26
11.15	11.15	11.16	11.16	11.15	11.16	11.16	11.16	♃	♀	♄	☉	☽	♂	☿	11.17	11.17	11.18	11.18	11.19	11.19	11.20
12.13	12.13	12.13	12.13	12.13	12.13	12.13	12.13	♂	☿	♃	♀	♄	☉	☽	12.13	12.13	12.13	12.13	12.13	12.13	12.13
1.11	1.11	1.11	1.10	1.10	1.09	1.09	1.09	☉	☽	♂	☿	♃	♀	♄	1.09	1.09	1.08	1.08	1.08	1.07	1.07
2.09	2.09	2.08	2.08	2.07	2.06	2.06	2.05	♀	♄	☉	☽	♂	☿	♃	2.05	2.04	2.04	2.03	2.02	2.01	2.00
3.07	3.07	3.06	3.05	3.04	3.03	3.02	3.01	☿	♃	♀	♄	☉	☽	♂	3.01	3.00	2.59	2.58	2.57	2.55	2.54
4.05	4.04	4.03	4.02	4.01	4.00	3.59	3.58	☽	♂	☿	♃	♀	♄	☉	3.57	3.56	3.54	3.52	3.51	3.49	3.46
5.03	5.02	5.01	5.00	4.58	4.56	4.55	4.54	♄	☉	☽	♂	☿	♃	♀	4.53	4.51	4.50	4.47	4.46	4.43	4.40

Night Hours; Sunset to Sunrise.

Lat. 27°	Lat. 29°	Lat. 31°	Lat. 33°	Lat. 35°	Lat. 37°	Lat. 39°	Lat. 41°	Su	M	Tu	W	Th	F	Sa	Lat. 43°	Lat. 45°	Lat. 47°	Lat. 49°	Lat. 51°	Lat. 53°	Lat. 55°
6.01	6.00	5.58	5.57	5.55	5.53	5.52	5.50	♃	♀	♄	☉	☽	♂	☿	5.49	5.47	5.45	5.42	5.40	5.37	5.34
7.03	7.02	7.00	7.00	6.58	6.56	6.55	6.54	♂	☿	♃	♀	♄	☉	☽	6.53	6.51	6.50	6.47	6.45	6.43	6.40
8.05	8.04	8.03	8.02	8.01	7.59	7.59	7.57	☉	☽	♂	☿	♃	♀	♄	7.57	7.55	7.54	7.52	7.51	7.49	7.47
9.07	9.06	9.05	9.05	9.04	9.03	9.02	9.01	♀	♄	☉	☽	♂	☿	♃	9.01	9.00	8.59	8.57	8.56	8.55	8.53
10.09	10.08	10.08	10.07	10.06	10.06	10.05	10.05	☿	♃	♀	♄	☉	☽	♂	10.04	10.04	10.03	10.02	10.01	10.00	9.59
11.11	11.10	11.10	11.10	11.09	11.09	11.09	11.08	☽	♂	☿	♃	♀	♄	☉	11.08	11.08	11.08	11.07	11.07	11.06	11.06
12.13	12.13	12.13	12.13	12.12	12.12	12.12	12.12	♄	☉	☽	♂	☿	♃	♀	12.12	12.12	12.12	12.12	12.12	12.12	12.12
1.14	1.15	1.15	1.15	1.15	1.15	1.15	1.16	♃	♀	♄	☉	☽	♂	☿	1.16	1.16	1.17	1.17	1.17	1.18	1.18
2.16	2.17	2.17	2.18	2.18	2.18	2.19	2.19	♂	☿	♃	♀	♄	☉	☽	2.20	2.20	2.21	2.22	2.23	2.24	2.25
3.18	3.19	3.20	3.20	3.21	3.22	3.22	3.23	☉	☽	♂	☿	♃	♀	♄	3.24	3.25	3.26	3.27	3.28	3.30	3.31
4.20	4.21	4.22	4.23	4.23	4.25	4.25	4.27	♀	♄	☉	☽	♂	☿	♃	4.27	4.29	4.30	4.32	4.33	4.35	4.37
5.22	5.23	5.25	5.25	5.26	5.28	5.29	5.30	☿	♃	♀	♄	☉	☽	♂	5.31	5.33	5.35	5.37	5.39	5.41	5.44

SEPTEMBER 1st to 7th, ANY YEAR, in South Latitude

MARCH 8th to 15th, ANY YEAR, in North Latitude

♄ Saturn; ♃ Jupiter; ♂ Mars; ☉ Sun; ♀ Venus; ☿ Mercury; ☽ Moon.

Day Hours; Sunrise to Sunset. Mean Time.

Lat. 27°	Lat. 29°	Lat. 31°	Lat. 33°	Lat. 35°	Lat. 37°	Lat. 39°	Lat. 41°	Su	M	Tu	W	Th	F	Sa	Lat. 43°	Lat. 45°	Lat. 47°	Lat. 49°	Lat. 51°	Lat. 53°	Lat. 55°
6.18	6.19	6.19	6.20	6.21	6.22	6.23	6.24	☉	☽	♂	☿	♃	♀	♄	6.25	6.26	6.28	6.29	6.31	6.33	6.35
7.17	7.18	7.18	7.18	7.19	7.20	7.21	7.21	♀	♄	☉	☽	♂	☿	♃	7.22	7.23	7.25	7.25	7.27	7.29	7.30
8.15	8.16	8.16	8.17	8.17	8.18	8.18	8.19	☿	♃	♀	♄	☉	☽	♂	8.19	8.20	8.21	8.22	8.23	8.24	8.25
9.14	9.15	9.15	9.15	9.15	9.15	9.16	9.16	☽	♂	☿	♃	♀	♄	☉	9.17	9.17	9.18	9.18	9.19	9.20	9.21
10.13	10.13	10.13	10.13	10.13	10.13	10.13	10.13	♄	☉	☽	♂	☿	♃	♀	10.14	10.14	10.14	10.15	10.15	10.16	10.16
11.11	11.12	11.11	11.11	11.11	11.11	11.11	11.11	♃	♀	♄	☉	☽	♂	☿	11.11	11.11	11.11	11.11	11.11	11.11	11.11
12.10	12.10	12.10	12.10	12.09	12.09	12.09	12.08	♂	☿	♃	♀	♄	☉	☽	12.08	12.08	12.08	12.08	12.08	12.07	12.07
1.09	1.09	1.08	1.08	1.07	1.06	1.06	1.05	☉	☽	♂	☿	♃	♀	♄	1.05	1.04	1.04	1.04	1.04	1.03	1.02
2.07	2.07	2.06	2.06	2.05	2.04	2.04	2.03	♀	♄	☉	☽	♂	☿	♃	2.02	2.01	2.01	2.00	2.00	1.58	1.57
3.06	3.06	3.05	3.04	3.03	3.02	3.01	3.00	☿	♃	♀	♄	☉	☽	♂	3.00	2.58	2.57	2.57	2.56	2.54	2.52
4.05	4.04	4.03	4.03	4.01	4.00	3.59	3.57	☽	♂	☿	♃	♀	♄	☉	3.57	3.55	3.54	3.54	3.52	3.50	3.48
5.03	5.03	5.02	5.01	4.59	4.57	4.56	4.55	♄	☉	☽	♂	☿	♃	♀	4.54	4.52	4.50	4.50	4.48	4.45	4.43

Night Hours; Sunset to Sunrise.

Lat. 27°	Lat. 29°	Lat. 31°	Lat. 33°	Lat. 35°	Lat. 37°	Lat. 39°	Lat. 41°	Su	M	Tu	W	Th	F	Sa	Lat. 43°	Lat. 45°	Lat. 47°	Lat. 49°	Lat. 51°	Lat. 53°	Lat. 55°
6.02	6.01	6.00	5.59	5.57	5.55	5.54	5.52	♃	♀	♄	☉	☽	♂	☿	5.51	5.49	5.47	5.46	5.44	5.41	5.38
7.03	7.02	7.02	7.01	6.59	6.57	6.56	6.55	♂	☿	♃	♀	♄	☉	☽	6.54	6.51	6.50	6.49	6.48	6.45	6.43
8.05	8.04	8.03	8.02	8.01	7.59	7.59	7.57	☉	☽	♂	☿	♃	♀	♄	7.56	7.55	7.54	7.53	7.52	7.49	7.47
9.06	9.05	9.05	9.04	9.03	9.02	9.01	9.00	♀	♄	☉	☽	♂	☿	♃	8.59	8.58	8.57	8.56	8.55	8.54	8.52
10.07	10.07	10.06	10.06	10.05	10.04	10.03	10.02	☿	♃	♀	♄	☉	☽	♂	10.02	10.01	10.00	10.00	9.59	9.58	9.56
11.08	11.08	11.08	11.07	11.07	11.06	11.06	11.05	☽	♂	☿	♃	♀	♄	☉	11.04	11.04	11.03	11.03	11.03	11.02	11.01
12.10	12.10	12.10	12.09	12.09	12.08	12.08	12.07	♄	☉	☽	♂	☿	♃	♀	12.07	12.07	12.07	12.07	12.07	12.06	12.05
1.11	1.11	1.11	1.11	1.10	1.10	1.10	1.10	♃	♀	♄	☉	☽	♂	☿	1.10	1.09	1.10	1.10	1.10	1.10	1.10
2.12	2.12	2.12	2.12	2.12	2.12	2.13	2.12	♂	☿	♃	♀	♄	☉	☽	2.12	2.12	2.13	2.13	2.14	2.14	2.14
3.13	3.14	3.14	3.14	3.14	3.15	3.15	3.15	☉	☽	♂	☿	♃	♀	♄	3.15	3.15	3.16	3.17	3.18	3.19	3.19
4.15	4.15	4.15	4.16	4.16	4.17	4.17	4.17	♀	♄	☉	☽	♂	☿	♃	4.18	4.18	4.20	4.20	4.22	4.23	4.23
5.16	5.17	5.17	5.17	5.18	5.19	5.20	5.20	☿	♃	♀	♄	☉	☽	♂	5.20	5.21	5.23	5.24	5.25	5.27	5.28

SEPTEMBER 8th to 15th, ANY YEAR, in South Latitude

MARCH 16th to 23rd, ANY YEAR, in North Latitude

♄ Saturn; ♃ Jupiter; ♂ Mars; ☉ Sun; ♀ Venus; ☿ Mercury; ☽ Moon.

Day Hours; Sunrise to Sunset. Mean Time.

Lat. 55°	Lat. 53°	Lat. 51°	Lat. 49°	Lat. 47°	Lat. 45°	Lat. 43°	Sa	F	Th	W	Tu	M	Su	Lat. 41°	Lat. 39°	Lat. 37°	Lat. 35°	Lat. 33°	Lat. 31°	Lat. 29°	Lat. 27°
6.15	6.14	6.13	6.13	6.12	6.12	6.12	♄	♀	♃	☿	♂	☽	☉	6.12	6.12	6.11	6.10	6.10	6.09	6.09	6.09
7.14	7.13	7.12	7.12	7.12	7.12	7.12	♃	☿	♂	☽	☉	♄	♀	7.12	7.12	7.11	7.10	7.10	7.09	7.09	7.09
8.13	8.13	8.12	8.12	8.11	8.11	8.11	♂	☽	☉	♄	♀	♃	☿	8.11	8.11	8.11	8.10	8.10	8.09	8.09	8.09
9.13	9.12	9.11	9.11	9.11	9.11	9.11	☉	♄	♀	♃	☿	♂	☽	9.11	9.11	9.10	9.10	9.10	9.09	9.09	9.09
10.12	10.11	10.10	10.11	10.10	10.10	10.10	♀	♃	☿	♂	☽	☉	♄	10.10	10.10	10.10	10.09	10.09	10.09	10.09	10.09
11.11	11.10	11.10	11.10	11.10	11.10	11.10	☿	♂	☽	☉	♄	♀	♃	11.10	11.10	11.10	11.09	11.09	11.09	11.09	11.09
12.10	12.10	12.09	12.10	12.09	12.10	12.10	☽	☉	♄	♀	♃	☿	♂	12.10	12.10	12.10	12.09	12.09	12.09	12.09	12.09
1.09	1.09	1.08	1.09	1.09	1.09	1.09	♄	♀	♃	☿	♂	☽	☉	1.09	1.09	1.09	1.09	1.09	1.08	1.08	1.09
2.08	2.08	2.08	2.08	2.08	2.09	2.09	♃	☿	♂	☽	☉	♄	♀	2.09	2.09	2.09	2.09	2.09	2.08	2.08	2.09
3.08	3.07	3.08	3.08	3.08	3.08	3.08	♂	☽	☉	♄	♀	♃	☿	3.08	3.08	3.09	3.09	3.09	3.08	3.08	3.09
4.07	4.07	4.06	4.07	4.07	4.08	4.08	☉	♄	♀	♃	☿	♂	☽	4.08	4.08	4.09	4.08	4.08	4.08	4.08	4.09
5.06	5.06	5.06	5.07	5.07	5.07	5.07	♀	♃	☿	♂	☽	☉	♄	5.07	5.07	5.08	5.08	5.08	5.08	5.08	5.09

Night Hours; Sunset to Sunrise.

Lat. 55°	Lat. 53°	Lat. 51°	Lat. 49°	Lat. 47°	Lat. 45°	Lat. 43°	Sa	F	Th	W	Tu	M	Su	Lat. 41°	Lat. 39°	Lat. 37°	Lat. 35°	Lat. 33°	Lat. 31°	Lat. 29°	Lat. 27°
6.05	6.05	6.05	6.06	6.06	6.07	6.07	☿	♂	☽	☉	♄	♀	♃	6.07	6.07	6.08	6.08	6.08	6.08	6.08	6.09
7.06	7.06	7.06	7.06	7.06	7.07	7.07	☽	☉	♄	♀	♃	☿	♂	7.07	7.07	7.08	7.08	7.08	7.08	7.08	7.09
8.06	8.06	8.06	8.07	8.07	8.08	8.08	♄	♀	♃	☿	♂	☽	☉	8.08	8.08	8.08	8.08	8.08	8.08	8.08	8.09
9.07	9.07	9.07	9.07	9.07	9.08	9.08	♃	☿	♂	☽	☉	♄	♀	9.08	9.08	9.08	9.08	9.08	9.08	9.08	9.09
10.07	10.07	10.07	10.08	10.07	10.08	10.08	♂	☽	☉	♄	♀	♃	☿	10.08	10.08	10.08	10.08	10.08	10.08	10.08	10.09
11.08	11.08	11.08	11.08	11.08	11.08	11.08	☉	♄	♀	♃	☿	♂	☽	11.08	11.08	11.08	11.08	11.08	11.08	11.08	11.09
12.09	12.09	12.08	12.09	12.08	12.09	12.09	♀	♃	☿	♂	☽	☉	♄	12.09	12.09	12.09	12.09	12.09	12.08	12.08	12.09
1.09	1.09	1.09	1.09	1.08	1.09	1.09	☿	♂	☽	☉	♄	♀	♃	1.09	1.09	1.09	1.09	1.09	1.08	1.08	1.08
2.10	2.10	2.09	2.09	2.09	2.09	2.09	☽	☉	♄	♀	♃	☿	♂	2.09	2.09	2.09	2.09	2.09	2.08	2.08	2.08
3.10	3.10	3.10	3.10	3.09	3.09	3.09	♄	♀	♃	☿	♂	☽	☉	3.09	3.09	3.09	3.09	3.09	3.08	3.08	3.08
4.11	4.11	4.10	4.10	4.09	4.10	4.10	♃	☿	♂	☽	☉	♄	♀	4.10	4.10	4.09	4.09	4.09	4.08	4.08	4.08
5.11	5.11	5.10	5.11	5.10	5.10	5.10	♂	☽	☉	♄	♀	♃	☿	5.10	5.10	5.09	5.09	5.09	5.08	5.08	5.08

SEPTEMBER 16th to 23rd, ANY YEAR, in South Latitude

MARCH 24th to 31st, ANY YEAR, in North Latitude

♄ Saturn; ♃ Jupiter; ♂ Mars; ☉ Sun; ♀ Venus; ☿ Mercury; ☽ Moon.

Day Hours; Sunrise to Sunset. Mean Time.

Lat. 27°	Lat. 29°	Lat. 31°	Lat. 33°	Lat. 35°	Lat. 37°	Lat. 39°	Lat. 41°	Su	M	Tu	W	Th	F	Sa	Lat. 43°	Lat. 45°	Lat. 47°	Lat. 49°	Lat. 51°	Lat. 53°	Lat. 55°
6.00	6.00	6.00	5.59	5.59	5.59	5.58	5.58	☉	☽	♂	☿	♃	♀	♄	5.57	5.57	5.57	5.56	5.55	5.54	5.53
7.01	7.01	7.01	7.00	7.00	7.00	6.59	6.59	♀	♄	☉	☽	♂	☿	♃	6.59	6.59	6.59	6.58	6.57	6.56	6.55
8.02	8.02	8.02	8.02	8.02	8.02	8.01	8.01	☿	♃	♀	♄	☉	☽	♂	8.00	8.00	8.00	8.00	7.59	7.58	7.58
9.03	9.04	9.04	9.03	9.03	9.03	9.02	9.02	☽	♂	☿	♃	♀	♄	☉	9.02	9.02	9.02	9.02	9.01	9.01	9.00
10.04	10.05	10.05	10.04	10.04	10.04	10.04	10.04	♄	☉	☽	♂	☿	♃	♀	10.03	10.04	10.04	10.03	10.03	10.03	10.02
11.05	11.06	11.06	11.06	11.06	11.06	11.05	11.05	♃	♀	♄	☉	☽	♂	☿	11.05	11.05	11.05	11.05	11.05	11.05	11.05
12.07	12.07	12.07	12.07	12.07	12.07	12.07	12.07	♂	☿	♃	♀	♄	☉	☽	12.07	12.07	12.07	12.07	12.07	12.07	12.07
1.08	1.08	1.08	1.08	1.08	1.08	1.08	1.08	☉	☽	♂	☿	♃	♀	♄	1.08	1.09	1.08	1.09	1.09	1.09	1.09
2.09	2.09	2.09	2.10	2.10	2.10	2.09	2.09	♀	♄	☉	☽	♂	☿	♃	2.10	2.10	2.10	2.11	2.11	2.11	2.12
3.10	3.11	3.11	3.11	3.11	3.11	3.11	3.11	☿	♃	♀	♄	☉	☽	♂	3.11	3.12	3.12	3.13	3.13	3.14	3.14
4.11	4.12	4.12	4.12	4.12	4.12	4.12	4.12	☽	♂	☿	♃	♀	♄	☉	4.13	4.14	4.14	4.14	4.15	4.16	4.16
5.12	5.13	5.13	5.14	5.14	5.14	5.14	5.14	♄	☉	☽	♂	☿	♃	♀	5.14	5.15	5.15	5.16	5.17	5.18	5.19

Night Hours; Sunset to Sunrise.

Lat. 27°	Lat. 29°	Lat. 31°	Lat. 33°	Lat. 35°	Lat. 37°	Lat. 39°	Lat. 41°	Su	M	Tu	W	Th	F	Sa	Lat. 43°	Lat. 45°	Lat. 47°	Lat. 49°	Lat. 51°	Lat. 53°	Lat. 55°
6.13	6.14	6.14	6.15	6.15	6.15	6.15	6.15	♃	♀	♄	☉	☽	♂	☿	6.16	6.17	6.17	6.18	6.19	6.20	6.21
7.12	7.13	7.13	7.14	7.14	7.14	7.13	7.13	♂	☿	♃	♀	♄	☉	☽	7.14	7.15	7.15	7.16	7.17	7.18	7.19
8.11	8.11	8.11	8.12	8.12	8.12	8.12	8.12	☉	☽	♂	☿	♃	♀	♄	8.13	8.13	8.13	8.14	8.15	8.15	8.16
9.10	9.10	9.10	9.11	9.11	9.11	9.10	9.10	♀	♄	☉	☽	♂	☿	♃	9.11	9.12	9.11	9.12	9.13	9.13	9.14
10.08	10.09	10.09	10.09	10.09	10.09	10.09	10.09	☿	♃	♀	♄	☉	☽	♂	10.09	10.10	10.09	10.10	10.10	10.11	10.11
11.07	11.07	11.07	11.08	11.08	11.08	11.07	11.07	☽	♂	☿	♃	♀	♄	☉	11.07	11.08	11.07	11.08	11.08	11.08	11.09
12.06	12.06	12.07	12.07	12.07	12.06	12.06	12.06	♄	☉	☽	♂	☿	♃	♀	12.06	12.06	12.06	12.06	12.06	12.06	12.06
1.05	1.05	1.05	1.05	1.05	1.05	1.04	1.04	♃	♀	♄	☉	☽	♂	☿	1.04	1.04	1.04	1.03	1.04	1.04	1.04
2.04	2.03	2.03	2.04	2.04	2.03	2.02	2.02	♂	☿	♃	♀	♄	☉	☽	2.02	2.02	2.02	2.01	2.02	2.01	2.01
3.03	3.02	3.02	3.02	3.02	3.02	3.01	3.01	☉	☽	♂	☿	♃	♀	♄	3.00	3.01	3.00	2.59	2.59	2.59	2.59
4.01	4.01	4.01	4.01	4.01	4.00	3.59	3.59	♀	♄	☉	☽	♂	☿	♃	3.59	3.59	3.58	3.57	3.57	3.57	3.56
5.00	4.59	4.59	4.59	4.59	4.59	4.58	4.58	☿	♃	♀	♄	☉	☽	♂	4.57	4.57	4.56	4.55	4.55	4.54	4.54

SEPTEMBER 24th to 30th, ANY YEAR, in South Latitude

APRIL 1st to 7th, ANY YEAR, in North Latitude

♄ Saturn; ♃ Jupiter; ♂ Mars; ☉ Sun; ♀ Venus; ☿ Mercury; ☽ Moon.

Day Hours; Sunrise to Sunset. Mean Time.

Lat. 55°	Lat. 53°	Lat. 51°	Lat. 49°	Lat. 47°	Lat. 45°	Lat. 43°	Sa	F	Th	W	Tu	M	Su	Lat. 41°	Lat. 39°	Lat. 37°	Lat. 35°	Lat. 33°	Lat. 31°	Lat. 29°	Lat. 27°
5.33	5.35	5.37	5.39	5.40	5.42	5.43	♄	♀	♃	☿	♂	☽	☉	5.44	5.46	5.47	5.48	5.49	5.50	5.50	5.51
6.38	6.40	6.41	6.43	6.44	6.46	6.47	♃	☿	♂	☽	☉	♄	♀	6.47	6.49	6.50	6.51	6.52	6.52	6.52	6.53
7.44	7.45	7.46	7.48	7.48	7.50	7.50	♂	☽	☉	♄	♀	♃	☿	7.51	7.52	7.53	7.54	7.54	7.55	7.55	7.55
8.48	8.50	8.51	8.52	8.52	8.53	8.54	☉	♄	♀	♃	☿	♂	☽	8.54	8.55	8.56	8.56	8.57	8.57	8.57	8.58
9.54	9.55	9.55	9.56	9.56	9.57	9.57	♀	♃	☿	♂	☽	☉	♄	9.58	9.58	9.59	9.59	9.59	10.00	9.59	10.00
10.59	11.00	11.00	11.00	11.00	11.01	11.01	☿	♂	☽	☉	♄	♀	♃	11.01	11.01	11.02	11.02	11.03	11.02	11.02	11.02
12.05	12.05	12.05	12.05	12.05	12.05	12.04	☽	☉	♄	♀	♃	☿	♂	12.05	12.05	12.05	12.05	12.05	12.05	12.04	12.04
1.10	1.09	1.09	1.09	1.09	1.08	1.08	♄	♀	♃	☿	♂	☽	☉	1.08	1.08	1.07	1.07	1.07	1.07	1.06	1.06
2.15	2.14	2.14	2.13	2.13	2.12	2.11	♃	☿	♂	☽	☉	♄	♀	2.11	2.11	2.10	2.10	2.10	2.09	2.09	2.08
3.20	3.19	3.18	3.17	3.17	3.16	3.15	♂	☽	☉	♄	♀	♃	☿	3.15	3.14	3.13	3.13	3.12	3.12	3.11	3.11
4.26	4.24	4.23	4.22	4.21	4.20	4.18	☉	♄	♀	♃	☿	♂	☽	4.18	4.17	4.16	4.16	4.15	4.14	4.13	4.13
5.31	5.29	5.27	5.26	5.25	5.24	5.22	♀	♃	☿	♂	☽	☉	♄	5.22	5.20	5.19	5.18	5.17	5.17	5.16	5.15

Night Hours; Sunset to Sunrise.

Lat. 55°	Lat. 53°	Lat. 51°	Lat. 49°	Lat. 47°	Lat. 45°	Lat. 43°	Sa	F	Th	W	Tu	M	Su	Lat. 41°	Lat. 39°	Lat. 37°	Lat. 35°	Lat. 33°	Lat. 31°	Lat. 29°	Lat. 27°
6.36	6.34	6.32	6.30	6.29	6.27	6.25	♂	♄	☉	☽	☿	♀	♃	6.25	6.23	6.22	6.21	6.20	6.19	6.18	6.17
7.31	7.29	7.27	7.26	7.25	7.23	7.21	☉	♃	♀	♄	☽	☿	♂	7.21	7.20	7.19	7.18	7.17	7.17	7.16	7.15
8.25	8.24	8.23	8.21	8.21	8.19	8.18	♀	♂	☿	♃	♄	☽	☉	8.18	8.17	8.16	8.15	8.15	8.14	8.13	8.13
9.20	9.19	9.18	9.17	9.16	9.15	9.14	☿	☉	☽	♂	♃	♄	♀	9.14	9.13	9.13	9.13	9.12	9.12	9.11	9.10
10.14	10.14	10.13	10.12	10.12	10.11	10.10	☽	♀	♄	☉	♂	♃	☿	10.11	10.10	10.10	10.10	10.09	10.09	10.08	10.08
11.09	11.09	11.08	11.08	11.08	11.07	11.07	♄	☿	♃	♀	☉	♂	☽	11.07	11.07	11.07	11.07	11.07	11.07	11.06	11.06
12.03	12.04	12.04	12.04	12.04	12.04	12.03	♃	☽	♂	☿	♀	☉	♄	12.04	12.04	12.04	12.04	12.04	12.04	12.04	12.05
12.58	12.58	12.59	12.59	12.59	1.00	12.59	♂	♄	☉	☽	☿	♀	♃	1.00	1.00	1.00	1.01	1.01	1.02	1.01	1.01
1.52	1.53	1.54	1.55	1.55	1.56	1.56	☉	♃	♀	♄	☽	☿	♂	1.56	1.57	1.57	1.58	1.59	1.59	1.59	1.59
2.47	2.48	2.49	2.50	2.51	2.52	2.52	♀	♂	☿	♃	♄	☽	☉	2.53	2.54	2.54	2.56	2.56	2.57	2.56	2.57
3.41	3.43	3.45	3.46	3.47	3.48	3.48	☿	☉	☽	♂	♃	♄	♀	3.49	3.51	3.51	3.53	3.53	3.54	3.54	3.55
4.36	4.38	4.40	4.41	4.42	4.44	4.45	☽	♀	♄	☉	♂	♃	☿	4.46	4.47	4.48	4.50	4.51	4.52	4.51	4.52

OCTOBER 1st to 7th, ANY YEAR, in South Latitude

APRIL 8th to 14th, ANY YEAR, in North Latitude

♄ Saturn; ♃ Jupiter; ♂ Mars; ☉ Sun; ♀ Venus; ☿ Mercury; ☽ Moon.

Day Hours; Sunrise to Sunset. Mean Time.

Lat. 27°	Lat. 29°	Lat. 31°	Lat. 33°	Lat. 35°	Lat. 37°	Lat. 39°	Lat. 41°	Su	M	Tu	W	Th	F	Sa	Lat. 43°	Lat. 45°	Lat. 47°	Lat. 49°	Lat. 51°	Lat. 53°	Lat. 55°
5.44	5.43	5.41	5.40	5.38	5.36	5.35	5.33	☉	☽	♂	☿	♃	♀	♄	5.32	5.30	5.27	5.24	5.22	5.19	5.15
6.47	6.46	6.45	6.44	6.42	6.40	6.40	6.38	♀	♄	☉	☽	♂	☿	♃	6.37	6.36	6.33	6.30	6.29	6.26	6.23
7.50	7.49	7.48	7.48	7.46	7.45	7.44	7.43	☿	♃	♀	♄	☉	☽	♂	7.42	7.41	7.39	7.37	7.36	7.34	7.31
8.53	8.53	8.52	8.51	8.50	8.49	8.49	8.48	☽	♂	☿	♃	♀	♄	☉	8.48	8.47	8.45	8.43	8.43	8.41	8.39
9.56	9.56	9.55	9.55	9.54	9.53	9.53	9.53	♄	☉	☽	♂	☿	♃	♀	9.53	9.52	9.51	9.50	9.49	9.48	9.47
10.59	10.59	10.59	10.59	10.58	10.58	10.58	10.58	♃	♀	♄	☉	☽	♂	☿	10.58	10.58	10.57	10.56	10.56	10.56	10.55
12.02	12.02	12.02	12.03	12.03	12.02	12.02	12.03	♂	☿	♃	♀	♄	☉	☽	12.03	12.03	12.03	12.03	12.03	12.03	12.03
1.05	1.05	1.06	1.06	1.07	1.06	1.07	1.07	☉	☽	♂	☿	♃	♀	♄	1.08	1.09	1.08	1.09	1.10	1.10	1.10
2.08	2.08	2.09	2.10	2.11	2.11	2.11	2.12	♀	♄	☉	☽	♂	☿	♃	2.13	2.14	2.14	2.15	2.17	2.18	2.18
3.11	3.12	3.13	3.14	3.15	3.15	3.16	3.17	☿	♃	♀	♄	☉	☽	♂	3.19	3.20	3.20	3.22	3.24	3.25	3.26
4.14	4.15	4.16	4.18	4.19	4.19	4.20	4.22	☽	♂	☿	♃	♀	♄	☉	4.24	4.25	4.26	4.28	4.30	4.32	4.34
5.17	5.18	5.20	5.21	5.23	5.24	5.25	5.27	♄	☉	☽	♂	☿	♃	♀	5.29	5.31	5.32	5.35	5.37	5.40	5.42

Night Hours; Sunset to Sunrise.

Lat. 27°	Lat. 29°	Lat. 31°	Lat. 33°	Lat. 35°	Lat. 37°	Lat. 39°	Lat. 41°	Su	M	Tu	W	Th	F	Sa	Lat. 43°	Lat. 45°	Lat. 47°	Lat. 49°	Lat. 51°	Lat. 53°	Lat. 55°
6.20	6.21	6.23	6.25	6.27	6.28	6.29	6.32	♃	♀	♄	☉	☽	♂	☿	6.34	6.36	6.38	6.41	6.44	6.47	6.50
7.17	7.18	7.19	7.21	7.23	7.24	7.24	7.27	♂	☿	♃	♀	♄	☉	☽	7.29	7.30	7.32	7.35	7.37	7.39	7.42
8.14	8.14	8.16	8.17	8.19	8.19	8.20	8.22	☉	☽	♂	☿	♃	♀	♄	8.23	8.25	8.26	8.28	8.30	8.32	8.34
9.11	9.11	9.12	9.13	9.15	9.15	9.15	9.17	♀	♄	☉	☽	♂	☿	♃	9.18	9.19	9.20	9.22	9.23	9.24	9.26
10.07	10.08	10.08	10.08	10.10	10.10	10.10	10.12	☿	♃	♀	♄	☉	☽	♂	10.13	10.13	10.14	10.15	10.16	10.18	10.18
11.04	11.04	11.05	11.05	11.06	11.06	11.06	11.07	☽	♂	☿	♃	♀	♄	☉	11.07	11.08	11.08	11.09	11.09	11.09	11.10
12.01	12.01	12.01	12.02	12.02	12.02	12.01	12.02	♄	☉	☽	♂	☿	♃	♀	12.02	12.02	12.02	12.02	12.02	12.02	12.02
12.58	12.58	12.57	12.58	12.58	12.57	12.56	12.56	♃	♀	♄	☉	☽	♂	☿	12.57	12.56	12.55	12.56	12.54	12.54	12.53
1.55	1.54	1.54	1.54	1.54	1.53	1.52	1.51	♂	☿	♃	♀	♄	☉	☽	1.51	1.51	1.49	1.49	1.47	1.46	1.45
2.52	2.51	2.50	2.50	2.50	2.48	2.47	2.46	☉	☽	♂	☿	♃	♀	♄	2.46	2.45	2.43	2.43	2.40	2.39	2.37
3.48	3.48	3.46	3.46	3.45	3.44	3.42	3.41	♀	♄	☉	☽	♂	☿	♃	3.41	3.39	3.37	3.35	3.33	3.31	3.29
4.45	4.44	4.43	4.42	4.41	4.39	4.37	4.36	☿	♃	♀	♄	☉	☽	♂	4.35	4.34	4.31	4.30	4.26	4.24	4.21

OCTOBER 8th to 14th, ANY YEAR, in South Latitude

APRIL 15th to 22nd, ANY YEAR, in North Latitude

♄ Saturn; ♃ Jupiter; ♂ Mars; ☉ Sun; ♀ Venus; ☿ Mercury; ☽ Moon.

Day Hours; Sunrise to Sunset. Mean Time.

Lat. 27°	Lat. 29°	Lat. 31°	Lat. 33°	Lat. 35°	Lat. 37°	Lat. 39°	Lat. 41°	Su	M	Tu	W	Th	F	Sa	Lat. 43°	Lat. 45°	Lat. 47°	Lat. 49°	Lat. 51°	Lat. 53°	Lat. 55°
5.37	5.35	5.33	5.31	5.29	5.27	5.24	5.22	☉	☽	♂	☿	♃	♀	♄	5.19	5.17	5.13	5.10	5.06	5.02	4.58
6.41	6.39	6.38	6.36	6.34	6.33	6.30	6.28	♀	♄	☉	☽	♂	☿	♃	6.26	6.24	6.21	6.18	6.15	6.12	6.08
7.45	7.43	7.42	7.41	7.40	7.38	7.36	7.35	☿	♃	♀	♄	☉	☽	♂	7.33	7.32	7.29	7.27	7.24	7.22	7.19
8.49	8.48	8.47	8.46	8.45	8.44	8.42	8.41	☽	♂	☿	♃	♀	♄	☉	8.40	8.39	8.37	8.35	8.33	8.31	8.29
9.53	9.52	9.51	9.51	9.50	9.49	9.48	9.48	♄	☉	☽	♂	☿	♃	♀	9.47	9.46	9.45	9.44	9.42	9.41	9.40
10.57	10.56	10.56	10.56	10.55	10.55	10.54	10.54	♃	♀	♄	☉	☽	♂	☿	10.54	10.54	10.53	10.52	10.51	10.51	10.50
12.01	12.00	12.00	12.01	12.01	12.01	12.01	12.01	♂	☿	♃	♀	♄	☉	☽	12.01	12.01	12.01	12.01	12.00	12.01	12.01
1.04	1.04	1.05	1.05	1.06	1.06	1.07	1.07	☉	☽	♂	☿	♃	♀	♄	1.07	1.08	1.08	1.09	1.09	1.10	1.11
2.08	2.08	2.09	2.10	2.11	2.12	2.13	2.13	♀	♄	☉	☽	♂	☿	♃	2.14	2.16	2.16	2.18	2.18	2.20	2.21
3.12	3.13	3.14	3.15	3.16	3.17	3.19	3.20	☿	♃	♀	♄	☉	☽	♂	3.21	3.23	3.24	3.26	3.27	3.30	3.32
4.16	4.17	4.18	4.20	4.22	4.23	4.25	4.26	☽	♂	☿	♃	♀	♄	☉	4.28	4.30	4.32	4.34	4.36	4.40	4.42
5.20	5.21	5.23	5.25	5.27	5.28	5.31	5.33	♄	☉	☽	♂	☿	♃	♀	5.35	5.38	5.40	5.43	5.45	5.49	5.53

Night Hours; Sunset to Sunrise.

Lat. 27°	Lat. 29°	Lat. 31°	Lat. 33°	Lat. 35°	Lat. 37°	Lat. 39°	Lat. 41°	Su	M	Tu	W	Th	F	Sa	Lat. 43°	Lat. 45°	Lat. 47°	Lat. 49°	Lat. 51°	Lat. 53°	Lat. 55°
6.24	6.25	6.27	6.30	6.32	6.34	6.37	6.39	♃	♀	♄	☉	☽	♂	☿	6.42	6.45	6.48	6.51	6.54	6.59	7.03
7.20	7.21	7.22	7.25	7.27	7.28	7.31	7.33	♂	☿	♃	♀	♄	☉	☽	7.35	7.38	7.40	7.42	7.45	7.49	7.52
8.16	8.17	8.18	8.20	8.21	8.23	8.25	8.26	☉	☽	♂	☿	♃	♀	♄	8.28	8.30	8.32	8.34	8.36	8.39	8.42
9.10	9.12	9.13	9.15	9.16	9.17	9.19	9.20	♀	♄	☉	☽	♂	☿	♃	9.21	9.23	9.24	9.25	9.27	9.29	9.31
10.08	10.08	10.09	10.10	10.11	10.11	10.12	10.13	☿	♃	♀	♄	☉	☽	♂	10.14	10.15	10.16	10.17	10.17	10.19	10.21
11.04	11.04	11.04	11.05	11.05	11.06	11.06	11.07	☽	♂	☿	♃	♀	♄	☉	11.07	11.08	11.08	11.08	11.08	11.09	11.10
12.00	12.00	12.00	12.00	12.00	12.00	12.00	12.00	♄	☉	☽	♂	☿	♃	♀	12.00	12.00	12.00	12.00	11.59	12.00	12.00
12.56	12.55	12.55	12.55	12.55	12.54	12.54	12.54	♃	♀	♄	☉	☽	♂	☿	12.53	12.53	12.52	12.51	12.50	12.50	12.49
1.52	1.51	1.50	1.50	1.49	1.49	1.48	1.47	♂	☿	♃	♀	♄	☉	☽	1.46	1.45	1.43	1.42	1.41	1.40	1.38
2.48	2.47	2.46	2.45	2.44	2.43	2.42	2.41	☉	☽	♂	☿	♃	♀	♄	2.39	2.38	2.35	2.34	2.32	2.30	2.28
3.44	3.43	3.41	3.40	3.39	3.37	3.35	3.34	♀	♄	☉	☽	♂	☿	♃	3.32	3.30	3.27	3.25	3.22	3.20	3.17
4.40	4.38	4.37	4.35	4.33	4.32	4.29	4.28	☿	♃	♀	♄	☉	☽	♂	4.25	4.23	4.19	4.17	4.13	4.10	4.07

OCTOBER 15th to 22nd, ANY YEAR, in South Latitude

APRIL 23rd to 30th, ANY YEAR, in North Latitude

♄ Saturn; ♃ Jupiter; ♂ Mars; ☉ Sun; ♀ Venus; ☿ Mercury; ☽ Moon.

Day Hours; Sunrise to Sunset. Mean Time.

Lat. 27°	Lat. 29°	Lat. 31°	Lat. 33°	Lat. 35°	Lat. 37°	Lat. 39°	Lat. 41°	Su	M	Tu	W	Th	F	Sa	Lat. 43°	Lat. 45°	Lat. 47°	Lat. 49°	Lat. 51°	Lat. 53°	Lat. 55°
5.28	5.25	5.23	5.21	5.19	5.16	5.13	5.09	☉	☽	♂	☿	♃	♀	♄	5.06	5.03	4.59	4.54	4.50	4.45	4.39
6.33	6.31	6.28	6.27	6.26	6.23	6.21	6.17	♀	♄	☉	☽	♂	☿	♃	6.15	6.12	6.09	6.05	6.02	5.57	5.52
7.38	7.36	7.35	7.34	7.32	7.30	7.28	7.26	☿	♃	♀	♄	☉	☽	♂	7.24	7.22	7.19	7.16	7.13	7.10	7.06
8.43	8.41	8.41	8.40	8.39	8.38	8.36	8.34	☽	♂	☿	♃	♀	♄	☉	8.32	8.31	8.29	8.26	8.25	8.22	8.19
9.48	9.47	9.46	9.46	9.46	9.45	9.44	9.42	♄	☉	☽	♂	☿	♃	♀	9.41	9.40	9.39	9.37	9.36	9.34	9.32
10.53	10.53	10.52	10.52	10.52	10.52	10.51	10.50	♃	♀	♄	☉	☽	♂	☿	10.50	10.49	10.49	10.48	10.48	10.47	10.46
11.59	11.58	11.58	11.59	11.59	11.59	11.59	11.59	♂	☿	♃	♀	♄	☉	☽	11.59	11.59	11.59	11.59	11.59	11.59	11.59
1.04	1.04	1.04	1.05	1.06	1.06	1.07	1.07	☉	☽	♂	☿	♃	♀	♄	1.07	1.08	1.08	1.09	1.11	1.11	1.12
2.09	2.09	2.10	2.11	2.12	2.13	2.14	2.15	♀	♄	☉	☽	♂	☿	♃	2.16	2.17	2.18	2.20	2.22	2.24	2.26
3.14	3.15	3.16	3.17	3.19	3.21	3.22	3.23	☿	♃	♀	♄	☉	☽	♂	3.25	3.26	3.28	3.31	3.34	3.36	3.39
4.19	4.20	4.21	4.24	4.26	4.28	4.30	4.32	☽	♂	☿	♃	♀	♄	☉	4.34	4.36	4.38	4.42	4.45	4.48	4.52
5.24	5.26	5.27	5.30	5.32	5.35	5.37	5.40	♄	☉	☽	♂	☿	♃	♀	5.42	5.45	5.48	5.52	5.57	6.01	6.06

Night Hours; Sunset to Sunrise.

Lat. 27°	Lat. 29°	Lat. 31°	Lat. 33°	Lat. 35°	Lat. 37°	Lat. 39°	Lat. 41°	Su	M	Tu	W	Th	F	Sa	Lat. 43°	Lat. 45°	Lat. 47°	Lat. 49°	Lat. 51°	Lat. 53°	Lat. 55°
6.29	6.31	6.33	6.36	6.39	6.42	6.45	6.48	♃	♀	♄	☉	☽	♂	☿	6.51	6.54	6.58	7.03	7.08	7.13	7.19
7.24	7.26	7.27	7.30	7.32	7.35	7.37	7.40	♂	☿	♃	♀	♄	☉	☽	7.42	7.45	7.48	7.52	7.56	8.00	8.00
8.19	8.20	8.21	8.23	8.25	8.27	8.29	8.31	☉	☽	♂	☿	♃	♀	♄	8.33	8.35	8.38	8.41	8.45	8.48	8.52
9.14	9.15	9.16	9.17	9.19	9.20	9.22	9.23	♀	♄	☉	☽	♂	☿	♃	9.25	9.26	9.28	9.31	9.33	9.35	9.39
10.09	10.09	10.10	10.11	10.12	10.13	10.14	10.15	☿	♃	♀	♄	☉	☽	♂	10.16	10.16	10.18	10.20	10.21	10.23	10.25
11.04	11.04	11.04	11.04	11.05	11.05	11.06	11.06	☽	♂	☿	♃	♀	♄	☉	11.07	11.07	11.08	11.09	11.10	11.10	11.12
11.59	11.58	11.58	11.58	11.58	11.58	11.58	11.58	♄	☉	☽	♂	☿	♃	♀	11.58	11.58	11.58	11.58	11.58	11.58	11.58
12.53	12.53	12.52	12.52	12.51	12.51	12.50	12.50	♃	♀	♄	☉	☽	♂	☿	12.49	12.48	12.47	12.47	12.46	12.45	12.45
1.48	1.47	1.46	1.45	1.44	1.43	1.42	1.41	♂	☿	♃	♀	♄	☉	☽	1.40	1.39	1.37	1.36	1.35	1.32	1.31
2.43	2.42	2.41	2.39	2.38	2.36	2.35	2.33	☉	☽	♂	☿	♃	♀	♄	2.32	2.29	2.27	2.26	2.23	2.20	2.18
3.38	3.36	3.35	3.33	3.31	3.29	3.27	3.25	♀	♄	☉	☽	♂	☿	♃	3.23	3.20	3.17	3.15	3.12	3.07	3.04
4.33	4.31	4.29	4.26	4.24	4.21	4.19	4.16	☿	♃	♀	♄	☉	☽	♂	4.14	4.10	4.07	4.04	4.00	3.55	3.51

OCTOBER 23rd to 31st, ANY YEAR, in South Latitude

MAY 1st to 7th, ANY YEAR, in North Latitude

♄ Saturn; ♃ Jupiter; ♂ Mars; ☉ Sun; ♀ Venus; ☿ Mercury; ☽ Moon.

Day Hours; Sunrise to Sunset. Mean Time.

Lat. 27°	Lat. 29°	Lat. 31°	Lat. 33°	Lat. 35°	Lat. 37°	Lat. 39°	Lat. 41°	Su	M	Tu	W	Th	F	Sa	Lat. 43°	Lat. 45°	Lat. 47°	Lat. 49°	Lat. 51°	Lat. 53°	Lat. 55°
5.22	5.19	5.16	5.13	5.10	5.06	5.03	4.59	☉	☽	♂	☿	♃	♀	♄	4.54	4.50	4.45	4.40	4.34	4.28	4.21
6.28	6.25	6.23	6.20	6.18	6.15	6.12	6.09	♀	♄	☉	☽	♂	☿	♃	6.05	6.01	5.57	5.53	5.48	5.43	5.37
7.34	7.32	7.30	7.28	7.26	7.23	7.21	7.19	☿	♃	♀	♄	☉	☽	♂	7.15	7.13	7.09	7.06	7.02	6.58	6.53
8.40	8.38	8.37	8.35	8.34	8.32	8.30	8.28	☽	♂	☿	♃	♀	♄	☉	8.26	8.24	8.21	8.19	8.16	8.13	8.09
9.46	9.45	9.44	9.43	9.42	9.40	9.39	9.38	♄	☉	☽	♂	☿	♃	♀	9.36	9.35	9.33	9.32	9.30	9.28	9.25
10.52	10.51	10.51	10.50	10.50	10.49	10.48	10.48	♃	♀	♄	☉	☽	♂	☿	10.47	10.46	10.45	10.45	10.44	10.43	10.41
11.58	11.58	11.58	11.58	11.58	11.58	11.58	11.58	♂	☿	♃	♀	♄	☉	☽	11.57	11.58	11.58	11.58	11.58	11.58	11.58
1.03	1.04	1.04	1.05	1.05	1.06	1.07	1.07	☉	☽	♂	☿	♃	♀	♄	1.08	1.09	1.10	1.10	1.11	1.12	1.14
2.09	2.10	2.11	2.12	2.13	2.15	2.16	2.17	♀	♄	☉	☽	♂	☿	♃	2.19	2.20	2.22	2.23	2.25	2.27	2.30
3.15	3.17	3.18	3.20	3.21	3.23	3.25	3.27	☿	♃	♀	♄	☉	☽	♂	3.29	3.31	3.34	3.36	3.37	3.42	3.46
4.21	4.23	4.25	4.27	4.29	4.32	4.34	4.37	☽	♂	☿	♃	♀	♄	☉	4.40	4.43	4.46	4.49	4.53	4.57	5.02
5.27	5.30	5.32	5.35	5.37	5.40	5.43	5.46	♄	☉	☽	♂	☿	♃	♀	5.50	5.54	5.58	6.02	6.07	6.12	6.18

Night Hours; Sunset to Sunrise.

Lat. 27°	Lat. 29°	Lat. 31°	Lat. 33°	Lat. 35°	Lat. 37°	Lat. 39°	Lat. 41°	Su	M	Tu	W	Th	F	Sa	Lat. 43°	Lat. 45°	Lat. 47°	Lat. 49°	Lat. 51°	Lat. 53°	Lat. 55°
6.33	6.36	6.39	6.42	6.45	6.49	6.52	6.56	♃	♀	♄	☉	☽	♂	☿	7.01	7.05	7.10	7.15	7.21	7.27	7.34
7.27	7.30	7.32	7.35	7.37	7.40	7.43	7.46	♂	☿	♃	♀	♄	☉	☽	7.50	7.54	7.58	8.02	8.07	8.12	8.18
8.21	8.23	8.25	8.27	8.29	8.32	8.34	8.36	☉	☽	♂	☿	♃	♀	♄	8.40	8.42	8.46	8.49	8.53	8.57	9.02
9.15	9.17	9.18	9.20	9.21	9.23	9.25	9.27	♀	♄	☉	☽	♂	☿	♃	9.29	9.31	9.34	9.36	9.39	9.42	9.45
10.09	10.10	10.11	10.12	10.13	10.14	10.15	10.17	☿	♃	♀	♄	☉	☽	♂	10.18	10.20	10.22	10.23	10.25	10.27	10.29
11.03	11.04	11.04	11.05	11.05	11.06	11.06	11.07	☽	♂	☿	♃	♀	♄	☉	11.08	11.08	11.10	11.10	11.11	11.12	11.13
11.57	11.57	11.57	11.57	11.57	11.57	11.57	11.57	♄	☉	☽	♂	☿	♃	♀	11.57	11.57	11.58	11.57	11.57	11.57	11.57
12.51	12.51	12.50	12.50	12.49	12.48	12.48	12.47	♃	♀	♄	☉	☽	♂	☿	12.46	12.46	12.45	12.44	12.42	12.41	12.40
1.45	1.44	1.43	1.42	1.41	1.40	1.39	1.37	♂	☿	♃	♀	♄	☉	☽	1.36	1.34	1.33	1.31	1.28	1.26	1.24
2.39	2.38	2.36	2.35	2.33	2.31	2.30	2.28	☉	☽	♂	☿	♃	♀	♄	2.25	2.23	2.21	2.18	2.14	2.11	2.08
3.33	3.31	3.29	3.27	3.25	3.22	3.20	3.18	♀	♄	☉	☽	♂	☿	♃	3.14	3.12	3.09	3.05	3.00	2.56	2.52
4.27	4.25	4.22	4.20	4.17	4.14	4.11	4.08	☿	♃	♀	♄	☉	☽	♂	4.04	4.00	3.57	3.52	3.46	3.41	3.35

NOVEMBER 1st to 7th, ANY YEAR, in South Latitude

MAY 8th to 15th, ANY YEAR, in North Latitude

♄ Saturn; ♃ Jupiter; ♂ Mars; ☉ Sun; ♀ Venus; ☿ Mercury; ☽ Moon.

Day Hours; Sunrise to Sunset. Mean Time.

Lat. 55°	Lat. 53°	Lat. 51°	Lat. 49°	Lat. 47°	Lat. 45°	Lat. 43°	Sa	F	Th	W	Tu	M	Su	Lat. 41°	Lat. 39°	Lat. 37°	Lat. 35°	Lat. 33°	Lat. 31°	Lat. 29°	Lat. 27°
4.06	4.14	4.22	4.29	4.34	4.40	4.45	♄	♀	♃	☿	♂	☽	☉	4.50	4.55	4.59	5.03	5.05	5.10	5.14	5.16
5.25	5.31	5.38	5.44	5.48	5.53	5.57	♃	☿	♂	☽	☉	♄	♀	6.01	6.05	6.09	6.12	6.14	6.18	6.21	6.23
6.43	6.48	6.54	6.58	7.02	7.06	7.09	♂	☽	☉	♄	♀	♃	☿	7.12	7.16	7.18	7.21	7.22	7.26	7.28	7.30
8.02	8.05	8.10	8.13	8.15	8.18	8.21	☉	♄	♀	♃	☿	♂	☽	8.23	8.26	8.28	8.30	8.31	8.33	8.36	8.36
9.20	9.22	9.25	9.28	9.29	9.31	9.33	♀	♃	☿	♂	☽	☉	♄	9.34	9.36	9.38	9.39	9.39	9.41	9.43	9.43
10.39	10.40	10.41	10.42	10.43	10.44	10.45	☿	♂	☽	☉	♄	♀	♃	10.45	10.47	10.47	10.48	10.48	10.49	10.50	10.50
11.57	11.57	11.57	11.57	11.57	11.57	11.57	☽	☉	♄	♀	♃	☿	♂	11.57	11.57	11.57	11.57	11.56	11.57	11.57	11.57
1.16	1.14	1.13	1.12	1.10	1.09	1.08	♄	♀	♃	☿	♂	☽	☉	1.08	1.07	1.07	1.06	1.05	1.04	1.04	1.03
2.34	2.31	2.29	2.26	2.24	2.22	2.20	♃	☿	♂	☽	☉	♄	♀	2.19	2.18	2.16	2.15	2.13	2.12	2.11	2.10
3.53	3.48	3.45	3.41	3.38	3.35	3.32	♂	☽	☉	♄	♀	♃	☿	3.30	3.28	3.26	3.24	3.22	3.20	3.19	3.17
5.11	5.05	5.00	4.56	4.52	4.48	4.44	☉	♄	♀	♃	☿	♂	☽	4.41	4.38	4.36	4.33	4.30	4.28	4.26	4.24
6.30	6.22	6.16	6.10	6.05	6.00	5.56	♀	♃	☿	♂	☽	☉	♄	5.52	5.49	5.45	5.42	5.39	5.35	5.33	5.30

Night Hours; Sunset to Sunrise.

Lat. 55°	Lat. 53°	Lat. 51°	Lat. 49°	Lat. 47°	Lat. 45°	Lat. 43°	Sa	F	Th	W	Tu	M	Su	Lat. 41°	Lat. 39°	Lat. 37°	Lat. 35°	Lat. 33°	Lat. 31°	Lat. 29°	Lat. 27°
7.48	7.39	7.32	7.25	7.19	7.13	7.08	☿	♂	☽	☉	♄	♀	♃	7.03	6.59	6.55	6.51	6.47	6.43	6.40	6.37
8.29	8.22	8.16	8.10	8.05	8.00	7.56	☽	☉	♄	♀	♃	☿	♂	7.52	7.49	7.45	7.42	7.39	7.35	7.33	7.30
9.11	9.05	9.00	8.55	8.51	8.47	8.44	♄	♀	♃	☿	♂	☽	☉	8.41	8.38	8.36	8.33	8.30	8.27	8.26	8.24
9.52	9.48	9.44	9.41	9.38	9.35	9.32	♃	☿	♂	☽	☉	♄	♀	9.30	9.28	9.26	9.24	9.22	9.20	9.18	9.17
10.33	10.30	10.28	10.26	10.24	10.22	10.20	♂	☽	☉	♄	♀	♃	☿	10.18	10.17	10.16	10.15	10.13	10.12	10.11	10.10
11.15	11.13	11.12	11.11	11.10	11.09	11.08	☉	♄	♀	♃	☿	♂	☽	11.07	11.07	11.06	11.06	11.05	11.04	11.04	11.03
11.56	11.56	11.56	11.56	11.56	11.56	11.56	♀	♃	☿	♂	☽	☉	♄	11.56	11.56	11.57	11.57	11.57	11.56	11.57	11.57
12.37	12.39	12.40	12.41	12.42	12.43	12.44	☿	♂	☽	☉	♄	♀	♃	12.45	12.46	12.46	12.47	12.48	12.48	12.49	12.50
1.19	1.22	1.24	1.26	1.28	1.30	1.32	☽	☉	♄	♀	♃	☿	♂	1.34	1.35	1.37	1.38	1.40	1.40	1.42	1.43
2.00	2.05	2.08	2.12	2.15	2.18	2.20	♄	♀	♃	☿	♂	☽	☉	2.23	2.24	2.27	2.29	2.31	2.33	2.35	2.36
2.41	2.47	2.52	2.57	3.01	3.05	3.08	♃	☿	♂	☽	☉	♄	♀	3.11	3.14	3.18	3.20	3.23	3.25	3.28	3.30
3.23	3.30	3.36	3.42	3.47	3.52	3.56	♂	☽	☉	♄	♀	♃	☿	4.00	4.04	4.08	4.11	4.14	4.17	4.20	4.23

NOVEMBER 8th to 15th, ANY YEAR, in South Latitude

MAY 16th to 23rd, ANY YEAR, in North Latitude

♄ Saturn; ♃ Jupiter; ♂ Mars; ☉ Sun; ♀ Venus; ☿ Mercury; ☽ Moon.

Day Hours; Sunrise to Sunset. Mean Time.

Lat. 27°	Lat. 29°	Lat. 31°	Lat. 33°	Lat. 35°	Lat. 37°	Lat. 39°	Lat. 41°	Su	M	Tu	W	Th	F	Sa	Lat. 43°	Lat. 45°	Lat. 47°	Lat. 49°	Lat. 51°	Lat. 53°	Lat. 55°
5.11	5.08	5.04	5.00	4.56	4.50	4.45	4.41	☉	☽	♂	☿	♃	♀	♄	4.36	4.30	4.23	4.16	4.09	4.00	3.51
6.19	6.16	6.13	6.09	6.06	6.01	5.57	5.54	♀	♄	☉	☽	♂	☿	♃	5.49	5.44	5.39	5.33	5.27	5.19	5.12
7.26	7.24	7.21	7.19	7.16	7.12	7.09	7.06	☿	♃	♀	♄	☉	☽	♂	7.03	6.59	6.54	6.50	6.45	6.39	6.33
8.34	8.32	8.30	8.28	8.26	8.23	8.21	8.19	☽	♂	☿	♃	♀	♄	☉	8.16	8.13	8.10	8.06	8.03	7.58	7.54
9.41	9.40	9.39	9.38	9.36	9.34	9.32	9.31	♄	☉	☽	♂	☿	♃	♀	9.30	9.28	9.25	9.23	9.21	9.18	9.15
10.49	10.48	10.47	10.47	10.46	10.45	10.44	10.44	♃	♀	♄	☉	☽	♂	☿	10.44	10.41	10.41	10.40	10.39	10.37	10.36
11.56	11.56	11.56	11.56	11.56	11.56	11.56	11.57	♂	☿	♃	♀	♄	☉	☽	11.57	11.57	11.57	11.57	11.57	11.57	11.57
1.04	1.04	1.05	1.06	1.07	1.07	1.08	1.09	☉	☽	♂	☿	♃	♀	♄	1.10	1.11	1.12	1.13	1.14	1.16	1.17
2.11	2.12	2.13	2.15	2.17	2.18	2.20	2.22	♀	♄	☉	☽	♂	☿	♃	2.23	2.25	2.28	2.30	2.32	2.35	2.38
3.19	3.20	3.22	3.25	3.27	3.29	3.32	3.34	☿	♃	♀	♄	☉	☽	♂	3.37	3.40	3.43	3.47	3.50	3.55	3.59
4.26	4.28	4.31	4.34	4.37	4.40	4.43	4.47	☽	♂	☿	♃	♀	♄	☉	4.50	4.54	4.59	5.04	5.08	5.14	5.20
5.33	5.36	5.39	5.44	5.47	5.51	5.55	5.59	♄	☉	☽	♂	☿	♃	♀	6.04	6.09	6.14	6.20	6.26	6.34	6.41

Night Hours; Sunset to Sunrise.

Lat. 27°	Lat. 29°	Lat. 31°	Lat. 33°	Lat. 35°	Lat. 37°	Lat. 39°	Lat. 41°	Su	M	Tu	W	Th	F	Sa	Lat. 43°	Lat. 45°	Lat. 47°	Lat. 49°	Lat. 51°	Lat. 53°	Lat. 55°
6.41	6.44	6.48	6.53	6.57	7.02	7.07	7.12	♃	♀	♄	☉	☽	♂	☿	7.17	7.23	7.30	7.37	7.44	7.53	8.02
7.34	7.36	7.39	7.44	7.47	7.51	7.55	7.59	♂	☿	♃	♀	♄	☉	☽	8.04	8.09	8.14	8.20	8.26	8.34	8.41
8.26	8.28	8.31	8.34	8.37	8.40	8.43	8.47	☉	☽	♂	☿	♃	♀	♄	8.50	8.54	8.59	9.03	9.08	9.14	9.20
9.19	9.20	9.22	9.25	9.27	9.29	9.32	9.34	♀	♄	☉	☽	♂	☿	♃	9.37	9.40	9.43	9.47	9.50	9.55	9.59
10.11	10.12	10.13	10.15	10.16	10.18	10.20	10.21	☿	♃	♀	♄	☉	☽	♂	10.23	10.25	10.27	10.30	10.32	10.35	10.38
11.04	11.04	11.05	11.06	11.06	11.07	11.08	11.09	☽	♂	☿	♃	♀	♄	☉	11.10	11.11	11.12	11.13	11.14	11.16	11.17
11.56	11.56	11.56	11.56	11.56	11.56	11.56	11.56	♄	☉	☽	♂	☿	♃	♀	11.56	11.56	11.56	11.56	11.56	11.56	11.56
12.49	12.48	12.47	12.47	12.46	12.45	12.44	12.43	♃	♀	♄	☉	☽	♂	☿	12.43	12.42	12.40	12.39	12.38	12.37	12.34
1.41	1.40	1.39	1.37	1.36	1.34	1.32	1.31	♂	☿	♃	♀	♄	☉	☽	1.29	1.27	1.25	1.22	1.20	1.17	1.13
2.34	2.32	2.30	2.28	2.26	2.23	2.21	2.18	☉	☽	♂	☿	♃	♀	♄	2.16	2.13	2.09	2.06	2.02	1.58	1.52
3.26	3.24	3.21	3.18	3.15	3.12	3.09	3.05	♀	♄	☉	☽	♂	☿	♃	3.02	2.58	2.53	2.49	2.44	2.38	2.31
4.19	4.16	4.13	4.09	4.05	4.01	3.57	3.53	☿	♃	♀	♄	☉	☽	♂	3.49	3.44	3.38	3.32	3.26	3.19	3.10

NOVEMBER 16th to 23rd, ANY YEAR, in South Latitude

MAY 24th to 31st, ANY YEAR, in North Latitude

♄ Saturn; ♃ Jupiter; ♂ Mars; ☉ Sun; ♀ Venus; ☿ Mercury; ☽ Moon.

Day Hours; Sunrise to Sunset. Mean Time.

Lat. 27°	Lat. 29°	Lat. 31°	Lat. 33°	Lat. 35°	Lat. 37°	Lat. 39°	Lat. 41°	Su	M	Tu	W	Th	F	Sa	Lat. 43°	Lat. 45°	Lat. 47°	Lat. 49°	Lat. 51°	Lat. 53°	Lat. 55°
5.08	5.04	5.00	4.55	4.51	4.46	4.41	4.35	☉	☽	♂	☿	♃	♀	♄	4.29	4.23	4.15	4.07	3.58	3.49	3.39
6.16	6.13	6.10	6.05	6.02	5.58	5.54	5.49	♀	♄	☉	☽	♂	☿	♃	5.44	5.39	5.32	5.25	5.18	5.10	5.02
7.24	7.22	7.19	7.16	7.13	7.10	7.06	7.02	☿	♃	♀	♄	☉	☽	♂	6.58	6.54	6.49	6.44	6.38	6.32	6.25
8.33	8.31	8.29	8.26	8.24	8.22	8.19	8.16	☽	♂	☿	♃	♀	♄	☉	8.13	8.10	8.06	8.02	7.57	7.53	7.48
9.41	9.39	9.38	9.36	9.35	9.33	9.32	9.29	♄	☉	☽	♂	☿	♃	♀	9.28	9.26	9.23	9.20	9.17	9.14	9.11
10.49	10.48	10.48	10.47	10.46	10.45	10.44	10.43	♃	♀	♄	☉	☽	♂	☿	10.42	10.41	10.40	10.38	10.37	10.35	10.34
11.57	11.57	11.57	11.57	11.57	11.57	11.57	11.57	♂	☿	♃	♀	♄	☉	☽	11.57	11.57	11.57	11.57	11.57	11.57	11.57
1.05	1.06	1.07	1.07	1.08	1.09	1.10	1.10	☉	☽	♂	☿	♃	♀	♄	1.12	1.13	1.14	1.15	1.16	1.18	1.20
2.13	2.15	2.16	2.18	2.19	2.21	2.22	2.24	♀	♄	☉	☽	♂	☿	♃	2.26	2.28	2.31	2.33	2.36	2.39	2.43
3.22	3.24	3.26	3.28	3.30	3.33	3.35	3.37	☿	♃	♀	♄	☉	☽	♂	3.41	3.44	3.48	3.51	3.56	4.00	4.06
4.30	4.32	4.35	4.38	4.41	4.44	4.48	4.51	☽	♂	☿	♃	♀	♄	☉	4.56	5.00	5.05	5.10	5.16	5.22	5.29
5.38	5.41	5.45	5.49	5.52	5.56	6.00	6.04	♄	☉	☽	♂	☿	♃	♀	6.10	6.15	6.22	6.28	6.35	6.43	6.52

Night Hours; Sunset to Sunrise.

Lat. 27°	Lat. 29°	Lat. 31°	Lat. 33°	Lat. 35°	Lat. 37°	Lat. 39°	Lat. 41°	Su	M	Tu	W	Th	F	Sa	Lat. 43°	Lat. 45°	Lat. 47°	Lat. 49°	Lat. 51°	Lat. 53°	Lat. 55°
6.46	6.50	6.54	6.59	7.03	7.08	7.13	7.18	♃	♀	♄	☉	☽	♂	☿	7.25	7.31	7.39	7.46	7.55	8.04	8.15
7.38	7.41	7.45	7.49	7.52	7.56	8.00	8.04	♂	☿	♃	♀	♄	☉	☽	8.10	8.15	8.22	8.28	8.35	8.43	8.52
8.30	8.32	8.35	8.38	8.41	8.44	8.48	8.51	☉	☽	♂	☿	♃	♀	♄	8.56	9.00	9.05	9.09	9.15	9.21	9.29
9.22	9.24	9.26	9.28	9.30	9.33	9.35	9.37	♀	♄	☉	☽	♂	☿	♃	9.41	9.44	9.48	9.51	9.56	10.00	10.06
10.13	10.15	10.16	10.18	10.19	10.21	10.22	10.24	☿	♃	♀	♄	☉	☽	♂	10.26	10.28	10.31	10.33	10.36	10.39	10.42
11.05	11.06	11.07	11.07	11.08	11.09	11.10	11.10	☽	♂	☿	♃	♀	♄	☉	11.11	11.12	11.14	11.14	11.16	11.17	11.19
11.57	11.57	11.57	11.57	11.57	11.57	11.57	11.57	♄	☉	☽	♂	☿	♃	♀	11.57	11.57	11.57	11.57	11.56	11.56	11.57
12.49	12.48	12.48	12.47	12.46	12.45	12.44	12.43	♃	♀	♄	☉	☽	♂	☿	12.42	12.41	12.39	12.38	12.36	12.35	12.33
1.41	1.39	1.38	1.36	1.35	1.33	1.32	1.29	♂	☿	♃	♀	♄	☉	☽	1.27	1.25	1.22	1.19	1.16	1.13	1.10
2.33	2.31	2.29	2.26	2.24	2.22	2.19	2.16	☉	☽	♂	☿	♃	♀	♄	2.12	2.09	2.05	2.01	1.57	1.52	1.47
3.24	3.22	3.19	3.16	3.13	3.10	3.06	3.02	♀	♄	☉	☽	♂	☿	♃	2.58	2.54	2.48	2.43	2.37	2.31	2.23
4.16	4.13	4.10	4.05	4.02	3.58	3.54	3.49	☿	♃	♀	♄	☉	☽	♂	3.43	3.38	3.31	3.24	3.17	3.09	3.00

NOVEMBER 24th to 30th, ANY YEAR, in South Latitude

JUNE 1st to 7th, ANY YEAR, in North Latitude

♄ Saturn; ♃ Jupiter; ♂ Mars; ☉ Sun; ♀ Venus; ☿ Mercury; ☽ Moon.

Day Hours; Sunrise to Sunset. Mean Time.

Lat. 27°	Lat. 29°	Lat. 31°	Lat. 33°	Lat. 35°	Lat. 37°	Lat. 39°	Lat. 41°	Su	M	Tu	W	Th	F	Sa	Lat. 43°	Lat. 45°	Lat. 47°	Lat. 49°	Lat. 51°	Lat. 53°	Lat. 55°
5.06	5.02	4.58	4.53	4.48	4.42	4.37	4.31	☉	☽	♂	☿	♃	♀	♄	4.24	4.17	4.09	4.00	3.51	3.40	3.29
6.15	6.11	6.08	6.04	6.00	5.55	5.51	5.46	♀	♄	☉	☽	♂	☿	♃	5.40	5.34	5.27	5.20	5.12	5.03	4.54
7.23	7.21	7.18	7.15	7.11	7.07	7.04	7.00	☿	♃	♀	♄	☉	☽	♂	6.55	6.51	6.45	6.39	6.33	6.26	6.19
8.32	8.30	8.28	8.26	8.23	8.20	8.18	8.15	☽	♂	☿	♃	♀	♄	☉	8.11	8.08	8.04	7.59	7.54	7.49	7.44
9.41	9.39	9.38	9.36	9.35	9.33	9.31	9.29	♄	☉	☽	♂	☿	♃	♀	9.27	9.24	9.22	9.18	9.15	9.12	9.08
10.49	10.49	10.48	10.47	10.46	10.45	10.45	10.44	♃	♀	♄	☉	☽	♂	☿	10.42	10.41	10.40	10.38	10.36	10.35	10.33
11.58	11.58	11.58	11.58	11.58	11.58	11.58	11.58	♂	☿	♃	♀	♄	☉	☽	11.58	11.58	11.58	11.58	11.58	11.58	11.58
1.07	1.07	1.08	1.09	1.10	1.11	1.12	1.13	☉	☽	♂	☿	♃	♀	♄	1.14	1.15	1.16	1.18	1.19	1.20	1.23
2.15	2.17	2.18	2.20	2.21	2.23	2.25	2.27	♀	♄	☉	☽	♂	☿	♃	2.29	2.32	2.34	2.37	2.40	2.43	2.48
3.24	3.26	3.28	3.31	3.33	3.36	3.39	3.42	☿	♃	♀	♄	☉	☽	♂	3.45	3.49	3.53	3.56	4.01	4.06	4.13
4.33	4.35	4.38	4.41	4.45	4.49	4.52	4.56	☽	♂	☿	♃	♀	♄	☉	5.01	5.05	5.11	5.15	5.22	5.26	5.37
5.41	5.45	5.48	5.52	5.56	6.01	6.06	6.11	♄	☉	☽	♂	☿	♃	♀	6.16	6.22	6.29	6.35	6.43	6.52	7.02

Night Hours; Sunset to Sunrise.

Lat. 27°	Lat. 29°	Lat. 31°	Lat. 33°	Lat. 35°	Lat. 37°	Lat. 39°	Lat. 41°	Su	M	Tu	W	Th	F	Sa	Lat. 43°	Lat. 45°	Lat. 47°	Lat. 49°	Lat. 51°	Lat. 53°	Lat. 55°
6.50	6.54	6.58	7.03	7.08	7.14	7.19	7.25	♃	♀	♄	☉	☽	♂	☿	7.32	7.39	7.47	7.55	8.04	8.15	8.27
7.41	7.45	7.48	7.52	7.56	8.01	8.05	8.10	♂	☿	♃	♀	♄	☉	☽	8.16	8.22	8.29	8.35	8.43	8.52	9.02
8.33	8.35	8.38	8.41	8.45	8.49	8.52	8.56	☉	☽	♂	☿	♃	♀	♄	9.01	9.05	9.11	9.16	9.22	9.29	9.37
9.24	9.26	9.28	9.30	9.33	9.36	9.38	9.41	♀	♄	☉	☽	♂	☿	♃	9.45	9.48	9.52	9.56	10.01	10.16	10.12
10.15	10.16	10.18	10.19	10.21	10.23	10.24	10.27	☿	♃	♀	♄	☉	☽	♂	10.29	10.31	10.34	10.36	10.39	10.43	10.47
11.06	11.07	11.08	11.08	11.09	11.10	11.11	11.12	☽	♂	☿	♃	♀	♄	☉	11.13	11.14	11.16	11.17	11.18	11.20	11.22
11.58	11.58	11.58	11.58	11.58	11.58	11.58	11.58	♄	☉	☽	♂	☿	♃	♀	11.58	11.58	11.58	11.57	11.57	11.57	11.57
12.50	12.48	12.47	12.47	12.46	12.45	12.43	12.43	♃	♀	♄	☉	☽	♂	☿	12.42	12.41	12.39	12.37	12.36	12.34	12.32
1.41	1.39	1.37	1.36	1.34	1.32	1.30	1.28	♂	☿	♃	♀	♄	☉	☽	1.26	1.24	1.21	1.18	1.15	1.11	1.07
2.32	2.29	2.27	2.25	2.22	2.19	2.16	2.14	☉	☽	♂	☿	♃	♀	♄	2.10	2.07	2.03	1.58	1.54	1.48	1.42
3.24	3.20	3.17	3.14	3.11	3.07	3.02	2.59	♀	♄	☉	☽	♂	☿	♃	2.55	2.50	2.45	2.38	2.32	2.25	2.17
4.15	4.10	4.07	4.03	3.59	3.54	3.49	3.45	☿	♃	♀	♄	☉	☽	♂	3.39	3.33	3.26	3.19	3.11	3.02	2.52

DECEMBER 1st to 7th, ANY YEAR, in South Latitude

JUNE 8th to 14th, ANY YEAR, in North Latitude

♄ Saturn; ♃ Jupiter; ♂ Mars; ☉ Sun; ♀ Venus; ☿ Mercury; ☽ Moon.

Day Hours; Sunrise to Sunset. Mean Time.

Lat. 27°	Lat. 29°	Lat. 31°	Lat. 33°	Lat. 35°	Lat. 37°	Lat. 39°	Lat. 41°	Su	M	Tu	W	Th	F	Sa	Lat. 43°	Lat. 45°	Lat. 47°	Lat. 49°	Lat. 51°	Lat. 53°	Lat. 55°
5.05	5.00	4.55	4.50	4.45	4.39	4.34	4.29	☉	☽	♂	☿	♃	♀	♄	4.21	4.14	4.05	3.56	3.46	3.35	3.23
6.14	6.10	6.06	6.01	5.57	5.52	5.48	5.43	♀	♄	☉	☽	♂	☿	♃	5.37	5.32	5.24	5.16	5.08	4.59	4.49
7.23	7.20	7.16	7.13	7.10	7.06	7.02	6.58	☿	♃	♀	♄	☉	☽	♂	6.54	6.49	6.43	6.37	6.30	6.23	6.15
8.32	8.29	8.27	8.24	8.22	8.19	8.17	8.14	☽	♂	☿	♃	♀	♄	☉	8.10	8.07	8.02	7.57	7.52	7.47	7.41
9.41	9.39	9.37	9.36	9.34	9.32	9.31	9.29	♄	☉	☽	♂	☿	♃	♀	9.26	9.24	9.21	9.17	9.14	9.11	9.07
10.50	10.49	10.48	10.47	10.46	10.45	10.45	10.44	♃	♀	♄	☉	☽	♂	☿	10.43	10.42	10.40	10.38	10.36	10.37	10.33
11.59	11.59	11.59	11.59	11.59	11.59	11.59	11.59	♂	☿	♃	♀	♄	☉	☽	11.59	11.59	11.59	11.59	11.59	11.59	11.59
1.08	1.09	1.09	1.10	1.11	1.12	1.13	1.14	☉	☽	♂	☿	♃	♀	♄	1.15	1.17	1.17	1.18	1.21	1.22	1.25
2.17	2.18	2.20	2.21	2.23	2.25	2.27	2.29	♀	♄	☉	☽	♂	☿	♃	2.32	2.34	2.36	2.39	2.43	2.46	2.51
3.26	3.28	3.30	3.33	3.35	3.38	3.42	3.45	☿	♃	♀	♄	☉	☽	♂	3.48	3.52	3.55	3.59	4.05	4.10	4.17
4.35	4.38	4.41	4.44	4.48	4.52	4.56	5.00	☽	♂	☿	♃	♀	♄	☉	5.04	5.09	5.14	5.19	5.27	5.34	5.43
5.44	5.47	5.51	5.56	6.00	6.05	6.10	6.15	♄	☉	☽	♂	☿	♃	♀	6.21	6.27	6.33	6.40	6.49	6.58	7.09

Night Hours; Sunset to Sunrise.

Lat. 27°	Lat. 29°	Lat. 31°	Lat. 33°	Lat. 35°	Lat. 37°	Lat. 39°	Lat. 41°	Su	M	Tu	W	Th	F	Sa	Lat. 43°	Lat. 45°	Lat. 47°	Lat. 49°	Lat. 51°	Lat. 53°	Lat. 55°
6.53	6.57	7.02	7.07	7.12	7.18	7.24	7.30	♃	♀	♄	☉	☽	♂	☿	7.37	7.44	7.52	8.00	8.11	8.22	8.35
7.44	7.47	7.51	7.56	8.00	8.05	8.10	8.15	♂	☿	♃	♀	♄	☉	☽	8.21	8.27	8.33	8.40	8.49	8.58	9.09
8.35	8.38	8.41	8.44	8.48	8.52	8.56	9.00	☉	☽	♂	☿	♃	♀	♄	9.05	9.09	9.14	9.19	9.27	9.34	9.43
9.26	9.28	9.30	9.33	9.35	9.38	9.42	9.45	♀	♄	☉	☽	♂	☿	♃	9.48	9.52	9.55	9.59	10.05	10.10	10.17
10.17	10.18	10.20	10.21	10.23	10.25	10.27	10.29	☿	♃	♀	♄	☉	☽	♂	10.32	10.34	10.36	10.39	10.43	10.46	10.51
11.08	11.08	11.09	11.10	11.11	11.12	11.13	11.14	☽	♂	☿	♃	♀	♄	☉	11.16	11.17	11.17	11.18	11.21	11.22	11.25
11.59	11.59	11.59	11.59	11.59	11.59	11.59	11.59	♄	☉	☽	♂	☿	♃	♀	11.59	11.59	11.59	11.59	11.59	11.59	11.59
12.50	12.49	12.48	12.47	12.46	12.45	12.45	12.44	♃	♀	♄	☉	☽	♂	☿	12.43	12.42	12.40	12.38	12.36	12.35	12.33
1.41	1.39	1.37	1.36	1.34	1.32	1.31	1.29	♂	☿	♃	♀	♄	☉	☽	1.27	1.24	1.21	1.17	1.14	1.11	1.07
2.32	2.29	2.27	2.24	2.22	2.19	2.17	2.14	☉	☽	♂	☿	♃	♀	♄	2.10	2.07	2.02	1.57	1.52	1.47	1.41
3.23	3.20	3.16	3.13	3.10	3.06	3.02	2.58	♀	♄	☉	☽	♂	☿	♃	2.54	2.49	2.43	2.37	2.30	2.23	2.15
4.14	4.10	4.06	4.01	3.57	3.52	3.48	3.43	☿	♃	♀	♄	☉	☽	♂	3.38	3.32	3.24	3.16	3.08	2.59	2.49

DECEMBER 8th to 14th, ANY YEAR, in South Latitude

JUNE 15th to 22nd, ANY YEAR, in North Latitude

♄ Saturn; ♃ Jupiter; ♂ Mars; ☉ Sun; ♀ Venus; ☿ Mercury; ☽ Moon.

Day Hours; Sunrise to Sunset. Mean Time.

Lat. 27°	Lat. 29°	Lat. 31°	Lat. 33°	Lat. 35°	Lat. 37°	Lat. 39°	Lat. 41°	Su	M	Tu	W	Th	F	Sa	Lat. 43°	Lat. 45°	Lat. 47°	Lat. 49°	Lat. 51°	Lat. 53°	Lat. 55°
5.05	5.00	4.55	4.50	4.45	4.39	4.33	4.26	☉	☽	♂	☿	♃	♀	♄	4.19	4.12	4.03	3.54	3.44	3.33	3.20
6.14	6.10	6.06	6.02	5.58	5.53	5.48	5.42	♀	♄	☉	☽	♂	☿	♃	5.36	5.30	5.23	5.15	5.07	4.58	4.47
7.23	7.20	7.17	7.13	7.10	7.06	7.02	6.57	☿	♃	♀	♄	☉	☽	♂	6.53	6.48	6.42	6.36	6.29	6.22	6.14
8.33	8.30	8.28	8.25	8.23	8.20	8.17	8.13	☽	♂	☿	♃	♀	♄	☉	8.10	8.06	8.02	7.57	7.52	7.47	7.40
9.42	9.40	9.38	9.37	9.35	9.33	9.31	9.29	♄	☉	☽	♂	☿	♃	♀	9.26	9.24	9.21	9.18	9.15	9.11	9.07
10.51	10.50	10.49	10.48	10.48	10.47	10.46	10.44	♃	♀	♄	☉	☽	♂	☿	10.43	10.42	10.41	10.39	10.37	10.36	10.34
12.00	12.00	12.00	12.00	12.00	12.00	12.00	12.00	♂	☿	♃	♀	♄	☉	☽	12.00	12.00	12.00	12.00	12.00	12.00	12.00
1.09	1.10	1.11	1.12	1.13	1.14	1.15	1.16	☉	☽	♂	☿	♃	♀	♄	1.17	1.18	1.20	1.21	1.23	1.25	1.27
2.18	2.20	2.22	2.23	2.25	2.27	2.29	2.31	♀	♄	☉	☽	♂	☿	♃	2.34	2.36	2.39	2.42	2.45	2.50	2.54
3.28	3.30	3.33	3.35	3.38	3.41	3.44	3.47	☿	♃	♀	♄	☉	☽	♂	3.51	3.54	3.59	4.03	4.08	4.14	4.21
4.37	4.40	4.43	4.47	4.50	4.54	4.58	5.03	☽	♂	☿	♃	♀	♄	☉	5.07	5.12	5.18	5.24	5.33	5.39	5.48
5.46	5.50	5.54	5.58	6.03	6.08	6.13	6.18	♄	☉	☽	♂	☿	♃	♀	6.24	6.30	6.38	6.45	6.53	7.03	7.14

Night Hours; Sunset to Sunrise.

Lat. 27°	Lat. 29°	Lat. 31°	Lat. 33°	Lat. 35°	Lat. 37°	Lat. 39°	Lat. 41°	Su	M	Tu	W	Th	F	Sa	Lat. 43°	Lat. 45°	Lat. 47°	Lat. 49°	Lat. 51°	Lat. 53°	Lat. 55°
6.55	7.00	7.05	7.10	7.15	7.21	7.27	7.34	♃	♀	♄	☉	☽	♂	☿	7.41	7.48	7.57	8.06	8.16	8.28	8.41
7.46	7.50	7.54	7.58	8.03	8.08	8.13	8.18	♂	☿	♃	♀	♄	☉	☽	8.24	8.30	8.38	8.45	8.53	9.03	9.14
8.37	8.40	8.43	8.47	8.50	8.54	8.58	9.03	☉	☽	♂	☿	♃	♀	♄	9.07	9.12	9.18	9.24	9.31	9.39	9.48
9.28	9.30	9.33	9.35	9.38	9.41	9.44	9.47	♀	♄	☉	☽	♂	☿	♃	9.51	9.54	9.59	10.03	10.08	10.14	10.21
10.18	10.20	10.22	10.23	10.25	10.27	10.29	10.31	☿	♃	♀	♄	☉	☽	♂	10.34	10.36	10.39	10.42	10.45	10.50	10.54
11.09	11.10	11.11	11.12	11.13	11.14	11.15	11.16	☽	♂	☿	♃	♀	♄	☉	11.17	11.18	11.20	11.21	11.23	11.25	11.27
12.00	12.00	12.00	12.00	12.00	12.00	12.00	12.00	♄	☉	☽	♂	☿	♃	♀	12.00	12.00	12.00	12.00	12.00	12.00	12.00
12.51	12.50	12.49	12.48	12.48	12.47	12.46	12.44	♃	♀	♄	☉	☽	♂	☿	12.43	12.42	12.41	12.39	12.37	12.36	12.34
1.42	1.40	1.38	1.37	1.35	1.33	1.31	1.29	♂	☿	♃	♀	♄	☉	☽	1.26	1.24	1.21	1.18	1.15	1.11	1.07
2.33	2.30	2.28	2.25	2.23	2.20	2.17	2.13	☉	☽	♂	☿	♃	♀	♄	2.10	2.06	2.02	1.57	1.52	1.47	1.40
3.23	3.20	3.17	3.13	3.10	3.06	3.02	2.57	♀	♄	☉	☽	♂	☿	♃	2.53	2.48	2.42	2.36	2.29	2.22	2.14
4.14	4.10	4.05	4.02	3.58	3.53	3.48	3.42	☿	♃	♀	♄	☉	☽	♂	3.36	3.30	3.23	3.15	3.07	2.58	2.47

DECEMBER 15th to 22nd, ANY YEAR, in South Latitude

JUNE 23rd to 30th, ANY YEAR, in North Latitude

♄ Saturn; ♃ Jupiter; ♂ Mars; ☉ Sun; ♀ Venus; ☿ Mercury; ☽ Moon.

Day Hours; Sunrise to Sunset. Mean Time.

Lat. 27°	Lat. 29°	Lat. 31°	Lat. 33°	Lat. 35°	Lat. 37°	Lat. 39°	Lat. 41°	Su	M	Tu	W	Th	F	Sa	Lat. 43°	Lat. 45°	Lat. 47°	Lat. 49°	Lat. 51°	Lat. 53°	Lat. 55°
5.07	5.02	4.57	4.52	4.47	4.41	4.35	4.28	☉	☽	♂	☿	♃	♀	♄	4.21	4.14	4.05	3.56	3.46	3.34	3.21
6.16	6.12	6.08	6.04	6.00	5.55	5.50	5.44	♀	♄	☉	☽	♂	☿	♃	5.38	5.32	5.25	5.17	5.09	4.59	4.48
7.26	7.22	7.19	7.16	7.12	7.08	7.04	7.00	☿	♃	♀	♄	☉	☽	♂	6.55	6.50	6.44	6.38	6.32	6.23	6.15
8.35	8.32	8.30	8.27	8.25	8.22	8.19	8.15	☽	♂	☿	♃	♀	♄	☉	8.12	8.08	8.04	7.59	7.54	7.48	7.42
9.44	9.42	9.41	9.39	9.37	9.35	9.33	9.31	♄	☉	☽	♂	☿	♃	♀	9.29	9.26	9.23	9.20	9.17	9.13	9.09
10.53	10.52	10.52	10.51	10.50	10.49	10.48	10.47	♃	♀	♄	☉	☽	♂	☿	10.46	10.44	10.43	10.41	10.40	10.37	10.36
12.03	12.03	12.03	12.03	12.03	12.03	12.03	12.03	♂	☿	♃	♀	♄	☉	☽	12.03	12.03	12.03	12.03	12.03	12.03	12.03
1.12	1.13	1.13	1.14	1.15	1.16	1.17	1.18	☉	☽	♂	☿	♃	♀	♄	1.19	1.21	1.22	1.24	1.25	1.28	1.29
2.21	2.23	2.24	2.26	2.28	2.30	2.32	2.34	♀	♄	☉	☽	♂	☿	♃	2.36	2.39	2.42	2.45	2.48	2.52	2.56
3.30	3.33	3.35	3.38	3.40	3.43	3.46	3.50	☿	♃	♀	♄	☉	☽	♂	3.53	3.57	4.01	4.06	4.11	4.17	4.23
4.40	4.43	4.46	4.50	4.53	4.57	5.01	5.06	☽	♂	☿	♃	♀	♄	☉	5.10	5.15	5.21	5.27	5.34	5.42	5.50
5.49	5.53	5.57	6.01	6.05	6.10	6.15	6.21	♄	☉	☽	♂	☿	♃	♀	6.27	6.33	6.40	6.48	6.56	7.06	7.17

Night Hours; Sunset to Sunrise.

Lat. 27°	Lat. 29°	Lat. 31°	Lat. 33°	Lat. 35°	Lat. 37°	Lat. 39°	Lat. 41°	Su	M	Tu	W	Th	F	Sa	Lat. 43°	Lat. 45°	Lat. 47°	Lat. 49°	Lat. 51°	Lat. 53°	Lat. 55°
6.58	7.02	7.08	7.13	7.18	7.24	7.30	7.37	♃	♀	♄	☉	☽	♂	☿	7.44	7.51	8.00	8.09	8.19	8.30	8.44
7.49	7.52	7.57	8.01	8.05	8.10	8.15	8.21	♂	☿	♃	♀	♄	☉	☽	8.27	8.33	8.40	8.48	8.56	9.05	9.17
8.40	8.42	8.46	8.50	8.53	8.57	9.01	9.06	☉	☽	♂	☿	♃	♀	♄	9.10	9.15	9.21	9.27	9.34	9.41	9.50
9.30	9.32	9.35	9.38	9.40	9.43	9.46	9.50	♀	♄	☉	☽	♂	☿	♃	9.53	9.57	10.01	10.06	10.11	10.16	10.23
10.21	10.22	10.24	10.26	10.28	10.30	10.32	10.34	☿	♃	♀	♄	☉	☽	♂	10.36	10.39	10.42	10.45	10.48	10.51	10.56
11.12	11.12	11.13	11.14	11.15	11.16	11.17	11.18	☽	♂	☿	♃	♀	♄	☉	11.19	11.21	11.22	11.24	11.25	11.27	11.29
12.03	12.03	12.03	12.03	12.03	12.03	12.03	12.03	♄	☉	☽	♂	☿	♃	♀	12.03	12.03	12.03	12.03	12.03	12.03	12.03
12.53	12.53	12.52	12.51	12.50	12.49	12.48	12.47	♃	♀	♄	☉	☽	♂	☿	12.46	12.44	12.43	12.41	12.40	12.37	12.36
1.44	1.43	1.41	1.39	1.36	1.35	1.33	1.31	♂	☿	♃	♀	♄	☉	☽	1.29	1.26	1.23	1.20	1.17	1.13	1.09
2.35	2.33	2.30	2.27	2.23	2.22	2.19	2.15	☉	☽	♂	☿	♃	♀	♄	2.12	2.08	2.04	1.59	1.54	1.48	1.42
3.26	3.23	3.19	3.16	3.11	3.08	3.04	3.00	♀	♄	☉	☽	♂	☿	♃	2.55	2.50	2.44	2.38	2.32	2.23	2.15
4.16	4.13	4.08	4.04	3.59	3.55	3.50	3.44	☿	♃	♀	♄	☉	☽	♂	3.38	3.32	3.25	3.17	3.09	2.59	2.48

DECEMBER 23rd to 31st, ANY YEAR, in South Latitude

JULY 1st to 7th, ANY YEAR, in North Latitude

♄ Saturn; ♃ Jupiter; ♂ Mars; ☉ Sun; ♀ Venus; ☿ Mercury; ☽ Moon.

Day Hours; Sunrise to Sunset. Mean Time.

Lat. 27°	Lat. 29°	Lat. 31°	Lat. 33°	Lat. 35°	Lat. 37°	Lat. 39°	Lat. 41°	Su	M	Tu	W	Th	F	Sa	Lat. 43°	Lat. 45°	Lat. 47°	Lat. 49°	Lat. 51°	Lat. 53°	Lat. 55°
5.08	5.04	4.59	4.54	4.49	4.43	4.37	4.31	☉	☽	♂	☿	♃	♀	♄	4.24	4.17	4.08	3.59	3.49	3.38	3.25
6.17	6.14	6.10	6.06	6.01	5.56	5.51	5.46	♀	♄	☉	☽	♂	☿	♃	5.41	5.35	5.27	5.20	5.12	5.02	4.52
7.26	7.24	7.21	7.17	7.14	7.10	7.06	7.02	☿	♃	♀	♄	☉	☽	♂	6.57	6.53	6.47	6.41	6.34	6.27	6.18
8.36	8.34	8.31	8.29	8.26	8.23	8.20	8.17	☽	♂	☿	♃	♀	♄	☉	8.14	8.10	8.06	8.01	7.57	7.51	7.45
9.45	9.44	9.42	9.40	9.39	9.37	9.35	9.32	♄	☉	☽	♂	☿	♃	♀	9.30	9.28	9.25	9.22	9.19	9.15	9.11
10.54	10.54	10.53	10.52	10.51	10.50	10.49	10.48	♃	♀	♄	☉	☽	♂	☿	10.47	10.46	10.44	10.43	10.42	10.40	10.38
12.03	12.04	12.04	12.04	12.04	12.04	12.04	12.04	♂	☿	♃	♀	♄	☉	☽	12.04	12.04	12.04	12.04	12.04	12.04	12.04
1.12	1.13	1.14	1.15	1.16	1.17	1.18	1.18	☉	☽	♂	☿	♃	♀	♄	1.20	1.21	1.23	1.24	1.27	1.28	1.31
2.21	2.23	2.25	2.27	2.28	2.30	2.32	2.34	♀	♄	☉	☽	♂	☿	♃	2.37	2.39	2.42	2.45	2.49	2.53	2.57
3.31	3.33	3.36	3.38	3.41	3.44	3.47	3.49	☿	♃	♀	♄	☉	☽	♂	3.53	3.57	4.01	4.06	4.12	4.17	4.24
4.40	4.43	4.47	4.50	4.53	4.57	5.02	5.04	☽	♂	☿	♃	♀	♄	☉	5.10	5.15	5.21	5.27	5.34	5.41	5.50
5.49	5.53	5.57	6.01	6.06	6.11	6.16	6.20	♄	☉	☽	♂	☿	♃	♀	6.26	6.32	6.40	6.47	6.57	7.06	7.17

Night Hours; Sunset to Sunrise.

Lat. 27°	Lat. 29°	Lat. 31°	Lat. 33°	Lat. 35°	Lat. 37°	Lat. 39°	Lat. 41°	Su	M	Tu	W	Th	F	Sa	Lat. 43°	Lat. 45°	Lat. 47°	Lat. 49°	Lat. 51°	Lat. 53°	Lat. 55°
6.58	7.03	7.08	7.13	7.18	7.24	7.30	7.35	♃	♀	♄	☉	☽	♂	☿	7.43	7.50	7.59	8.08	8.19	8.30	8.43
7.49	7.53	7.57	8.02	8.06	8.11	8.16	8.20	♂	☿	♃	♀	♄	☉	☽	8.27	8.32	8.40	8.47	8.57	9.06	9.17
8.40	8.43	8.47	8.50	8.53	8.57	9.01	9.05	☉	☽	♂	☿	♃	♀	♄	9.10	9.15	9.21	9.27	9.34	9.42	9.50
9.31	9.34	9.36	9.39	9.41	9.44	9.47	9.49	♀	♄	☉	☽	♂	☿	♃	9.54	9.57	10.01	10.06	10.12	10.17	10.24
10.22	10.24	10.25	10.27	10.29	10.31	10.33	10.34	☿	♃	♀	♄	☉	☽	♂	10.37	10.39	10.42	10.55	10.49	10.53	10.57
11.13	11.14	11.15	11.16	11.16	11.17	11.18	11.19	☽	♂	☿	♃	♀	♄	☉	11.21	11.21	11.23	11.24	11.27	11.29	11.31
12.04	12.04	12.04	12.04	12.04	12.04	12.04	12.04	♄	☉	☽	♂	☿	♃	♀	12.04	12.04	12.04	12.04	12.04	12.04	12.04
12.54	12.54	12.53	12.53	12.52	12.51	12.50	12.48	♃	♀	♄	☉	☽	♂	☿	12.48	12.46	12.44	12.42	12.42	12.40	12.38
1.45	1.44	1.43	1.41	1.39	1.37	1.35	1.33	♂	☿	♃	♀	♄	☉	☽	1.31	1.28	1.25	1.22	1.20	1.16	1.12
2.36	2.35	2.32	2.30	2.27	2.24	2.21	2.18	☉	☽	♂	☿	♃	♀	♄	2.15	2.10	2.06	2.01	1.57	1.53	1.45
3.27	3.25	3.21	3.18	3.15	3.11	3.07	3.03	♀	♄	☉	☽	♂	☿	♃	2.58	2.53	2.47	2.41	2.37	2.28	2.19
4.18	4.15	4.12	4.07	4.02	3.57	3.52	3.47	☿	♃	♀	♄	☉	☽	♂	3.42	3.35	3.27	3.20	3.12	3.03	2.52

JANUARY 1st to 7th, ANY YEAR, in South Latitude

JULY 8th to 15th, ANY YEAR, in North Latitude

♄ Saturn; ♃ Jupiter; ♂ Mars; ☉ Sun; ♀ Venus; ☿ Mercury; ☽ Moon.

Day Hours; Sunrise to Sunset. Mean Time.

Lat. 27°	Lat. 29°	Lat. 31°	Lat. 33°	Lat. 35°	Lat. 37°	Lat. 39°	Lat. 41°	Su	M	Tu	W	Th	F	Sa	Lat. 43°	Lat. 45°	Lat. 47°	Lat. 49°	Lat. 51°	Lat. 53°	Lat. 55°
5.10	5.07	5.03	4.58	4.53	4.47	4.41	4.35	☉	☽	♂	☿	♃	♀	♄	4.28	4.21	4.12	4.03	3.54	3.43	3.31
6.19	6.17	6.13	6.09	6.05	6.00	5.55	5.50	♀	♄	☉	☽	♂	☿	♃	5.44	5.38	5.31	5.23	5.16	5.07	4.57
7.28	7.26	7.24	7.20	7.17	7.13	7.09	7.05	☿	♃	♀	♄	☉	☽	♂	7.00	6.56	6.49	6.43	6.38	6.30	6.22
8.37	8.36	8.34	8.32	8.29	8.26	8.23	8.20	☽	♂	☿	♃	♀	♄	☉	8.16	8.13	8.08	8.04	8.00	7.54	7.48
9.46	9.45	9.44	9.43	9.41	9.39	9.37	9.35	♄	☉	☽	♂	☿	♃	♀	9.32	9.30	9.27	9.24	9.22	9.17	9.13
10.55	10.55	10.54	10.54	10.53	10.52	10.51	10.50	♃	♀	♄	☉	☽	♂	☿	10.48	10.47	10.45	10.44	10.44	10.41	10.39
12.04	12.05	12.05	12.05	12.05	12.05	12.05	12.05	♂	☿	♃	♀	♄	☉	☽	12.05	12.05	12.05	12.05	12.05	12.05	12.05
1.13	1.14	1.15	1.16	1.17	1.18	1.18	1.19	☉	☽	♂	☿	♃	♀	♄	1.21	1.22	1.23	1.25	1.26	1.28	1.30
2.22	2.24	2.26	2.27	2.29	2.31	2.32	2.34	♀	♄	☉	☽	♂	☿	♃	2.37	2.39	2.41	2.45	2.48	2.52	2.56
3.31	3.33	3.36	3.39	3.41	3.44	3.46	3.49	☿	♃	♀	♄	☉	☽	♂	3.53	3.56	4.00	4.05	4.10	4.15	4.21
4.40	4.43	4.46	4.50	4.53	4.57	5.00	5.04	☽	♂	☿	♃	♀	♄	☉	5.09	5.14	5.19	5.25	5.32	5.39	5.47
5.49	5.52	5.57	6.01	6.05	6.10	6.14	6.19	♄	☉	☽	♂	☿	♃	♀	6.25	6.31	6.37	6.45	6.53	7.02	7.12

Night Hours; Sunset to Sunrise.

Lat. 27°	Lat. 29°	Lat. 31°	Lat. 33°	Lat. 35°	Lat. 37°	Lat. 39°	Lat. 41°	Su	M	Tu	W	Th	F	Sa	Lat. 43°	Lat. 45°	Lat. 47°	Lat. 49°	Lat. 51°	Lat. 53°	Lat. 55°
6.58	7.02	7.07	7.12	7.17	7.23	7.28	7.34	♃	♀	♄	☉	☽	♂	☿	7.41	7.48	7.56	8.05	8.15	8.26	8.38
7.49	7.53	7.57	8.01	8.05	8.10	8.14	8.19	♂	☿	♃	♀	♄	☉	☽	8.25	8.31	8.37	8.45	8.53	9.03	9.13
8.40	8.43	8.46	8.50	8.53	8.57	9.00	9.04	☉	☽	♂	☿	♃	♀	♄	9.09	9.14	9.19	9.25	9.32	9.39	9.47
9.32	9.34	9.36	9.39	9.41	9.44	9.47	9.49	♀	♄	☉	☽	♂	☿	♃	9.53	9.56	10.00	10.05	10.10	10.16	10.22
10.23	10.24	10.26	10.27	10.29	10.31	10.33	10.34	☿	♃	♀	♄	☉	☽	♂	10.37	10.39	10.42	10.45	10.48	10.52	10.56
11.14	11.15	11.15	11.16	11.17	11.18	11.19	11.19	☽	♂	☿	♃	♀	♄	☉	11.21	11.22	11.23	11.25	11.27	11.29	11.31
12.05	12.05	12.05	12.05	12.05	12.05	12.05	12.05	♄	☉	☽	♂	☿	♃	♀	12.05	12.05	12.05	12.05	12.05	12.05	12.05
12.56	12.56	12.55	12.54	12.53	12.52	12.51	12.50	♃	♀	♄	☉	☽	♂	☿	12.48	12.47	12.46	12.44	12.43	12.42	12.40
1.47	1.46	1.44	1.43	1.41	1.39	1.37	1.35	♂	☿	♃	♀	♄	☉	☽	1.32	1.30	1.27	1.24	1.22	1.18	1.14
2.39	2.37	2.34	2.32	2.29	2.26	2.24	2.20	☉	☽	♂	☿	♃	♀	♄	2.16	2.13	2.09	2.04	2.00	1.55	1.49
3.30	3.27	3.24	3.20	3.17	3.13	3.10	3.05	♀	♄	☉	☽	♂	☿	♃	3.00	2.56	2.50	2.44	2.38	2.31	2.23
4.21	4.18	4.13	4.09	4.05	4.00	3.56	3.50	☿	♃	♀	♄	☉	☽	♂	3.44	3.38	3.32	3.24	3.17	3.08	2.58

JANUARY 8th to 15th, ANY YEAR, in South Latitude

JULY 16th to 23rd, ANY YEAR, in North Latitude

♄ Saturn; ♃ Jupiter; ♂ Mars; ☉ Sun; ♀ Venus; ☿ Mercury; ☽ Moon.

Day Hours; Sunrise to Sunset. Mean Time.

Lat. 27°	Lat. 29°	Lat. 31°	Lat. 33°	Lat. 35°	Lat. 37°	Lat. 39°	Lat. 41°	Su	M	Tu	W	Th	F	Sa	Lat. 43°	Lat. 45°	Lat. 47°	Lat. 49°	Lat. 51°	Lat. 53°	Lat. 55°
5.15	5.11	5.07	5.04	4.58	4.52	4.47	4.41	☉	☽	♂	☿	♃	♀	♄	4.34	4.28	4.20	4.11	4.02	3.52	3.41
6.24	6.20	6.17	6.14	6.09	6.04	6.00	5.55	♀	♄	☉	☽	♂	☿	♃	5.49	5.44	5.38	5.30	5.23	5.14	5.05
7.32	7.29	7.27	7.24	7.21	7.17	7.13	7.10	☿	♃	♀	♄	☉	☽	♂	7.05	7.01	6.55	6.49	6.43	6.37	6.29
8.41	8.39	8.37	8.25	8.32	8.29	8.26	8.24	☽	♂	☿	♃	♀	♄	☉	8.20	8.17	8.13	8.09	8.04	7.59	7.53
9.49	9.48	9.46	9.45	9.43	9.41	9.39	9.38	♄	☉	☽	♂	☿	♃	♀	9.35	9.33	9.30	9.28	9.24	9.21	9.17
10.58	10.57	10.56	10.56	10.55	10.53	10.52	10.52	♃	♀	♄	☉	☽	♂	☿	10.50	10.49	10.48	10.47	10.45	10.43	10.41
12.06	12.06	12.06	12.06	12.06	12.06	12.06	12.06	♂	☿	♃	♀	♄	☉	☽	12.06	12.06	12.06	12.06	12.06	12.06	12.06
1.15	1.15	1.16	1.17	1.17	1.18	1.19	1.21	☉	☽	♂	☿	♃	♀	♄	1.21	1.22	1.23	1.25	1.26	1.28	1.30
2.23	2.24	2.26	2.28	2.29	2.30	2.32	2.35	♀	♄	☉	☽	♂	☿	♃	2.36	2.38	2.41	2.44	2.46	2.50	2.54
3.32	3.34	3.36	3.39	3.40	3.42	3.45	3.49	☿	♃	♀	♄	☉	☽	♂	3.51	3.54	3.58	4.04	4.07	4.12	4.18
4.40	4.43	4.45	4.49	4.51	4.55	4.58	5.04	☽	♂	☿	♃	♀	♄	☉	5.07	5.11	5.16	5.23	5.27	5.35	5.42
5.49	5.52	5.55	6.00	6.03	6.07	6.11	6.17	♄	☉	☽	♂	☿	♃	♀	6.22	6.27	6.33	6.42	6.48	6.57	7.06

Night Hours; Sunset to Sunrise.

Lat. 27°	Lat. 29°	Lat. 31°	Lat. 33°	Lat. 35°	Lat. 37°	Lat. 39°	Lat. 41°	Su	M	Tu	W	Th	F	Sa	Lat. 43°	Lat. 45°	Lat. 47°	Lat. 49°	Lat. 51°	Lat. 53°	Lat. 55°
6.57	7.01	7.05	7.10	7.14	7.19	7.24	7.32	♃	♀	♄	☉	☽	♂	☿	7.37	7.43	7.51	8.01	8.08	8.19	8.30
7.49	7.52	7.55	8.00	8.03	8.07	8.11	8.18	♂	☿	♃	♀	♄	☉	☽	8.22	8.27	8.34	8.42	8.48	8.57	9.06
8.40	8.43	8.45	8.49	8.51	8.55	8.58	9.04	☉	☽	♂	☿	♃	♀	♄	9.07	9.11	9.16	9.23	9.27	9.35	9.42
9.32	9.34	9.36	9.39	9.40	9.43	9.45	9.50	♀	♄	☉	☽	♂	☿	♃	9.52	9.55	9.59	10.04	10.07	10.13	10.18
10.23	10.24	10.26	10.28	10.29	10.30	10.32	10.35	☿	♃	♀	♄	☉	☽	♂	10.36	10.38	10.41	10.45	10.46	10.51	10.54
11.15	11.15	11.16	11.17	11.17	11.18	11.19	11.21	☽	♂	☿	♃	♀	♄	☉	11.21	11.22	11.24	11.26	11.26	11.29	11.30
12.06	12.06	12.06	12.06	12.06	12.06	12.06	12.06	♄	☉	☽	♂	☿	♃	♀	12.06	12.06	12.06	12.06	12.06	12.06	12.06
12.58	12.57	12.56	12.56	12.55	12.54	12.53	12.53	♃	♀	♄	☉	☽	♂	☿	12.51	12.50	12.49	12.47	12.45	12.44	12.43
1.49	1.48	1.47	1.46	1.43	1.42	1.40	1.39	♂	☿	♃	♀	♄	☉	☽	1.36	1.34	1.31	1.28	1.25	1.22	1.19
2.41	2.39	2.37	2.36	2.32	2.30	2.27	2.25	☉	☽	♂	☿	♃	♀	♄	2.21	2.18	2.14	2.09	2.04	2.00	1.55
3.32	3.29	3.27	3.25	3.21	3.17	3.14	3.10	♀	♄	☉	☽	♂	☿	♃	3.05	3.01	2.56	2.50	2.44	2.38	2.31
4.24	4.20	4.17	4.15	4.09	4.05	4.01	3.56	☿	♃	♀	♄	☉	☽	♂	3.50	3.45	3.39	3.31	3.23	3.16	3.07

JANUARY 16th to 23rd, ANY YEAR, in South Latitude

JULY 24th to 31st, ANY YEAR, in North Latitude

♄ Saturn; ♃ Jupiter; ♂ Mars; ☉ Sun; ♀ Venus; ☿ Mercury; ☽ Moon.

Day Hours; Sunrise to Sunset. Mean Time.

Lat. 27°	Lat. 29°	Lat. 31°	Lat. 33°	Lat. 35°	Lat. 37°	Lat. 39°	Lat. 41°	Su	M	Tu	W	Th	F	Sa	Lat. 43°	Lat. 45°	Lat. 47°	Lat. 49°	Lat. 51°	Lat. 53°	Lat. 55°
5.19	5.15	5.11	5.07	5.03	4.58	4.53	4.47	☉	☽	♂	☿	♃	♀	♄	4.42	4.36	4.29	4.22	4.13	4.04	3.53
6.27	6.24	6.20	6.17	6.14	6.09	6.05	6.01	♀	♄	☉	☽	♂	☿	♃	5.56	5.51	5.45	5.39	5.32	5.24	5.15
7.35	7.32	7.29	7.27	7.24	7.21	7.18	7.13	☿	♃	♀	♄	☉	☽	♂	7.10	7.06	7.02	6.57	6.51	6.45	6.37
8.43	8.41	8.39	8.37	8.35	8.32	8.30	8.27	☽	♂	☿	♃	♀	♄	☉	8.24	8.21	8.18	8.14	8.10	8.05	7.59
9.50	9.49	9.48	9.46	9.45	9.44	9.42	9.40	♄	☉	☽	♂	☿	♃	♀	9.38	9.36	9.34	9.32	9.28	9.25	9.21
10.58	10.58	10.57	10.56	10.56	10.55	10.54	10.53	♃	♀	♄	☉	☽	♂	☿	10.52	10.51	10.50	10.49	10.47	10.46	10.43
12.06	12.06	12.06	12.06	12.06	12.06	12.06	12.06	♂	☿	♃	♀	♄	☉	☽	12.06	12.06	12.06	12.06	12.06	12.06	12.06
1.14	1.15	1.15	1.16	1.17	1.18	1.19	1.19	☉	☽	♂	☿	♃	♀	♄	1.21	1.22	1.23	1.24	1.25	1.26	1.28
2.22	2.23	2.24	2.26	2.28	2.29	2.31	2.32	♀	♄	☉	☽	♂	☿	♃	2.35	2.37	2.39	2.41	2.44	2.47	2.50
3.30	3.32	3.34	3.36	3.38	3.41	3.43	3.46	☿	♃	♀	♄	☉	☽	♂	3.49	3.52	3.55	3.59	4.03	4.07	4.12
4.37	4.42	4.43	4.45	4.49	4.52	4.56	4.59	☽	♂	☿	♃	♀	♄	☉	5.03	5.07	5.12	5.16	5.21	5.27	5.34
5.45	5.49	5.52	5.55	5.59	6.04	6.08	6.12	♄	☉	☽	♂	☿	♃	♀	6.17	6.22	6.28	6.34	6.40	6.48	6.56

Night Hours; Sunset to Sunrise.

Lat. 27°	Lat. 29°	Lat. 31°	Lat. 33°	Lat. 35°	Lat. 37°	Lat. 39°	Lat. 41°	Su	M	Tu	W	Th	F	Sa	Lat. 43°	Lat. 45°	Lat. 47°	Lat. 49°	Lat. 51°	Lat. 53°	Lat. 55°
6.53	6.57	7.01	7.05	7.10	7.15	7.20	7.25	♃	♀	♄	☉	☽	♂	☿	7.31	7.37	7.44	7.51	7.59	8.08	8.18
7.45	7.49	7.52	7.55	8.00	8.04	8.08	8.12	♂	☿	♃	♀	♄	☉	☽	8.17	8.22	8.28	8.34	8.40	8.48	8.56
8.37	8.40	8.43	8.46	8.49	8.52	8.56	8.59	☉	☽	♂	☿	♃	♀	♄	9.03	9.07	9.12	9.16	9.22	9.27	9.34
9.30	9.32	9.34	9.36	9.39	9.41	9.44	9.46	♀	♄	☉	☽	♂	☿	♃	9.49	9.52	9.56	9.59	10.03	10.07	10.12
10.22	10.23	10.25	10.26	10.28	10.30	10.31	10.33	☿	♃	♀	♄	☉	☽	♂	10.35	10.37	10.39	10.42	10.44	10.47	10.50
11.14	11.15	11.16	11.16	11.18	11.18	11.19	11.20	☽	♂	☿	♃	♀	♄	☉	11.21	11.22	11.23	11.24	11.25	11.26	11.28
12.06	12.06	12.06	12.06	12.06	12.07	12.07	12.07	♄	☉	☽	♂	☿	♃	♀	12.07	12.07	12.07	12.07	12.07	12.06	12.07
12.58	12.58	12.57	12.57	12.57	12.55	12.55	12.53	♃	♀	♄	☉	☽	♂	☿	12.53	12.52	12.51	12.50	12.48	12.46	12.45
1.50	1.50	1.48	1.47	1.46	1.43	1.43	1.40	♂	☿	♃	♀	♄	☉	☽	1.39	1.37	1.35	1.32	1.29	1.25	1.23
2.43	2.41	2.39	2.37	2.36	2.32	2.31	2.27	☉	☽	♂	☿	♃	♀	♄	2.25	2.22	2.19	2.15	2.10	2.05	2.01
3.35	3.33	3.30	3.28	3.25	3.21	3.18	3.14	♀	♄	☉	☽	♂	☿	♃	3.11	3.07	3.02	2.58	2.52	2.45	2.39
4.27	4.24	4.21	4.18	4.15	4.09	4.06	4.01	☿	♃	♀	♄	☉	☽	♂	3.57	3.52	3.46	3.40	3.33	3.24	3.17

JANUARY 24th to 31st, ANY YEAR, in South Latitude

AUGUST 1st to 7th, ANY YEAR, in North Latitude

♄ Saturn; ♃ Jupiter; ♂ Mars; ☉ Sun; ♀ Venus; ☿ Mercury; ☽ Moon.

Day Hours; Sunrise to Sunset. Mean Time.

Lat. 55°	Lat. 53°	Lat. 51°	Lat. 49°	Lat. 47°	Lat. 45°	Lat. 43°	Sa	F	Th	W	Tu	M	Su	Lat. 41°	Lat. 39°	Lat. 37°	Lat. 35°	Lat. 33°	Lat. 31°	Lat. 29°	Lat. 27°
4.07	4.16	4.24	4.31	4.38	4.44	4.50	♄	♀	♃	☿	♂	☽	☉	4.55	5.00	5.05	5.09	5.13	5.16	5.20	5.23
5.27	5.34	5.41	5.47	5.53	5.58	6.03	♃	☿	♂	☽	☉	♄	♀	6.07	6.11	6.15	6.19	6.22	6.24	6.28	6.30
6.47	6.53	6.58	7.03	7.07	7.11	7.15	♂	☽	☉	♄	♀	♃	☿	7.19	7.22	7.25	7.28	7.31	7.33	7.35	7.38
8.06	8.11	8.15	8.18	8.22	8.25	8.28	☉	♄	♀	♃	☿	♂	☽	8.31	8.33	8.36	8.38	8.40	8.41	8.43	8.45
9.26	9.29	9.32	9.34	9.37	9.39	9.41	♀	♃	☿	♂	☽	☉	♄	9.42	9.44	9.46	9.47	9.48	9.49	9.51	9.52
10.46	10.47	10.49	10.50	10.51	10.52	10.53	☿	♂	☽	☉	♄	♀	♃	10.54	10.55	10.56	10.57	10.57	10.57	10.58	10.59
12.06	12.06	12.06	12.06	12.06	12.06	12.06	☽	☉	♄	♀	♃	☿	♂	12.06	12.06	12.06	12.06	12.06	12.06	12.06	12.07
1.25	1.24	1.22	1.21	1.21	1.20	1.19	♄	♀	♃	☿	♂	☽	☉	1.18	1.17	1.16	1.16	1.15	1.14	1.14	1.14
2.45	2.42	2.39	2.37	2.35	2.33	2.31	♃	☿	♂	☽	☉	♄	♀	2.30	2.28	2.26	2.25	2.24	2.22	2.21	2.21
4.05	4.00	3.56	3.53	3.50	3.47	3.44	♂	☽	☉	♄	♀	♃	☿	3.42	3.39	3.37	3.35	3.33	3.30	3.29	3.28
5.25	5.19	5.13	5.09	5.05	5.01	4.57	☉	♄	♀	♃	☿	♂	☽	4.53	4.50	4.47	4.44	4.41	4.39	4.37	4.36
6.44	6.37	6.30	6.24	6.19	6.14	6.09	♀	♃	☿	♂	☽	☉	♄	6.05	6.01	5.57	5.54	5.50	5.47	5.45	5.43

Night Hours; Sunset to Sunrise.

Lat. 55°	Lat. 53°	Lat. 51°	Lat. 49°	Lat. 47°	Lat. 45°	Lat. 43°	Sa	F	Th	W	Tu	M	Su	Lat. 41°	Lat. 39°	Lat. 37°	Lat. 35°	Lat. 33°	Lat. 31°	Lat. 29°	Lat. 27°
8.04	7.55	7.47	7.40	7.34	7.28	7.22	☿	♂	☽	☉	♄	♀	♃	7.17	7.12	7.07	7.03	6.59	6.55	6.52	6.50
8.44	8.37	8.30	8.24	8.19	8.15	8.09	☽	☉	♄	♀	♃	☿	♂	8.05	8.01	7.57	7.54	7.50	7.47	7.44	7.43
9.25	9.19	9.13	9.09	9.05	9.01	8.57	♄	♀	♃	☿	♂	☽	☉	8.54	8.50	8.47	8.44	8.41	8.39	8.37	8.36
10.05	10.01	9.57	9.53	9.50	9.48	9.44	♃	☿	♂	☽	☉	♄	♀	9.42	9.39	9.37	9.35	9.33	9.31	9.29	9.29
10.46	10.43	10.40	10.37	10.36	10.34	10.32	♂	☽	☉	♄	♀	♃	☿	10.30	10.28	10.26	10.25	10.24	10.22	10.22	10.21
11.26	11.25	11.23	11.22	11.21	11.21	11.19	☉	♄	♀	♃	☿	♂	☽	11.18	11.17	11.16	11.16	11.15	11.14	11.14	11.14
12.06	12.06	12.06	12.06	12.06	12.06	12.06	♀	♃	☿	♂	☽	☉	♄	12.06	12.06	12.06	12.06	12.06	12.06	12.07	12.07
12.47	12.48	12.49	12.50	12.52	12.54	12.54	☿	♂	☽	☉	♄	♀	♃	12.55	12.55	12.56	12.57	12.57	12.58	12.59	1.00
1.27	1.30	1.32	1.35	1.37	1.40	1.41	☽	☉	♄	♀	♃	☿	♂	1.43	1.44	1.46	1.47	1.48	1.50	1.51	1.53
2.08	2.12	2.16	2.19	2.23	2.27	2.29	♄	♀	♃	☿	♂	☽	☉	2.31	2.33	2.36	2.38	2.40	2.42	2.44	2.46
2.48	2.54	2.59	3.03	3.08	3.13	3.16	♃	☿	♂	☽	☉	♄	♀	3.20	3.22	3.25	3.28	3.31	3.33	3.36	3.38
3.29	3.36	3.42	3.48	3.54	4.00	4.04	♂	☽	☉	♄	♀	♃	☿	4.08	4.11	4.15	4.19	4.22	4.25	4.29	4.31

FEBRUARY 1st to 7th, ANY YEAR, in South Latitude

AUGUST 8th to 15th, ANY YEAR, in North Latitude

♄ Saturn; ♃ Jupiter; ♂ Mars; ☉ Sun; ♀ Venus; ☿ Mercury; ☽ Moon.

Day Hours; Sunrise to Sunset. Mean Time.

Lat. 27°	Lat. 29°	Lat. 31°	Lat. 33°	Lat. 35°	Lat. 37°	Lat. 39°	Lat. 41°	Su	M	Tu	W	Th	F	Sa	Lat. 43°	Lat. 45°	Lat. 47°	Lat. 49°	Lat. 51°	Lat. 53°	Lat. 55°
5.27	5.24	5.20	5.17	5.14	5.10	5.06	5.02	☉	☽	♂	☿	♃	♀	♄	4.59	4.53	4.47	4.41	4.34	4.27	4.20
6.33	6.31	6.28	6.25	6.23	6.19	6.16	6.13	♀	♄	☉	☽	♂	☿	♃	6.10	6.05	6.00	5.55	5.49	5.43	5.38
7.40	7.38	7.35	7.33	7.31	7.29	7.26	7.23	☿	♃	♀	♄	☉	☽	♂	7.21	7.17	7.13	7.09	7.04	7.00	6.55
8.46	8.45	8.43	8.41	8.40	8.38	8.36	8.34	☽	♂	☿	♃	♀	♄	☉	8.33	8.29	8.26	8.23	8.20	8.16	8.13
9.53	9.52	9.50	9.49	9.48	9.47	9.45	9.44	♄	☉	☽	♂	☿	♃	♀	9.44	9.41	9.39	9.37	9.35	9.32	9.30
10.59	10.59	10.58	10.57	10.57	10.56	10.55	10.55	♃	♀	♄	☉	☽	♂	☿	10.55	10.53	10.52	10.51	10.50	10.49	10.48
12.06	12.06	12.05	12.05	12.06	12.06	12.05	12.05	♂	☿	♃	♀	♄	☉	☽	12.06	12.06	12.06	12.06	12.05	12.05	12.06
1.12	1.12	1.13	1.13	1.14	1.15	1.15	1.16	☉	☽	♂	☿	♃	♀	♄	1.17	1.18	1.19	1.19	1.20	1.21	1.23
2.18	2.19	2.20	2.21	2.23	2.24	2.25	2.26	♀	♄	☉	☽	♂	☿	♃	2.28	2.30	2.32	2.33	2.35	2.38	2.41
3.25	3.26	3.28	3.29	3.31	3.33	3.35	3.37	☿	♃	♀	♄	☉	☽	♂	3.40	3.42	3.45	3.47	3.51	3.54	3.58
4.31	4.33	4.35	4.37	4.40	4.43	4.44	4.47	☽	♂	☿	♃	♀	♄	☉	4.51	4.54	4.58	5.01	5.06	5.10	5.16
5.38	5.40	5.43	5.45	5.48	5.52	5.54	5.58	♄	☉	☽	♂	☿	♃	♀	6.02	6.06	6.11	6.15	6.21	6.27	6.33

Night Hours; Sunset to Sunrise.

Lat. 27°	Lat. 29°	Lat. 31°	Lat. 33°	Lat. 35°	Lat. 37°	Lat. 39°	Lat. 41°	Su	M	Tu	W	Th	F	Sa	Lat. 43°	Lat. 45°	Lat. 47°	Lat. 49°	Lat. 51°	Lat. 53°	Lat. 55°
6.44	6.47	6.50	6.53	6.57	7.01	7.04	7.08	♃	♀	♄	☉	☽	♂	☿	7.13	7.18	7.24	7.29	7.36	7.43	7.51
7.38	7.40	7.43	7.45	7.49	7.52	7.54	7.58	♂	☿	♃	♀	♄	☉	☽	8.02	8.06	8.11	8.15	8.21	8.27	8.34
8.31	8.33	8.35	8.37	8.40	8.43	8.45	8.47	☉	☽	♂	☿	♃	♀	♄	8.51	8.54	8.58	9.01	9.06	9.11	9.16
9.25	9.26	9.28	9.29	9.32	9.34	9.35	9.37	♀	♄	☉	☽	♂	☿	♃	9.39	9.42	9.45	9.48	9.51	9.55	9.59
10.18	10.19	10.20	10.21	10.23	10.24	10.25	10.26	☿	♃	♀	♄	☉	☽	♂	10.28	10.30	10.32	10.34	10.36	10.38	10.41
11.12	11.12	11.13	11.13	11.15	11.15	11.15	11.16	☽	♂	☿	♃	♀	♄	☉	11.17	11.18	11.19	11.20	11.21	11.22	11.24
12.06	12.06	12.06	12.06	12.06	12.06	12.06	12.06	♄	☉	☽	♂	☿	♃	♀	12.06	12.06	12.06	12.06	12.06	12.06	12.06
12.59	12.59	12.58	12.58	12.58	12.57	12.56	12.55	♃	♀	♄	☉	☽	♂	☿	12.54	12.54	12.53	12.52	12.51	12.50	12.49
1.53	1.52	1.51	1.50	1.49	1.48	1.46	1.45	♂	☿	♃	♀	♄	☉	☽	1.43	1.42	1.40	1.38	1.36	1.34	1.32
2.46	2.45	2.43	2.42	2.41	2.39	2.36	2.34	☉	☽	♂	☿	♃	♀	♄	2.32	2.30	2.27	2.25	2.21	2.18	2.14
3.40	3.38	3.36	3.34	3.32	3.29	3.27	3.24	♀	♄	☉	☽	♂	☿	♃	3.21	3.18	3.14	3.11	3.06	3.01	2.57
4.33	4.31	4.28	4.26	4.24	4.20	4.17	4.13	☿	♃	♀	♄	☉	☽	♂	4.09	4.06	4.01	3.57	3.51	3.45	3.39

FEBRUARY 8th to 15th, ANY YEAR, in South Latitude

AUGUST 16th to 23rd, ANY YEAR, in North Latitude

♄ Saturn; ♃ Jupiter; ♂ Mars; ☉ Sun; ♀ Venus; ☿ Mercury; ☽ Moon.

Day Hours; Sunrise to Sunset. Mean Time.

Lat. 55°	Lat. 53°	Lat. 51°	Lat. 49°	Lat. 47°	Lat. 45°	Lat. 43°	Sa	F	Th	W	Tu	M	Su	Lat. 41°	Lat. 39°	Lat. 37°	Lat. 35°	Lat. 33°	Lat. 31°	Lat. 29°	Lat. 27°
4.35	4.41	4.47	4.52	4.57	5.02	5.06	♄	♀	♃	☿	♂	☽	☉	5.10	5.14	5.17	5.20	5.23	5.26	5.28	5.31
5.50	5.55	6.00	6.04	6.08	6.12	6.16	♃	☿	♂	☽	☉	♄	♀	6.19	6.22	6.25	6.27	6.30	6.32	6.34	6.37
7.05	7.09	7.13	7.16	7.19	7.23	7.25	♂	☽	☉	♄	♀	♃	☿	7.28	7.31	7.33	7.35	7.37	7.39	7.40	7.42
8.20	8.23	8.25	8.28	8.30	8.33	8.35	☉	♄	♀	♃	☿	♂	☽	8.37	8.39	8.41	8.42	8.44	8.45	8.46	8.48
9.34	9.36	9.38	9.40	9.41	9.43	9.45	♀	♃	☿	♂	☽	☉	♄	9.46	9.47	9.48	9.49	9.50	9.52	9.52	9.53
10.49	10.50	10.51	10.52	10.52	10.54	10.54	☿	♂	☽	☉	♄	♀	♃	10.55	10.56	10.56	10.57	10.57	10.58	10.58	10.59
12.04	12.04	12.04	12.04	12.04	12.04	12.04	☽	☉	♄	♀	♃	☿	♂	12.04	12.04	12.04	12.04	12.04	12.04	12.04	12.04
1.19	1.18	1.16	1.15	1.15	1.14	1.14	♄	♀	♃	☿	♂	☽	☉	1.13	1.12	1.12	1.11	1.11	1.10	1.10	1.10
2.34	2.32	2.29	2.27	2.26	2.25	2.23	♃	☿	♂	☽	☉	♄	♀	2.22	2.21	2.20	2.19	2.18	2.17	2.16	2.15
3.49	3.46	3.42	3.39	3.37	3.35	3.33	♂	☽	☉	♄	♀	♃	☿	3.31	3.29	3.28	3.26	3.25	3.23	3.22	3.21
5.03	4.59	4.55	4.51	4.48	4.45	4.43	☉	♄	♀	♃	☿	♂	☽	4.40	4.37	4.35	4.33	4.31	4.29	4.28	4.26
6.18	6.13	6.07	6.03	5.59	5.56	5.52	♀	♃	☿	♂	☽	☉	♄	5.49	5.46	5.43	5.41	5.38	5.36	5.34	5.32

Night Hours; Sunset to Sunrise.

Lat. 55°	Lat. 53°	Lat. 51°	Lat. 49°	Lat. 47°	Lat. 45°	Lat. 43°	Sa	F	Th	W	Tu	M	Su	Lat. 41°	Lat. 39°	Lat. 37°	Lat. 35°	Lat. 33°	Lat. 31°	Lat. 29°	Lat. 27°
7.33	7.27	7.20	7.15	7.10	7.06	7.02	☿	♂	☽	☉	♄	♀	♃	6.58	6.54	6.51	6.48	6.45	6.42	6.40	6.37
8.18	8.13	8.07	8.03	7.59	7.56	7.52	☽	☉	♄	♀	♃	☿	♂	7.49	7.46	7.43	7.41	7.38	7.36	7.34	7.32
9.04	9.00	8.55	8.52	8.48	8.46	8.43	♄	♀	♃	☿	♂	☽	☉	8.40	8.37	8.35	8.33	8.31	8.29	8.28	8.26
9.49	9.46	9.42	9.40	9.37	9.36	9.33	♃	☿	♂	☽	☉	♄	♀	9.31	9.29	9.28	9.26	9.25	9.23	9.22	9.21
10.34	10.31	10.29	10.28	10.26	10.25	10.24	♂	☽	☉	♄	♀	♃	☿	10.22	10.21	10.20	10.19	10.18	10.17	10.16	10.15
11.19	11.19	11.17	11.16	11.15	11.15	11.14	☉	♄	♀	♃	☿	♂	☽	11.13	11.12	11.12	11.11	11.11	11.10	11.10	11.10
12.05	12.05	12.04	12.05	12.05	12.05	12.05	♀	♃	☿	♂	☽	☉	♄	12.04	12.04	12.04	12.04	12.04	12.04	12.05	12.05
12.50	12.51	12.51	12.53	12.54	12.55	12.55	☿	♂	☽	☉	♄	♀	♃	12.55	12.56	12.56	12.57	12.57	12.58	12.59	12.59
1.35	1.38	1.39	1.41	1.43	1.45	1.45	☽	☉	♄	♀	♃	☿	♂	1.46	1.47	1.48	1.49	1.50	1.51	1.53	1.54
2.20	2.24	2.26	2.29	2.32	2.35	2.36	♄	♀	♃	☿	♂	☽	☉	2.37	2.39	2.41	2.42	2.44	2.45	2.47	2.48
3.06	3.10	3.13	3.18	3.21	3.24	3.26	♃	☿	♂	☽	☉	♄	♀	3.28	3.31	3.33	3.35	3.37	3.38	3.41	3.43
3.51	3.57	4.01	4.06	4.10	4.14	4.17	♂	☽	☉	♄	♀	♃	☿	4.19	4.22	4.25	4.27	4.30	4.32	4.35	4.37

FEBRUARY 16th to 23rd, ANY YEAR, in South Latitude

AUGUST 24th to 31st, ANY YEAR, in North Latitude

♄ Saturn; ♃ Jupiter; ♂ Mars; ☉ Sun; ♀ Venus; ☿ Mercury; ☽ Moon.

Day Hours; Sunrise to Sunset. Mean Time.

Lat. 55°	Lat. 53°	Lat. 51°	Lat. 49°	Lat. 47°	Lat. 45°	Lat. 43°	Sa	F	Th	W	Tu	M	Su	Lat. 41°	Lat. 39°	Lat. 37°	Lat. 35°	Lat. 33°	Lat. 31°	Lat. 29°	Lat. 27°
4.49	4.54	4.59	5.04	5.07	5.11	5.14	♄	♀	♃	☿	♂	☽	☉	5.17	5.20	5.23	5.26	5.28	5.31	5.33	5.35
6.01	6.05	6.09	6.14	6.16	6.19	6.22	♃	☿	♂	☽	☉	♄	♀	6.24	6.27	6.30	6.32	6.34	6.36	6.38	6.40
7.13	7.17	7.20	7.23	7.25	7.28	7.30	♂	☽	☉	♄	♀	♃	☿	7.32	7.34	7.36	7.38	7.39	7.41	7.43	7.44
8.25	8.28	8.30	8.33	8.34	8.36	8.38	☉	♄	♀	♃	☿	♂	☽	8.39	8.41	8.43	8.44	8.45	8.47	8.48	8.49
9.37	9.39	9.41	9.43	9.43	9.45	9.46	♀	♃	☿	♂	☽	☉	♄	9.47	9.48	9.49	9.50	9.51	9.52	9.52	9.53
10.49	10.50	10.51	10.52	10.52	10.53	10.54	☿	♂	☽	☉	♄	♀	♃	10.54	10.55	10.56	10.56	10.56	10.57	10.57	10.58
12.02	12.02	12.02	12.02	12.02	12.02	12.02	☽	☉	♄	♀	♃	☿	♂	12.02	12.02	12.02	12.02	12.02	12.02	12.02	12.02
1.14	1.13	1.12	1.12	1.11	1.10	1.09	♄	♀	♃	☿	♂	☽	☉	1.09	1.09	1.09	1.08	1.08	1.07	1.07	1.07
2.26	2.24	2.22	2.21	2.20	2.18	2.17	♃	☿	♂	☽	☉	♄	♀	2.16	2.16	2.15	2.14	2.13	2.12	2.12	2.11
3.38	3.35	3.33	3.31	3.29	3.27	3.25	♂	☽	☉	♄	♀	♃	☿	3.24	3.23	3.22	3.20	3.19	3.18	3.17	3.16
4.50	4.47	4.43	4.41	4.38	4.35	4.33	☉	♄	♀	♃	☿	♂	☽	4.31	4.30	4.28	4.26	4.25	4.23	4.21	4.20
6.02	5.58	5.54	5.50	5.47	5.44	5.41	♀	♃	☿	♂	☽	☉	♄	5.39	5.37	5.35	5.32	5.30	5.28	5.26	5.25

Night Hours; Sunset to Sunrise.

Lat. 55°	Lat. 53°	Lat. 51°	Lat. 49°	Lat. 47°	Lat. 45°	Lat. 43°	Sa	F	Th	W	Tu	M	Su	Lat. 41°	Lat. 39°	Lat. 37°	Lat. 35°	Lat. 33°	Lat. 31°	Lat. 29°	Lat. 27°
7.14	7.09	7.04	7.00	6.56	6.52	6.49	☿	♂	☽	☉	♄	♀	♃	6.46	6.44	6.41	6.38	6.36	6.33	6.31	6.29
8.02	7.58	7.54	7.50	7.47	7.44	7.41	☽	☉	♄	♀	♃	☿	♂	7.39	7.37	7.35	7.32	7.30	7.28	7.26	7.25
8.50	8.46	8.44	8.41	8.38	8.35	8.33	♄	♀	♃	☿	♂	☽	☉	8.31	8.30	8.28	8.26	8.25	8.23	8.22	8.20
9.38	9.35	9.33	9.31	9.29	9.27	9.26	♃	☿	♂	☽	☉	♄	♀	9.24	9.23	9.22	9.20	9.19	9.18	9.17	9.16
10.26	10.25	10.23	10.22	10.20	10.19	10.18	♂	☽	☉	♄	♀	♃	☿	10.17	10.16	10.15	10.14	10.14	10.13	10.12	10.11
11.14	11.13	11.13	11.12	11.11	11.10	11.10	☉	♄	♀	♃	☿	♂	☽	11.09	11.09	11.09	11.08	11.08	11.08	11.07	11.07
12.02	12.02	12.02	12.02	12.02	12.02	12.02	♀	♃	☿	♂	☽	☉	♄	12.02	12.02	12.02	12.02	12.02	12.02	12.02	12.02
12.51	12.51	12.52	12.53	12.53	12.54	12.54	☿	♂	☽	☉	♄	♀	♃	12.55	12.56	12.56	12.57	12.57	12.57	12.58	12.58
1.39	1.39	1.42	1.43	1.44	1.45	1.46	☽	☉	♄	♀	♃	☿	♂	1.47	1.49	1.50	1.51	1.51	1.52	1.53	1.54
2.27	2.28	2.32	2.34	2.35	2.37	2.39	♄	♀	♃	☿	♂	☽	☉	2.40	2.42	2.43	2.45	2.46	2.47	2.48	2.49
3.15	3.18	3.22	3.24	3.26	3.29	3.31	♃	☿	♂	☽	☉	♄	♀	3.33	3.35	3.37	3.39	3.40	3.42	3.44	3.45
4.03	4.06	4.11	4.15	4.17	4.20	4.23	♂	☽	☉	♄	♀	♃	☿	4.25	4.28	4.30	4.33	4.35	4.37	4.39	4.40

FEBRUARY 24th to 28th or 29th, ANY YEAR, in South Latitude

SEPTEMBER 1st to 7th, ANY YEAR, in North Latitude

♄ Saturn; ♃ Jupiter; ♂ Mars; ⊙ Sun; ♀ Venus; ☿ Mercury; ☽ Moon.

Day Hours; Sunrise to Sunset. Mean Time.

Lat. 55°	Lat. 53°	Lat. 51°	Lat. 49°	Lat. 47°	Lat. 45°	Lat. 43°	Sa	F	Th	W	Tu	M	Su	Lat. 41°	Lat. 39°	Lat. 37°	Lat. 35°	Lat. 33°	Lat. 31°	Lat. 29°	Lat. 27°
5.04	5.08	5.12	5.15	5.18	5.21	5.23	♄	♀	♃	☿	♂	☽	⊙	5.26	5.28	5.30	5.32	5.34	5.36	5.38	5.39
6.13	6.17	6.20	6.22	6.25	6.28	6.29	♃	☿	♂	☽	⊙	♄	♀	6.32	6.33	6.35	6.37	6.38	6.40	6.42	6.43
7.22	7.25	7.28	7.30	7.32	7.34	7.35	♂	☽	⊙	♄	♀	♃	☿	7.37	7.39	7.40	7.41	7.43	7.44	7.45	7.46
8.32	8.34	8.36	8.37	8.39	8.41	8.41	⊙	♄	♀	♃	☿	♂	☽	8.43	8.44	8.45	8.46	8.47	8.48	8.49	8.50
9.41	9.42	9.44	9.45	9.46	9.47	9.47	♀	♃	☿	♂	☽	⊙	♄	9.48	9.49	9.50	9.51	9.51	9.52	9.53	9.53
10.49	10.51	10.52	10.52	10.53	10.54	10.53	☿	♂	☽	⊙	♄	♀	♃	10.54	10.54	10.55	10.55	10.56	10.56	10.56	10.57
12.00	12.00	12.00	12.00	12.00	12.00	12.00	☽	⊙	♄	♀	♃	☿	♂	12.00	12.00	12.00	12.00	12.00	12.00	12.00	12.00
1.09	1.08	1.07	1.07	1.06	1.06	1.06	♄	♀	♃	☿	♂	☽	⊙	1.05	1.05	1.05	1.05	1.04	1.04	1.04	1.04
2.18	2.16	2.15	2.14	2.13	2.13	2.12	♃	☿	♂	☽	⊙	♄	♀	2.11	2.10	2.10	2.09	2.09	2.08	2.07	2.07
3.28	3.25	3.23	3.22	3.20	3.20	3.18	♂	☽	⊙	♄	♀	♃	☿	3.16	3.15	3.15	3.14	3.13	3.12	3.11	3.11
4.37	4.33	4.31	4.29	4.27	4.26	4.24	⊙	♄	♀	♃	☿	♂	☽	4.22	4.21	4.20	4.19	4.17	4.16	4.15	4.14
5.46	5.42	5.39	5.37	5.34	5.33	5.30	♀	♃	☿	♂	☽	⊙	♄	5.28	5.26	5.25	5.23	5.22	5.20	5.18	5.18

Night Hours; Sunset to Sunrise.

Lat. 55°	Lat. 53°	Lat. 51°	Lat. 49°	Lat. 47°	Lat. 45°	Lat. 43°	Sa	F	Th	W	Tu	M	Su	Lat. 41°	Lat. 39°	Lat. 37°	Lat. 35°	Lat. 33°	Lat. 31°	Lat. 29°	Lat. 27°
6.54	6.50	6.47	6.44	6.41	6.39	6.36	☿	♂	☽	⊙	♄	♀	♃	6.33	6.31	6.30	6.28	6.26	6.24	6.22	6.21
7.45	7.42	7.39	7.37	7.34	7.33	7.30	☽	⊙	♄	♀	♃	☿	♂	7.28	7.26	7.25	7.23	7.22	7.20	7.18	7.18
8.36	8.33	8.31	8.29	8.27	8.26	8.24	♄	♀	♃	☿	♂	☽	⊙	8.22	8.21	8.20	8.19	8.17	8.16	8.15	8.14
9.27	9.25	9.24	9.22	9.21	9.20	9.18	♃	☿	♂	☽	⊙	♄	♀	9.17	9.16	9.15	9.14	9.13	9.12	9.11	9.11
10.18	10.17	10.16	10.15	10.14	10.13	10.12	♂	☽	⊙	♄	♀	♃	☿	10.11	10.10	10.10	10.09	10.09	10.08	10.07	10.07
11.09	11.08	11.08	11.07	11.07	11.07	11.06	⊙	♄	♀	♃	☿	♂	☽	11.06	11.05	11.05	11.05	11.04	11.04	11.04	11.04
12.00	12.00	12.00	12.00	12.00	12.00	12.00	♀	♃	☿	♂	☽	⊙	♄	12.00	12.00	12.00	12.00	12.00	12.00	12.00	12.00
12.51	12.52	12.52	12.53	12.53	12.54	12.54	☿	♂	☽	⊙	♄	♀	♃	12.55	12.55	12.55	12.55	12.56	12.56	12.56	12.57
1.42	1.43	1.44	1.45	1.46	1.48	1.48	☽	⊙	♄	♀	♃	☿	♂	1.49	1.50	1.50	1.51	1.51	1.52	1.53	1.53
2.33	2.35	2.37	2.38	2.40	2.41	2.42	♄	♀	♃	☿	♂	☽	⊙	2.44	2.45	2.45	2.46	2.47	2.48	2.49	2.50
3.24	3.27	3.29	3.31	3.33	3.35	3.36	♃	☿	♂	☽	⊙	♄	♀	3.38	3.39	3.40	3.41	3.43	3.44	3.45	3.46
4.15	4.18	4.21	4.23	4.26	4.28	4.30	♂	☽	⊙	♄	♀	♃	☿	4.33	4.34	4.35	4.37	4.38	4.40	4.42	4.43

MARCH 1st to 7th, ANY YEAR, in South Latitude

SEPTEMBER 8th to 14th, ANY YEAR, in North Latitude

♄ Saturn; ♃ Jupiter; ♂ Mars; ☉ Sun; ♀ Venus; ☿ Mercury; ☽ Moon.

Day Hours; Sunrise to Sunset. Mean Time.

Lat. 55°	Lat. 53°	Lat. 51°	Lat. 49°	Lat. 47°	Lat. 45°	Lat. 43°	Sa	F	Th	W	Tu	M	Su	Lat. 41°	Lat. 39°	Lat. 37°	Lat. 35°	Lat. 33°	Lat. 31°	Lat. 29°	Lat. 27°
5.17	5.20	5.23	5.25	5.27	5.29	5.31	♄	♀	♃	☿	♂	☽	☉	5.33	5.35	5.36	5.37	5.38	5.39	5.41	5.42
6.24	6.26	6.29	6.30	6.32	6.34	6.35	♃	☿	♂	☽	☉	♄	♀	6.37	6.39	6.40	6.40	6.41	6.42	6.44	6.45
7.30	7.32	7.35	7.36	7.37	7.38	7.40	♂	☽	☉	♄	♀	♃	☿	7.41	7.43	7.43	7.44	7.45	7.45	7.47	7.47
8.37	8.39	8.40	8.41	8.42	8.43	8.44	☉	♄	♀	♃	☿	♂	☽	8.45	8.46	8.47	8.47	8.48	8.48	8.50	8.50
9.44	9.45	9.46	9.46	9.47	9.48	9.48	♀	♃	☿	♂	☽	☉	♄	9.49	9.50	9.50	9.51	9.51	9.51	9.52	9.53
10.50	10.51	10.52	10.52	10.52	10.52	10.53	☿	♂	☽	☉	♄	♀	♃	10.53	10.54	10.54	10.54	10.54	10.54	10.55	10.55
11.58	11.58	11.58	11.58	11.58	11.58	11.58	☽	☉	♄	♀	♃	☿	♂	11.58	11.58	11.58	11.58	11.58	11.58	11.58	11.58
1.05	1.04	1.03	1.03	1.03	1.03	1.02	♄	♀	♃	☿	♂	☽	☉	1.02	1.01	1.01	1.01	1.01	1.01	1.01	1.01
2.11	2.10	2.09	2.09	2.08	2.07	2.07	♃	☿	♂	☽	☉	♄	♀	2.06	2.05	2.05	2.04	2.04	2.04	2.04	2.03
3.18	3.16	3.15	3.14	3.13	3.12	3.11	♂	☽	☉	♄	♀	♃	☿	3.10	3.09	3.08	3.08	3.08	3.07	3.07	3.06
4.25	4.23	4.21	4.19	4.18	4.17	4.15	☉	♄	♀	♃	☿	♂	☽	4.14	4.13	4.12	4.11	4.11	4.10	4.09	4.09
5.31	5.28	5.26	5.25	5.23	5.21	5.20	♀	♃	☿	♂	☽	☉	♄	5.18	5.16	5.15	5.15	5.14	5.13	5.12	5.11

Night Hours; Sunset to Sunrise.

Lat. 55°	Lat. 53°	Lat. 51°	Lat. 49°	Lat. 47°	Lat. 45°	Lat. 43°	Sa	F	Th	W	Tu	M	Su	Lat. 41°	Lat. 39°	Lat. 37°	Lat. 35°	Lat. 33°	Lat. 31°	Lat. 29°	Lat. 27°
6.37	6.34	6.32	6.29	6.27	6.25	6.23	☿	♂	☽	☉	♄	♀	♃	6.22	6.20	6.19	6.18	6.17	6.16	6.15	6.14
7.31	7.28	7.26	7.24	7.22	7.20	7.19	☽	☉	♄	♀	♃	☿	♂	7.18	7.16	7.16	7.15	7.14	7.13	7.12	7.11
8.24	8.22	8.21	8.19	8.17	8.16	8.15	♄	♀	♃	☿	♂	☽	☉	8.14	8.13	8.12	8.11	8.11	8.10	8.09	8.09
9.18	9.16	9.15	9.13	9.12	9.11	9.10	♃	☿	♂	☽	☉	♄	♀	9.10	9.09	9.09	9.08	9.08	9.07	9.07	9.06
10.11	10.10	10.10	10.08	10.07	10.07	10.06	♂	☽	☉	♄	♀	♃	☿	10.06	10.05	10.05	10.05	10.04	10.04	10.04	10.03
11.05	11.04	11.04	11.03	11.02	11.02	11.02	☉	♄	♀	♃	☿	♂	☽	11.02	11.02	11.02	11.01	11.01	11.01	11.01	11.01
11.58	11.58	11.58	11.58	11.58	11.58	11.58	♀	♃	☿	♂	☽	☉	♄	11.58	11.58	11.58	11.58	11.58	11.58	11.58	11.58
12.52	12.52	12.53	12.53	12.53	12.53	12.53	☿	♂	☽	☉	♄	♀	♃	12.54	12.54	12.55	12.55	12.55	12.55	12.55	12.55
1.45	1.46	1.47	1.48	1.48	1.48	1.49	☽	☉	♄	♀	♃	☿	♂	1.50	1.51	1.51	1.51	1.52	1.52	1.52	1.53
2.39	2.40	2.42	2.42	2.43	2.44	2.45	♄	♀	♃	☿	♂	☽	☉	2.46	2.47	2.48	2.48	2.49	2.49	2.50	2.50
3.32	3.34	3.36	3.37	3.38	3.39	3.41	♃	☿	♂	☽	☉	♄	♀	3.42	3.43	3.44	3.45	3.45	3.46	3.47	3.47
4.26	4.28	4.31	4.32	4.33	4.35	4.36	♂	☽	☉	♄	♀	♃	☿	4.38	4.40	4.41	4.41	4.42	4.43	4.44	4.45

MARCH 8th to 14th, ANY YEAR, in South Latitude

SEPTEMBER 15th to 22nd, ANY YEAR, in North Latitude

♄ Saturn; ♃ Jupiter; ♂ Mars; ☉ Sun; ♀ Venus; ☿ Mercury; ☽ Moon.

Day Hours; Sunrise to Sunset. Mean Time.

Lat. 27°	Lat. 29°	Lat. 31°	Lat. 33°	Lat. 35°	Lat. 37°	Lat. 39°	Lat. 41°	Su	M	Tu	W	Th	F	Sa	Lat. 43°	Lat. 45°	Lat. 47°	Lat. 49°	Lat. 51°	Lat. 53°	Lat. 55°
5.45	5.44	5.44	5.43	5.42	5.41	5.40	5.39	☉	☽	♂	☿	♃	♀	♄	5.38	5.37	5.36	5.35	5.34	5.32	5.31
6.47	6.46	6.46	6.45	6.44	6.43	6.43	6.42	♀	♄	☉	☽	♂	☿	♃	6.41	6.40	6.39	6.38	6.38	6.36	6.35
7.48	7.48	7.48	7.47	7.46	7.46	7.45	7.44	☿	♃	♀	♄	☉	☽	♂	7.44	7.43	7.42	7.42	7.41	7.40	7.39
8.50	8.50	8.50	8.49	8.49	8.48	8.48	8.47	☽	♂	☿	♃	♀	♄	☉	8.46	8.46	8.45	8.45	8.45	8.43	8.43
9.52	9.51	9.51	9.51	9.51	9.50	9.50	9.49	♄	☉	☽	♂	☿	♃	♀	9.49	9.49	9.48	9.48	9.48	9.47	9.47
10.53	10.53	10.53	10.53	10.53	10.53	10.53	10.52	♃	♀	♄	☉	☽	♂	☿	10.52	10.52	10.51	10.52	10.52	10.51	10.51
11.55	11.55	11.55	11.55	11.55	11.55	11.55	11.55	♂	☿	♃	♀	♄	☉	☽	11.55	11.55	11.55	11.55	11.55	11.55	11.55
12.57	12.57	12.57	12.57	12.57	12.57	12.58	12.57	☉	☽	♂	☿	♃	♀	♄	12.57	12.57	12.57	12.58	12.59	12.58	12.59
1.58	1.59	1.59	1.59	1.59	2.00	2.00	2.00	♀	♄	☉	☽	♂	☿	♃	2.00	2.00	2.01	2.02	2.02	2.02	2.03
3.00	3.01	3.01	3.01	3.02	3.02	3.03	3.03	☿	♃	♀	♄	☉	☽	♂	3.03	3.03	3.04	3.05	3.06	3.06	3.07
4.02	4.02	4.02	4.03	4.04	4.04	4.05	4.05	☽	♂	☿	♃	♀	♄	☉	4.06	4.06	4.07	4.08	4.09	4.10	4.11
5.03	5.04	5.04	5.05	5.06	5.07	5.08	5.08	♄	☉	☽	♂	☿	♃	♀	5.08	5.09	5.10	5.12	5.13	5.13	5.15

Night Hours; Sunset to Sunrise.

Lat. 27°	Lat. 29°	Lat. 31°	Lat. 33°	Lat. 35°	Lat. 37°	Lat. 39°	Lat. 41°	Su	M	Tu	W	Th	F	Sa	Lat. 43°	Lat. 45°	Lat. 47°	Lat. 49°	Lat. 51°	Lat. 53°	Lat. 55°
6.05	6.06	6.06	6.07	6.08	6.09	6.10	6.10	♃	♀	♄	☉	☽	♂	☿	6.11	6.12	6.13	6.14	6.16	6.17	6.19
7.03	7.04	7.04	7.05	7.06	7.07	7.08	7.08	♂	☿	♃	♀	♄	☉	☽	7.08	7.09	7.10	7.11	7.13	7.13	7.15
8.02	8.03	8.03	8.03	8.04	8.05	8.05	8.05	☉	☽	♂	☿	♃	♀	♄	8.06	8.07	8.07	8.08	8.09	8.10	8.11
9.00	9.01	9.01	9.01	9.02	9.02	9.03	9.03	♀	♄	☉	☽	♂	☿	♃	9.03	9.04	9.04	9.05	9.06	9.06	9.07
9.59	9.59	9.59	9.59	10.00	10.00	10.00	10.00	☿	♃	♀	♄	☉	☽	♂	10.01	10.01	10.01	10.02	10.02	10.03	10.03
10.57	10.57	10.57	10.57	10.58	10.58	10.58	10.58	☽	♂	☿	♃	♀	♄	☉	10.58	10.58	10.58	10.59	10.59	10.59	10.59
11.56	11.56	11.56	11.56	11.56	11.56	11.56	11.56	♄	☉	☽	♂	☿	♃	♀	11.56	11.56	11.56	11.56	11.56	11.56	11.56
12.54	12.54	12.54	12.54	12.53	12.53	12.53	12.53	♃	♀	♄	☉	☽	♂	☿	12.53	12.53	12.53	12.52	12.52	12.52	12.52
1.52	1.52	1.52	1.52	1.51	1.51	1.51	1.51	♂	☿	♃	♀	♄	☉	☽	1.50	1.50	1.50	1.49	1.49	1.48	1.48
2.51	2.50	2.50	2.50	2.49	2.49	2.48	2.48	☉	☽	♂	☿	♃	♀	♄	2.48	2.47	2.47	2.46	2.45	2.45	2.44
3.49	3.49	3.49	3.48	3.47	3.47	3.46	3.46	♀	♄	☉	☽	♂	☿	♃	3.45	3.45	3.44	3.43	3.42	3.41	3.40
4.48	4.47	4.47	4.46	4.45	4.44	4.43	4.43	☿	♃	♀	♄	☉	☽	♂	4.43	4.42	4.41	4.40	4.39	4.38	4.36

MARCH 15th to 22nd, ANY YEAR, in South Latitude

SEPTEMBER 23th to 30th, ANY YEAR, in North Latitude

♄ Saturn; ♃ Jupiter; ♂ Mars; ☉ Sun; ♀ Venus; ☿ Mercury; ☽ Moon.

Day Hours; Sunrise to Sunset. Mean Time.

Lat. 55°	Lat. 53°	Lat. 51°	Lat. 49°	Lat. 47°	Lat. 45°	Lat. 43°	Sa	F	Th	W	Tu	M	Su	Lat. 41°	Lat. 39°	Lat. 37°	Lat. 35°	Lat. 33°	Lat. 31°	Lat. 29°	Lat. 27°
5.46	5.46	5.46	5.47	5.47	5.47	5.47	♄	♀	♃	☿	♂	☽	☉	5.48	5.48	5.48	5.48	5.48	5.48	5.48	5.48
6.47	6.47	6.47	6.48	6.48	6.48	6.48	♃	☿	♂	☽	☉	♄	♀	6.49	6.49	6.49	6.49	6.49	6.49	6.49	6.49
7.48	7.48	7.48	7.49	7.49	7.49	7.49	♂	☽	☉	♄	♀	♃	☿	7.50	7.50	7.49	7.49	7.49	7.49	7.49	7.49
8.49	8.49	8.49	8.50	8.50	8.50	8.50	☉	♄	♀	♃	☿	♂	☽	8.50	8.50	8.50	8.50	8.50	8.50	8.50	8.50
9.50	9.50	9.50	9.50	9.50	9.50	9.50	♀	♃	☿	♂	☽	☉	♄	9.51	9.51	9.51	9.51	9.51	9.51	9.51	9.51
10.51	10.51	10.51	10.51	10.51	10.51	10.51	☿	♂	☽	☉	♄	♀	♃	10.52	10.52	10.51	10.51	10.51	10.51	10.51	10.51
11.52	11.52	11.52	11.52	11.52	11.52	11.52	☽	☉	♄	♀	♃	☿	♂	11.52	11.52	11.52	11.52	11.52	11.52	11.52	11.52
12.53	12.53	12.53	12.53	12.53	12.53	12.53	♄	♀	♃	☿	♂	☽	☉	12.53	12.53	12.53	12.53	12.53	12.53	12.53	12.53
1.54	1.54	1.54	1.54	1.54	1.54	1.54	♃	☿	♂	☽	☉	♄	♀	1.54	1.54	1.53	1.53	1.53	1.53	1.53	1.53
2.55	2.55	2.55	2.55	2.55	2.55	2.55	♂	☽	☉	♄	♀	♃	☿	2.55	2.55	2.54	2.54	2.54	2.54	2.54	2.54
3.56	3.56	3.56	3.55	3.55	3.55	3.55	☉	♄	♀	♃	☿	♂	☽	3.56	3.56	3.55	3.55	3.55	3.55	3.55	3.55
4.57	4.57	4.57	4.56	4.56	4.56	4.56	♀	♃	☿	♂	☽	☉	♄	4.56	4.56	4.55	4.55	4.55	4.55	4.55	4.55

Night Hours; Sunset to Sunrise.

Lat. 55°	Lat. 53°	Lat. 51°	Lat. 49°	Lat. 47°	Lat. 45°	Lat. 43°	Sa	F	Th	W	Tu	M	Su	Lat. 41°	Lat. 39°	Lat. 37°	Lat. 35°	Lat. 33°	Lat. 31°	Lat. 29°	Lat. 27°
5.58	5.58	5.58	5.57	5.57	5.57	5.57	☿	♂	☽	☉	♄	♀	♃	5.57	5.57	5.56	5.56	5.56	5.56	5.56	5.56
6.57	6.57	6.57	6.56	6.56	6.56	6.56	☽	☉	♄	♀	♃	☿	♂	6.56	6.56	6.55	6.55	6.55	6.55	6.55	6.55
7.56	7.56	7.56	7.56	7.56	7.56	7.56	♄	♀	♃	☿	♂	☽	☉	7.56	7.56	7.55	7.55	7.55	7.55	7.55	7.55
8.56	8.56	8.56	8.55	8.55	8.55	8.55	♃	☿	♂	☽	☉	♄	♀	8.55	8.55	8.54	8.54	8.54	8.54	8.54	8.54
9.55	9.55	9.55	9.54	9.54	9.54	9.54	♂	☽	☉	♄	♀	♃	☿	9.54	9.54	9.54	9.54	9.54	9.54	9.54	9.54
10.54	10.54	10.54	10.53	10.53	10.53	10.53	☉	♄	♀	♃	☿	♂	☽	10.54	10.54	10.53	10.53	10.53	10.53	10.53	10.53
11.53	11.53	11.53	11.53	11.53	11.53	11.53	♀	♃	☿	♂	☽	☉	♄	11.53	11.53	11.53	11.53	11.53	11.53	11.53	11.53
12.52	12.52	12.52	12.52	12.52	12.52	12.52	☿	♂	☽	☉	♄	♀	♃	12.52	12.52	12.52	12.52	12.52	12.52	12.52	12.52
1.51	1.51	1.51	1.51	1.51	1.51	1.51	☽	☉	♄	♀	♃	☿	♂	1.52	1.52	1.51	1.51	1.51	1.51	1.51	1.51
2.51	2.51	2.51	2.50	2.50	2.50	2.50	♄	♀	♃	☿	♂	☽	☉	2.51	2.51	2.51	2.51	2.51	2.51	2.51	2.51
3.50	3.50	3.50	3.50	3.50	3.50	3.50	♃	☿	♂	☽	☉	♄	♀	3.50	3.50	3.50	3.50	3.50	3.50	3.50	3.50
4.49	4.49	4.49	4.49	4.49	4.49	4.49	♂	☽	☉	♄	♀	♃	☿	4.50	4.50	4.50	4.50	4.50	4.50	4.50	4.50

MARCH 23rd to 31st, ANY YEAR, in South Latitude

OCTOBER 1st to 7th, ANY YEAR, in North Latitude

♄ Saturn; ♃ Jupiter; ♂ Mars; ☉ Sun; ♀ Venus; ☿ Mercury; ☽ Moon.

Day Hours; Sunrise to Sunset. Mean Time.

Lat. 27°	Lat. 29°	Lat. 31°	Lat. 33°	Lat. 35°	Lat. 37°	Lat. 39°	Lat. 41°	Su	M	Tu	W	Th	F	Sa	Lat. 43°	Lat. 45°	Lat. 47°	Lat. 49°	Lat. 51°	Lat. 53°	Lat. 55°
5.52	5.53	5.53	5.54	5.54	5.55	5.56	5.56	☉	☽	♂	☿	♃	♀	♄	5.57	5.58	5.58	5.59	6.00	6.00	6.01
6.52	6.52	6.52	6.53	6.53	6.54	6.55	6.55	♀	♄	☉	☽	♂	☿	♃	6.56	6.57	6.57	6.57	6.58	6.58	6.59
7.51	7.52	7.52	7.53	7.53	7.53	7.54	7.54	☿	♃	♀	♄	☉	☽	♂	7.55	7.55	7.55	7.56	7.57	7.56	7.57
8.51	8.51	8.51	8.52	8.52	8.52	8.53	8.53	☽	♂	☿	♃	♀	♄	☉	8.53	8.54	8.54	8.54	8.55	8.55	8.55
9.50	9.51	9.51	9.51	9.51	9.51	9.52	9.52	♄	☉	☽	♂	☿	♃	♀	9.52	9.53	9.52	9.53	9.53	9.53	9.54
10.50	10.50	10.50	10.50	10.50	10.50	10.50	10.51	♃	♀	♄	☉	☽	♂	☿	10.51	10.51	10.51	10.51	10.51	10.51	10.52
11.50	11.50	11.50	11.50	11.50	11.50	11.50	11.50	♂	☿	♃	♀	♄	☉	☽	11.50	11.50	11.50	11.50	11.50	11.49	11.50
12.49	12.49	12.49	12.49	12.49	12.49	12.48	12.48	☉	☽	♂	☿	♃	♀	♄	12.48	12.49	12.48	12.48	12.48	12.47	12.47
1.49	1.48	1.48	1.48	1.48	1.48	1.47	1.47	♀	♄	☉	☽	♂	☿	♃	1.47	1.47	1.47	1.46	1.46	1.45	1.46
2.48	2.48	2.48	2.47	2.47	2.47	2.46	2.46	☿	♃	♀	♄	☉	☽	♂	2.46	2.46	2.45	2.45	2.44	2.44	2.44
3.48	3.47	3.47	3.47	3.47	3.46	3.45	3.45	☽	♂	☿	♃	♀	♄	☉	3.45	3.45	3.44	3.43	3.43	3.42	3.42
4.47	4.47	4.47	4.46	4.46	4.45	4.44	4.44	♄	☉	☽	♂	☿	♃	♀	4.43	4.43	4.42	4.42	4.41	4.40	4.40

Night Hours; Sunset to Sunrise.

Lat. 27°	Lat. 29°	Lat. 31°	Lat. 33°	Lat. 35°	Lat. 37°	Lat. 39°	Lat. 41°	Su	M	Tu	W	Th	F	Sa	Lat. 43°	Lat. 45°	Lat. 47°	Lat. 49°	Lat. 51°	Lat. 53°	Lat. 55°
5.47	5.46	5.46	5.45	5.45	5.44	5.43	5.43	♃	♀	♄	☉	☽	♂	☿	5.42	5.42	5.41	5.40	5.39	5.38	5.37
6.47	6.47	6.47	6.46	6.46	6.45	6.44	6.44	♂	☿	♃	♀	♄	☉	☽	6.43	6.43	6.43	6.42	6.41	6.40	6.39
7.48	7.47	7.47	7.47	7.47	7.46	7.45	7.45	☉	☽	♂	☿	♃	♀	♄	7.45	7.45	7.44	7.43	7.42	7.42	7.41
8.48	8.48	8.48	8.47	8.48	8.47	8.47	8.47	♀	♄	☉	☽	♂	☿	♃	8.46	8.46	8.46	8.45	8.44	8.44	8.43
9.50	9.48	9.48	9.48	9.48	9.48	9.48	9.48	☿	♃	♀	♄	☉	☽	♂	9.47	9.48	9.47	9.46	9.46	9.46	9.45
10.49	10.49	10.49	10.49	10.49	10.49	10.49	10.49	☽	♂	☿	♃	♀	♄	☉	10.49	10.49	10.49	10.48	10.47	10.48	10.47
11.50	11.50	11.50	11.50	11.50	11.50	11.50	11.50	♄	☉	☽	♂	☿	♃	♀	11.50	11.50	11.50	11.50	11.50	11.50	11.50
12.50	12.50	12.50	12.51	12.51	12.51	12.51	12.51	♃	♀	♄	☉	☽	♂	☿	12.51	12.52	12.52	12.52	12.52	12.51	12.52
1.50	1.51	1.51	1.52	1.52	1.52	1.52	1.52	♂	☿	♃	♀	♄	☉	☽	1.53	1.53	1.53	1.53	1.53	1.53	1.54
2.51	2.51	2.51	2.52	2.53	2.53	2.54	2.54	☉	☽	♂	☿	♃	♀	♄	2.54	2.55	2.55	2.55	2.55	2.55	2.56
3.51	3.52	3.52	3.53	3.53	3.54	3.55	3.55	♀	♄	☉	☽	♂	☿	♃	3.55	3.56	3.56	3.56	3.57	3.57	3.58
4.52	4.52	4.52	4.53	4.54	4.55	4.56	4.56	☿	♃	♀	♄	☉	☽	♂	4.57	4.58	4.58	4.58	4.58	4.59	5.00

APRIL 1st to 7th, ANY YEAR, in South Latitude

OCTOBER 8th to 15th, ANY YEAR, in North Latitude

♄ Saturn; ♃ Jupiter; ♂ Mars; ☉ Sun; ♀ Venus; ☿ Mercury; ☽ Moon.

Day Hours; Sunrise to Sunset. Mean Time.

Lat. 27°	Lat. 29°	Lat. 31°	Lat. 33°	Lat. 35°	Lat. 37°	Lat. 39°	Lat. 41°	Su	M	Tu	W	Th	F	Sa	Lat. 43°	Lat. 45°	Lat. 47°	Lat. 49°	Lat. 51°	Lat. 53°	Lat. 55°
5.56	5.57	5.58	5.59	6.00	6.01	6.02	6.03	☉	☽	♂	☿	♃	♀	♄	6.04	6.06	6.08	6.09	6.11	6.13	6.15
6.55	6.55	6.56	6.57	6.58	6.59	7.00	7.00	♀	♄	☉	☽	♂	☿	♃	7.01	7.03	7.05	7.05	7.07	7.09	7.10
7.53	7.54	7.55	7.55	7.56	7.57	7.57	7.58	☿	♃	♀	♄	☉	☽	♂	7.58	8.00	8.01	8.02	8.03	8.05	8.06
8.52	8.52	8.53	8.53	8.54	8.54	8.55	8.55	☽	♂	☿	♃	♀	♄	☉	8.56	8.57	8.58	8.58	8.59	9.00	9.01
9.50	9.51	9.51	9.51	9.52	9.52	9.52	9.52	♄	☉	☽	♂	☿	♃	♀	9.53	9.54	9.54	9.55	9.55	9.56	9.57
10.49	10.49	10.49	10.49	10.50	10.50	10.50	10.50	♃	♀	♄	☉	☽	♂	☿	10.50	10.51	10.51	10.51	10.51	10.52	10.52
11.48	11.48	11.48	11.48	11.48	11.48	11.48	11.47	♂	☿	♃	♀	♄	☉	☽	11.48	11.48	11.48	11.48	11.48	11.48	11.48
12.46	12.46	12.46	12.46	12.45	12.45	12.45	12.44	☉	☽	♂	☿	♃	♀	♄	12.45	12.44	12.44	12.44	12.44	12.43	12.43
1.45	1.44	1.44	1.44	1.43	1.43	1.43	1.42	♀	♄	☉	☽	♂	☿	♃	1.42	1.41	1.41	1.40	1.40	1.39	1.38
2.43	2.43	2.42	2.42	2.41	2.41	2.40	2.39	☿	♃	♀	♄	☉	☽	♂	2.40	2.38	2.37	2.37	2.36	2.35	2.34
3.42	3.41	3.41	3.40	3.39	3.39	3.38	3.36	☽	♂	☿	♃	♀	♄	☉	3.37	3.35	3.34	3.32	3.32	3.31	3.29
4.40	4.40	4.39	4.38	4.37	4.36	4.35	4.34	♄	☉	☽	♂	☿	♃	♀	4.34	4.32	4.30	4.29	4.28	4.26	4.25

Night Hours; Sunset to Sunrise.

Lat. 27°	Lat. 29°	Lat. 31°	Lat. 33°	Lat. 35°	Lat. 37°	Lat. 39°	Lat. 41°	Su	M	Tu	W	Th	F	Sa	Lat. 43°	Lat. 45°	Lat. 47°	Lat. 49°	Lat. 51°	Lat. 53°	Lat. 55°
5.39	5.38	5.37	5.36	5.35	5.34	5.33	5.31	♃	♀	♄	☉	☽	♂	☿	5.30	5.29	5.27	5.26	5.24	5.22	5.20
6.40	6.40	6.39	6.38	6.37	6.36	6.36	6.34	♂	☿	♃	♀	♄	☉	☽	6.33	6.32	6.31	6.30	6.28	6.26	6.25
7.42	7.41	7.41	7.40	7.39	7.39	7.38	7.37	☉	☽	♂	☿	♃	♀	♄	7.36	7.35	7.34	7.34	7.32	7.31	7.30
8.43	8.43	8.43	8.42	8.42	8.41	8.41	8.39	♀	♄	☉	☽	♂	☿	♃	8.39	8.39	8.38	8.37	8.36	8.34	8.34
9.45	9.45	9.44	9.44	9.44	9.43	9.43	9.42	☿	♃	♀	♄	☉	☽	♂	9.42	9.42	9.41	9.41	9.40	9.39	9.39
10.46	10.46	10.46	10.46	10.46	10.46	10.46	10.45	☽	♂	☿	♃	♀	♄	☉	10.45	10.45	10.45	10.45	10.44	10.43	10.44
11.48	11.48	11.48	11.48	11.48	11.48	11.48	11.48	♄	☉	☽	♂	☿	♃	♀	11.48	11.48	11.48	11.48	11.48	11.48	11.48
12.49	12.49	12.50	12.50	12.50	12.50	12.51	12.50	♃	♀	♄	☉	☽	♂	☿	12.50	12.51	12.52	12.52	12.53	12.53	12.53
1.50	1.51	1.52	1.52	1.52	1.53	1.53	1.53	♂	☿	♃	♀	♄	☉	☽	1.53	1.54	1.55	1.56	1.57	1.57	1.58
2.52	2.52	2.54	2.54	2.55	2.55	2.56	2.57	☉	☽	♂	☿	♃	♀	♄	2.56	2.58	2.59	3.00	3.01	3.02	3.03
3.53	3.54	3.55	3.56	3.57	3.57	3.58	4.00	♀	♄	☉	☽	♂	☿	♃	3.59	4.01	4.02	4.04	4.05	4.06	4.08
4.55	4.55	4.57	4.58	4.59	5.00	5.01	5.02	☿	☽	♄	♃	♂	☉	♀	5.02	5.04	5.06	5.07	5.09	5.11	5.12

APRIL 8th to 15th, ANY YEAR, in South Latitude

OCTOBER 16th to 23rd, ANY YEAR, in North Latitude

♄ Saturn; ♃ Jupiter; ♂ Mars; ☉ Sun; ♀ Venus; ☿ Mercury; ☽ Moon.

Day Hours; Sunrise to Sunset. Mean Time.

Lat. 27°	Lat. 29°	Lat. 31°	Lat. 33°	Lat. 35°	Lat. 37°	Lat. 39°	Lat. 41°	Su	M	Tu	W	Th	F	Sa	Lat. 43°	Lat. 45°	Lat. 47°	Lat. 49°	Lat. 51°	Lat. 53°	Lat. 55°
6.00	6.01	6.03	6.04	6.06	6.08	6.10	6.12	☉	☽	♂	☿	♃	♀	♄	6.14	6.16	6.19	6.22	6.24	6.27	6.30
6.58	6.58	7.00	7.01	7.03	7.04	7.06	7.08	♀	♄	☉	☽	♂	☿	♃	7.09	7.11	7.13	7.16	7.18	7.20	7.23
7.55	7.56	7.57	7.58	7.59	8.01	8.02	8.03	☿	♃	♀	♄	☉	☽	♂	8.05	8.06	8.08	8.10	8.11	8.13	8.15
8.53	8.53	8.54	8.55	8.56	8.57	8.58	8.59	☽	♂	☿	♃	♀	♄	☉	9.00	9.01	9.02	9.04	9.05	9.06	9.08
9.50	9.51	9.51	9.52	9.52	9.53	9.54	9.54	♄	☉	☽	♂	☿	♃	♀	9.55	9.56	9.57	9.58	9.58	9.59	10.00
10.48	10.48	10.48	10.49	10.49	10.49	10.50	10.50	♃	♀	♄	☉	☽	♂	☿	10.50	10.51	10.51	10.52	10.52	10.52	10.53
11.46	11.46	11.46	11.46	11.46	11.46	11.46	11.46	♂	☿	♃	♀	♄	☉	☽	11.46	11.46	11.46	11.46	11.45	11.45	11.45
12.44	12.43	12.43	12.42	12.42	12.42	12.41	12.41	☉	☽	♂	☿	♃	♀	♄	12.41	12.40	12.40	12.39	12.39	12.38	12.38
1.42	1.40	1.40	1.39	1.39	1.38	1.37	1.37	♀	♄	☉	☽	♂	☿	♃	1.36	1.35	1.34	1.33	1.32	1.31	1.30
2.39	2.38	2.37	2.36	2.35	2.34	2.33	2.32	☿	♃	♀	♄	☉	☽	♂	2.31	2.30	2.29	2.27	2.26	2.24	2.23
3.37	3.35	3.34	3.33	3.33	3.31	3.29	3.28	☽	♂	☿	♃	♀	♄	☉	3.27	3.25	3.23	3.21	3.19	3.17	3.15
4.34	4.33	4.31	4.30	4.29	4.27	4.25	4.23	♄	☉	☽	♂	☿	♃	♀	4.22	4.20	4.18	4.15	4.13	4.10	4.08

Night Hours; Sunset to Sunrise.

Lat. 27°	Lat. 29°	Lat. 31°	Lat. 33°	Lat. 35°	Lat. 37°	Lat. 39°	Lat. 41°	Su	M	Tu	W	Th	F	Sa	Lat. 43°	Lat. 45°	Lat. 47°	Lat. 49°	Lat. 51°	Lat. 53°	Lat. 55°
5.31	5.30	5.28	5.27	5.25	5.23	5.21	5.19	♃	♀	♄	☉	☽	♂	☿	5.17	5.15	5.12	5.09	5.06	5.03	5.00
6.34	6.33	6.31	6.30	6.29	6.27	6.25	6.24	♂	☿	♃	♀	♄	☉	☽	6.22	6.20	6.18	6.15	6.13	6.10	6.08
7.36	7.35	7.34	7.33	7.32	7.31	7.29	7.28	☉	☽	♂	☿	♃	♀	♄	7.27	7.26	7.23	7.21	7.19	7.17	7.15
8.39	8.38	8.37	8.37	8.36	8.35	8.34	8.33	♀	♄	☉	☽	♂	☿	♃	8.32	8.31	8.29	8.28	8.26	8.25	8.23
9.41	9.41	9.40	9.40	9.39	9.38	9.38	9.37	☿	♃	♀	♄	☉	☽	♂	9.37	9.36	9.35	9.34	9.33	9.32	9.31
10.44	10.43	10.43	10.43	10.43	10.42	10.42	10.42	☽	♂	☿	♃	♀	♄	☉	10.42	10.41	10.40	10.40	10.39	10.39	10.38
11.46	11.46	11.46	11.46	11.46	11.46	11.46	11.46	♄	☉	☽	♂	☿	♃	♀	11.46	11.46	11.46	11.46	11.46	11.46	11.46
12.49	12.49	12.49	12.49	12.50	12.50	12.50	12.51	♃	♀	♄	☉	☽	♂	☿	12.51	12.52	12.52	12.52	12.53	12.53	12.54
1.51	1.51	1.52	1.52	1.53	1.54	1.54	1.55	♂	☿	♃	♀	♄	☉	☽	1.56	1.57	1.57	1.58	1.59	2.00	2.01
2.54	2.54	2.55	2.56	2.57	2.58	2.59	3.00	☉	☽	♂	☿	♃	♀	♄	3.01	3.02	3.03	3.05	3.06	3.08	3.09
3.56	3.57	3.58	3.59	4.00	4.01	4.03	4.04	♀	♄	☉	☽	♂	☿	♃	4.06	4.08	4.09	4.11	4.13	4.15	4.17
4.57	4.59	5.01	5.02	5.04	5.05	5.07	5.09	☿	♃	♀	♄	☉	☽	♂	5.11	5.13	5.14	5.17	5.19	5.22	5.24

APRIL 16th to 23rd, ANY YEAR, in South Latitude

OCTOBER 24th to 31st, ANY YEAR, in North Latitude

♄ Saturn; ♃ Jupiter; ♂ Mars; ☉ Sun; ♀ Venus; ☿ Mercury; ☽ Moon.

Day Hours; Sunrise to Sunset. Mean Time.

Lat. 27°	Lat. 29°	Lat. 31°	Lat. 33°	Lat. 35°	Lat. 37°	Lat. 39°	Lat. 41°	Su	M	Tu	W	Th	F	Sa	Lat. 43°	Lat. 45°	Lat. 47°	Lat. 49°	Lat. 51°	Lat. 53°	Lat. 55°
6.05	6.07	6.09	6.11	6.13	6.15	6.18	6.21	☉	☽	♂	☿	♃	♀	♄	6.24	6.27	6.31	6.34	6.38	6.42	6.47
7.02	7.03	7.05	7.07	7.08	7.10	7.12	7.15	♀	♄	☉	☽	♂	☿	♃	7.17	7.20	7.23	7.26	7.29	7.32	7.37
7.58	8.00	8.01	8.02	8.03	8.05	8.07	8.09	☿	♃	♀	♄	☉	☽	♂	8.11	8.13	8.15	8.17	8.20	8.23	8.26
8.55	8.56	8.57	8.58	8.59	9.00	9.01	9.03	☽	♂	☿	♃	♀	♄	☉	9.04	9.06	9.07	9.09	9.11	9.13	9.16
9.51	9.52	9.53	9.53	9.54	9.54	9.55	9.56	♄	☉	☽	♂	☿	♃	♀	9.57	9.58	10.00	10.01	10.02	10.03	10.05
10.48	10.48	10.49	10.49	10.49	10.49	10.50	10.50	♃	♀	♄	☉	☽	♂	☿	10.51	10.51	10.52	10.52	10.53	10.54	10.55
11.45	11.45	11.45	11.44	11.44	11.44	11.44	11.44	♂	☿	♃	♀	♄	☉	☽	11.44	11.44	11.44	11.44	11.44	11.44	11.44
12.41	12.41	12.40	12.40	12.39	12.39	12.38	12.38	☉	☽	♂	☿	♃	♀	♄	12.37	12.37	12.36	12.36	12.35	12.34	12.34
1.38	1.37	1.36	1.35	1.34	1.34	1.33	1.32	♀	♄	☉	☽	♂	☿	♃	1.31	1.30	1.28	1.27	1.26	1.25	1.23
2.34	2.33	2.32	2.31	2.30	2.29	2.27	2.26	☿	♃	♀	♄	☉	☽	♂	2.24	2.23	2.21	2.19	2.17	2.15	2.13
3.31	3.30	3.28	3.26	3.25	3.23	3.20	3.19	☽	♂	☿	♃	♀	♄	☉	3.17	3.15	3.13	3.11	3.08	3.05	3.02
4.27	4.26	4.24	4.22	4.20	4.18	4.16	4.13	♄	☉	☽	♂	☿	♃	♀	4.11	4.08	4.05	4.02	3.59	3.56	3.52

Night Hours; Sunset to Sunrise.

Lat. 27°	Lat. 29°	Lat. 31°	Lat. 33°	Lat. 35°	Lat. 37°	Lat. 39°	Lat. 41°	Su	M	Tu	W	Th	F	Sa	Lat. 43°	Lat. 45°	Lat. 47°	Lat. 49°	Lat. 51°	Lat. 53°	Lat. 55°
5.24	5.22	5.20	5.17	5.15	5.13	5.10	5.07	♃	♀	♄	☉	☽	♂	☿	5.04	5.01	4.57	4.54	4.50	4.46	4.41
6.28	6.26	6.24	6.22	6.20	6.18	6.16	6.13	♂	☿	♃	♀	♄	☉	☽	6.11	6.08	6.05	6.02	5.59	5.56	5.52
7.31	7.30	7.28	7.26	7.25	7.24	7.22	7.20	☉	☽	♂	☿	♃	♀	♄	7.18	7.16	7.13	7.11	7.08	7.06	7.02
8.35	8.34	8.33	8.31	8.30	8.29	8.27	8.26	♀	♄	☉	☽	♂	☿	♃	8.24	8.23	8.21	8.19	8.18	8.16	8.13
9.38	9.37	9.37	9.35	9.35	9.34	9.33	9.32	☿	♃	♀	♄	☉	☽	♂	9.31	9.30	9.29	9.28	9.27	9.25	9.24
10.42	10.41	10.41	10.40	10.40	10.39	10.39	10.38	☽	♂	☿	♃	♀	♄	☉	10.38	10.37	10.37	10.36	10.36	10.35	10.34
11.45	11.45	11.45	11.45	11.45	11.45	11.45	11.45	♄	☉	☽	♂	☿	♃	♀	11.45	11.45	11.45	11.45	11.45	11.45	11.45
12.49	12.49	12.49	12.49	12.49	12.50	12.50	12.51	♃	♀	♄	☉	☽	♂	☿	12.51	12.52	12.52	12.53	12.54	12.55	12.56
1.52	1.53	1.53	1.54	1.54	1.55	1.56	1.57	♂	☿	♃	♀	♄	☉	☽	1.58	1.59	2.00	2.01	2.03	2.05	2.06
2.56	2.57	2.58	2.58	2.59	3.00	3.02	3.03	☉	☽	♂	☿	♃	♀	♄	3.05	3.06	3.08	3.10	3.13	3.15	3.17
3.59	4.00	4.02	4.03	4.04	4.06	4.08	4.10	♀	♄	☉	☽	♂	☿	♃	4.12	4.14	4.16	4.18	4.22	4.24	4.28
5.03	5.04	5.06	5.07	5.09	5.11	5.13	5.16	☿	♃	♀	♄	☉	☽	♂	5.18	5.21	5.24	5.27	5.31	5.34	5.38

APRIL 24th to 30th, ANY YEAR, in South Latitude

NOVEMBER 1st to 7th, ANY YEAR, in North Latitude

♄ Saturn; ♃ Jupiter; ♂ Mars; ☉ Sun; ♀ Venus; ☿ Mercury; ☽ Moon.

Day Hours; Sunrise to Sunset. Mean Time.

Lat. 27°	Lat. 29°	Lat. 31°	Lat. 33°	Lat. 35°	Lat. 37°	Lat. 39°	Lat. 41°	Su	M	Tu	W	Th	F	Sa	Lat. 43°	Lat. 45°	Lat. 47°	Lat. 49°	Lat. 51°	Lat. 53°	Lat. 55°
6.10	6.12	6.14	6.17	6.20	6.24	6.27	6.31	☉	☽	♂	☿	♃	♀	♄	6.34	6.38	6.42	6.46	6.51	6.57	7.03
7.06	7.07	7.09	7.11	7.14	7.17	7.20	7.23	♀	♄	☉	☽	♂	☿	♃	7.26	7.29	7.32	7.36	7.40	7.45	7.49
8.01	8.03	8.04	8.06	8.08	8.11	8.13	8.15	☿	♃	♀	♄	☉	☽	♂	8.17	8.20	8.23	8.25	8.28	8.33	8.36
8.57	8.58	8.59	9.00	9.02	9.04	9.05	9.07	☽	♂	☿	♃	♀	♄	☉	9.09	9.11	9.13	9.15	9.17	9.20	9.23
9.53	9.53	9.54	9.55	9.53	9.57	9.58	9.59	♄	☉	☽	♂	☿	♃	♀	10.00	10.02	10.03	10.04	10.06	10.08	10.10
10.48	10.48	10.49	10.49	10.50	10.50	10.51	10.51	♃	♀	♄	☉	☽	♂	☿	10.52	10.53	10.53	10.54	10.54	10.56	10.56
11.44	11.44	11.44	11.44	11.44	11.44	11.44	11.44	♂	☿	♃	♀	♄	☉	☽	11.44	11.44	11.44	11.44	11.44	11.44	11.44
12.40	12.39	12.38	12.38	12.37	12.37	12.36	12.36	☉	☽	♂	☿	♃	♀	♄	12.35	12.34	12.34	12.33	12.32	12.31	12.30
1.35	1.34	1.33	1.32	1.31	1.30	1.29	1.28	♀	♄	☉	☽	♂	☿	♃	1.27	1.25	1.24	1.22	1.20	1.19	1.16
2.31	2.29	2.28	2.27	2.25	2.23	2.22	2.20	☿	♃	♀	♄	☉	☽	♂	2.18	2.16	2.14	2.12	2.09	2.07	2.03
3.27	3.25	3.23	3.21	3.19	3.17	3.15	3.12	☽	♂	☿	♃	♀	♄	☉	3.10	3.07	3.05	3.01	2.58	2.55	2.50
4.22	4.20	4.18	4.16	4.13	4.10	4.07	4.04	♄	☉	☽	♂	☿	♃	♀	4.01	3.58	3.55	3.51	3.46	3.42	3.36

Night Hours; Sunset to Sunrise.

Lat. 27°	Lat. 29°	Lat. 31°	Lat. 33°	Lat. 35°	Lat. 37°	Lat. 39°	Lat. 41°	Su	M	Tu	W	Th	F	Sa	Lat. 43°	Lat. 45°	Lat. 47°	Lat. 49°	Lat. 51°	Lat. 53°	Lat. 55°
5.18	5.15	5.13	5.10	5.07	5.03	5.00	4.56	♃	♀	♄	☉	☽	♂	☿	4.53	4.49	4.45	4.40	4.35	4.30	4.23
6.22	6.20	6.18	6.16	6.13	6.10	6.07	6.04	♂	☿	♃	♀	♄	☉	☽	6.02	5.58	5.55	5.51	5.47	5.42	5.37
7.27	7.25	7.23	7.21	7.19	7.17	7.15	7.12	☉	☽	♂	☿	♃	♀	♄	7.10	7.07	7.05	7.01	6.58	6.55	6.50
8.31	8.30	8.29	8.27	8.26	8.24	8.22	8.20	♀	♄	☉	☽	♂	☿	♃	8.19	8.17	8.15	8.12	8.10	8.07	8.04
9.35	9.34	9.34	9.33	9.32	9.30	9.29	9.28	☿	♃	♀	♄	☉	☽	♂	9.27	9.26	9.24	9.23	9.21	9.20	9.17
10.40	10.39	10.39	10.38	10.38	10.37	10.37	10.36	☽	♂	☿	♃	♀	♄	☉	10.36	10.35	10.34	10.33	10.33	10.32	10.31
11.44	11.44	11.44	11.44	11.44	11.44	11.44	11.44	♄	☉	☽	♂	☿	♃	♀	11.44	11.44	11.44	11.44	11.44	11.44	11.44
12.48	12.49	12.49	12.50	12.50	12.51	12.51	12.52	♃	♀	♄	☉	☽	♂	☿	12.53	12.53	12.54	12.55	12.56	12.57	12.58
1.53	1.54	1.54	1.55	1.56	1.58	1.59	2.00	♂	☿	♃	♀	♄	☉	☽	2.01	2.02	2.04	2.05	2.07	2.09	2.11
2.57	2.59	3.00	3.01	3.03	3.05	3.06	3.08	☉	☽	♂	☿	♃	♀	♄	3.10	3.12	3.14	3.16	3.19	3.22	3.25
4.01	4.03	4.05	4.07	4.09	4.11	4.13	4.16	♀	♄	☉	☽	♂	☿	♃	4.18	4.21	4.23	4.27	4.30	4.34	4.38
5.06	5.08	5.10	5.12	5.15	5.18	5.21	5.24	☿	♃	♀	♄	☉	☽	♂	5.27	5.30	5.33	5.37	5.42	5.47	5.52

MAY 1st to 7th, ANY YEAR, in South Latitude

NOVEMBER 8th to 14th, ANY YEAR, in North Latitude

♄ Saturn; ♃ Jupiter; ♂ Mars; ☉ Sun; ♀ Venus; ☿ Mercury; ☽ Moon.

Day Hours; Sunrise to Sunset. Mean Time.

Lat. 27°	Lat. 29°	Lat. 31°	Lat. 33°	Lat. 35°	Lat. 37°	Lat. 39°	Lat. 41°	Su	M	Tu	W	Th	F	Sa	Lat. 43°	Lat. 45°	Lat. 47°	Lat. 49°	Lat. 51°	Lat. 53°	Lat. 55°
6.15	6.18	6.21	6.24	6.27	6.31	6.34	6.38	☉	☽	♂	☿	♃	♀	♄	6.43	6.47	6.53	6.58	7.04	7.10	7.17
7.10	7.12	7.15	7.17	7.20	7.23	7.26	7.29	♀	♄	☉	☽	♂	☿	♃	7.33	7.36	7.41	7.46	7.51	7.56	8.01
8.05	8.07	8.09	8.11	8.13	8.15	8.17	8.20	☿	♃	♀	♄	☉	☽	♂	8.23	8.26	8.30	8.33	8.37	8.41	8.46
8.59	9.01	9.02	9.04	9.05	9.07	9.09	9.11	☽	♂	☿	♃	♀	♄	☉	9.13	9.15	9.19	9.21	9.24	9.27	9.30
9.54	9.55	9.56	9.57	9.58	9.59	10.00	10.02	♄	☉	☽	♂	☿	♃	♀	10.03	10.05	10.07	10.09	10.10	10.12	10.15
10.49	10.49	10.50	10.50	10.51	10.51	10.52	10.53	♃	♀	♄	☉	☽	♂	☿	10.53	10.54	10.56	10.56	10.57	10.58	10.59
11.44	11.44	11.44	11.44	11.44	11.44	11.44	11.44	♂	☿	♃	♀	♄	☉	☽	11.44	11.44	11.44	11.44	11.44	11.44	11.44
12.38	12.38	12.37	12.37	12.36	12.36	12.35	12.34	☉	☽	♂	☿	♃	♀	♄	12.34	12.33	12.33	12.32	12.30	12.29	12.28
1.33	1.32	1.31	1.30	1.29	1.28	1.27	1.25	♀	♄	☉	☽	♂	☿	♃	1.24	1.22	1.21	1.19	1.17	1.15	1.12
2.28	2.26	2.25	2.23	2.22	2.20	2.18	2.16	☿	♃	♀	♄	☉	☽	♂	2.14	2.12	2.10	2.07	2.03	2.00	1.57
3.23	3.21	3.19	3.17	3.15	3.12	3.10	3.07	☽	♂	☿	♃	♀	♄	☉	3.04	3.01	2.58	2.55	2.50	2.46	2.41
4.17	4.15	4.11	4.10	4.07	4.04	4.01	3.58	♄	☉	☽	♂	☿	♃	♀	3.54	3.51	3.47	3.42	3.36	3.31	3.26

Night Hours; Sunset to Sunrise.

Lat. 27°	Lat. 29°	Lat. 31°	Lat. 33°	Lat. 35°	Lat. 37°	Lat. 39°	Lat. 41°	Su	M	Tu	W	Th	F	Sa	Lat. 43°	Lat. 45°	Lat. 47°	Lat. 49°	Lat. 51°	Lat. 53°	Lat. 55°
5.12	5.09	5.06	5.03	5.00	4.56	4.53	4.49	♃	♀	♄	☉	☽	♂	☿	4.44	4.40	4.35	4.30	4.23	4.17	4.10
6.17	6.15	6.12	6.10	6.07	6.04	6.02	5.58	♂	☿	♃	♀	♄	☉	☽	5.54	5.51	5.47	5.42	5.37	5.32	5.26
7.23	7.21	7.19	7.17	7.15	7.12	7.10	7.07	☉	☽	♂	☿	♃	♀	♄	7.04	7.02	6.58	6.55	6.50	6.46	6.42
8.28	8.27	8.25	8.24	8.22	8.20	8.19	8.17	♀	♄	☉	☽	♂	☿	♃	8.14	8.12	8.10	8.07	8.04	8.01	7.57
9.33	9.32	9.31	9.30	9.29	9.28	9.27	9.26	☿	♃	♀	♄	☉	☽	♂	9.24	9.23	9.21	9.20	9.17	9.15	9.13
10.39	10.38	10.38	10.37	10.37	10.36	10.36	10.35	☽	♂	☿	♃	♀	♄	☉	10.34	10.34	10.33	10.32	10.31	10.30	10.29
11.44	11.44	11.44	11.44	11.44	11.44	11.44	11.44	♄	☉	☽	♂	☿	♃	♀	11.44	11.44	11.44	11.44	11.44	11.44	11.44
12.49	12.50	12.50	12.51	12.51	12.52	12.53	12.53	♃	♀	♄	☉	☽	♂	☿	12.54	12.55	12.56	12.57	12.58	12.59	1.00
1.55	1.56	1.57	1.58	1.59	2.00	2.01	2.02	♂	☿	♃	♀	♄	☉	☽	2.04	2.06	2.08	2.09	2.12	2.14	2.16
3.00	3.02	3.03	3.05	3.06	3.08	3.10	3.12	☉	☽	♂	☿	♃	♀	♄	3.14	3.17	3.19	3.22	3.25	3.28	3.32
4.05	4.07	4.09	4.11	4.13	4.16	4.18	4.21	♀	♄	☉	☽	♂	☿	♃	4.24	4.28	4.31	4.34	4.39	4.43	4.48
5.11	5.13	5.16	5.18	5.21	5.24	5.27	5.30	☿	♃	♀	♄	☉	☽	♂	5.34	5.38	5.42	5.47	5.52	5.57	6.03

MAY 8th to 14th, ANY YEAR, in South Latitude

NOVEMBER 15th to 22nd, ANY YEAR, in North Latitude

♄ Saturn; ♃ Jupiter; ♂ Mars; ☉ Sun; ♀ Venus; ☿ Mercury; ☽ Moon.

Day Hours; Sunrise to Sunset. Mean Time.

Lat. 27°	Lat. 29°	Lat. 31°	Lat. 33°	Lat. 35°	Lat. 37°	Lat. 39°	Lat. 41°	Su	M	Tu	W	Th	F	Sa	Lat. 43°	Lat. 45°	Lat. 47°	Lat. 49°	Lat. 51°	Lat. 53°	Lat. 55°
6.20	6.23	6.26	6.30	6.34	6.38	6.43	6.47	☉	☽	♂	☿	♃	♀	♄	6.52	6.57	7.03	7.09	7.16	7.23	7.31
7.14	7.17	7.19	7.22	7.26	7.29	7.33	7.37	♀	♄	☉	☽	♂	☿	♃	7.41	7.45	7.50	7.55	8.01	8.07	8.12
8.08	8.10	8.12	8.15	8.18	8.20	8.24	8.26	☿	♃	♀	♄	☉	☽	♂	8.30	8.33	8.37	8.41	8.46	8.50	8.55
9.02	9.04	9.05	9.07	9.09	9.11	9.14	9.16	☽	♂	☿	♃	♀	♄	☉	9.18	9.21	9.24	9.26	9.30	9.34	9.38
9.56	9.57	9.58	10.00	10.01	10.02	10.04	10.05	♄	☉	☽	♂	☿	♃	♀	10.07	10.09	10.11	10.13	10.15	10.17	10.20
10.50	10.51	10.51	10.52	10.53	10.53	10.54	10.55	♃	♀	♄	☉	☽	♂	☿	10.56	10.57	10.58	10.59	11.00	11.01	11.02
11.45	11.45	11.45	11.45	11.45	11.45	11.45	11.45	♂	☿	♃	♀	♄	☉	☽	11.45	11.45	11.45	11.45	11.45	11.45	11.45
12.39	12.38	12.38	12.37	12.36	12.36	12.35	12.34	☉	☽	♂	☿	♃	♀	♄	12.33	12.32	12.31	12.30	12.29	12.28	12.27
1.33	1.32	1.31	1.29	1.28	1.27	1.26	1.24	♀	♄	☉	☽	♂	☿	♃	1.22	1.20	1.18	1.16	1.14	1.12	1.09
2.27	2.25	2.24	2.22	2.20	2.18	2.16	2.13	☿	♃	♀	♄	☉	☽	♂	2.11	2.08	2.05	2.02	1.59	1.55	1.52
3.21	3.19	3.17	3.14	3.12	3.09	3.06	3.03	☽	♂	☿	♃	♀	♄	☉	3.00	2.56	2.52	2.48	2.44	2.39	2.34
4.15	4.12	4.10	4.07	4.03	4.00	3.57	3.52	♄	☉	☽	♂	☿	♃	♀	3.48	3.44	3.39	3.34	3.28	3.22	3.16

Night Hours; Sunset to Sunrise.

Lat. 27°	Lat. 29°	Lat. 31°	Lat. 33°	Lat. 35°	Lat. 37°	Lat. 39°	Lat. 41°	Su	M	Tu	W	Th	F	Sa	Lat. 43°	Lat. 45°	Lat. 47°	Lat. 49°	Lat. 51°	Lat. 53°	Lat. 55°
5.09	5.06	5.03	4.59	4.55	4.51	4.47	4.42	♃	♀	♄	☉	☽	♂	☿	4.37	4.32	4.26	4.20	4.13	4.06	3.57
6.15	6.12	6.10	6.07	6.03	6.00	5.57	5.53	♂	☿	♃	♀	♄	☉	☽	5.48	5.44	5.39	5.34	5.28	5.23	5.15
7.21	7.19	7.17	7.14	7.12	7.09	7.07	7.03	☉	☽	♂	☿	♃	♀	♄	7.00	6.57	6.53	6.48	6.44	6.39	6.33
8.27	8.25	8.24	8.22	8.20	8.18	8.16	8.14	♀	♄	☉	☽	♂	☿	♃	8.11	8.09	8.06	8.03	7.59	7.56	7.51
9.33	9.32	9.31	9.30	9.28	9.27	9.26	9.24	☿	♃	♀	♄	☉	☽	♂	9.23	9.21	9.19	9.17	9.14	9.12	9.09
10.39	10.38	10.38	10.37	10.37	10.36	10.36	10.35	☽	♂	☿	♃	♀	♄	☉	10.34	10.33	10.32	10.31	10.30	10.29	10.27
11.45	11.45	11.45	11.45	11.45	11.45	11.45	11.45	♄	☉	☽	♂	☿	♃	♀	11.45	11.45	11.45	11.45	11.45	11.45	11.45
12.50	12.51	12.52	12.53	12.54	12.55	12.55	12.56	♃	♀	♄	☉	☽	♂	☿	12.57	12.58	12.59	12.59	1.00	1.02	1.03
1.56	1.57	1.59	2.00	2.02	2.03	2.05	2.07	♂	☿	♃	♀	♄	☉	☽	2.08	2.10	2.12	2.13	2.16	2.18	2.21
3.02	3.04	3.06	3.08	3.10	3.12	3.15	3.17	☉	☽	♂	☿	♃	♀	♄	3.20	3.22	3.25	3.28	3.31	3.35	3.39
4.08	4.10	4.13	4.16	4.18	4.21	4.25	4.28	♀	♄	☉	☽	♂	☿	♃	4.31	4.35	4.39	4.42	4.46	4.51	4.57
5.14	5.17	5.20	5.23	5.27	5.30	5.34	5.38	☿	♃	♀	♄	☉	☽	♂	5.43	5.47	5.52	5.56	6.02	6.08	6.15

MAY 15th to 22nd, ANY YEAR, in South Latitude

NOVEMBER 23rd to 30th, ANY YEAR, in North Latitude

♄ Saturn; ♃ Jupiter; ♂ Mars; ☉ Sun; ♀ Venus; ☿ Mercury; ☽ Moon.

Day Hours; Sunrise to Sunset. Mean Time.

Lat. 27°	Lat. 29°	Lat. 31°	Lat. 33°	Lat. 35°	Lat. 37°	Lat. 39°	Lat. 41°	Su	M	Tu	W	Th	F	Sa	Lat. 43°	Lat. 45°	Lat. 47°	Lat. 49°	Lat. 51°	Lat. 53°	Lat. 55°
6.27	6.30	6.34	6.38	6.42	6.46	6.51	6.56	☉	☽	♂	☿	♃	♀	♄	7.01	7.07	7.14	7.21	7.29	7.38	7.47
7.20	7.23	7.26	7.30	7.33	7.36	7.40	7.44	♀	♄	☉	☽	♂	☿	♃	7.49	7.54	7.59	8.05	8.12	8.19	8.27
8.14	8.16	8.18	8.21	8.24	8.26	8.29	8.33	☿	♃	♀	♄	☉	☽	♂	8.36	8.40	8.45	8.49	8.55	9.01	9.07
9.07	9.09	9.10	9.13	9.15	9.16	9.19	9.21	☽	♂	☿	♃	♀	♄	☉	9.24	9.27	9.30	9.34	9.38	9.42	9.47
10.00	10.01	10.02	10.04	10.05	10.06	10.08	10.09	♄	☉	☽	♂	☿	♃	♀	10.11	10.13	10.15	10.18	10.21	10.24	10.27
10.54	10.54	10.54	10.56	10.56	10.56	10.57	10.58	♃	♀	♄	☉	☽	♂	☿	10.59	11.00	11.01	11.02	11.04	11.05	11.07
11.47	11.47	11.47	11.47	11.47	11.47	11.47	11.47	♂	☿	♃	♀	♄	☉	☽	11.47	11.47	11.47	11.47	11.47	11.47	11.47
12.40	12.40	12.39	12.39	12.37	12.37	12.36	12.35	☉	☽	♂	☿	♃	♀	♄	12.35	12.34	12.32	12.31	12.29	12.28	12.26
1.34	1.33	1.31	1.30	1.28	1.27	1.25	1.24	♀	♄	☉	☽	♂	☿	♃	1.22	1.20	1.18	1.15	1.12	1.09	1.06
2.27	2.26	2.23	2.22	2.19	2.17	2.15	2.12	☿	♃	♀	♄	☉	☽	♂	2.10	2.07	2.03	2.00	1.55	1.51	1.46
3.20	3.18	3.15	3.14	3.10	3.07	3.04	3.00	☽	♂	☿	♃	♀	♄	☉	2.57	2.53	2.48	2.44	2.38	2.32	2.26
4.14	4.11	4.07	4.05	4.00	3.57	3.53	3.49	♄	☉	☽	♂	☿	♃	♀	3.45	3.40	3.34	3.28	3.21	3.14	3.06

Night Hours; Sunset to Sunrise.

Lat. 27°	Lat. 29°	Lat. 31°	Lat. 33°	Lat. 35°	Lat. 37°	Lat. 39°	Lat. 41°	Su	M	Tu	W	Th	F	Sa	Lat. 43°	Lat. 45°	Lat. 47°	Lat. 49°	Lat. 51°	Lat. 53°	Lat. 55°
5.07	5.04	4.59	4.55	4.51	4.46	4.41	4.36	♃	♀	♄	☉	☽	♂	☿	4.31	4.25	4.18	4.11	4.04	3.55	3.46
6.14	6.11	6.07	6.03	6.00	5.56	5.52	5.48	♂	☿	♃	♀	♄	☉	☽	5.44	5.39	5.33	5.27	5.21	5.14	5.06
7.20	7.19	7.15	7.12	7.10	7.06	7.03	7.00	☉	☽	♂	☿	♃	♀	♄	6.56	6.52	6.48	6.43	6.38	6.32	6.26
8.27	8.26	8.23	8.21	8.19	8.16	8.14	8.11	♀	♄	☉	☽	♂	☿	♃	8.09	8.06	8.03	7.59	7.56	7.51	7.47
9.34	9.33	9.31	9.30	9.28	9.26	9.25	9.23	☿	♃	♀	♄	☉	☽	♂	9.22	9.20	9.17	9.15	9.13	9.10	9.07
10.40	10.40	10.39	10.38	10.38	10.36	10.36	10.35	☽	♂	☿	♃	♀	♄	☉	10.34	10.33	10.32	10.31	10.30	10.28	10.27
11.47	11.47	11.47	11.47	11.47	11.47	11.47	11.47	♄	☉	☽	♂	☿	♃	♀	11.47	11.47	11.47	11.47	11.47	11.47	11.47
12.54	12.55	12.55	12.56	12.56	12.57	12.57	12.58	♃	♀	♄	☉	☽	♂	☿	1.00	1.01	1.02	1.03	1.04	1.06	1.07
2.00	2.02	2.03	2.04	2.06	2.07	2.08	2.10	♂	☿	♃	♀	♄	☉	☽	2.12	2.14	2.17	2.19	2.21	2.24	2.27
3.07	3.09	3.11	3.13	3.15	3.17	3.19	3.22	☉	☽	♂	☿	♃	♀	♄	3.25	3.28	3.32	3.35	3.39	3.43	3.48
4.14	4.17	4.19	4.22	4.24	4.27	4.30	4.34	♀	♄	☉	☽	♂	☿	♃	4.38	4.42	4.46	4.51	4.56	5.02	5.08
5.20	5.24	5.27	5.30	5.34	5.37	5.41	5.45	☿	♃	♀	♄	☉	☽	♂	5.50	5.55	6.01	6.07	6.13	6.20	6.28

MAY 23rd to 31st, ANY YEAR, in South Latitude

DECEMBER 1st to 7th, ANY YEAR, in North Latitude

♄ Saturn; ♃ Jupiter; ♂ Mars; ☉ Sun; ♀ Venus; ☿ Mercury; ☽ Moon.

Day Hours; Sunrise to Sunset. Mean Time.

Lat. 55°	Lat. 53°	Lat. 51°	Lat. 49°	Lat. 47°	Lat. 45°	Lat. 43°	Sa	F	Th	W	Tu	M	Su	Lat. 41°	Lat. 39°	Lat. 37°	Lat. 35°	Lat. 33°	Lat. 31°	Lat. 29°	Lat. 27°
8.00	8.50	7.41	7.32	7.25	7.18	7.12	♄	♀	♃	☿	♂	☽	☉	7.05	6.59	6.54	6.49	6.45	6.40	6.36	6.32
8.38	8.30	8.22	8.15	8.09	8.03	7.58	♃	☿	♂	☽	☉	♄	♀	7.52	7.47	7.43	7.39	7.36	7.32	7.28	7.25
9.16	9.10	9.04	8.58	8.53	8.48	8.44	♂	☽	☉	♄	♀	♃	☿	8.40	8.35	8.32	8.29	8.26	8.23	8.20	8.18
9.54	9.50	9.45	9.41	9.37	9.34	9.31	☉	♄	♀	♃	☿	♂	☽	9.27	9.24	9.21	9.18	9.17	9.15	9.13	9.11
10.32	10.29	10.26	10.23	10.21	10.19	10.17	♀	♃	☿	♂	☽	☉	♄	10.14	10.12	10.10	10.09	10.08	10.06	10.05	10.03
11.10	11.09	11.08	11.06	11.05	11.04	11.03	☿	♂	☽	☉	♄	♀	♃	11.01	11.00	10.59	10.59	10.58	10.58	10.57	10.56
11.49	11.49	11.49	11.49	11.49	11.49	11.49	☽	☉	♄	♀	♃	☿	♂	11.49	11.49	11.49	11.49	11.49	11.49	11.49	11.49
12.27	12.29	12.30	12.32	12.33	12.34	12.35	♄	♀	♃	☿	♂	☽	☉	12.36	12.37	12.38	12.38	12.40	12.41	12.41	12.42
1.05	1.09	1.12	1.15	1.17	1.19	1.21	♃	☿	♂	☽	☉	♄	♀	1.23	1.26	1.27	1.28	1.30	1.32	1.33	1.35
1.43	1.49	1.53	1.58	2.01	2.05	2.08	♂	☽	☉	♄	♀	♃	☿	2.10	2.14	2.16	2.18	2.21	2.24	2.26	2.28
2.21	2.28	2.34	2.40	2.45	2.50	2.54	☉	♄	♀	♃	☿	♂	☽	2.58	3.02	3.05	3.08	3.12	3.15	3.18	3.20
2.59	3.08	3.16	3.23	3.29	3.35	3.40	♀	♃	☿	♂	☽	☉	♄	3.45	3.51	3.54	3.58	4.02	4.07	4.10	4.13

Night Hours; Sunset to Sunrise.

Lat. 55°	Lat. 53°	Lat. 51°	Lat. 49°	Lat. 47°	Lat. 45°	Lat. 43°	Sa	F	Th	W	Tu	M	Su	Lat. 41°	Lat. 39°	Lat. 37°	Lat. 35°	Lat. 33°	Lat. 31°	Lat. 29°	Lat. 27°
3.37	3.48	3.57	4.06	4.13	4.20	4.26	☿	♂	☽	☉	♄	♀	♃	4.32	4.38	4.43	4.48	4.53	4.58	5.02	5.06
4.59	5.08	5.16	5.23	5.29	5.35	5.40	☽	☉	♄	♀	♃	☿	♂	5.45	5.50	5.54	5.58	6.02	6.07	6.10	6.13
6.21	6.29	6.35	6.41	6.45	6.50	6.54	♄	♀	♃	☿	♂	☽	☉	6.58	7.02	7.05	7.08	7.12	7.15	7.18	7.21
7.43	7.49	7.53	7.58	8.01	8.05	8.08	♃	☿	♂	☽	☉	♄	♀	8.11	8.14	8.16	8.19	8.21	8.24	8.26	8.28
9.05	9.09	9.12	9.15	9.17	9.20	9.22	♂	☽	☉	♄	♀	♃	☿	9.23	9.25	9.27	9.29	9.31	9.32	9.34	9.35
10.27	10.29	10.31	10.32	10.33	10.35	10.36	☉	♄	♀	♃	☿	♂	☽	10.36	10.37	10.38	10.39	10.40	10.41	10.42	10.42
11.49	11.49	11.49	11.49	11.49	11.49	11.49	♀	♃	☿	♂	☽	☉	♄	11.49	11.49	11.49	11.49	11.49	11.49	11.49	11.49
1.12	1.10	1.08	1.07	1.06	1.04	1.03	☿	♂	☽	☉	♄	♀	♃	1.02	1.01	1.00	12.59	12.59	12.58	12.57	12.57
2.34	2.29	2.27	2.24	2.22	2.19	2.17	☽	☉	♄	♀	♃	☿	♂	2.15	2.13	2.11	2.09	2.08	2.07	2.05	2.04
3.56	3.50	3.46	3.41	3.38	3.34	3.31	♄	♀	♃	☿	♂	☽	☉	3.28	3.25	3.22	3.20	3.18	3.15	3.13	3.11
5.18	5.11	5.05	4.59	4.54	4.49	4.45	♃	☿	♂	☽	☉	♄	♀	4.40	4.36	4.33	4.30	4.27	4.24	4.21	4.19
6.40	6.31	6.23	6.16	6.10	6.04	5.59	♂	☽	☉	♄	♀	♃	☿	5.53	5.48	5.44	5.40	5.37	5.32	5.29	5.26

JUNE 1st to 7th, ANY YEAR, in South Latitude

DECEMBER 8th to 15th, ANY YEAR, in North Latitude

♄ Saturn; ♃ Jupiter; ♂ Mars; ⊙ Sun; ♀ Venus; ☿ Mercury; ☽ Moon.

Day Hours; Sunrise to Sunset. Mean Time.

Lat. 27°	Lat. 29°	Lat. 31°	Lat. 33°	Lat. 35°	Lat. 37°	Lat. 39°	Lat. 41°	Su	M	Tu	W	Th	F	Sa	Lat. 43°	Lat. 45°	Lat. 47°	Lat. 49°	Lat. 51°	Lat. 53°	Lat. 55°
6.38	6.42	6.46	6.51	6.55	7.01	7.06	7.12	⊙	☽	♂	☿	♃	♀	♄	7.19	7.25	7.33	7.41	7.50	7.59	8.10
7.30	7.34	7.37	7.41	7.44	7.50	7.54	7.59	♀	♄	⊙	☽	♂	☿	♃	8.05	8.10	8.16	8.23	8.30	8.38	8.47
8.23	8.25	8.28	8.31	8.34	8.38	8.41	8.45	☿	♃	♀	♄	⊙	☽	♂	8.50	8.54	8.59	9.05	9.11	9.17	9.24
9.15	9.17	9.19	9.22	9.23	9.27	9.29	9.32	☽	♂	☿	♃	♀	♄	⊙	9.36	9.39	9.43	9.47	9.51	9.55	10.01
10.07	10.09	10.10	10.12	10.13	10.15	10.17	10.19	♄	⊙	☽	♂	☿	♃	♀	10.21	10.23	10.26	10.28	10.31	10.34	10.38
11.00	11.00	11.01	11.02	11.02	11.04	11.04	11.05	♃	♀	♄	⊙	☽	♂	☿	11.07	11.08	11.09	11.10	11.12	11.13	11.15
11.52	11.52	11.52	11.52	11.52	11.52	11.52	11.52	♂	☿	♃	♀	♄	⊙	☽	11.52	11.52	11.52	11.52	11.52	11.52	11.52
12.44	12.44	12.43	12.42	12.41	12.41	12.40	12.39	⊙	☽	♂	☿	♃	♀	♄	12.38	12.37	12.35	12.34	12.32	12.30	12.28
1.37	1.35	1.34	1.32	1.30	1.29	1.27	1.25	♀	♄	⊙	☽	♂	☿	♃	1.23	1.21	1.18	1.16	1.13	1.09	1.05
2.29	2.27	2.25	2.23	2.20	2.18	2.15	2.12	☿	♃	♀	♄	⊙	☽	♂	2.09	2.06	2.02	1.58	1.53	1.48	1.42
3.21	3.19	3.16	3.13	3.09	3.06	3.03	2.59	☽	♂	☿	♃	♀	♄	⊙	2.54	2.50	2.45	2.39	2.33	2.27	2.19
4.14	4.10	4.07	4.03	3.59	3.55	3.50	3.45	♄	⊙	☽	♂	☿	♃	♀	3.40	3.35	3.28	3.21	3.14	3.05	2.56

Night Hours; Sunset to Sunrise.

Lat. 27°	Lat. 29°	Lat. 31°	Lat. 33°	Lat. 35°	Lat. 37°	Lat. 39°	Lat. 41°	Su	M	Tu	W	Th	F	Sa	Lat. 43°	Lat. 45°	Lat. 47°	Lat. 49°	Lat. 51°	Lat. 53°	Lat. 55°
5.06	5.02	4.58	4.53	4.48	4.43	4.38	4.32	♃	♀	♄	⊙	☽	♂	☿	4.25	4.19	4.11	4.03	3.54	3.44	3.33
6.14	6.10	6.07	6.03	5.59	5.55	5.50	5.45	♂	☿	♃	♀	♄	⊙	☽	5.40	5.35	5.28	5.21	5.14	5.05	4.56
7.21	7.19	7.16	7.13	7.09	7.06	7.03	6.59	⊙	☽	♂	☿	♃	♀	♄	6.54	6.50	6.45	6.40	6.34	6.27	6.20
8.29	8.27	8.25	8.23	8.20	8.18	8.15	8.12	♀	♄	⊙	☽	♂	☿	♃	8.09	8.06	8.02	7.58	7.53	7.48	7.43
9.37	9.35	9.34	9.32	9.31	9.29	9.28	9.26	☿	♃	♀	♄	⊙	☽	♂	9.23	9.21	9.19	9.16	9.13	9.09	9.06
10.44	10.44	10.43	10.42	10.41	10.41	10.40	10.39	☽	♂	☿	♃	♀	♄	⊙	10.38	10.37	10.36	10.34	10.33	10.31	10.29
11.52	11.52	11.52	11.52	11.52	11.52	11.52	11.52	♄	⊙	☽	♂	☿	♃	♀	11.52	11.52	11.52	11.52	11.52	11.52	11.52
1.00	1.00	1.01	1.02	1.03	1.04	1.05	1.06	♃	♀	♄	⊙	☽	♂	☿	1.07	1.08	1.09	1.11	1.12	1.13	1.16
2.07	2.09	2.10	2.12	2.13	2.16	2.17	2.19	♂	☿	♃	♀	♄	⊙	☽	2.22	2.24	2.26	2.29	2.32	2.35	2.39
3.15	3.17	3.19	3.22	3.24	3.27	3.30	3.33	⊙	☽	♂	☿	♃	♀	♄	3.36	3.39	3.43	3.47	3.52	3.56	4.02
4.23	4.25	4.28	4.31	4.35	4.39	4.42	4.46	♀	♄	⊙	☽	♂	☿	♃	4.51	4.55	5.00	5.06	5.12	5.17	5.26
5.30	5.34	5.37	5.41	5.45	5.50	5.55	6.00	☿	♃	♀	♄	⊙	☽	♂	6.05	6.10	6.17	6.24	6.31	6.39	6.49

JUNE 8th to 15th, ANY YEAR, in South Latitude

DECEMBER 16th to 23rd, ANY YEAR, in North Latitude

♄ Saturn; ♃ Jupiter; ♂ Mars; ☉ Sun; ♀ Venus; ☿ Mercury; ☽ Moon.

Day Hours; Sunrise to Sunset. Mean Time.

Lat. 27°	Lat. 29°	Lat. 31°	Lat. 33°	Lat. 35°	Lat. 37°	Lat. 39°	Lat. 41°	Su	M	Tu	W	Th	F	Sa	Lat. 43°	Lat. 45°	Lat. 47°	Lat. 49°	Lat. 51°	Lat. 53°	Lat. 55°
6.42	6.47	6.51	6.56	7.01	7.07	7.12	7.18	☉	☽	♂	☿	♃	♀	♄	7.25	7.32	7.40	7.48	7.57	8.08	8.20
7.34	7.39	7.42	7.46	7.50	7.55	7.59	8.04	♀	♄	☉	☽	♂	☿	♃	8.10	8.16	8.23	8.29	8.37	8.46	8.56
8.27	8.30	8.33	8.36	8.39	8.43	8.46	8.51	☿	♃	♀	♄	☉	☽	♂	8.55	9.00	9.05	9.11	9.17	9.24	9.32
9.19	9.22	9.23	9.26	9.28	9.32	9.33	9.37	☽	♂	☿	♃	♀	♄	☉	9.40	9.44	9.48	9.52	9.56	10.02	10.08
10.11	10.13	10.14	10.16	10.17	10.20	10.20	10.23	♄	☉	☽	♂	☿	♃	♀	10.25	10.28	10.30	10.33	10.36	10.40	10.44
11.03	11.05	11.05	11.06	11.06	11.08	11.07	11.09	♃	♀	♄	☉	☽	♂	☿	11.10	11.12	11.13	11.14	11.16	11.18	11.20
11.56	11.56	11.56	11.56	11.56	11.56	11.56	11.56	♂	☿	♃	♀	♄	☉	☽	11.56	11.56	11.56	11.56	11.56	11.56	11.56
12.48	12.48	12.46	12.45	12.45	12.44	12.43	12.42	☉	☽	♂	☿	♃	♀	♄	12.41	12.39	12.38	12.37	12.35	12.33	12.31
1.40	1.39	1.37	1.35	1.34	1.32	1.31	1.28	♀	♄	☉	☽	♂	☿	♃	1.26	1.23	1.21	1.18	1.15	1.11	1.07
2.32	2.31	2.28	2.25	2.23	2.21	2.17	2.14	☿	♃	♀	♄	☉	☽	♂	2.11	2.07	2.03	1.59	1.55	1.49	1.43
3.25	3.22	3.19	3.15	3.12	3.09	3.04	3.01	☽	♂	☿	♃	♀	♄	☉	2.56	2.51	2.46	2.41	2.35	2.27	2.19
4.17	4.14	4.09	4.05	4.01	3.57	3.51	3.47	♄	☉	☽	♂	☿	♃	♀	3.41	3.35	3.28	3.22	3.14	3.05	2.55

Night Hours; Sunset to Sunrise.

Lat. 27°	Lat. 29°	Lat. 31°	Lat. 33°	Lat. 35°	Lat. 37°	Lat. 39°	Lat. 41°	Su	M	Tu	W	Th	F	Sa	Lat. 43°	Lat. 45°	Lat. 47°	Lat. 49°	Lat. 51°	Lat. 53°	Lat. 55°
5.09	5.05	5.00	4.55	4.50	4.44	4.39	4.33	♃	♀	♄	☉	☽	♂	☿	4.26	4.19	4.11	4.03	3.54	3.43	3.31
6.17	6.14	6.09	6.05	6.01	5.56	5.52	5.47	♂	☿	♃	♀	♄	☉	☽	5.41	5.35	5.29	5.22	5.14	5.05	4.55
7.25	7.22	7.19	7.15	7.12	7.08	7.05	7.01	☉	☽	♂	☿	♃	♀	♄	6.56	6.51	6.46	6.41	6.35	6.27	6.19
8.33	8.31	8.28	8.26	8.23	8.20	8.18	8.15	♀	♄	☉	☽	♂	☿	♃	8.11	8.08	8.04	8.00	7.55	7.50	7.44
9.40	9.39	9.37	9.36	9.34	9.32	9.30	9.28	☿	♃	♀	♄	☉	☽	♂	9.26	9.24	9.21	9.18	9.15	9.12	9.08
10.48	10.48	10.47	10.46	10.45	10.44	10.43	10.42	☽	♂	☿	♃	♀	♄	☉	10.41	10.40	10.39	10.37	10.36	10.34	10.32
11.56	11.56	11.56	11.56	11.56	11.56	11.56	11.56	♄	☉	☽	♂	☿	♃	♀	11.56	11.56	11.56	11.56	11.56	11.56	11.56
1.04	1.05	1.05	1.06	1.07	1.08	1.09	1.10	♃	♀	♄	☉	☽	♂	☿	1.11	1.12	1.14	1.15	1.16	1.18	1.20
2.12	2.14	2.15	2.16	2.18	2.20	2.22	2.24	♂	☿	♃	♀	♄	☉	☽	2.26	2.28	2.31	2.34	2.37	2.40	2.44
3.20	3.22	3.24	3.27	3.29	3.32	3.35	3.38	☉	☽	♂	☿	♃	♀	♄	3.41	3.45	3.49	3.53	3.57	4.03	4.09
4.27	4.31	4.33	4.37	4.40	4.44	4.47	4.51	♀	♄	☉	☽	♂	☿	♃	4.56	5.01	5.06	5.11	5.17	5.25	5.53
5.35	5.39	5.43	5.47	5.51	5.56	6.00	6.05	☿	♃	♀	♄	☉	☽	♂	6.11	6.17	6.24	6.30	6.38	6.47	6.57

JUNE 16th to 23rd, ANY YEAR, in South Latitude

DECEMBER 24th to 31st, ANY YEAR, in North Latitude

♄ Saturn; ♃ Jupiter; ♂ Mars; ☉ Sun; ♀ Venus; ☿ Mercury; ☽ Moon.

Day Hours; Sunrise to Sunset. Mean Time.

Lat. 27°	Lat. 29°	Lat. 31°	Lat. 33°	Lat. 35°	Lat. 37°	Lat. 39°	Lat. 41°	Su	M	Tu	W	Th	F	Sa	Lat. 43°	Lat. 45°	Lat. 47°	Lat. 49°	Lat. 51°	Lat. 53°	Lat. 55°
6.47	6.51	6.55	7.00	7.05	7.11	7.17	7.23	☉	☽	♂	☿	♃	♀	♄	7.30	7.37	7.45	7.53	8.02	8.13	8.25
7.39	7.42	7.46	7.50	7.54	7.59	8.04	8.09	♀	♄	☉	☽	♂	☿	♃	8.14	8.21	8.28	8.34	8.42	8.51	9.01
8.31	8.34	8.37	8.40	8.43	8.47	8.51	8.55	☿	♃	♀	♄	☉	☽	♂	9.00	9.05	9.10	9.15	9.21	9.29	9.37
9.23	9.25	9.27	9.30	9.32	9.35	9.38	9.40	☽	♂	☿	♃	♀	♄	☉	9.45	9.49	9.53	9.56	10.01	10.06	10.12
10.15	10.17	10.18	10.20	10.21	10.23	10.25	10.27	♄	☉	☽	♂	☿	♃	♀	10.30	10.32	10.35	10.37	10.40	10.44	10.48
11.07	11.08	11.09	11.10	11.10	11.11	11.12	11.13	♃	♀	♄	☉	☽	♂	☿	11.15	11.16	11.17	11.18	11.20	11.22	11.24
12.00	12.00	12.00	12.00	12.00	12.00	12.00	12.00	♂	☿	♃	♀	♄	☉	☽	12.00	12.00	12.00	12.00	12.00	12.00	12.00
12.52	12.51	12.50	12.49	12.49	12.48	12.47	12.46	☉	☽	♂	☿	♃	♀	♄	12.44	12.43	12.43	12.41	12.39	12.37	12.35
1.44	1.42	1.41	1.39	1.38	1.36	1.34	1.32	♀	♄	☉	☽	♂	☿	♃	1.29	1.28	1.25	1.22	1.19	1.15	1.11
2.36	2.34	2.32	2.29	2.27	2.24	2.21	2.18	☿	♃	♀	♄	☉	☽	♂	2.14	2.12	2.08	2.03	1.58	1.53	1.47
3.28	3.25	3.23	3.19	3.16	3.12	3.08	3.04	☽	♂	☿	♃	♀	♄	☉	2.59	2.55	2.50	2.44	2.38	2.31	2.23
4.20	4.17	4.13	4.09	4.05	4.00	3.55	3.50	♄	☉	☽	♂	☿	♃	♀	3.44	3.39	3.33	3.25	3.17	3.08	2.58

Night Hours; Sunset to Sunrise.

Lat. 27°	Lat. 29°	Lat. 31°	Lat. 33°	Lat. 35°	Lat. 37°	Lat. 39°	Lat. 41°	Su	M	Tu	W	Th	F	Sa	Lat. 43°	Lat. 45°	Lat. 47°	Lat. 49°	Lat. 51°	Lat. 53°	Lat. 55°
5.12	5.08	5.04	4.59	4.54	4.48	4.42	4.36	♃	♀	♄	☉	☽	♂	☿	4.29	4.23	4.15	4.06	3.57	3.46	3.34
6.20	6.17	6.13	6.09	6.05	6.00	5.55	5.50	♂	☿	♃	♀	♄	☉	☽	5.44	5.39	5.33	5.25	5.17	5.08	4.58
7.28	7.25	7.23	7.19	7.16	7.12	7.08	7.04	☉	☽	♂	☿	♃	♀	♄	6.59	6.55	6.50	6.44	6.38	6.31	6.23
8.36	8.34	8.32	8.30	8.27	8.24	8.21	8.18	♀	♄	☉	☽	♂	☿	♃	8.14	8.12	8.08	8.03	7.58	7.53	7.47
9.44	9.42	9.41	9.40	9.38	9.36	9.34	9.32	☿	♃	♀	♄	☉	☽	♂	9.29	9.28	9.25	9.22	9.19	9.15	9.11
10.52	10.51	10.51	10.50	10.49	10.48	10.47	10.46	☽	♂	☿	♃	♀	♄	☉	10.44	10.44	10.43	10.41	10.39	10.37	10.35
12.00	12.00	12.00	12.00	12.00	12.00	12.00	12.00	♄	☉	☽	♂	☿	♃	♀	12.00	12.00	12.00	12.00	12.00	12.00	12.00
1.07	1.08	1.09	1.10	1.11	1.12	1.12	1.13	♃	♀	♄	☉	☽	♂	☿	1.15	1.16	1.18	1.18	1.20	1.22	1.24
2.15	2.17	2.19	2.20	2.22	2.24	2.25	2.27	♂	☿	♃	♀	♄	☉	☽	2.30	2.32	2.35	2.37	2.40	2.44	2.48
3.23	3.25	3.28	3.31	3.33	3.36	3.38	3.41	☉	☽	♂	☿	♃	♀	♄	3.45	3.49	3.53	3.56	4.01	4.06	4.12
4.31	4.34	4.37	4.41	4.44	4.48	4.51	4.55	♀	♄	☉	☽	♂	☿	♃	5.00	5.05	5.10	5.15	5.21	5.29	5.37
5.39	5.42	5.47	5.51	5.55	6.00	6.04	6.09	☿	♃	♀	♄	☉	☽	♂	6.15	6.21	6.28	6.34	6.42	6.51	7.01

JUNE 24th to 30th, ANY YEAR, in South Latitude

Time Correction Tables

Cities in the United States

Time Zone Column

Some states have more than one time zone within them. Pay attention to the zone number. Here is the key for the time zones.

Zone 5   Eastern Standard Time EST

Zone 6   Central Standard Time CST

Zone 7   Mountain Standard Time MST

Zone 8   Pacific Standard Time PST

Zone 9   Alaska Standard Time AST

Zone 10 Hawaii Standard Time HST

Time Correction Column

A plus (+) sign preceding the number means that you *add* that number of minutes to the standard clock time to get Local Mean Time.

A minus (−) sign preceding the number means that you *subtract* that number of minutes to the standard clock time to get Local Mean Time.

The times given in the planetary hour tables are in Local Mean Time (LMT).

Latitude Column

The latitudes are given here in degrees and minutes. You will need to round off the latitude to the nearest odd-numbered degree in order to use the planetary hour tables. For example, 34°01′ is closest to 35°. On the other hand, while you would normally round off 33.38° to 34°, in this case you would stay with 33°, because that is the closest *odd-numbered* latitude.

ALABAMA

City	Time Zone	Time Cor.	Lat. North	
		mins.	°	′
Alexander City	6	+16	32	57
Anniston	6	+16	33	38
Birmingham	6	+12	33	30
Decatur	6	+12	34	35
Dothan	6	+18	31	13
Eufaula	6	+19	31	53
Fairfield	6	+13	33	29
Florence	6	+09	84	47
Gadsden	6	+16	34	01
Huntsville	6	+14	34	44
Mobile	6	+08	30	42
Montgomery	6	+15	32	21
Phenix City	5	−40	32	29
Selma	6	+12	32	24
Tuscaloosa	6	+10	33	11

ALASKA

City	Time Zone	Time Cor.	Lat. North	
Anchorage	9	−59	61	13
Barrow	9	−1:27	71	17
Bethel	9	−1:47	60	50
College	9	−51	64	51
Fairbanks	9	−51	64	50
Galena	9	−1:28	64	44
Juneau	9	+03	58	18
King Cove	9	−1:49	55	30
Kodiak	9	−1:10	57	47
Nome	9	−2:02	64	30

ARIZONA

City	Time Zone	Time Cor.	Lat. North	
Bisbee	7	−20	31	27
Casa Grande	7	−27	32	53
Chandler	7	−27	32	18
Clifton	7	−17	33	03
Douglas	7	−18	31	21
Flagstaff	7	−27	35	11
Fredonia	7	−30	36	57
Kingsman	7	−36	35	11
Lake Havasu City	7	−37	33	25
Mesa	7	−27	33	05

ARIZONA *(continued)*

City	Time Zone	Time Cor.	Lat. North	
		mins.	°	′
Nogales	7	−24	31	20
Phoenix	7	−28	33	27
Prescott	7	−30	34	32
Scottsdale	7	−28	33	31
Sierra Vista	7	−21	31	33
Sun City	7	−29	33	36
Tempe	7	−28	33	24
Tucson	7	−24	32	13
Yuma	7	−38	32	43

ARKANSAS

City	Time Zone	Time Cor.	Lat. North	
Batesville	6	−07	35	46
Benton	6	−10	34	34
Blytheville	6	−00	35	56
Camden	6	−11	33	35
Conway	6	−09	35	05
El Dorado	6	−11	33	13
Fayetteville	6	−17	36	04
Forrest City	6	−03	35	00
Fort Smith	6	−I8	35	23
Harrison	6	−12	36	14
Hope	6	−14	33	40
Hot Springs	6	−12	34	30
Jonesboro	6	−03	35	50
Little Rock	6	−09	34	43
Paragould	6	−02	36	03
Pine Bluff	6	−08	34	14
Texarkana	6	−16	33	26
West Memphis	6	−01	35	08

CALIFORNIA

City	Time Zone	Time Cor.	Lat. North	
Alameda	8	−09	37	46
Alturas	8	−02	41	29
Anaheim	8	+08	33	50
Bakersfield	8	+04	35	22
Barstow	8	+12	34	54
Berkeley	8	−09	3	52
Beverly Hills	8	+06	34	04
Burbank	8	+07	34	11

CALIFORNIA (continued)

City	Time Zone	Time Cor.	Lat. North	
		mins.	°	′
Chino	8	+09	34	00
Crescent City	8	–17	41	45
El Centro	8	+08	32	48
Eureka	8	–17	40	48
Freemont	8	–08	37	33
Fresno	8	+01	36	45
Fullerton	8	+08	33	52
Glendale	8	+07	34	09
Inglewood	8	+06	33	58
Long Beach	8	+07	33	46
Los Angeles	8	+07	34	03
Madera	8	–00	36	58
Modesto	8	–04	37	38
Napa	8	–09	38	18
Oakland	8	–09	37	48
Oceanside	8	+10	33	12
Ontario	8	+09	34	04
Palm Springs	8	+14	33	50
Palo Alto	8	–09	37	26
Pasadena	8	+07	34	09
Pomona	8	+09	34	03
Porterville	8	+04	36	03
Redding	8	–10	40	35
Redlands	8	+11	34	04
Richmond	8	–09	37	56
Riverside	8	+10	33	57
Sacramento	8	–06	38	35
Salinas	8	–07	36	41
San Bernardino	8	+11	34	07
San Diego	8	+11	32	43
San Francisco	8	–10	37	47
San Jose	8	–08	37	20
San Leandro	8	–09	37	44
San Mateo	8	–09	37	34
Santa Ana	8	+08	33	44
Santa Barbara	8	+01	34	25
Santa Cruz	8	–08	36	59
Santa Monica	8	+06	34	01
Santa Rosa	8	–11	38	26
South Lake Tahoe	8	+00	38	57

CALIFORNIA *(continued)*

City	Time Zone	Time Cor.	Lat. North	
		mins.	°	'
Stockton	8	–05	37	57
Ukiah	8	–13	39	09
Vallejo	8	–09	38	06
West Hollywood	8	+07	34	05
Whittier	8	+08	33	59

COLORADO

City	Time Zone	Time Cor.	Lat. North	
Alamosa	7	–03	37	28
Aspen	7	–07	39	11
Boulder	7	–01	40	02
Burlington	7	+11	39	18
Canon City	7	–01	38	24
Colorado Springs	7	+01	38	50
Denver	7	+00	39	44
Dove Creek	7	-16	37	46
Durango	7	-12	37	17
Englewood	7	+00	39	38
Fort Collins	7	–00	40	35
Grand Junction	7	–14	39	04
Greeley	7	+01	40	25
La Junta	7	+06	37	59
Longmont	7	–00	40	10
Meeker	7	–12	40	02
Pueblo	7	+02	38	15
Salida	7	–04	38	32
Trinidad	7	+02	37	10
Wray	7	+11	40	04

CONNECTICUT

City	Time Zone	Time Cor.	Lat. North	
Bridgeport	5	+07	41	10
Bristol	5	+08	41	40
Danbury	5	+06	41	19
Derby	5	+08	41	20
Hartford	5	+09	41	45
Meriden	5	+09	41	32
Middletown	5	+09	41	34
Milford	5	+08	41	13

CONNECTICUT (*continued*)

City	Time Zone	Time Cor.	Lat. North	
		mins.	°	'
New Britain	5	+09	41	40
New Haven	5	+08	41	18
New London	5	+12	41	21
Norwalk	5	+06	41	07
Stamford	5	+06	41	03
Torrington	5	+08	41	48
Waterbury	5	+08	41	33
West Haven	5	+08	41	16
Willimantic	5	+11	41	45

DELAWARE

Brookside	5	−03	39	40
Dover	5	−02	39	09
Lewes	5	−01	38	46
Newark	5	−03	39	41
Wilmington	5	−02	39	45

DISTRICT OF COLUMBIA

Washington	5	−08	38	54

FLORIDA

Bartow	5	−27	27	54
Boca Raton	5	−20	26	21
Clearwater	5	−21	27	58
Daytona Beach	5	−24	29	12
Fort Lauderdale	5	−21	26	07
Fort Walton Beach	6	+14	30	24
Gainesville	5	−29	29	39
Haines City	5	−26	28	06
Jacksonville	5	−27	30	20
Key West	5	−27	24	33
Lakeland	5	−28	28	03
Miami	5	−21	25	46
Naples	5	−27	26	08
Orlando	5	−26	28	32
Palm Bay	5	−22	28	02

FLORIDA (continued)

City	Time Zone	Time Cor.	Lat. North
		mins.	° '
Pensacola	6	+11	30 25
Sarasota	5	–30	27 20
St. Petersburg	5	–31	27 46
Tallahassee	5	–37	30 26
Tampa	5	–30	27 57
Warrington	6	+11	30 23

GEORGIA

City	Time Zone	Time Cor.	Lat. North
Albany	5	–37	31 35
Americus	5	–37	32 04
Athens	5	–34	33 58
Atlanta	5	–38	33 45
Augusta	5	–28	33 28
Brunswick	5	–26	31 09
Columbus	5	–40	32 28
Covington	5	–35	33 36
Decatur	5	–37	33 46
Douglas	5	–31	31 30
Gainesville	5	–35	34 17
Griffin	5	–37	33 15
LaGrange	5	–40	33 02
Macon	5	–35	32 50
Marietta	5	–38	33 57
Rome	5	–41	34 15
Savannah	5	–24	32 05
Thomasville	5	–36	30 50
Valdosta	5	–33	30 50
Waycross	5	–29	31 12

HAWAII

City	Time Zone	Time Cor.	Lat. North
Hana	10	–24	20 45
Hanalei	10	–38	22 12
Hilo	10	–20	19 43
Honolulu	10	–31	21 18
Kahului	10	–26	20 54
Kalaupapa	10	–28	21 11
Kawaihae	10	–23	20 02
Kilauea	10	–38	22 13

HAWAII *(continued)*

City	Time Zone	Time Cor.	Lat. North
		mins.	° ′
Lihue	10	−37	21 59
Pearl City	10	−32	21 24
Wailuku	10	−26	20 53
Waipahu	10	−32	21 23

IDAHO

City	Time Zone	Time Cor.	Lat. North
Boise	7	−45	43 37
Bonners Ferry	8	+45	48 41
Caldwell	7	−47	43 40
Coeur d'Alene	8	+13	47 41
Dubois	7	−29	44 11
Grangeville	8	+16	45 56
Idaho Falls	7	−28	43 28
Lewiston	8	+12	46 25
Moscow	8	+12	46 44
Nampa	7	−46	43 32
Pocatello	7	−30	42 52
Rexburg	7	−27	43 50
Salmon	7	−38	45 10
Twin Falls	7	−38	42 34
Wallace	8	+16	47 28

ILLINOIS

City	Time Zone	Time Cor.	Lat. North
Aurora	6	+07	41 45
Belleville	6	+00	38 31
Bloomington	6	+00	40 29
Brookfield	6	+09	41 49
Canton	6	−00	40 33
Carbondale	6	+03	37 44
Centralia	6	+03	38 31
Champaign	6	+07	40 07
Chicago	6	+09	41 51
Cicero	6	+09	41 51
Decatur	6	+04	39 50
Des Plaines	6	+08	42 02
Dixon	6	+02	41 50
East St. Louis	6	−01	38 37
Effingham	6	+06	39 07

ILLINOIS *(continued)*

City	Time Zone	Time Cor.	Lat. North	
		mins.	°	′
Elgin	6	+07	42	02
Evanston	6	+09	42	02
Freeport	6	+02	42	18
Galesburg	6	–01	40	57
Jacksonville	6	–01	39	44
Joliet	6	+08	41	31
LaGrange	6	+08	41	48
Lincoln	6	+02	40	09
Macomb	6	–03	40	28
Moline	6	–02	41	30
Ottawa	6	+05	41	21
Peoria	6	+02	40	42
Quincy	6	–06	39	56
Rockford	6	+04	42	16
Springfield	6	+01	39	48
Waukegan	6	+09	42	22

INDIANA

City	Time Zone	Time Cor.	Lat. North	
Anderson	5	–43	40	06
Bloomington	5	–46	39	09
Columbus	5	–44	39	12
Connersville	5	–41	39	38
Crawfordsville	5	–47	40	02
Crown Point	6	+10	41	25
East Chicago	6	+10	41	38
Elkhart	5	–44	41	41
Evansville	6	+10	37	59
Fort Wayne	5	–40	41	08
Franklin	5	–44	39	29
Gary	6	+11	41	36
Goshen	5	–43	41	35
Hammond	6	+10	41	35
Indianapolis	5	–45	39	46
Kokomo	5	–44	40	29
Lafayette	5	–47	40	25
Marion	5	–43	40	33
Muncie	5	–41	40	11

INDIANA *(continued)*

City	Time Zone	Time Cor.	Lat. North	
		mins.	°	′
Portage	6	+11	41	34
Seymour	5	−44	38	58
Shelbyville	5	−43	39	31
South Bend	5	−45	41	41
Terre Haute	5	−50	39	28
Vincennes	5	−50	38	41

IOWA

City	Time Zone	Time Cor.	Lat. North	
Ames	6	−14	42	02
Burlington	6	−04	40	48
Carroll	6	−19	42	04
Cedar Rapids	6	−07	42	00
Clinton	6	−01	41	51
Council Bluffs	6	−23	41	16
Davenport	6	−02	41	31
Decorah	6	−07	43	18
Des Moines	6	−14	41	36
Dubuque	6	−03	42	30
Fort Dodge	6	−17	42	30
Fort Madison	6	−05	40	38
Iowa City	6	−06	41	40
Marshalltown	6	−12	42	03
Mason City	6	−13	43	09
Muscatine	6	−04	41	25
Oskaloosa	6	−11	41	18
Ottumwa	6	−09	41	00
Sioux City	6	−26	42	30
Spencer	6	−21	43	08
Waterloo	6	−09	42	30

KANSAS

City	Time Zone	Time Cor.	Lat. North	
Arkansas City	6	−28	37	04
Atchison	6	−20	39	34
Coffeyville	6	−28	37	02
Colby	6	−44	39	24
Dodge City	6	−40	37	45
El Dorado	6	−27	37	49
Garden City	6	−43	37	58

KANSAS *(continued)*

City	Time Zone	Time Cor.	Lat. North
		mins.	° ′
Great Bend	6	–35	38 22
Hays	6	–38	38 53
Hutchinson	6	–32	38 03
Independence	6	–23	37 14
Kansas City	6	–19	39 06
Lawrence	6	–21	38 58
Liberal	6	–44	37 03
Manhattan	6	–26	39 11
Olanthe	6	–19	38 53
Phillipsburg	6	–37	39 45
Pittsburg	6	–19	37 25
Salina	6	–30	38 50
Topeka	6	–23	39 03
Wichita	6	–29	37 41

KENTUCKY

City	Time Zone	Time Cor.	Lat. North
Ashland	5	–31	38 28
Bowling Green	6	+14	37 00
Covington	5	–38	39 05
Danville	5	–39	37 39
Elizabethtown	5	–43	37 42
Fort Thomas	5	–38	39 04
Frankfort	5	–39	38 12
Glasgow	6	+16	37 00
Hazard	5	–33	37 15
Henderson	6	+10	37 50
Hopkinsville	6	+10	36 52
Lexington	5	–38	38 03
Louisville	5	–43	38 15
Madisonville	6	+10	37 20
Middlesborough	5	–35	36 36
Newport	5	–38	39 05
Owensboro	6	+12	37 46
Paducah	6	+06	37 05
Somerset	5	–38	37 05
Winchester	5	–27	37 59

LOUISIANA

City	Time Zone	Time Cor.	Lat. North
		mins.	° '
Abbeville	6	−09	29 58
Alexandria	6	−10	31 19
Bastrop	6	−08	32 47
Baton Rouge	6	−05	30 27
Bogalusa	6	+01	30 47
Hammond	6	−02	30 30
Houma	6	−02	29 36
Jonesboro	6	−11	32 14
Lafayette	6	−08	30 14
Lake Charles	6	−13	30 14
Minden	6	−13	32 31
Monroe	6	−08	32 31
New Orleans	6	−00	29 58
Opelousas	6	−08	30 32
Shreveport	6	−15	32 30
Tallulah	6	−05	32 24

MAINE

City	Time Zone	Time Cor.	Lat. North
Auburn	5	+19	44 06
Augusta	5	+21	44 19
Bangor	5	+25	44 48
Biddeford	5	+18	43 30
Brunswick	5	+20	43 55
Caribou	5	+28	46 52
Dover-Foxcroft	5	+23	45 11
Frenchville	5	+27	46 41
Houlton	5	+29	46 08
Lewiston	5	+19	44 06
Machias	5	+30	44 43
Millinocket	5	+25	45 39
Portland	5	+19	43 40
Presque Isle	5	+28	46 41
Sanford	5	+17	43 26
Stratton	5	+18	45 08
Waterville	5	+21	44 33

MARYLAND

City	Time Zone	Time Cor.	Lat. North	
		mins.	°	′
Annapolis	5	–06	38	59
Baltimore	5	–06	39	17
Bethesda	5	–08	38	59
Cambridge	5	–04	38	34
Catonsville	5	–07	39	16
Cumberland	5	–15	39	39
Frederick	5	–10	39	25
Hagerstown	5	–11	39	38
Oakland	5	–18	38	20
Ocean City	5	–00	38	20
Potomac	5	–09	39	01
Salisbury	5	–02	38	22
Seabrook	5	–07	38	59
Silver Spring	5	–09	39	00

MASSACHUSETTS

City	Time Zone	Time Cor.	Lat. North	
Amesbury	5	+16	42	50
Amherst	5	+10	42	22
Attleboro	5	+15	41	57
Boston	5	+16	42	21
Cambridge	5	+16	42	22
Fall River	5	+15	41	42
Framingham	5	+14	42	17
Gloucester	5	+17	42	37
Hyannis	5	+19	41	40
Lawrence	5	+15	42	42
Lowell	5	+15	42	39
New Bedford	5	+16	41	37
North Adams	5	+08	42	27
Pittsfield	5	+07	42	27
Plymouth	5	+17	41	57
Quincy	5	+16	42	15
Salem	5	+16	42	28
Springfield	5	+10	42	06
Taunton	5	+16	41	54
Worcester	5	+13	42	16

MICHIGAN

City	Time Zone	Time Cor.	Lat. North	
		mins.	°	'
Adrian	5	−36	41	54
Ann Arbor	5	−35	42	17
Battle Creek	5	−41	42	19
Bay City	5	−36	43	36
Big Rapids	5	−42	43	42
Benton Harbor	5	−46	42	09
Cadillac	5	−42	44	15
Cheboygan	5	−38	45	38
Detroit	5	−32	42	20
Flint	5	−35	43	01
Grand Rapids	5	−43	42	58
Houghton	5	−54	47	07
Jackson	5	−38	42	15
Kalamazoo	5	−42	42	17
Lansing	5	−38	42	44
Marquette	5	−50	46	33
Midland	5	−37	43	37
Mount Clemens	5	−31	42	36
Muskegon	5	−45	43	14
Niles	5	−45	41	50
Owosso	5	−37	43	00
Pontiac	5	−33	42	38
Port Huron	5	−30	42	58
Saginaw	5	−36	43	25
Sault Ste. Marie	5	−37	46	20
Traverse City	5	−42	44	46
Wyoming	5	−43	42	55

MINNESOTA

Albert Lea	6	−13	43	40
Austin	6	−12	43	40
Baudette	6	−18	48	42
Brainerd	6	−17	46	21
Crookston	6	−26	47	46
Duluth	6	−08	46	47
Fairmont	6	−18	43	39
Faribault	6	−13	44	18
Fergus Falls	6	−24	46	17

MINNESOTA *(continued)*

City	Time Zone	Time Cor.	Lat. North	
		mins.	°	′
Grand Marais	6	−01	47	45
Grand Rapids	6	−14	47	14
Hibbing	6	−12	47	25
Mahnomen	6	−24	47	19
Mankato	6	−16	44	10
Marshall	6	−23	44	27
Minneapolis	6	−13	44	59
Minnetonka	6	−14	44	55
Moorhead	6	−27	46	52
Northfield	6	−13	44	27
Ortonville	6	−26	45	18
Owatonna	6	−13	44	05
Rochester	6	−10	44	01
Silver Bay	6	−05	47	18
St. Cloud	6	−17	45	34
St. Paul	6	−12	44	58
Winona	6	−07	44	03
Worthington	6	−22	43	37

MISSISSIPPI

Biloxi	6	+04	30	24
Brookhaven	6	−02	31	35
Canton	6	−00	32	37
Clarksdale	6	−02	34	12
Cleveland	6	−03	33	45
Columbus	6	+06	33	30
Corinth	6	+06	34	56
Greenville	6	−04	33	25
Greenwood	6	−01	33	31
Gulfport	6	+04	30	22
Hattiesburg	6	+03	31	20
Jackson	6	−01	32	17
Kosciusko	6	+02	33	03
Laurel	6	+03	31	42
McComb	6	−02	31	15

MISSISSIPPI (continued)

City	Time Zone	Time Cor.	Lat. North
		mins.	° '
Meridian	6	+05	32 22
Natchez	6	−05	31 35
Picayune	6	+01	30 31
Tupelo	6	+05	34 15
Vicksburg	6	−03	32 21
Yazoo City	6	−02	32 51

MISSOURI

City	Time Zone	Time Cor.	Lat. North
Cape Girardeau	6	+02	37 18
Carthage	6	−17	37 11
Chillicothe	6	−14	39 49
Columbia	6	−09	38 57
Fulton	6	−08	38 51
Hannibal	6	−05	39 42
Independence	6	−18	39 05
Jefferson City	6	−09	38 35
Joplin	6	−18	37 05
Kansas City	6	−18	39 06
Kennett	6	−00	36 14
Kirksville	6	−20	70 11
Marshall	6	−13	39 07
Maryville	6	−20	40 21
Moberly	6	−10	39 25
Poplar Bluff	6	−02	37 56
Rolla	6	−07	37 57
Sedalia	6	−13	38 42
Sikeston	6	+02	36 53
Springfield	6	−13	37 13
St. Charles	6	−02	38 47
St. Joseph	6	−19	38 47
St. Louis	6	−01	38 38
West Plains	6	−01	36 44

MONTANA

City	Time Zone	Time Cor.	Lat. North
Anaconda	7	−32	46 08
Billings	7	−14	45 47
Bozeman	7	−24	45 41
Butte	7	−30	46 00

MONTANA *(continued)*

City	Time Zone	Time Cor.	Lat. North	
		mins.	°	′
Dillon	7	–31	45	13
Forsyth	7	–07	46	16
Great Falls	7	–25	47	30
Havre	7	–19	48	33
Helena	7	–28	46	36
Kalispell	7	–37	48	12
Lewistown	7	–18	47	04
Libby	7	–42	48	23
Malta	7	–11	46	24
Miles City	7	–03	46	24
Missoula	7	–36	46	52
Plentywood	7	+02	48	46
Red Lodge	7	–17	45	11
Shelby	7	–27	48	30
Sidney	7	+03	47	43
Wolf Point	7	–03	48	05

NEBRASKA

City	Time Zone	Time Cor.	Lat. North	
Beatrice	6	–27	40	16
Broken Bow	6	–39	41	24
Chadron	7	+08	42	50
Columbus	6	–29	41	26
Fairbury	6	–29	40	09
Falls City	6	–24	40	03
Fremont	6	–26	41	26
Grand Island	6	–33	40	55
Hastings	6	–33	40	35
Hyannis	7	+13	42	00
Lincoln	6	–27	40	48
McCook	6	–42	40	12
Norfolk	6	–30	42	02
North Platte	6	–43	41	07
Ogallala	7	+13	41	15
Omaha	6	–24	41	16
Papillion	6	–24	41	09
Scottsbluff	7	+08	41	52
Sidney	7	+08	41	09
Valentine	6	–42	42	52

NEVADA

City	Time Zone	Time Cor.	Lat. North	
		mins.	°	'
Austin	8	+12	39	30
Boulder City	8	+21	35	59
Carson City	8	+01	39	10
Elko	8	+17	40	50
Ely	8	+20	39	15
Goldfield	8	+11	37	42
Hawthorne	8	+05	38	31
Henderson	8	+20	36	02
Lake Tahoe	8	+00	39	01
Las Vegas	8	+20	36	10
Pioche	8	+22	37	56
Reno	8	+01	39	32
Sparks	8	+01	39	32
Sun Valley	8	+01	39	36
Vya	8	+01	41	35
Winchester	8	+20	36	08
Winnamucca	8	+09	40	58

NEW HAMPSHIRE

City	Time Zone	Time Cor.	Lat. North	
Berlin	5	+15	44	28
Claremont	5	+10	43	23
Concord	5	+14	43	12
Dover	5	+16	43	12
Exeter	5	+16	42	59
Keene	5	+11	42	56
Laconia	5	+14	43	32
Lancaster	5	+14	44	29
Lebanon	5	+11	43	38
Manchester	5	+14	43	00
Nashua	5	+14	42	46
Portsmouth	5	+17	43	04
Rochester	5	+16	43	18
Woodsville	5	+12	44	09

NEW JERSEY

City	Time Zone	Time Cor.	Lat. North	
		mins.	°	′
Atlantic City	5	+02	39	22
Bridgeton	5	−01	39	25
Camden	5	−01	39	56
Cape May	5	+00	38	56
Clifton	5	+03	40	51
East Orange	5	+03	40	46
Elizabeth	5	+03	40	40
Englewood	5	+04	40	54
Hackensack	5	+04	40	52
Hoboken	5	+04	40	45
Jersey City	5	+04	40	44
Morristown	5	+02	40	48
Newark	5	+03	40	44
New Brunswick	5	+02	40	29
Passaic	5	+03	40	51
Paterson	5	+03	40	55
Perth Amboy	5	+03	40	31
Princeton	5	+01	40	20
Rutherford	5	+04	40	50
Trenton	5	+01	40	13
Vineland	5	−00	39	29

NEW MEXICO

Alamogordo	7	−04	32	54
Albuquerque	7	−07	35	05
Artesia	7	+02	32	50
Carlsbad	7	+03	32	25
Clayton	7	+07	36	27
Clovis	7	+07	34	24
Deming	7	−11	32	16
Farmington	7	−13	36	44
Gallup	7	−15	35	32
Hobbs	7	+07	32	19
Las Cruces	7	−07	32	19
Las Vegas	7	−01	35	36
Los Alamos	7	−05	35	53
Raton	7	+02	36	54
Reserve	7	−15	33	43

NEW MEXICO *(continued)*

City	Time Zone	Time Cor.	Lat. North	
		mins.	°	′
Roswell	7	+02	33	24
Santa Fe	7	−04	35	41
Silver City	7	−13	32	46
Tucumcari	7	+05	35	10

NEW YORK

City	Time Zone	Time Cor.	Lat. North	
Albany	5	+05	42	39
Auburn	5	−06	42	56
Batavia	5	−13	43	00
Binghamton	5	−04	42	06
Buffalo	5	−15	42	53
Cortland	5	−05	42	36
Dunkirk	5	−17	42	29
Elmira	5	−07	42	06
Freeport	5	+06	40	39
Geneva	5	−08	42	52
Glens Falls	5	+05	43	26
Ithaca	5	−06	42	26
Jamestown	5	−17	42	06
Kingston	5	+04	41	56
Lake Placid	5	+04	44	17
Lockport	5	−15	43	10
Long Beach	5	+05	40	35
Massena	5	00	44	58
Mastic	5	+09	40	48
New York	5	+04	40	43
Niagara Falls	5	−16	43	06
Ogdensburg	5	−02	44	42
Olean	5	−14	42	05
Oswego	5	−06	43	27
Poughkeepsie	5	+04	41	42
Rochester	5	−10	43	09
Rome	5	−02	43	13
Saratoga Springs	5	+05	43	05
Schenectady	5	+04	42	49
Syracuse	5	−05	43	03
Tonawanda	5	−15	43	01
Utica	5	−01	43	06
Watertown	5	−04	43	58

NORTH CAROLINA

City	Time Zone	Time Cor.	Lat. North	
		mins.	°	'
Albermarle	5	–21	35	21
Asheville	5	–30	35	36
Burlington	5	–18	36	05
Charlotte	5	–23	35	14
Durham	5	–16	36	00
Elizabeth City	5	–05	36	18
Fayetteville	5	–15	35	03
Gastonia	5	–25	35	16
Goldsboro	5	–12	35	23
Greensboro	5	–19	36	04
Kannapolis	5	–22	35	29
Laurinburg	5	–18	34	46
Murphy	5	+36	35	05
Raleigh	5	–14	35	46
Rocky Mount	5	11	35	56
Salisbury	5	–22	35	40
Thomasville	5	–20	35	53
Wilmington	5	–12	34	13
Winston-Salem	5	–21	36	06

NORTH DAKOTA

City	Time Zone	Time Cor.	Lat. North	
Ashley	6	–38	46	01
Bismarck	6	–43	46	48
Bottineau	6	–42	48	50
Bowman	7	+06	46	11
Carson	7	+14	48	55
Crosby	6	–53	46	25
Dickinson	7	+09	46	52
Fargo	6	–27	46	53
Grafton	6	–30	48	25
Grand Forks	6	–28	47	55
Jamestown	6	–35	46	55
Langdon	6	–33	48	46
Mandan	6	–43	46	50
Minot	6	–45	48	14
Rugby	6	–40	48	22
Williston	6	–54	48	08

OHIO

City	Time Zone	Time Cor.	Lat. North	
		mins.	°	′
Akron	5	−26	41	05
Ashtabula	5	−23	41	52
Barberton	5	−26	41	01
Cambridge	5	−26	40	02
Canton	5	−25	40	48
Chillicothe	5	−32	39	20
Cincinnati	5	−38	39	10
Cleveland	5	−27	41	30
Columbus	5	−32	39	58
Dayton	5	−37	39	45
Defiance	5	−37	41	17
Findlay	5	−35	41	03
Hamilton	5	−38	39	24
Lakewood	5	−27	41	29
Lorain	5	−29	41	27
Mansfield	5	−30	40	46
Marietta	5	−26	39	25
Marion	5	−33	40	35
Middletown	5	−38	39	31
Portsmouth	5	−32	38	44
Sandusky	5	−30	41	27
Springfield	5	−35	39	56
Steubenville	5	−23	40	22
Toledo	5	−34	41	40
Youngstown	5	−22	41	06
Zanesville	5	−28	39	56

OKLAHOMA

Ada	6	−27	34	46
Altus	6	−37	34	38
Ardmore	6	−29	34	10
Bartelsville	6	−24	36	45
Boise City	6	−50	36	44
Clinton	6	−36	35	31
Enid	6	−31	36	24
Guthrie	6	−30	35	53
Guymon	6	−46	36	41
Lawton	6	−34	34	36
Miami	6	−20	37	52
Midwest City	6	30	35	27
Muskogee	6	−21	35	45

OKLAHOMA *(continued)*

City	Time Zone	Time Cor.	Lat. North	
		mins.	°	′
Norman	6	–30	35	13
Oklahoma City	6	–30	35	28
Okmulgee	6	–24	35	38
Ponca City	6	–28	36	42
Sapulpa	6	–24	36	00
Stillwater	6	–28	36	07
Tahlequah	6	–20	35	55
Tulsa	6	–24	36	09
Woodward	6	–38	36	26

OREGON

City	Time Zone	Time Cor.	Lat. North	
Albany	8	–12	44	38
Ashland	8	–11	42	12
Astoria	8	–15	46	11
Baker	8	+08	44	47
Beavertown	8	–11	45	29
Coos Bay	8	–17	43	22
Corvallis	8	–13	44	34
Dalles	8	–05	45	36
Eugene	8	–12	44	03
Grants Pass	8	–13	42	26
Gresham	8	–10	45	30
Hillsboro	8	–12	45	31
Klamath Falls	8	–07	42	13
La Grande	8	+08	45	19
Lebanon	8	–12	44	32
McMinnville	8	–13	45	13
Medford	8	–11	42	19
Oregon City	8	–10	45	21
Pendleton	8	+05	45	40
Portland	8	–11	45	30
Roseburg	8	–13	43	13
Salem	8	–12	44	57
The Dalles	8	––04	45	35
Vale	7	–49	43	59

PENNSYLVANIA

City	Time Zone	Time Cor.	Lat. North	
		mins.	°	′
Allentown	5	−02	40	37
Altoona	5	−13	40	31
Ardmore	5	−01	40	00
Bethlehem	5	−01	40	37
Bristol	5	+01	40	06
Carbondale	5	−02	41	34
Carlisle	5	−09	40	12
Chambersburg	5	−11	39	56
Du Bois	5	−15	41	07
Erie	5	−20	42	08
Hanover	5	−08	39	48
Harrisburg	5	−07	40	16
Hazleton	5	−04	70	57
Jeanette	5	−18	40	20
Johnstown	5	−16	40	20
Lancaster	5	−05	40	02
McKeesport	5	−19	40	21
Meadville	5	−20	41	39
New Castle	5	−21	41	00
Philadelphia	5	−01	39	57
Pittsburgh	5	−20	40	26
Reading	5	−03	40	20
Scranton	5	−02	41	24
Wilkes-Barre	5	−08	41	14
Willlamsport	5	−08	41	14
York	5	−07	39	58

RHODE ISLAND

City	Time Zone	Time Cor.	Lat. North	
Cranston	5	+14	41	47
East Providence	5	+14	41	49
Newport	5	+15	41	29
Pawtucket	5	+14	41	53
Providence	5	+14	41	50
Warwick	5	+14	41	41
Westerly	5	+13	41	23
Woonsocket	5	+14	42	00

SOUTH CAROLINA

City	Time Zone	Time Cor.	Lat. North	
		mins.	°	'
Aiken	5	–27	33	34
Anderson	5	–31	34	30
Charleston	5	–20	32	47
Columbia	5	–24	34	00
Conway	5	–16	33	50
Florence	5	–19	34	12
Gaffney	5	–26	35	04
Greenville	5	–29	34	51
Lancaster	5	–23	34	43
Myrtle Beach	5	–16	33	41
Newberry	5	–26	34	16
Orangeburg	5	–23	33	29
Port Royal	5	–23	32	23
Rock Hill	5	–24	34	55
Spartanburg	5	–27	34	57
Summerville	5	–21	33	01
Sumter	5	–21	33	56

SOUTH DAKOTA

Aberdeen	6	–33	45	28
Belle Fourche	7	+04	44	40
Brookings	6	–27	44	19
Buffalo	7	+06	45	35
Chamberlain	6	–37	43	48
Dupree	7	+14	45	03
Hot Springs	7	+06	43	26
Huron	6	–32	44	22
Mitchell	6	–32	43	43
Mobridge	6	–41	45	32
Pierre	6	–41	44	22
Rapid City	7	+07	44	05
Sioux Falls	6	–27	43	33
Sisseton	6	–28	45	39
Vermillion	6	–30	42	47
Watertown	6	–28	44	54
Yankton	6	–29	42	53

TENNESSEE

City	Time Zone	Time Cor.	Lat. North	
		mins.	°	′
Athens	5	–38	34	27
Chattanooga	5	–41	35	03
Clarksville	6	+10	36	32
Cleveland	5	–39	35	10
Columbia	6	+12	35	37
Cookeville	6	+18	36	10
Dyersburg	6	+02	36	02
Franklin	6	+12	35	55
Jackson	6	+05	35	37
Johnson City	5	–29	36	19
Kingsport	5	–30	38	33
Knoxville	5	–36	35	58
Lawrenceburg	6	+11	35	14
Memphis	6	+00	35	09
Mufreesboro	6	+14	35	51
Nashville	6	+13	36	10
Paris	6	+07	36	18
Shelbyville	6	+14	35	29
Springfield	6	+12	38	31

TEXAS

Abilene	6	–39	32	26
Amarillo	6	–47	35	13
Austin	6	–31	30	16
Beaumont	6	–16	30	05
Big Spring	6	–46	32	15
Brownsville	6	–30	25	54
Corpus Christi	6	–30	27	48
Dallas	6	–27	32	47
Denison	6	–26	33	45
Denton	6	–29	33	12
Dumas	6	–48	35	51
Eagle Pass	6	–42	28	42
El Paso	7	–06	31	46
Fort Worth	6	–29	32	44
Freeport	6	–21	28	57
Galveston	6	–19	29	18
Grand Prairie	6	–28	32	45
Harlingen	6	–31	26	11
Houston	6	–21	29	45
Kingsville	6	–31	27	30

TEXAS *(continued)*

City	Time Zone	Time Cor.	Lat. North	
		mins.	°	′
Laredo	6	−38	27	30
Longview	6	−19	32	30
Lubbock	6	−47	33	35
Lufkin	6	−19	33	35
Marfa	6	−56	30	18
McAllen	6	−33	26	12
Mesquite	6	−26	32	46
Midland	6	−48	32	00
Odessa	6	−50	31	51
Pecos	6	−54	31	25
Port Arthur	6	−16	29	54
Port Lavaca	6	−26	28	37
San Angelo	6	−42	31	28
San Antonio	6	−34	29	25
Sweetwater	6	−42	32	28
Temple	6	−29	31	05
Texarkana	6	−16	33	25
Tyler	6	−21	32	21
Victoria	6	−28	28	48
Waco	6	−29	31	33
Wichita Falls	6	−34	33	55

UTAH

Brigham City	7	−28	41	31
Cedar City	7	−32	37	41
Cottonwood	7	−17	39	04
Logan	7	−27	41	44
Magna	7	−28	40	42
Mexican Hat	7	−19	37	09
Monticello	7	−28	40	40
Ogden	7	−28	41	13
Orem	7	−27	40	18
Price	7	−23	39	36
Provo	7	−27	40	14
Salt Lake City	7	−28	40	46
Spanish Fork	7	−26	40	07
Springville	7	−26	40	10
Tooele	7	−29	40	32
Vernal	7	−18	40	27

VERMONT

City	Time Zone	Time Cor.	Lat. North
		mins.	° ′
Bennington	5	+07	42 53
Burlington	5	+07	44 30
Montpelier	5	+10	44 15
Newport	5	+11	44 56
Rutland	5	+08	43 37
Springfield	5	+10	43 18
St. Albans	5	+08	44 49

VIRGINIA

City	Time Zone	Time Cor.	Lat. North
Alexandria	5	−08	38 48
Arlington	5	−08	38 53
Bristol	5	−29	36 36
Charlottesville	5	−14	38 02
Danville	5	−18	36 35
Fredericksburg	5	−10	38 18
Front Royal	5	−13	38 55
Harrisonburg	5	−15	38 27
Lynchburg	5	−17	37 23
Newport News	5	−06	36 59
Norfolk	5	−06	36 51
Petersburg	5	−10	37 14
Radford	5	−22	37 10
Portsmouth	5	−05	36 47
Richmond	5	−10	37 33
Roanoke	5	−20	37 16
Staunton	5	−16	38 09
Virginia Beach	5	−04	36 51
Waynesboro	5	−16	38 04
Williamsburg	5	−07	37 16
Winchester	5	−13	39 11

WASHINGTON

City	Time Zone	Time Cor.	Lat. North
Aberdeen	8	−15	46 58
Anacortes	8	−10	48 31
Bellingham	8	−10	48 46
Bremerton	8	−11	47 34
Centralia	8	−12	46 43
Colville	8	+08	48 33
Ellensburg	8	−02	47 00

WASHINGTON *(continued)*

City	Time Zone	Time Cor.	Lat. North	
		mins.	°	′
Everett	8	–09	47	59
Kelso	8	–12	46	09
Kennewick	8	+03	46	13
Longview	8	–12	46	08
Mount Vernon	8	–09	48	24
Olympia	8	–12	47	02
Pasco	8	+04	46	14
Port Angeles	8	–14	48	07
Pullman	8	+11	46	44
Puyallup	8	–09	47	11
Richland	8	+03	46	17
Seattle	8	–10	47	36
Spokane	8	+10	47	40
Tacoma	8	–10	47	15
Vancouver	8	–11	45	38
Walla Walla	8	+07	46	04
Wenatchee	8	–01	47	25

WEST VIRGINIA

City	Time Zone	Time Cor.	Lat. North	
Beckley	5	–25	37	47
Bluefield	5	–25	37	16
Charleston	5	–26	38	21
Clarksburg	5	–21	39	17
Elkins	5	–19	38	56
Fairmont	5	–21	39	29
Huntington	5	–30	38	25
Keyser	5	–16	39	26
Martinsburg	5	–12	39	27
Morgantown	5	–20	39	38
Moundsville	5	–23	39	55
Parkersville	5	–26	39	16
Weirton	5	–22	40	25
Wheeling	5	–23	40	04
Williamson	5	–29	37	40

WISCONSIN

City	Time Zone	Time Cor.	Lat. North	
Appleton	6	+06	44	16
Ashland	6	–04	46	35
Beaver Dam	6	+05	43	27
Beloit	6	+04	42	30
Chippewa Falls	6	–05	44	56

WISCONSIN *(continued)*

City	Time Zone	Time Cor.	Lat. North	
		mins.	°	'
De Pere	6	+08	44	27
Eau Claire	6	−06	44	49
Fond du Lac	6	+06	43	46
Green Bay	6	+08	44	31
Janesville	6	+04	42	41
Kenosha	6	+09	42	35
La Crosse	6	−05	43	48
Madison	6	+02	43	04
Manitowoc	6	+09	44	05
Marinette	6	+09	45	06
Marshfield	6	−01	44	40
Milwaukee	6	+08	43	02
Monroe	6	+01	42	36
Oshkosh	6	+06	44	01
Racine	6	+09	42	44
Sheboygan	6	+09	43	45
Superior	6	−08	46	43
Watertown	6	+05	43	12
Waukesha	6	+07	43	01
Wausau	6	+01	44	58
West Bend	6	+07	43	25

WYOMING

City	Time Zone	Time Cor.	Lat. North	
Casper	7	−05	42	52
Cheyenne	7	+01	41	08
Cody	7	−16	44	32
Evanston	7	−24	41	16
Gilette	7	−02	44	17
Green River	7	−18	41	32
Jackson	7	−23	43	29
Lander	7	−15	42	50
Laramie	7	−02	41	19
Medicine Bow	7	−05	41	54
Newcastle	7	+03	43	51
Rawlins	7	−09	41	47
Sheridan	7	−08	44	46
Thermopolis	7	−13	43	39
Torrington	7	+03	42	04

International Cities

This table gives the latitudes and time corrections necessary to use the planetary hour tables for a selection of international cities. The selection is rather arbitrary—a limited list of cities that, in the author's opinion, are so well-known that the city names are as familiar as the names of the countries. Cities are given in alphabetical order, followed by the country. You may be able to time-correct fairly accurately for a city that is not on this list by finding a city in the same time zone that is at approximately the same latitude and longitude.

The first column of numbers, under the heading "Time Zone," is the standard time zone for the city. Each zone is assigned a number according to its distance from the zero point at Greenwich, England. A minus (–) sign in front of a zone number means that the city is east of Greenwich, or *east* longitude. Zone numbers without the minus sign are in *west* longitude time zones. Remember these zones assume standard time. Many countries have summer time changes similar to daylight saving time in the United States. Be aware of local time variations in order to determine if an additional correction might be needed during some times of the year.

The second column of numbers, under the heading "Time Cor.," is the number of minutes for which you must correct your standard clock time in each city in order to obtain the Local Mean Time needed to use the planetary hour tables. A plus (+) sign means you must add the given number of minutes to standard clock time to get LMT. A minus sign means you must subtract the given number of minutes from standard time to get LMT.

The third column, "Lat.," shows the latitude of the city. To use the planetary hour tables, round off the city latitude to the nearest latitude column in the tables. The tables have columns for each two degrees of latitude, in *odd* numbers only. For example, even though 31 N 57 is closest to 32°, you would still look under the 31° column in the planetary hour tables, because 31 is the closest *odd* number. On the other hand, 16 N 51 would be rounded off to 17°. Since the lowest latitude given on the tables is 27°, you will have to interpolate. Notice that the minutes of latitude decrease about 2 minutes per column. Imagine 5 more columns, going from latitude 27° down to latitude 17°. At two minutes each, figure 10 minutes less than whatever time is given under latitude 27°.

For southern latitude locations, such as 36 S 52, be sure to take note of the date range given at the *bottom* each of the planetary hour table. The dates for each table are different for southern latitudes than for northern latitudes.

INTERNATIONAL CITIES

City	Time Zone	Time Cor.	Lat.	Long.
		mins.	° ′	
Amman, Jordan	–2:0	+0:24	31 N 57	35 E 56
Acapulco, Mexico	6:0	–0:40	16 N 51	99 W 55
Addis Ababa, Ethiopia	–3:0	–0:25	9 N 2	38 E 42
Alexandria, Egypt	–2:0	–0:24	31 N 12	29 E 54
Algiers, Algeria	–1:0	–0:48	36 N 47	3 E 3
Amsterdam, Netherlands	–1:0	–0:40	52 N 22	4 E 54
Athens, Greece	–2:0	–0:25	37 N 58	23 E 43
Auckland, New Zealand	–12:0	–0:21	36 S 52	174 E 46
Baghdad, Iraq	–3:0	–0:02	33 N 21	44 E 25
Bangkok, Thailand	–7:0	–0:18	13 N 45	100 E 31
Barcelona, Spain	–1:0	–0:51	41 N 23	2 E 11
Beijing, China	–8:0	–0:14	39 N 55	116 E 25
Beirut, Lebanon	–2:0	+0:22	33 N 53	35 E 30
Belfast, N. Ireland	0:0	–0:24	54 N 35	5 W 55
Belgrade, Serbia	–1:0	+0:22	44 N 50	20 E 30
Berlin, Germany	–1:0	–0:07	52 N 30	13 E 22
Bogotá, Columbia	5:0	+0:04	4 N 36	74 W 5
Bombay, India	–5:30	–0:39	18 N 58	72 E 50
Bonn, Germany	–1:0	–0:32	50 N 44	7 E 5
Brasília, Brazil	3:0	–0:12	15 S 47	47 W 55
Bucharest, Romania	–2:0	–0:16	44 N 26	26 E 6
Budapest, Hungary	–1:0	+0:16	47 N 30	19 E 5
Buenos Aires, Argentina	3:0	–0:54	34 S 36	58 W 27
Cairo, Egypt	–2:0	+0:05	30 N 3	31 E 15
Calcutta, India	–5:30	+0:23	22 N 32	88 E 22
Calgary, Canada	7:0	–0:36	51 N 3	114 W 5
Cape Town, S. Africa	–2:0	–0:46	33 S 55	18 E 22
Caracas, Venezuela	4:0	–0:28	10 N 30	66 W 56

INTERNATIONAL CITIES (continued)

City	Time Zone	Time Cor.	Lat.	Long.
		mins.	° ′	
Casablanca, Morocco	0:0	–0:30	33 N 39	7 W 35
Chongqing, China	–8:0	–0:55	29 N 34	106 E 35
Copenhagen, Denmark	–1:0	–0:10	55 N 40	12 E 35
Damascus, Syria	–2:0	+0:25	33 N 30	36 E 18
Delhi, India	–5:30	–0:21	28 N 40	77 E 13
Dover, England	0:0	+0:05	51 N 8	1 E 19
Dublin, Ireland	0:0	–0:25	53 N 20	6 W 15
Düsseldorf, Germany	–1:0	–0:33	51 N 12	6 E 47
Edinburgh, Scotland	0:0	–0:13	55 N 57	3 W 13
Edmonton, Canada	7:0	–0:34	53 N 33	113 W 28
Florence, Italy	–1:0	–0:15	43 N 46	11 E 15
Frankfurt, Germany	–1:0	–0:25	50 N 7	8 E 40
Geneva, Switzerland	–1:0	–0:35	46 N 12	6 E 9
Glasgow, Scotland	0:0	–0:17	55 N 53	4 W 15
Guadalajara, Mexico	6:0	–0:53	20 N 40	103 W 20
Guatemala City, Guatemala	6:0	–0:02	14 N 38	90 W 31
Halifax, Canada	4:0	–0:14	44 N 39	63 W 36
Hanoi, Vietnam	–7:0	+0:03	21 N 2	105 E 51
Havana, Cuba	5:0	–0:29	23 N 8	82 W 22
Helsinki, Finland	–2:0	–0:20	60 N 10	24 E 58
Hiroshima, Japan	–9:0	–0:10	34 N 24	132 E 27
Hong Kong, (Victoria) China	–8:0	–0:23	22 N 17	114 E 9
Inverness, Scotland	0:0	–0:17	57 N 27	4 W 15
Istanbul, Turkey	–2:0	–0:04	41 N 1	28 E 58
Jerusalem, Israel	–2:0	+0:21	31 N 46	35 E 14
Johannesburg, South Africa	–2:0	–0:08	26 S 15	28 E 0
Kabul, Afgahanistan	–4:30	+0:07	34 N 31	69 E 12
Kathmandu, Nepal	–5:45	–0:04	27 N 43	85 E 19
Kiev, Ukraine	–2:0	+0:02	50 N 26	30 E 31
Kraków, Poland	–1:0	+0:20	50 N 3	19 E 58
La Paz, Bolivia	4:0	–0:33	16 S 30	68 W 9
Lima, Peru	5:0	–0:08	12 S 3	77 W 3
Lisbon, Portugal	0:0	–0:37	38 N 43	9 W 8
Liverpool, England	0:0	–0:12	53 N 25	2 W 55
London, England	0:0	–0:01	51 N 30	0 W 10
Luanda, Angola	–1:0	–0:07	8 S 48	13 E 14
Luxembourg, Luxembourg	–1:0	–0:35	49 N 36	6 E 9
Madrid, Spain	–1:0	–1:15	40 N 24	3 W 41

INTERNATIONAL CITIES (*continued*)

City	Time Zone	Time Cor.	Lat.	Long.
		mins.	° ′	
Manila, Philippines	−8:0	+0:04	14 N 35	121 E 0
Marrakech, Morocco	0:0	−0:32	31 N 38	8 W 0
Marseille, France	−1:0	−0:38	43 N 18	5 E 24
Mecca, Saudi Arabia	−3:0	−0:21	21 N 27	39 E 49
Melbourne, Australia	−10:0	−0:20	37 S 49	144 E 58
Mexico City, Mexico	6:0	−0:37	19 N 24	99 W 9
Milan, Italy	−1:0	−0:23	45 N 28	9 E 12
Monaco, Monaco	−1:0	−0:30	43 N 42	7 E 23
Montevideo, Uruguay	3:0	−0:45	34 S 53	56 W 11
Montréal, Canada	5:0	+0:06	45 N 31	73 W 34
Moscow, Russia	−3:0	−0:30	55 N 45	37 E 35
Munich, Germany	−1:0	−0:14	48 N 8	11 E 34
Nairobi, Kenya	−3:0	−0:33	1 S 17	36 E 49
Naples, Italy	−1:0	−0:03	40 N 51	14 E 17
Nice, France	−1:0	−0:31	43 N 42	7 E 15
Oslo, Norway	−1:0	−0:17	59 N 55	10 E 45
Ottawa, Canada	5:0	−0:03	45 N 25	75 W 42
Panama City, Panama	5:0	−0:18	8 N 58	79 W 32
Paris, France	−1:0	−0:51	48 N 52	2 E 20
Port-au-Prince, Haiti	5:0	+0:11	18 N 32	72 W 20
Prague, Czech Republic	−1:0	−0:02	50 N 5	14 E 26
Puerto Vallarta, Mexico	6:0	−1:01	20 N 37	105 W 15
Québec, Canada	5:0	+0:15	46 N 49	71 W 14
Rio de Janeiro, Brazil	3:0	+0:07	22 S 54	43 W 14
Rome, Italy	−1:0	−0:10	41 N 54	12 E 29
Rotterdam, Netherlands	−1:0	−0:42	51 N 55	4 E 28
San José, Costa Rica	6:0	+0:24	9 N 56	84 W 5
San Juan, Puerto Rico	4:0	−0:24	18 N 28	66 W 7
Santiago, Chile	4:0	−0:43	33 S 27	70 W 40
Santo Domingo, Dominican Republic	4:0	−0:40	18 N 28	69 W 54
São Paulo, Brazil	3:0	−0:06	23 S 32	46 W 37
Sarajevo, Bosnia	−1:0	+0:14	43 N 52	18 E 25
Seoul, S. Korea	−9:0	−0:32	37 N 33	126 E 58
Seville, Spain	−1:0	−1:24	37 N 23	5 W 59
Shanghai, China	−8:0	+0:06	31 N 14	121 E 28
Singapore, Singapore	−8:0	−1:05	1 N 17	103 E 51
St. Petersburg, Russia	−3:0	−0:59	59 N 55	30 E 15
Stockholm, Sweden	−1:0	+0:12	59 N 20	18 E 3

INTERNATIONAL CITIES *(continued)*

City	Time Zone	Time Cor.	Lat.	Long.
		mins.	° ′	
Sydney, Australia	−10:0	+0:05	33 S 52	151 E 13
T'aipei, China	−8:0	+0:06	25 N 3	121 E 30
T'aipei, Taiwan	−8:0	+0:06	25 N 3	121 E 30
Tehran, Iran	−3:30	−0:04	35 N 40	51 E 26
Tel Aviv, Israel	−2:0	+0:19	32 N 4	34 E 46
Tijuana, Mexico	8:0	+0:12	32 N 32	117 W 1
Tokyo, Japan	−9:0	+0:19	35 N 42	139 E 46
Toronto, Canada	5:0	−0:18	43 N 39	79 W 23
Vancouver, Canada	8:0	−0:12	49 N 16	123 W 7
Venice, Italy	−1:0	−0:11	45 N 27	12 E 21
Veracruz, Mexico	8:0	+0:20	32 N 25	115 W 5
Vienna, Austria	−1:0	+0:05	48 N 13	16 E 20
Warsaw, Poland	−1:0	+0:24	52 N 15	21 E 0
Xi'an, China	−8:0	−0:45	34 N 15	108 E 52
Zurich, Switzerland	−1:0	−0:26	47 N 23	8 E 32

5

Quick Timing with an Astrological Calendar

In the introduction, I promised you some hints for "quick and dirty" electional astrology. Here they are. You will need an astrological calendar. I will base my instructions on Llewellyn's *Astrological Pocket Planner*. Llewellyn's *Daily Planetary Guide* will also work. Both of these calendar/day planner publications have the aspect times listed, in both Eastern and Pacific Standard Times. If you live in Central or Mountain Standard Time, you'll have to make a mental adjustment to account for the time change. For Central Standard Time, your actual clock time for the aspect is one hour less than the listed calendar time for Eastern Standard Time; for Mountain Standard Time, your actual clock time for the aspect is two hours less than Eastern (or one hour more than Pacific).

The *Daily Planetary Guide* lists the aspects with times on each day. The calendar section of the *Astrological Pocket Planner* only has times for the Moon's phases and sign, but in the back of the book there's a complete daily aspect listing that includes aspect times. This small book is the easiest resource to carry with you.

You will need to know how to read the astrological glyphs for the planets, signs, and primary aspects. Here they are.

Astrology Glyphs

Sun	☉	Aries	♈
Moon	☽	Taurus	♉
Mercury	☿	Gemini	♊
Venus	♀	Cancer	♋
Mars	♂	Leo	♌
Jupiter	♃	Virgo	♍
Saturn	♄	Libra	♎
Uranus	♅	Scorpio	♏
Neptune	♆	Sagittarius	♐
Pluto	♇	Capricorn	♑
conjunction	☌	Aquarius	♒
sextile	⚹	Pisces	♓
square	□	Moon void of course	v/c
trine	△	retrograde planet	℞
opposition	☍	(℞ after planet glyph)	

There are other minor aspects listed in the example resources, and also the glyphs for the four major asteroids, but just disregard them.

I look at asteroids and minor aspects for other types of astrological work. Horary and electional astrology are different, though, and they have their own sets of rules. Only the lights (the Sun and Moon) and the eight planets are used. Some *really* traditional astrologers will only use the Sun through Saturn. The only aspects used are the Ptolemaic aspects (named for the ancient Greek astrologer Ptolemy): the conjunction, sextile, square, trine, and opposition.[1]

The idea of looking at a chart for the moment that a question is asked (horary) or deliberately setting a chart for the moment you intend to do something (electional) is the closest astrology comes to being an oracle. Astrologers differ quite a bit in regard to which set of rules they follow, but one thing I think all of them would tell you is *don't thwart the oracle!* What this means is that once you have decided on the rules you will follow, then look at the chart (or calendar) and follow your preset rules.

The planets will not always say what you'd like them to say. Nevertheless, always make sure to follow your preset rules! Don't try to manipulate the oracle by adding in an extra asteroid or minor aspect in the hopes that it will then tell you something you like better. When you do that, the oracle can quite easily become a trickster.

By this reasoning, if you philosophically disagree with the simplified system I present here, and you really prefer to consider the minor aspects and/or asteroids (or any other factor), fine. You have the free will to choose. *But,* if you want this "oracle" to work, then you must use your rules *consistently.* If you don't like what you are seeing with your final outcome based on an asteroid or minor aspect, don't then decide, "Oh, that's not really part of traditional horary/electional anyway—I'll just disregard it." Beware—this would be thwarting the oracle, turning it into a trickster that will trip you up.

If your quick look at the astrological factors, according to the method given in this chapter, speaks to you clearly, then use it. If it doesn't, or if the message is unclear, use another form of guidance as to what you should do.

If you don't like what the planets are saying for a given time, you can choose a better time. However, if you absolutely must act within that time frame, don't despair. Remember that the power is not with the planets, it is within you! You can study the themes of the string of aspects leading to the final outcome and accept the challenge to proceed according to the highest manifestation of those themes. You can take the high road, behave in an ethical manner, and even work appropriate magick to influence a more favorable outcome. As long as you do that, things are likely to work out for the best anyway, despite an apparent unfavorable indication from the planets. On the other hand, if the outcome is not what you would prefer, look at the situation for the lesson to be derived from it, accept that perhaps you needed that lesson, reflect and learn from it, and move on.

Rules for the Moon Void of Course

The time period for the Moon void of course begins when the calendar shows the symbol "☽ v/c" and ends when you see "☽ enters ♉" (or any sign). The Moon is said to be void of course after it makes its last aspect to the other planets in the sign it is in until it enters the next sign. Use this no-aspect time period to attend to routine matters, or for continuing projects you've already begun. It's a good time for thinking things over, and also for meditation or for ritual activities where the intent is worship. I've led some wonderful rituals during void-of-course Moons. Do not, however, choose this time to work magick for mundane purposes. For this, it is best to wait until the Moon enters a new sign.

By the same token, wait until the void period is over before initiating any mundane activity in which you want action or results. For example, applying for a job is not an activity likely to work out as you hope if you do it during a Moon void—it would be best to wait to take action until the Moon is back on course. On the other hand, if what you want is for nothing out of the ordinary to happen, go ahead and do it. For example, you want nothing but routine with your income tax return—no audit—so sending it off during a Moon void is okay, and likely even a good choice. Purchases follow a similar rule. Routine grocery shopping is fine, but buying a new car during the void is a bad idea.

Rules for the Phases of the Moon

Review the material in chapter 3 on Moon timing for details on keeping your desired activity in sync with the phases of the Moon. In general, when you are glancing at an astrological calendar to determine if this is a good day to act, you are more than likely thinking of doing something that will move you forward, so the waxing Moon is much more favorable than the waning Moon. If you can wait a few days until the Moon will be waxing again, it's best to do so. If you can't wait, then tailor your intent to the waning Moon theme. Be aware that for initiating activity, the onset of the New Moon is an instinctive and therefore somewhat unreliable period, when things are not completely thought through. Unless you really trust your instincts and they have usually proven right, it might be best to set your activity for several hours after the given time for the New Moon, or even for the day after, so that things have time to jell. This may vary depending on the string of aspects.

Rules for Aspects

Action proceeds according to the succession of aspects from when the Moon enters a sign until it is void of course. The *outcome* is symbolized by the last aspect the Moon makes before it changes signs. Therefore, *the final aspect of the Moon within a sign is highly important.*

The conjunction is the strongest aspect. Whether it is "good" or not depends on which planet the Moon is conjunct, and whether that planet's theme (see chapter 2) supports your purpose—especially when the conjunction is the final aspect.

Sextiles and trines mean a smooth flow of action and, if the final aspect, a favorable outcome.

Squares mean that something about the situation is challenging. This does not necessarily mean "bad"; just perhaps not as easy as you'd like, so be aware. *A square as final aspect is generally to be avoided.* It could work out with some combinations of planets, but with others, is best avoided.

Oppositions are generally not as challenging as squares, but should still be noted as potentially challenging, *especially if the final aspect.* Something needs to be balanced, or someone may be in opposition or antagonistic to your intent.

Only applying aspects matter. If the time at which you want to act is in the middle of a sequence of aspects while the Moon is passing through a sign, the only aspects you should consider in projecting the potential success of your action are those that happen *after* your chosen time.

Rules for Retrogrades

If a retrograde planet is involved in the string of aspects you are considering, and it rules the matter in question (see chapter 2 for what each planet rules), use extra caution. The outer planets are all retrograde for many months out of every year, so you can hardly avoid them. Fast-moving planets (Mercury, Venus, or Mars) retrograde for shorter periods of time, but these times can be more problematic, especially for the things or situations they rule. Again, sometimes you just can't avoid retrogrades, but be aware of them and use additional caution.

For this timing technique, if you are using *Llewellyn's 2001 Astrological Pocket Planner*, you will be using the Moon timing information given on the days in the main calendar section of the *Pocket Planner* (where there's room to make notes), and you will also be using the aspectarian pages in the back of the book.

In seeking an advantageous time, first scan the main calendar section for a day when the Moon is in the appropriate phase for what you want to do, and if it is reasonable for your time frame, also look for the Moon in an appropriate sign. Make a note of the time it enters that sign and the time it goes void of course. Now turn to the same day in the back of the book and jot down all the aspects (σ, $\ast$, $\square$, $\triangle$, and σ^{o} *only* for traditional electional astrology) between when the Moon enters the sign and when it goes void, and what time each aspect occurs. Within that time frame, next look for the best planetary hour for your intent. If you take action during that planetary hour, the remaining aspects that occur after the time you've chosen can be read for insight into how the process is likely to unfold. The final aspect of the Moon before it goes void of course indicates the outcome.

I have used this method both to decide at a glance whether a day was most likely good for a mundane purpose, such as making an important call, pushing or holding back in a negotiation, scheduling a social event, or other things of this type. If a mundane matter was of major importance, I would do a full election chart and also do an update on my natal chart—but when one is busy, and I usually am, there just isn't time. For many matters, the choice is do—or do charts! For such things, the quick calendar glance is a worthwhile tool. I have also used this same quick method to design rituals or spells, the better to flow with the cosmic current, one might say. I will give you examples of the method for both mundane and magickal purposes, using randomly selected days for the months of October through December of 2001. Demonstrations usually make things much clearer than a mere set of instructions.

The demonstrations given here use Eastern Standard Time for looking at the *Astrological Pocket Planner*, and the latitude 42 N 44 (Kensington, NH) for the planetary hours. Should you decide to use any of the information given here for the demonstration dates, remember that times will be off unless you adjust for your own time zone and location.

Electional Timing Examples for Mundane Matters
A Time to Make a Phone Call

You are determined to make an important phone call this week to someone you need to persuade to make a change, a decision in your favor. You expect that the communication might be tense, but you really can't put it off much longer. The call must be made during business hours sometime between Monday, October 22 and Friday, October 26, 2001, and it is now Monday morning. When should you make this call?

As you scan the pages of your *2001 Astrological Pocket Planner*, you see that the Moon begins the week in Capricorn. Okay, this might work, although Capricorn tends to stick to tradition . . . but whoa! It says "☿ D" (see figure 3). Mercury is stationary direct today, but not until 7:24 P.M. tonight. "Too late for my call," you are thinking, "and I don't want to make it on the retrograde. Better wait until at least Tuesday."

On Tuesday, the Moon is still in Capricorn. Turning to the aspectarian for October, you see that there's only one aspect to consider during that business day: Moon conjunct Mars at 3:11 P.M. Turning back to the calendar page, you see that 3:11 P.M. is also "☽ v/c," the Moon void of course. There's not much help here. You'd want to make the call before the Moon is void, which means you'd have only the applying aspect to Mars. That's action, but it's also

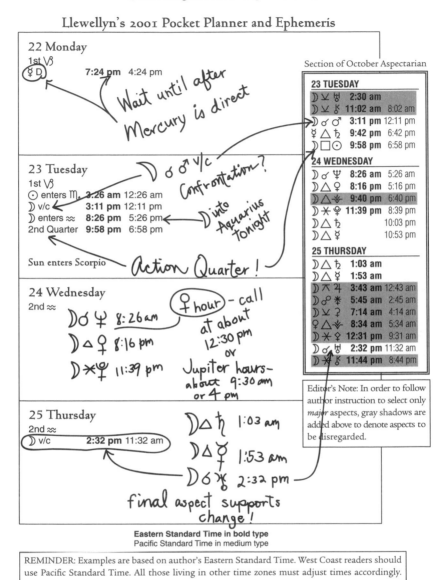

Figure 3. A Time to Make a Phone Call.

potentially confrontational and you'd prefer an easier approach. "Well," you might say, "I hate to procrastinate, but the Moon goes into Aquarius Tuesday evening, a sign more supportive of openness to change, and just after that it begins the second quarter, the 'crisis of action.' That's also supportive of what I want to accomplish. I think I'll look at the string of aspects for Aquarius."

Turn back to the aspectarian. The first aspect of the Moon is the square to the Sun (the second quarter). Jot down the string of aspects on the calendar pages (as is shown in the illustration) so you don't have to keep thumbing back and forth in the *Pocket Planner*. Use only Ptolemaic aspects, including the times they occur.

At a glance, then, what do we have? After the conjunction to Neptune, which is too early anyway, we have an easy flow and supportive string of sextile and trine aspects, ending with a conjunction to Uranus. Uranus is the planet of change. Good! Any time you choose to call before the void at 2:32 P.M. on Thursday would be okay, though it would be best to take advantage of the applying trines to Venus and Mercury by calling on Wednesday. Don't be afraid of the aspects to Pluto and Saturn, for Pluto supports change and Saturn supports the discipline necessary to manifest desired change. The best choice on Wednesday takes advantage of the amicable and pleasant applying trine to Venus.

Now let's look for a good planetary hour. Wednesday is Mercury's day—good for communication. A Venus hour would be good for rapport on this phone call. Looking in the planetary hour tables for October 16 to 23, you see that for Wednesday, at latitude 43°, the Venus hour begins at 11:46 A.M. and ends at 12:41 P.M. If you think you might have trouble getting through to the person you're calling at lunch time, the Jupiter hours should also be good times, from 9:15 A.M. to 9:45 A.M. or around 3:45 P.M. to 4:15 P.M. (Note that I am choosing times that are safely in the middle of each planetary hour, since for the purpose of this example I am glancing at the more generalized perpetual planetary hour tables in this book, rather than running a computer list based on exact time and location.)

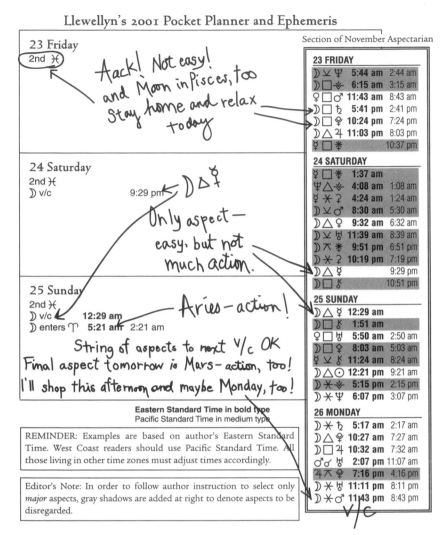

Figure 4. A Time to Shop.

A Time to Shop

You are tempted to fight the crowds to do some holiday shopping on the day after Thanksgiving. The advertised sales are great. You decide to check the aspects first to see how easy or difficult this day might be. On Friday, November 23, 2001, the Moon is in

Pisces all day long. Scanning ahead, you note that the Moon is void of course on Sunday at 12:29 A.M., and enters Aries at 5:21 A.M. Looking at the aspects that would be applying as you shop on Friday, you see the Moon square Saturn at 5:41 P.M. and the Moon square Pluto at 10:24 P.M. (see figure 4). Aack! Do you still want to fight those crowds on Friday? I wouldn't. Better to work quietly alone, clean up from the holiday, rest, read, meditate, dream . . . take a nice Piscean day off. Saturday looks a little easier, with the only applying aspect being the final one before the Moon goes void: the Moon trine Mercury. Still, you might feel more like charging out to deal with those crowds when the Moon is in Aries on Sunday—and the Aries aspect string is more suggestive of action and accomplishment, too.

Electional Timing Examples for Magick

A Time for Letting Go

While we're looking at November in our *2001 Astrological Pocket Planner*, let's scan for a good time to do a banishing ritual. While Mother Nature is letting go of the old in preparation for rebirth, it makes sense that it's an excellent season for us to do the same. On Wednesday and Thursday, November 14 and 15, 2001, we see the notations for the New Moon, and we also note that the New Moon time marks the void of course, as well (see figure 5). November's main Sun sign is Scorpio, the sign of death and rebirth, so we know that this New Moon (Sun conjunct Moon) must be the Scorpio New Moon. How perfect! We can do a banishing ritual with the Moon dark in Scorpio. Our final aspect before the void of course will be the New Moon, with its promise of rebirth and new beginnings.

Note that the New Moon void of course is at 1:40 A.M. Eastern Standard Time on Thursday, but at 10:40 P.M. Pacific Standard Time on Wednesday. That means Tuesday evening, with the Moon in Scorpio, but not so close yet to the New Moon, is a better choice

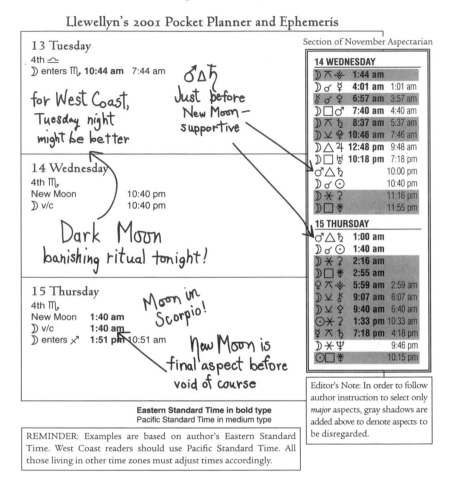

Figure 5. A Time for Letting Go.

if you're on the West Coast. For those of you on the East Coast, Wednesday evening would also be fine.

Scanning the aspectarian, we find generally supportive aspects of the Moon, with Mars trine Saturn occurring just before the New Moon, confirming this timing as a good choice for our intent. If you also wish to choose an appropriate planetary hour, look for Mars in the nocturnal hours for your area, in keeping with the Scorpio theme.

For a simple and appropriate working, consecrate a black candle to your purpose. You could tie knots in a black thread, binding yourself to a resolution to break an unwanted habit, and then wind the thread around the candle to burn with it. Or you could write out what you want to release on a parchment paper and burn it in a metal bowl. If any other person is involved in any way in your choice to let go, be sure that you add "with harm to none" to your intent. Conclude by letting your black candle burn all the way down. Make sure it is in a metal holder and in a very safe place (like behind a fireplace grate or in the middle of a shower stall) unless you plan to stay right near it (and awake!) all the while it is burning.

A Time for Charging Success and Prosperity

In scanning for a good time to charge the new, notice that on Christmas Day there's a waxing Moon in Taurus, the sign most easily associated with prosperity (see figure 6). It's a second-quarter Moon, a time for action and building energy. This is a day in which many people will be involved with family gatherings—perhaps not the best time for spellwork. But I have an idea for a little spell that can combine the intent of success and prosperity for the year ahead with seasonal fun for the family. Let's look to see if other aspects support this time. Aha! At 11:10 P.M. on December 25, 2001, the Moon sextiles Jupiter. This can work!

Supportive aspects to Mars and Mercury follow, and the final void-of-course aspect is the Moon square Uranus. Well, that final one might cause me to reconsider for some types of mundane matters, but I consider it no good reason not to use our chosen December 25 evening time for this particular ritual. It could just mean the potential for a surprising opportunity lies ahead, if one is alert and accepts the challenge to go with it. Squares are action, they can work positively—especially when one's intent is positive and spiritually focused.

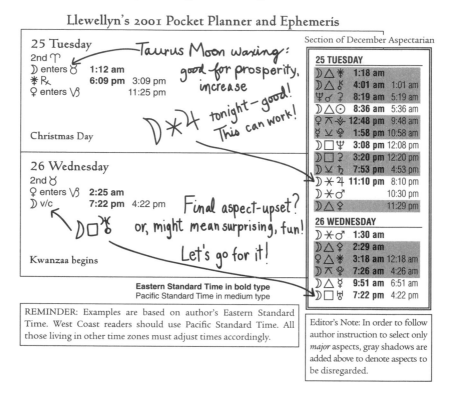

Figure 6. A Time for Charging Success and Prosperity.

In making a lovely potpourri of fragrant seasonal ingredients, you are including a wealth of prosperity correspondences. You can make it alone that evening, before the Moon sextiles Jupiter, or do it as a group project. Gather the ingredients ahead of time, or you might wish to ask everyone who will be present to bring an ingredient to contribute. At that time of the year, pine needles are easy to find, even if pine is not native to your area. Use fresh, fragrant pine as a base. Other things that are good to add include juniper with berries, cedar, cypress, cinnamon sticks, whole cloves, rosemary leaves, basil, sage, small pine cones, winter berry (if you can find some wild), and gold and silver glitter.

Assemble all your ingredients, along with a large bowl, cauldron, or pan to mix them in. If you are alone or with a group that is familiar with or receptive to magick, a formal circle-casting can be performed around your work area, and you could call on the Lady of the Moon to aid you in understanding and fulfilling this Taurus Full Moon theme.

If your group is not familiar with magick, you still ethically need their consent to participate in it. If they are not receptive at all, work later and alone. If they are receptive, here is an explanation that should be comfortable for everyone's enjoyment and participation with appropriate intent, as well as being simple enough for children to understand.

> *We've just passed the time of year, the winter solstice, long dark nights came to an end, and from now on, the sunlight will be steadily increasing, each day getting a little longer. In ancient times, the winter solstice was called the rebirth of the Sun, and it was considered a time of new beginnings. I've asked you to bring evergreen and spices so that we can make a special potpourri together. By doing this, we can bless and give energy to our ideas for new beginnings for the new year to come. Everyone can take some home and keep it in a bowl where the good smells will be a reminder of the plans we've shared, and of what we plan to do to make them happen. If you like, you can keep a little bit in a closed container as a success charm.*

As all of you together break the ingredients into small pieces and combine them, keep the conversation directed to each person's plans, hopes, and dreams for the year to come. Encourage lively and upbeat conversation, supporting each other's dreams and what steps may be taken toward making them happen. In this way, the potpourri is charged with intent. If the group is receptive, you could take the container out under the Taurus Full Moon (or visualize her if weather does not permit going out to see her) and hold it aloft while saying:

> *O Lady of the Taurus Moon*
> *Bless my potpourri*
> *For insight gained while making it*

I give my thanks to thee
Your wisdom I will follow
Toward success, prosperity
Send now your light that I may share
This magick, blessed be!

Have little bags ready so everyone can take home a share of the finished potpourri. If you are doing this ritual alone, share your success and prosperity by making up little decorated bags of potpourri to give as gifts.

---

1. For readers who may be very new to astrology, an "aspect" is an angular relationship between two planets. Depending on the angle, aspects have different meanings. For example, 90° is called a square, and its primary keyword is "challenging"; 120° is a trine, and its primary keyword is "ease." Faster-moving planets make aspects to slower-moving planets. When the faster-moving planet is approaching the angle to the slower-moving planet, the aspect is said to be "applying." After it passes the exact angle, it is said to be "separating."

6

Planetary Meditations

Meditation is an excellent way to bring yourself into greater attunement with the planets, or with any archetypal energy, for that matter. Meditation and visualization are also highly significant keys to your ability to be effective at magickal work. This chapter assists you with guided meditations for deeper understanding of each of the ten "planets" of classic astrology. Read them as a stimulation for your own imaginative use in creating alternative meditations, or, if you wish, read them aloud into a tape recorder to play later while you meditate.

As a general rule for your times of meditation, find a place of privacy and do what you can to cut yourself off from interruption. Take the phone off the hook, and if you share your space with others, ask that they not disturb you. Meditation is a time for *you*, a time when it is right to be selfish and insist on undisturbed time, privacy, and silence. It is something you do for yourself, to restore your soul, to learn, and to open yourself to hearing the wisdom of the Universe, the sound of the spheres. If prayer is talking *to* God (however you perceive him, her, or it, and by whatever name), meditation is when you *listen* and learn, and become One with the divine, the Whole. There is no more important thing you can do than this.

Think of the planets as faces and expressions of the One. The One is All—too awesome to understand in its entirety. In the introduction to Doreen Valiente's "Charge of the Goddess," it is said that Her body encompasses the Universe. Still, the Goddess, God, Athena, Pan, Jehovah, Allah, Yahweh . . . no matter what name we may use, in truth all gods and goddesses are One—our human attempt to name the unknowable. In the limitations of our physical selves, we can see only certain facets of that which is essentially unknowable, and this is no doubt why the human mind seeks to personalize deity and give it names and personalities, thus to bring it down to a more comprehensible concept.

The planets are bodies in our solar system, they are age-old archetypal entities for faces of deity, and they are symbols for aspects of our inner selves. Meditate upon the planets to receive insight into how you may best express each of them in fulfillment of your life purpose and spiritual growth.

Becoming the Sun

Sit comfortably in a chair with your feet flat on the ground and your hands open, palms up on your knees. Breathe slowly and deeply. Begin to concentrate on the palm of your dominant hand. Visualize a ball of energy forming there. As you focus, the ball becomes warmer, and gradually it grows. It grows so large that soon you are feeling it balanced in both your palms. Feel the energy and heat, build it. The ball becomes larger and larger until it begins to encompass you. Visualize the ball growing until it completely surrounds you. You are a ball of glowing energy, solar energy, shining from the source of power, the life force within you. Like the Sun, you are the center of your own personal Universe. All things are seen from your perspective. Absolutely everything and everyone in your world revolves around you, reflecting you.

Visualize what and whom you find currently revolving around you. Notice which of these shine brightly back at you, and acknowledge them with an inner smile. Notice which of them are dimmed, or even nearly hidden from your view, as if covered by a cloud. Why might the clouds be there? Do you want them there? After all, you needn't focus your full energy everywhere at all times. If you want certain clouds to remain, thank them, and move on in your viewing.

Note if your energy feels somehow diminished by a particularly dark cloud. If so, why? After all, you are the Sun—nothing in your Universe can drain your power unless you permit it to do so. Build your energy, shine more brightly, and banish that cloud so that you can see clearly what lies beyond it. Can a stronger projection of the warmth and light of your being keep the cloud away and cause the person or thing beyond it to reflect your light back to you? Try it! In your imagination, can you now see light returning to you? If so, acknowledge the light with an inner smile and remember.

Begin to notice your breathing—slow, deep abdominal inhales through your nose, hold, and slow exhales through your mouth. At your own speed, return to normal consciousness.

When you return to your world, remembering your visualization of creating increased light in the area of life from which you banished the dark cloud, and project light, love, and warmth in that direction. Increased light will most likely be reflected back to you.

If, however, despite your very best efforts, the cloud keeps returning, then go back into meditation. This time, banish the dark cloud again and replace it with a dense but fluffy and happy cloud that hides the unresponsive situation from your view. You do not have to focus your energy toward anything that drains it. You are the power! Nothing can make you unhappy unless you empower it to do so. It is quite possible to share the world with a problem area or person, and even interact as necessary, while not allowing it to touch your inner being. Just let it orbit on by you, think of your happy cloud shield, and refocus. Direct your light and energy toward areas of your life that shine back at you!

Becoming the Moon

Since the Moon is associated with memory, roots, the subconscious mind, and soul purpose, this Moon meditation will be a past-life regression, assisting you in gaining insight from a former life that will be meaningful to you in the present and teach you something about the emotions that emerge from the deep mysteries within your soul. Allow your intuition free rein. The very first thing that comes to your mind as you hear questions asked of you is what you are to remember.

Sit or lie down comfortably and relax, breathing deeply and steadily. Close your eyes. In your mind's eye, see yourself in a dark forest clearing, in the dark of the Moon. Only the stars show through the trees overhead, but you have a lantern that enables you to see that around the clearing there are many paths you could take. From this magical forest clearing, you have the opportunity to choose a pathway into your distant past. Your body will remain right here, comfortable and safe, but your Spirit can travel freely, safely, and completely without fear through the magical forest, visiting other nights and other phases of the Moon in lives you have lived before.

Choose a path and begin walking along it. At the count of twelve, you will be deep in an altered state of consciousness. You will emerge from the path and find yourself in the past: 1, 2, 3, 4 relaxing and deepening, 5, 6, 7, 8, deeper and deeper, 9, 10, 11, and 12.

Step out of the forest and look to the sky. Do you see the Moon? What phase is it in? If you are not sure, remember its shape so you can draw it later. Look around and describe the place you find yourself in. Look down at your feet. Are you wearing shoes? What kind of shoes? Something is within your scene that allows you to see your reflection. What is it? Look at yourself. Are you male or female? About how old are you? What is your name? Describe yourself. Describe how you are feeling at this moment. What are your emotions and concerns? Look around you again. Is anyone else there? If so, who? How do you feel about that person or persons?

Now it is nearly dawn. Look toward the sunrise and describe it. What do you expect to do on this day? How do you feel about it?

If your Spirit could live again, in the far-distant future, in another lifetime, another body, what would you say to that being? The very first thing that comes to your mind is instinctively the right thing for you to say.

As your present self receives this final message from your past self, your Spirit moves back toward the forest path and enters it: 12, 11, 10, relaxed and remembering, 8, 7, remembering all you have learned, 6, 5, and you are back in the clearing, 4, 3, 2, and 1. You're back in your body, comfortable and relaxed. You will remember all you learned from your past self as you open your eyes.

Write down all your remembrances so that you can reflect on them later. The phase of the Moon that you saw when you first entered your past life will be an additional clue to its message. Review the interpretations of the Moon phases in chapter 3 for clues.

Becoming Mercury

Let's try a thinking meditation to help with a problem you need to resolve—a change to which you must adapt, or a decision that must be made, perhaps regarding the best approach to take in a difficult communication.

In a relaxed position, close your eyes and breathe deeply for a few moments, paying close attention to your breathing. Inhale slowly through your nose, allowing your abdomen to expand. Hold for three heartbeats and then exhale very slowly through your mouth. As you feel more and more relaxed, and your breathing, still deep and slow, becomes automatic, visualize yourself on a cliff overlooking a beautiful landscape in the distance. Feel the breeze blowing across your body, refreshing you. Overhead are billowy clouds, shot through with the rays of the Sun. Suddenly, out of a Sun ray, a figure appears, gliding effortlessly toward you, ever more closely, a figure with winged feet—Mercury!

Mercury speaks: "You are perplexed about a problem . . . perhaps you feel of two minds, or even three? I come to you as the messenger from your Sun. Though my style may vary a bit, it's my job to help you think and communicate in a manner that fulfills your highest purpose. Let's look at your problem from some different perspectives. I have a little magick to help you do so."

With that, Mercury whizzes around you three times in a flash of golden light. Feel the wind he raises! Suddenly, you find that you are not one person, but three! Without knowing exactly how, you recognize each of the three of you as being an aspect of your consciousness: Young Self (subconscious), Adult Self (conscious mind), and High Self (superconsciousness).

Mercury speaks: "Now, Young Self, you will represent just what you most want in this situation. Speak of your desires, your wishes, your fears, and your fantasies. Hold nothing back. Cry, if you need to. Stamp your feet! Young you may be, but your wants are important. Better to get them out in the open now than to cry or otherwise behave badly after one of these other selves makes a decision you are unwilling to accept.

"Adult Self, you will represent the practical matters to be considered. Speak of the situation as it is, as logically and honestly as you possibly can. Speak of the facts, the pros and cons, and of what the result is likely to be, whichever way you decide to resolve the problem. Keep in mind that no matter what you decide, if Young Self is not at all in agreement, your decision may be for naught. You must listen carefully to the desires and fears expressed. Like any good parent with a child, you must listen and learn as you give loving guidance if you are to convince Young Self that your way is the right way.

"High Self, you are the one who represents the Path you have chosen to walk in this life. You are the Spiritual Self, the voice of conscience, the God/dess within. Serve as a mediator here, but gently and firmly state your case if either of these other two selves seem to be verging too far off the Path. You are the one who knows how much they may regret it later if the ultimate decision is in violation of conscience.

"The objective here is consensus. Discuss this matter thoroughly among you, with a willingness to both listen and speak. When you come to an agreement on a resolution to your problem, you will find yourselves as One once again." In a flash of wind and light, Mercury speeds off toward the center of the Sun.

Now, take as long as you like to carry on your discussion among your three selves. As the right choice becomes clear to you, feel your selves merging into one, bathed in a beautiful golden ray of the Sun. As a last light breeze blows around you, give silent thanks, and at your own speed, open your eyes and return to the world, confident that what you have decided to do is the right solution.

Becoming Mercury in Virgo

Mercury, especially in Virgo, is also about skill-building. Some sports champions have learned that meditating can assist them in finetuning their technique. Whatever you are trying to learn to do, whether it be a sport, a game, an art, a study, or mastering your computer, practice not just physically, but also in your mind. Try sessions of meditation where you first center yourself with any of the breathing or relaxation techniques that open the various guided meditations in this chapter, and invoke the power of Mercury and perhaps also that of Venus or Mars, as is appropriate to your particular skill-building objective. Then, in the meditative altered state of consciousness, visualize yourself performing beautifully whatever skill you are working to acquire. In your mind, go through all the motions in detail, doing them over again, if need be, until they flow perfectly. Enjoy that for a few moments, and then thank the higher powers and return to normal consciousness. What you have accomplished in your mind will manifest in improved physical performance.

Becoming Venus

Relax into a comfortable position, close your eyes, and breathe deeply. Imagine that you are outdoors in a lovely garden just as the

Sun has set. You can still feel its warmth in the air and enjoy the last bright, fiery colors of its light, but on your bare feet, the lush grass feels cool and moist from a short rainshower that ended just awhile ago. A cool, refreshing breeze ruffles the leaves and petals of the flowers. As you look upward, a bright point of light pops out in the darkening sky above you—Venus, evening star, first star— and the little childhood verse comes quickly to your mind as you say, "Starlight, star bright, first star I see tonight. I wish I may, I wish I might, have the wish I wish tonight!" Suddenly the light expands, and the Goddess appears, descending from the star point to a point below the star to the left, where she hovers in the sky before you and says, "Tell me what you wish, for I am Goddess of your earthly realm and I am that which you desire. What do you desire?" As you deal with your surprise and wonder how you should respond to her, the Goddess ascends upward toward a point to the right of the original star point, but still beneath it, and you see that her path is tracing a pentagram of light in the sky, the pentagram of invoking Earth–Spirit to manifestation. Now from the point of water, she says, "And I am the mystery of the waters, and the mystery of desire within your heart. From me all things proceed, and onto me they shall return." With that she glides gracefully to the left, hovering at the point of air, and continues, "Mind that your desire be attuned both to beauty and strength, to both power and compassion. Let there be honor and humility, mirth and reverence within you, for I am also the Goddess of balance in all things, the balance to which your soul must aspire."

Take a moment now to think of your wish, and feel in your soul if it is right for you at this time. Think also of the steps you may need to take to achieve your wish, as you gaze at the Goddess gliding down toward the fire point, where she says, "I wish you may, I wish you might, but the power to grant your wish lies not outside you, my child, but within. Have you the courage, the faith, the will to do what you must to achieve it? Know that my love is within you, and my love is the fire of your Spirit and of mine." Feel the warmth of that love build within you as you see the Goddess return to the point of starlight. As she vanishes within that bright point of light, hear her voice speak these final words to you: "And remember, I am with you always and I am that which you will find at the end of desire!"

Think quietly of your wish and of what you will do to fulfill it for a few more moments as you gaze at the star and remember the words of the Goddess. Then again be conscious of the fresh breeze across your body, the lush grass beneath your feet, and the beauty of the night as you return to your world, at your own speed, and open your eyes.

Becoming Mars

Try a moving meditation for Mars. An Aries woman in my coven led a meditation for our Beltane ritual that was truly inspiring and very sensual. It worked well in a group, but a similar idea would be perfect for a solitary practitioner seeking to become attuned with Mars energy.

Choose a good drumming tape or CD to play. Stand in the center of the room as your music begins. Visualize Mars as a bright, reddish star point of light far above your head and feel a red ray beaming down toward you, entering your body through the top of your head. Feel it warm, glowing, and flowing throughout your body, infusing you with warrior energy, banishing all fear, strengthening your will. Now visualize a tendril of that energy extending down from your feet like a tap root, rapidly growing down, down, down through the floor, through the soil, through the layers of Earth to the center molten core—the heart of the Earth Mother. Feel her energy coursing upward, entering your body, and flowing throughout. You are connected—Mars energy, Earth energy. Feel the power, the sensuality, and the warmth, and hear the irresistible rhythm of the drums as you begin to move your body with it. Think no more. Just feel. Move. Dance! You are the energy. Flow with it! Feel it in every cell of your body. Be alive! Move.

This is a meditation in which you can trance and become one with the energy you are creating. Continue moving and let yourself go. Experiment. Be free. Let the music take you to the point where you feel inside you the courage to take on whatever it is that you have invoked the power of Mars to create in your life. When you feel it within, then slow your movements gradually, sink to the floor, and ground your energy by allowing it to flow back into the Earth, while keeping what you need of it for yourself.

Becoming Jupiter

Sit comfortably with your feet flat on the floor and your hands relaxed on your lap. Close your eyes and visualize the number nine. Breathe steadily and slowly. As the nine dissolves and turns into an eight, you feel increasingly relaxed. Allow the eight to dissolve and be replaced with a seven. As soon as the seven becomes clear, dissolve it and replace it with a six. Continue on to zero, and with each number, become more and more relaxed: 5, 4, 3, 2, 1, and 0.

You are walking through a pathway with an arched ceiling held up by pairs of white stone columns. Each pair of columns is a bit taller than the one that came before, the ceiling arching higher and higher. With growing anticipation, you see that beyond the ninth pair of columns is the entrance to a grand temple. Let's count them as we pass: 1, 2, 3, 4, 5, 6, 7, 8, and 9. You are at the entrance to the temple and carved across the top of the door arch are the words "Temple of Wisdom." Enter. You find a gleaming, inlaid marble floor, and a soaring vaulted ceiling. Lighted purple candles in tall holders encrusted with amethysts line the walls and illuminate your view of the altar. In the center of the altar is a large oil lamp, which, like the candleholders, is encrusted with sparkling amethysts. Behind the lamp is a beautifully carved mirror, and beside the lamp is a long, golden fire wand. Light the lamp. As you gaze into its flame, you see that beyond the flame your reflection appears in the mirror. But wait! The reflection is like you, but not quite. The person in the mirror is older, and a light of great and profound wisdom shines from the eyes, which look back at you with great love and infinite understanding. The reflection in the mirror speaks:

"I am your Elder Self, your High Self. Within me dwells the wisdom gained from all your life's experience and growth, as well as that of all lives you have lived before. Although knowledge is not wisdom, knowledge used rightly may lead you to wisdom. If it may benefit you to know what you seek to know about your present concerns, then I will tell you. What do you seek to know? Mind you, I will answer no more than nine questions at this time. Begin."

Silently visualize yourself asking your Elder High Self your questions. After each question, pause and listen for the answer. The first clear, intuitive thought that comes to your mind will be the voice of your Elder High Self. If no answer to a particular question comes, or your instant thoughts are contradictory and unclear, trust that greater growth will come to you in this matter by learning through your own experience.

After you have completed your questions—no more than nine—thank your Elder High Self with a respectful bow for the knowledge you have been given, and resolve to use that knowledge wisely, with fairness, according to the free will of all, and with harm to none. Extinguish the oil lamp with the golden snuffer you now see on the altar, turn, and walk out of the temple. Pass the ninth set of columns and, counting backward, progress to where you began. With each column you pass, you gradually return to normal consciousness: 8, 7, 6, 5, 4, 3, 2, 1, and open your eyes.

Becoming Saturn

This will be a meditation of protection. It can be used for shielding yourself against any influence you feel may be limiting you—even against your own impulses. In such a case, you are inside your shield, and what you want to avoid, such as unhealthy food, cigarettes, or alcohol, will be visualized outside your shield.

Draw a physical boundary around your chosen place of meditation with sprinkled salt, a cord laid out on the floor, or, if outdoors, a line drawn with a stick on the ground or a circle of small rocks. Sit comfortably within your protective boundary and close your eyes.

Take several deep breaths. Allow your abdomen to expand slowly as you breathe deeply inward through your nose, and then slowly exhale by blowing gently through your mouth. Try not to think about anything but your breathing at this time. Just continue breathing and you will notice that you feel increasingly relaxed.

Become aware, in your mind's eye, of the physical circle you created around yourself. See it begin to glow with a translucent light, an aura of protective energy, and slowly rise above the floor to circle around the center of the spot where you are sitting. As the aura glows brighter, see the ring gradually become multiple rings, swirling around you with light energy, just like the rings of Saturn, protecting you. Then, concentric rings begin to form above and below the original rings. Eventually, they become smaller and smaller until you now have a complete sphere of light swirling around you, completely shielding you from any unwanted outside influences. The swirls of light have fused into a force field. You can see through the field whenever you wish, but nothing outside can get through it to you—unless you deliberately choose to let it in.

Now see the influences you wish to avoid outside your sphere of protection. If you wish not to see them, just make the light completely opaque, and they are gone from sight. Know that absolutely nothing can come in where you are unless you deliberately reach through your shield to get it. You feel comfortable and secure within your sphere, and you are completely in control of it. You can banish your sphere at will, and when you feel you need it, you have only to say to yourself, "Light rings of Saturn, come!", and it is back.

As you gaze through your shield at the influences outside, they begin to look tawdry, lacking in light, and not so attractive at all, from your position of protected strength within your shield. You wonder why you ever allowed them to limit you. Resolve never to do so again, and to quickly recall your shield if you are so tempted.

Now begin to breathe deeply again as before and slowly, at your own speed, return to normal consciousness.

Becoming Uranus

Lie down, and cover yourself if the air is cool. Relax and breathe deeply and steadily. Imagine yourself becoming lighter and lighter, barely feeling the surface on which you lie. With every breath you take, your relaxation increases and you become lighter and lighter. You are weightless, floating. Float gently to the ceiling, and look at the space you are in from that perspective. Can you see your body lying in that space? The space is warm and protected. You need not be concerned about it or about you. You are connected by a silver strand of Spirit and can return whenever you like, but not just now—you are enjoying your freedom! Find a way to go outdoors. If no windows or doors are open, it is of no matter. You can fly right through the wall! You are now outdoors. Float upward until you can see your house. Now look around at the trees, play with the clouds, and jump over a rainbow. Roll around sideways. Feel free. Free! Where would you like to go? What would you like to see? Go there! In Spirit, anything is possible. (Pause for a few moments to enjoy your freedom.)

Now float back to view your everyday world. From this perspective, viewing your life back on the ground, in your body, what freedoms do you most value? What restrictions on your freedom do you willingly accept? If some restrictions feel overly repressive, what can you do to change yourself—your life—to feel a greater sense of freedom? From your lofty perspective, you can see all aspects of your life. Take whatever time you need to look them over. When you return to your body, you will remember, and will feel energized toward creative change.

When you are ready, take a deep breath and count to eight, and you will be back in your body once again, safe and comfortable, feeling a new sense of energy and freedom of Spirit: 1, 2, 3, 4, 5, 6, 7, and 8. Welcome back!

Becoming Neptune

Neptune is about escape from reality, such as through the joy of pure fantasy and imagination. Sometimes, especially if you've been overworked or stressed, a voyage into fantasy can be just the right thing to do to restore your energy and perspective. It can also be a way of reenvisioning what you'd like your life to be about.

In a comfortable position, close your eyes and visualize a sandy beach near the ocean. Feel the sand under your bare feet and the fresh sea air. It is a lovely moonlit night, with stars twinkling overhead. Walk down toward the surf, with each step becoming more and more relaxed. Now the sand becomes moist beneath your feet, from the waves that have flowed over it and then back out to sea. At the water's edge, you come to a small sailboat, and now just a little way off the coast, you see an island in the mist. Pinpoints of light shining through the mist are inviting, and somehow you know and intuitively trust that it will be safe and wonderful to go there.

Get into the sailboat, and as soon as you are settled within it, a gentle breeze catches the sails and floats you away to the island. As you come ever closer, you see through the mist that the lights are coming from a wonderful castle with towers reaching through the clouds. Visualize your castle in the clouds exactly as you'd like it to be in the most beautiful of your dreams. This is the castle of your ideals and visions. Your boat docks and you walk onto the island. View the castle from the outside and then go into it. Visualize the castle however you would like it to be. See people inside it, if you choose, or be there alone. Imagine sounds, feelings, and tastes. Furnish the castle with the things that serve your most cherished purpose in life. Open yourself to the vision, and let it flow.

Now dawn begins to break and you know you must go back to the shore. Leave the castle and enter your sailboat. As you do so, the gentle breeze rises up again, catches the sails, and takes you safely back to the beach. As you walk back across the beach to where you began, gradually return to normal consciousness.

Bring your fantasy into the reality of your world by journaling the main things you remember from your sail to the island castle. What did you see as your most cherished purpose? What elements of your reality are in sync with your vision? What steps could you take to grow into your vision and use it to establish a more clearly defined purpose and direction for your life? As you write, reflect on what you have written, and then think about and act upon the intuitive wisdom gained, you have used the fantasy of Neptune in a manner that can serve your highest ideals.

Becoming Pluto

Stretch out on the floor and do a progressive tighten-and-release exercise to relax and enter an altered state. Starting with your feet, tense your muscles as tightly as you can, hold for a few seconds, and then release. Move up your body, tightening and releasing as you go: legs, lower torso, upper torso, arms, hands (make fists), neck and shoulders, and face (make a really ugly face). Now just lie there, relaxed, and breathe very deeply, allowing your abdomen to rise with each inhale, and exhaling slowly through your mouth. Count down from nine breaths to zero—slowly, with each count, going deeper and deeper into a relaxed state: 9, 8, 7, 6, 5, 4, 3, 2, 1, and 0. Your astral self is now miniaturizing and entering the attic of your mind. Picture your attic, filled with myriad cluttered momentos of all your stored experiences of life and all the things you have saved to remind you of your successes, failures, loves, hates, hurts, sorrows, obligations, guilts, and confusions. They are yours. Take a few moments to look them over. Don't just look at what is on the surface—dig. Pick things up to see what's underneath. Open that old trunk over there and go through it. Dig, probe, and discover. (If you are recording this or someone is reading it for you as you meditate, pause here for about three to five minutes for personal review. Background meditation music is appropriate here.)

Now, do you really need to keep all this stuff? Are there some things here that no longer serve you, that, in fact, may be hindering your growth? Some old guilts or hurts you've been nursing, but really don't need anymore? Some things to which you've felt obligated in the past for which responsibility would now be better given over to someone else? Some hates that really don't deserve your passion? Wouldn't your mind be clearer, more powerful, and better able to focus on what you love and should be doing for your growth without all this clutter? Visualize a great big window right over there on that back wall. Now, take some time to sort things out. Get rid of all the old clutter that you no longer want or need. Throw it right out the window. Do it now! Be ruthless! You know it's time to let go of that junk. (Pause for another three to five minutes.)

Now allow your astral body to pause a moment to admire the good things you have kept, and perhaps dust them off a bit. (Pause for one minute.) You are now leaving the attic of your mind and traveling to the heap of things you have thrown out the window. They are now magically in the middle of an open expanse of sandy beach where nothing is nearby that can be damaged by their destruction. You have a fire wand. Set them on fire. Send them into a mighty blaze and watch them burn into a fine ash. Gather up the ash in that bucket over there to your right. Now walk down into the waves of the ocean, wade in just a little way, until the water laps up around your lower legs, and when the next wave comes in, give the ashes back to the womb of the Mother, from whence all things have come and onto whom all things must return. Give thanks to her for the lessons you have learned in the past that you are now releasing, and for taking them back now that you no longer need them in your life. Tell her that you are releasing them with the intent of harm to no one, and with love, forgiveness, and thanks. Pause for a moment as you watch the waves carry away all that you have released, then turn and slowly walk nine steps back onto the beach and back into normal consciousness: 1, 2, 3, 4, 5, 6, 7, 8, and 9.

7

Planetary Rituals

The rituals in this chapter are active magickal workings based on the themes of each of the ten "planets" of classical astrology. They are designed as solitary rituals, but could also be adapted to group work.

Unlike the meditations, for these workings you should make an effort to choose timing that emphasizes the appropriate planet. At the beginning of each ritual, I will list the most ideal timing elements. To insist on all the best factors at the same time would mean only one "right" time in a year, and then only if that planet is also emphasized by aspect. Obviously, this is much too limiting. Common sense says you use as many of the timing elements as are practical for your purpose, but definitely don't obsess over it! After all, the appropriate planetary hour is available multiple times each day—you should at least be able to take advantage of that without too much trouble. The appropriate day occurs every week, and the corresponding Moon comes once a month. If it just isn't convenient to match up planetary hours, days, and Moon signs, then at least try to use combinations that are compatible. The easiest way to do this is to refer to the elemental correspondences summarized in appendix 2. Generally, the same element is the easiest match. If that's not possible, then blend fire with air and earth with water.

Whatever you do, though (just as I said for the meditations), set aside this time of ritual just for you. Plan ahead and arrange your life so that you will not be interrupted. Do these rituals exactly as given, if you wish, but do not—I repeat, *not*—feel that this is the only way, or even the best way, that these rituals can be successfully carried out.

I'm offering these suggestions for rituals to stimulate your own creativity. With them for starters, along with review of the planetary interpretations and correspondences given earlier in this book, and your own developing experience, you can design your own rituals that will work just as well, and perhaps even better.

Pre-written rituals such as these can work for you and help you learn, even if you are completely new to astrology. As an added bonus for students of astrology, you will find that intuitive work with the planetary themes will vastly enrich your ability to understand the charts you study. Take it from this astrologer, who formerly specialized in highly technical Uranian and Cosmobiology techniques, but found through working ritual how profoundly valuable the most basic of astrological understanding can be.

Through planetary meditations and rituals in this book, you can get in touch with the themes and energies of the planets as an experiential and intuitive accompaniment to your study of your own birth chart. All the planets are in your chart, in patterns and arrangements that are unique to you. All planetary themes have a wide range in which they can be expressed. Nothing is inherently "bad" or "good." The manner of their expression is up to you, and your aim should be to strive to achieve the best expression for your soul purpose and spiritual growth. Although astrology can be useful for many secular and mundane purposes, I believe that its highest purpose is fulfilled when we use it to grow in Spirit.

The Ethics of Magick

Positive magick means you focus on working on yourself. As you will see, none of these workings are directed outward to attempt, in any manner, to force your will on the minds or behavior of other individuals. As you seek and implement creative changes within yourself, your outer world will begin to respond to the new you naturally. That is one meaning of the phrase "As within, so without."

Change yourself. Do not attempt to change others. Even the most altruistic healing magick should not be forced on someone else without his or her consent. It is not for you to decide what that other soul wants and needs for its progress on its path. Even for someone who cannot speak for himself or herself (such as someone in a coma), send only your loving and healing energy near, so that the soul may reach out and accept or refuse it, as it chooses.

Mind well the Wiccan Rede in all that you do, especially in the work of magick: *Bide ye the Wiccan Rede ye must, in perfect love and perfect trust. Eight words the Wiccan Rede fulfills: As it harms none, do as ye will.*

Most phrasings of the Rede also speak of the rule of three, which relates to concepts of karma. Essentially, its meaning is that whatever you put out into the Universe returns to you threefold—but do not think of such "karma" as only relating to other lifetimes. The boomerang effect of the threefold law can be quite dramatic. I've heard it referred to as "instant karma" by several friends as they became more adept at spellworking—sometimes ruefully, when they had not given sufficient care and preparation in the forming of their intent.

Work only to effect creative change within yourself. Especially until you have thoroughly studied magick and are fully aware of what you are doing, please always add to your intent, in your words and in your heart and mind, the extra phrases "as it harm none" and "according to the free will of all."

The Magick of the Sun
Most Ideal Timing
On Sunday; in the hour of the Sun; when the Moon is in Leo (or the exaltation sign, Aries); at the New Moon or Full Moon in Leo

(or Aries). Also, when your Sun is receiving important aspects from other planets, or when the transiting Sun is making significant aspects to your chart and you feel a special need to build your confidence, generosity, pride, and creativity; or if you feel the need for a general type of healing, such as to increase your vitality and strength.

This ritual was created on a Sunday in the hour of the Sun, with the Moon in Leo. It is a greeting to the sunrise, and ideally should be done at dawn, although it could be done at any time you feel the need for it.

Preparation

Plan to wake up early on a Sunday morning to welcome the Sun in the hour of the Sun! You who are "larks" (in contrast to those who are sleep-in "owls") may enjoy this ritual so much that you'll do it often. (The owls may want to substitute Thursdays, when the Sun hour is the third planetary hour after dawn.) You don't need any tools at all, just a sunrise you can see.

Rising Sun Ritual

Stand outdoors facing the rising Sun. Cross your hands across your chest and bow to the Sun, then stretch your arms up as high as you can reach, stand on your tiptoes—stretch—and then spread your arms out as wide as you can reach, and take three long, deep breaths, inhaling fully through your nose, and then blowing slowly out through your mouth. Speak:

Hail! I greet you, Lord of Day,
Sun that shines so bright
I feel your rays now fill my soul
With energy and light.
Like you, may I be constant,
If clouds should come my way,
And shine on still, with inner light,
All throughout this day.

Pause for a few moments, as you view the lights of dawn and the Sun rising higher in the sky. Reflect on the constancy of the Sun, and the fact that all life on Earth depends on the Sun's warmth, energy, and light to thrive. The Sun is the center of our planetary system, and all the other planets respond to it and reflect its light. Know that you, too, are the center of your world, and your world responds to you. Resolve to be like the Sun's light.

> Bow once more to the Sun. Stretch your arms up high, saying, *As above* . . .
> Now stretch down to touch the ground, saying, *So below* . . .
> Stand up and touch both hands on your heart, saying, *As within* . . .
> Now stretch your arms out wide, saying, *So without* . . .
> With your arms still stretched wide, turn slowly in a clockwise circle, saying, *As the Universe* . . .
> Returning to face the Sun, cross your hands across your chest once more, and conclude, *So the soul!*

Now go forth into your day, and bring light to your world!

Setting Sun Ritual

Repeat the same bow-and-stretch exercise, as for the greeting to the rising Sun, but now stand facing toward the setting Sun. Say:

> *Farewell I bid you, Lord of Day,*
> *Soon hidden from my sight,*
> *Though shining still, with constancy*
> *Throughout the coming night.*
> *Within my heart I'll keep you,*
> *Source of my energy*
> *Until the dawn, go with my thanks*
> *All hail and blessed be.*

Spend a few more moments in silent reflection on what you have accomplished and learned during the day now passing. Acknowledge what you might have done better, and resolve that next time you will. Acknowledge and compliment yourself on what you did well.

Now conclude with the same "As above, so below . . ." exercise as for the rising Sun, and go forth into the evening, knowing confidently that the power of the Sun is within you, throughout the night and always.

Solar Return Ritual

Astrologers cast a yearly chart for the moment the Sun returns to the same position it held in one's birth chart. This puts the transits (positions of the planets in the sky at that exact moment) in a context that is very personal to the individual to whom the chart belongs. The location for such a chart is usually cast for where the person actually is at the time of the Solar Return. Astrologers differ on what is the best choice of location for a Solar Return chart—some say the birth location, some say the place of residence, and some say where the person actually is on his or her birthday. A few think the latter option is so significant that they will actually plan a vacation to go spend their birthdays at a location that will give them a "good" Solar Return!

I have tested all these options, and my experience is that they all "work" to some extent, but that the chart for where I actually am at the exact moment of the Sun's return shows best what the primary focus for the coming year will be.

The Solar Return chart is interpreted as a forecast of what the year ahead will bring, and as an indicator of what themes are most significant to you and your life. Now, if that is true, doesn't it seem likely that what you are actually doing and thinking at the moment of your Sun's return should be highly significant or even magickal? I do. Doing a ritual at the time of your Solar Return, to set your intent for the best possible outcome of the planetary themes of your Solar Return chart, can be quite effective—and also a lot less expensive than traveling for your birthday to whatever distant place might be the best possible location for your Solar Return chart!

A Solar Return ritual is one that should be personally designed and tailored to the Solar Return chart. If you are not trained in astrology, it would be helpful to ask an astrologer to help you with an interpretation of the main points of your Solar Return. If you are a beginner, you'll likely be able to derive the main themes from the chart yourself. Here are the most important things to consider.

1. The house position of the Sun.

2. Planets in very close major aspect to the Sun.

3. Planets in close conjunction to any of the four angles.[1]

4. The Ascendant or Midheaven of the Solar Return chart in the same degree as one of your natal chart planets.

Use the themes of the planets on angles or in close aspect to the Sun to plan your personal ritual to emphasize the best qualities of those planets. Use ideas from chapter 2 on planets—what they rule and what they represent—and also from chapters 6 and 7 on individual planetary meditations and rituals.

In any case, even if you do not choose to study your Solar Return chart, be aware that it exists, and that what is happening at the time the Sun is in the same degree and minute as in your birth chart has symbolic significance for the year ahead. It is useful to know what that exact time is. It may be on your birthday, or, in some years, it may be on the day before or after. You can get a Solar Return chart calculated with many astrological software programs or from practically any chart service. Look at the time the Sun returns, and see that you are doing and thinking something positive at that time. I remember one year I even got up at 3:30 A.M. to sit and meditate with a white candle at the moment of my Sun's return. It is a magickal moment!

The Magick of the Moon
Most Ideal Timing

On Monday; in the hour of the Moon; when the Moon is in Cancer (or the exaltation sign, Taurus); at the New Moon or Full Moon in

Cancer (or Taurus). Also, when your Moon is receiving important aspects from other planets, or when the transiting Moon is making significant aspects to your chart and you feel a special need to increase your nurturing qualities or understand your own feelings. Another great time to do a Moon ritual is at your Lunar Return—the time each month that the transiting Moon comes to exactly the same position in the zodiac as the Moon in your birth chart.

Most of the rituals in this chapter are fairly elaborate, with a formal casting of the circle, invocations, and tools. You don't need any of these things, though. It's your attitude and intent that sets anything you choose to do apart from the mundane and makes it a spiritual experience and a magickal working. The first ritual given here doesn't use any of the usual ritual tools—not even one. No circle is cast, and no formal words of invocation are spoken. I created it for my Lunar Return, but you can adapt it to fit your own situation. I think that working at your Lunar Return can be an especially powerful time each month. I also wish to illustrate that there can be a lot more depth to solitary rituals than little spellworkings for such things as prosperity or the like.

My older, more experienced readers will know all this, but I know from letters I've received that many readers of rituals and spells are youthful and often looking for easy answers. Well, life is complex, and often the things you most need to work through spiritually just cannot be reduced to a prewritten ritual that addresses a superficial problem. Perhaps you want to do a spell for money, but what does money represent to you? What is it that you *really* want? Perhaps you think a love spell will bring you happiness . . . but romance is often fleeting, and then what? How well do you know yourself? You are a complex being, with many twists and turns on your path to spiritual growth. Books can give you ideas, but your most powerful solitary rituals will be personally designed by you, as you probe for new layers of understanding of your own soul through what you do in your world, what you learn from it, and how you grow spiritually. That is all that really matters.

At the end of this section, I'll give you another short ritual that you can use, with minor adaptation, at any phase of the Moon.

My Personal Lunar Return Ritual

Preparation

This Moon ritual was one of the last ones I got around to writing for this chapter. I suppose I put it off because I've done so many Moon rituals—at every Full Moon and most New Moons—that I'd not yet been inspired with a new idea that would be unique to this book. When I had finished all but a few of the rituals, I went through my planetary hour computer list and highlighted favorable days on which I would create the rest of the rituals in order to make a self-imposed deadline to turn in this manuscript to Llewellyn. I had marked off the first Saturday and Sunday in September to write the Moon ritual because the Moon was in Cancer then, and there was absolutely no Monday within my deadline period that had the Moon in either Cancer or Taurus.

On that Saturday morning, I woke up shortly before sunrise (still in the hour of the Moon) with an idea for the Moon meditation. As I lay there contemplating it, I remembered that this was the day I had designated to create the Moon ritual. My next thought was "Why did I decide to do this on a Saturday? Oh, yeah, because there was no good Monday and the Moon is in Cancer today. Cancer? My Moon is in Cancer. Hey, my Lunar Return must be today. I wonder when it comes in." So I went to the computer, ran my Lunar Return chart, and looked at it. "Aha! It's at 1:11 P.M. Perfect! It's even within the hour of the Moon. I should have thought of this before. I've done Solar Return rituals to highlight the best of the potential for the year ahead, so why not bring out the best of the month ahead in ritual, too . . ."

As I looked at the chart, I realized that the simplest and most obvious things in it were practically screaming about significant issues in my life that were coming to a head. It seemed obvious to me that I'd awakened with thoughts that were leading me to this because I needed not only to create a Moon ritual, but to actually *do* this ritual—now, today!

My Lunar Return chart had the Moon in the seventh house of marriage. Its aspects, plus the planets on the angles and the Ascendant and Midheaven correspondences with my natal chart, were all significant and pinpointed the major competing areas of my life at the moment—career, marriage, and my role as daughter/caregiver in an increasingly difficult situation. My once very wise and creative mom, who'd been living with us for over a year and a half because it was no longer safe for her to live alone, was sadly slipping into an increasingly debilitating, Alzheimer's-type dementia. I was feeling drained, restricted, and burned out, especially because of the situation with my mother, and knew that my husband was also feeling the stress. It was not the first time I had allowed myself to become drained because of a reluctance to let go or say "no" at the appropriate time.

The Libran themes in my Lunar Return chart demanded to know, "Where is the balance point? Where are the appropriate personal boundaries?"

Opening Meditation

My Lunar Return ritual began right after breakfast, and my first tool was a pair of garden clippers. (I hope you will appreciate the symbolism of what follows without detailed explanation—just think about it.) My opening meditation was to attack a large honeysuckle vine growing over a trellis that had been itself attacked by aphids over the last several weeks of hot summer. I had been paying little attention to it, because I was so preoccupied with my inner turmoil over what to do about mom.

With serious intent to meditate—to flow into the action of trimming the sick and dead parts of the bush while turning my thoughts over to the Lady—I began. As I cut away the parts that were draining the energy of the plant, in order to restore it to health, the voice inside told me that my own health and Spirit were being drained and that I must "cut away" something in my life in order to protect my health. If I accidentally snipped a branch that contained a few good leaves or a blossom, the voice inside told me, "Forgive yourself. Sometimes it is impossible to completely avoid the loss of something positive at the same time that you are letting go of that which is causing harm. The leaves will grow back; blossoms will come again. The plant will be better off for your having done this."

Eventually, I finished. The vine was much reduced in size, but what was left on the trellis looked pretty healthy again. Knowing the plant would be much healthier with a little time, I went inside and called my husband, who was at his office. I told him to please not ask any questions now, but to expect me to pick him up around noon; I wanted him to go somewhere with me, and we needed to be there by 1:00 P.M.

Ritual Cleansing

I next took a "ritual shower" that served as both a very necessary clean-up from my clipping meditation and as a spiritual cleansing and a letting go. As I stood in the shower, the water washing away any remaining doubts about what needed to be done, I reached out for the Spirit of my mother and told her that I loved her and appreciated all she had done for me in the past. Then I told her that I knew that she would not like what I must do now, but I knew it was the right thing for her as well as for me, and I hoped that she would forgive me. I then, with a sharp hand motion downward across my navel, cut the psychic umbilical cord that had become too draining for me to maintain. Feeling a new sense of inner serenity, I completed my shower, dressed, prepared lunch for Mom, told her that I'd be gone for two or three hours that afternoon, and then left to pick up my husband.

The Working

I asked Jim to suggest a pretty spot near the ocean where we could talk quietly in relative privacy. He said he knew just the place, and as we drove there, I told him about my Lunar Return chart, what it meant to me, and how I'd like him to participate in my ritual.

During the exact time of my lunar return, and for more than an hour after that, we sat in a shady spot under a pine tree overlooking a cliff where the waters of the North Atlantic splashed against the rocks below. It was a beautiful sunny day, with a fresh ocean breeze. We had a wonderful talk about Mom and the fact that moving her to an assisted-living home was the best thing to do now, both for her and for us, and that I was ready to handle that, on both an inner and outer level. We talked about what each of us wanted from our relationship and for our future, both within our individual career goals and as a couple, and for our children and grandchildren. It was a perfectly magical—and magickal—time.

Conclusion

Concluding the ritual, we grounded the energy by walking down the beach to have lunch at a little seafood restaurant. I felt very satisfied that my ritual had fulfilled all the aspects of what I had seen in my Lunar Return chart, and I felt sure that the situation with my mother would resolve itself soon, in the right way and in the right manner, and that it would harm none.

Epilogue

No, the ritual didn't work immediately, but it worked, primarily by helping me internally, as was intended. In the days and weeks following, my mood was much more relaxed and serene, and my mother gradually slipped into another phase of her illness that, if not easy, was at least considerably more mellow. I interviewed at several assisted-living homes and found an excellent one just in time, since we were beginning a long-planned renovation on our house that would mean no working kitchen for weeks. The construction noise and mess were very unsettling for Mom, so while she'd always been dead set against the idea of actually living in such a home, she agreed to go into one on a respite basis "just until the worst of the mess was past." As it turned out, she found that she really enjoyed the people and the planned daily activities at the home. It was very easy to stretch out the "completion" of the renovation for a few weeks until she no longer asked when she was coming home. She began to think of her new residence as her home, and became a cheerful hostess when I came to visit. She has been there for nearly a year now. I visit her twice a week and sometimes bring her to our home for an afternoon. Though her memory continues to decline, it is obvious that she is content, and so am I.

Moon Bathing Ritual

This ritual was written on a Monday, in the hour of the Moon, with the Moon in Taurus.

Preparation

You'll need lots of candles, some recorded mood music, some uninterrupted time, and water. If the water can be outdoors in a natural body of water, such as a swimming pool or spa in the moonlight, great. If not, a bathtub will do just fine, and you can have the added pleasure of adding bath salts.

A Recipe for Bath Salts

Bath salts can be very special when you make your own. Mix together three parts Epsom salt and one part baking soda with enough drops of essential oil to scent the mixture nicely. Jasmine is wonderful. Sandalwood is nice, added to the blend. Lemon is also good, or lotus. Fresh herbs or flower petals of an appropriate Moon correspondence can be added. Mix all the ingredients together thoroughly. You'll need a handful for this bath; the rest can be saved in a glass jar for another bath.

Prepare anything else you'll need for bathing: a towel, of course, perhaps a robe, or perhaps sandals and a bathing suit if you'll be doing your ritual outdoors where nudity would not be acceptable. Also have a little jar of bubbles available, such as those sold for children.

The Ritual

Begin your mood music. Arrange your candles all around where you'll be bathing and light them, saying to each, *I light thee in honor of Lady Moon, and charge thee to my rite.*

If you are bathing in a tub, toss in your bath salts. If in a pool where this would not be acceptable, you could still toss in a few flowers or flower petals. Step into the water and sink slowly into it, savoring the sensations. Gaze at the Moon if you are fortunate enough to be able to view her from your bathing place. If not, close your eyes and visualize her. Float as weightlessly as possible, moving slowly with the music, as you feel the sensations of water flowing around your body and the emotions and feeling flowing within you. Let them ebb and flow as the tides that are pulled by the Moon.

If you are in a pool, you can water dance. One time I participated in a very magical ritual with two other people in a backyard pool. With candles all around the edge of the pool and the Moon overhead, we joined hands and went round and round to the music in a dreamy, trancelike state.

There are no chants or verses to say in this ritual—just flow with the water, guided by your music and your mood, in a dreamy meditation. Blow soap bubbles into the air above you. Watch these little shimmering "Moons" float through the air. Catch some in your hands; allow others to settle on the water or other parts of your body. Gaze at the rainbow colors they form. Relax, trance if you will, and open yourself to whatever message the Goddess may send you, within your dreamlike, meditative state.

Continue until you intuitively feel it is time to conclude. Then silently and slowly rise out of the water and raise your arms to form a crescent toward the Moon. Say, *Lady Moon, I honor thee and thank thee for your presence within my rite and within my soul.*

Wrap yourself in a comfortable towel or robe, and then extinguish each of your candles.

The Magick of Mercury

Most Ideal Timing

On Wednesday; in the hour of Mercury; when the Moon is in Gemini or Virgo (or the exaltation sign, Aquarius); at the New Moon or Full Moon in Gemini, Virgo, or Aquarius. Also, when your natal Mercury is receiving important aspects from other planets, or when transiting Mercury is making significant aspects to your chart and you feel a special need for logical reasoning or improvement in your ability to communicate.

This ritual was created on a Wednesday, with the Moon in Gemini, beginning in the hour of Mercury. Transiting Mercury was applying to a trine with transiting Jupiter.

Preparation

The Mercury ritual, like the Mercury meditation, will focus on problem solving, but in a more active, either/or mode. This is for when you are waffling between two specific choices and need help deciding which one is best. (It is possible that you may have to choose between more than one alternative, and, if so, adjust the ritual accordingly.) Since Mercury rules logic and rational thought, that is the process we will invoke in arriving at a decision, but, in ritual, the intuitive mind always plays a significant role, as well. Understand that this ritual could be adapted to many different questions: Which partner or job or house or course of study (or whatever) shall I choose? Which strategy would work best in communicating with _____? Shall I accept or resist an impending change? Shall I push my luck and go for it, or wait for a possibly better time? The possibilities are endless—decision-making is a fact of daily life. This is for making the big decisions, in which you seek higher guidance.

For those of you who wish to add (or substitute) a goddess name for Mercury, I suggest Minerva, who as Roman goddess of wisdom and technical skill, is a logical goddess image for the Mercury theme.

You will need a brown candle, a yellow candle, holders for each (a metal holder for the brown one—you'll be burning it all the way down), an anointing oil, salt, water in a small bowl, a smudge stick or censer and incense, a feather, and matches or a lighter. Additionally, have something available with which you can make two (or more) circles on the floor or ground, around a yard or so in diameter. If you are working outdoors, you could draw the circles with a stick or perhaps form them with petals or pebbles. Indoors, you might use lengths of yarn, cord, or ribbon. An athame may also be used, if you choose (it is not necessary).

For oils, use peppermint, lavender, or lemon verbena. For incense, you could use a sage smudge or, alternatively, combine lavender buds with either dragon's blood or benzoin resin and burn it on charcoal in a censer.

If you are working on a decision that involves more than two alternatives, you may also want to prepare a visual symbol that will help you easily focus on where you are (the mystery of what I mean by this will be understandable when you read the working). Such a symbol might be a small sign with a word or two on it, in big letters, that reminds you of the main idea of your alternative choice, such as "go for it" and "stay put," for example.

Lay out your tools on a small altar table in the east, facing east. The center of your circle area remains open for now. If you wish, you may also set out whatever tools, candles, or other markers you customarily use for the four watchtowers.

The Ritual

Creating Sacred Space

Using your athame or your finger, draw a banishing pentagram over the water container (start at the bottom left corner, moving to the top point, down, and so on) while saying, *O element of Water, I do banish and cast out all that is impure and unclean that you may be a fitting tool for my magick.* Make an upward casting-away motion with your athame or hand. Draw three small circles above you, gathering en-

Figure 7. Banishing Earth Pentagram.

ergy from the Universe, and then plunge the tip of your athame or your pointer and middle fingers into the water and visualize energy pouring into it. Say, *And I do charge you in the name of Mercury (Minerva)*.

Over the salt container, draw a pentagram and repeat the same procedure. *O element of Earth, I do banish and cast out all that is impure and unclean that you may be a fitting tool for my magick*. Make an upward casting-away motion with your athame or hand. Now draw three small circles above you, gathering energy from the Universe, and then plunge the tip of your athame or your pointer and middle fingers into the salt and visualize energy pouring into it. Say, *And I do charge you in the name of Mercury (Minerva)*.

Light the sage smudge or, if you are using charcoal, light the charcoal and sprinkle incense onto it. Drawing your pentagram over both fire and incense, say, *O elements of Fire and Air, I do banish and cast out all that is impure and unclean that you may be a fitting tool for my magick*. Make the casting-away motion, gather energy, and charge the elements. You can touch the tip of your athame to the fire, or hold your hand above it, visualizing the energy flowing into it. Say, *And I do charge you in the name of Mercury (Minerva)*.

Pick up a pinch of salt and stir it into the water, saying, *I now do combine this salt of the Earth with this Water that together they form the elixir of life, womb of the Mother, from which we have all come and unto which we must return.*

Pick up the container of salted water and, beginning with the east and moving clockwise around the circle, sprinkle the water as you go, saying, *With Earth and Water I do cleanse and bless this circle, charging that it be a place of protection and of inner communion with the Mighty Ones.*

Pick up the burning smudge stick or censer and carry it clockwise around the circle, wafting smoke toward the perimeter with the feather. Say, *With Fire and Air I do cleanse and bless this circle, charging that it be a place of inspiration and clarity received from the Mighty Ones.*

Invocation of Mercury and Minerva

Stand in the center of your circle, facing east. Hold your hands up toward the sky and say, *O Mighty One, whose breath stirs the fresh breezes of mental clarity, be with me in this rite! In my uncertainty, I seek your aid in a decision I must make. You who are messenger of light and truth and intellect, flow through me, connect me with the source of Universal Mind that I may see and know what is my best choice. Guide me in the path of wisdom. Be with me now!*

Pause for a moment to feel the energy flow through you, and return to the altar.

The Working

Take each of the candles out of its holder and, one by one, do the following. Sprinkle the candle with the salted water, saying, *With Earth and Water I cleanse this tool.* Pass the candle through the incense smoke, saying, *With Fire and Air I cleanse this tool.* Using a few drops of oil, anoint the candle. Start in the center and rub the oil from center to top and from center to bottom, all the time thinking of the decision you must make and the two alternatives between which you must choose. Now, sprinkle the candle with salted water once more, saying, *With Earth and Water I charge this magickal tool and arm it with my will.* Pass it through the incense smoke, saying, *With Fire and Air I charge this magickal tool and arm it with my will.* Put both candles back in their holders. Light the brown candle only. The yellow one you will light at a later time. As you light the brown candle, visualize that your decision will be firmly made through this rite, and say:

> *My indecisiveness is past*
> *This rite will set me free*
> *As candle burns, its light will show*
> *The truth of what I seek to know*
> *And I will see what's right for me*
> *An' it harm none, so mote it be.*

Take whatever tool you have prepared to make two (or more) circles on the floor or ground. The circles must be made large enough for you to stand in and be placed a few feet apart, generally in the center of the sacred space you have created. As you form the circles, visualize each one as representing a specific alternative you could choose in coming to your decision. Place each visual symbol (if you have prepared them) at the edge of its circle.

Now pause for a moment, take three deep breaths, and step into one of your circles. As you step into it, take a moment to pause again, breathe deeply, and take on the role of that choice. Become it. Let it be as if you had made your decision and are completely confident of your choice. When you are in this circle, you can advocate your choice brilliantly, so do so—out loud! Use hand gestures or other body movements to emphasize your points. Say the reasons why this is the best of all possible choices.

Change to the other circle, and take on its role, advocating it just as firmly. Become that choice! If there are more than two circles, continue with each.

Now go back to the circle where you began. Addressing the other circle (or circles), tear down that argument. Give the reasons why that other idea won't work, or wouldn't be for the best, or is scary—or whatever else you can think of against it. Then change circles, take on the other role, and do the same.

By this time, one of your arguments is likely to begin making the most sense even to your indecisive self. Time for final rebuttal. Go to each circle again, taking on its role. Defend the counter arguments and, once again, make your "pro" points.

When you are finished, if you clearly feel that one circle is the winner of the debate, go stand in it for a moment and stretch to the sky, feeling the power and relief flow through you, and then ground the energy by touching the Earth, feeling her power and sharing yours, giving thanks.

If by chance you still are not completely sure, trust in the power of your own intuition. Stand in each circle silently for a moment. Stretch to the sky and feel the lights of the Universe flowing into you. Feel the energy of Earth Mother beneath your feet flow upward into you. Which circle *feels* the best to you? Trust that one and give thanks.

Closing

Go back to your altar and light the yellow candle, saying:

> *O Messenger of Light and Truth,*
> *My thanks I give to thee,*
> *I understand my choice, my path,*
> *With crystal clarity*
> *This light shall be my beacon*
> *To guide me onward, blessed be!*

Let the yellow candle burn for a short period of peaceful meditation and then extinguish it—but keep it handy. If you feel yourself wavering a bit in the decision you made in ritual, or if you just need an added boost of Spirit to move onward, or perhaps a little time to meditate on the next best step to take in doing so, light the candle again to aid you.

The Magick of Venus

Most Ideal Timing

On Friday; in the hour of Venus; when the Moon is in Taurus or Libra (or the exaltation sign, Pisces); at the New Moon or Full Moon in Taurus, Libra, or Pisces. Also, when your natal Venus is receiving important aspects from other planets, or when transiting Venus is making significant aspects to your chart and you feel a special need for attracting or expressing love. (Venus is a good choice for prosperity workings, too, and is best within Taurean symbolism.)

This ritual for preparing a Venus love mist, and also the ritual for charging the Venus love mist that follows, were conceived on a Friday with the Moon in Taurus, just as I was awakening in the morning hour of Venus. I actually sat down to write them on a Monday with the Moon in Pisces, applying to a trine with Venus, in the hour of Venus.

Preparation

In this ritual working, you will be making a Venus love mist, which you can use whenever you feel the need to alleviate stress, obtain better balance, banish negative energy around you, and build the power of love within you.

You will need a spray bottle. This could be a bottle that held a household cleaner you've emptied and washed out thoroughly, or you can buy one. You will also need small amounts of some essential oils of your choice that have a Venus correspondence. I suggest cherry, ylang ylang, rose, rose geranium, tonka, vanilla, verbena, vetivert, or wisteria. It would also be useful to look up their specific magickal correspondences in a good reference book, such as *Cunningham's Encyclopedia of Magical Herbs*, so that you will be

aware of which scents have the traditional meanings that most
suit your intent.

It would be best to choose from among those oil fragrances
that most appeal to you, and experiment with your own blends.
Bring whatever assortment you have into your ritual circle to do
this. If your choice is limited, rose and vanilla are easy to obtain
and make a nice love blend—I'd go stronger on the rose, lighter on
the vanilla, perhaps three or four parts rose to one part vanilla.

If your oil containers do not have individual droppers, you
should also assemble an eye dropper, a small container of dena-
tured alcohol, and a container of water, so you can clean the eye
dropper when changing from one oil to another. Fill the spray bottle with water, preferably spring water or clean-catch rain water. If
that's not possible, tap water is fine. Also, get a piece of paper and a
pencil or pen.

If at all possible, choose a time to work when you will be able to
see Venus visible in the sky, either morning or evening star. If this
is not possible, you will be preparing your love mist in ritual, but
actually completing it when you charge your mist under the star.

In your circle area, trace out a large pentagram on the ground
or floor that you can walk along (use petals, salt, or cords). Place a
white candle at the Spirit point, and symbols of the elements at
their points—salt at the earth point, water at the water point, incense at the air point, and either a quartz crystal or a lighted red
votive candle at the fire point. Orient the point of Spirit to compass east if you desire greater emphasis on the Libra-ruled Venus
in your intent (balance, fairness, beauty, partnership, and love in
marriage). Orient the point of Spirit to compass north if you desire greater emphasis on Taurus-ruled Venus in your intent (magnetism, sensuality, comfort, acquisition, and security.) Use
patchouli incense for an "earthy" Venus, and rose incense for the
Libran themes.

The other points of the pentagram will then fall in between the
normal directional quarters, which is okay. We are not focusing on

the cross of matter here. We are working with the pentagram, which is closely associated with the planet Venus—over a period of eight years, the repeated orbital pattern of Venus forms the five points of the pentagram.[2]

Assemble the tools for your working in the center of the pentagram, on a small altar table. You could decorate your altar with flowers, a goddess image . . . as you wish.

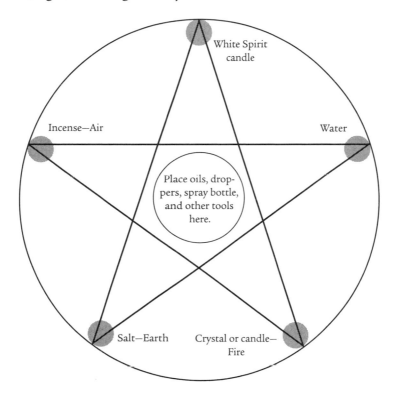

Figure 8. Pentagram Plan for Venus Tools and Altar.

Finding Venus in the Sky

Look for Venus in the morning sky just before dawn or in the evening sky just after sunset. You can find out on what dates she is to be either morning or evening star by consulting your astrological calendar. Also, if your local newspaper has a skywatch column, you'll likely find it there. Venus is easy to spot, for she is the brightest "star" you'll see, and usually the first. She'll be along the arc across the southern sky that is the ecliptic. As evening star, she'll be not far above the setting sun, or, as morning star, approximately above where the sun will rise. Since Venus is really a planet, her light will be steady, rather than twinkling.

The Ritual

Opening Meditation and Creating Sacred Space

Ground and center yourself. You could use the Becoming Venus meditation for this, or use your own favorite method. When you feel ready, stand facing your white candle at the point of Spirit. Have a match or fire wand ready. Stretch as high as you can and look upward toward the sky, toward Venus if you can see the star, or visualize it, if you can't. Say, *As above . . .* Now, drop to the ground, kneeling with both hands on it and, head bowed, say, *So below . . .* Rise up, lift your hands out wide, and circle slowly in place, saying, *As the Universe . . .* Cross your arms across you chest and say, *So the soul. In perfect love and perfect trust, let the Spirit flow within.* Light the white candle. Turn clockwise in place and face the earth point. Walk straight to it, pick up the salt container, and circle the pentagram clockwise, sprinkling salt as you go and visualizing a protective shield around your working area. When you return to the earth point, replace the salt container, turn clockwise and walk in a straight line toward the water point. Pick up the water container and again walk clockwise to circle your pentagram, sprinkling water as you go and visualizing that the area be cleansed of anything that does not serve your intent. Replace the water container, turn clockwise, and walk in a straight line toward the air point. Pick up the burning incense and again circle your pentagram clockwise, moving the incense in a constantly graceful clockwise circle. Visualize the incense as helping you clarify your thoughts and intent. Replace the incense, turn clockwise, and walk in a straight line to the fire point. Pick up the crystal point or candle and once again walk the circle clockwise, holding the symbol aloft and visualizing a circle of love and light energy being formed around your working area. Replace the symbol at the fire point, turn clockwise, and walk in a straight line back to the white candle at the point of Spirit. Take up the white candle and carry it clockwise around the circle one final time, chanting as you go:

> *Balance, attraction, love and light*
> *Venus be with me in this rite.*

The Working

Replace the white candle, turn clockwise, and go to your altar, circling around it to sit facing the white candle. You will now choose a blend of oils to your liking. Trust in the Spirit you have invoked to guide you as to the right blend. Smell each of the oils. Try holding two or three close to each other so you can test how they might blend together. When you feel ready, take the spray cap off your bottle of water and put a few drops of your chosen oils in the bottle. Allow your intuition to be guided by the Spirit of Venus as to how much of each oil to add—*but*, be sure to count your drops and immediately write down how much of each oil you put in, so that you will be able to duplicate your recipe later whenever you like. *Also*, if you are using only one eyedropper, be sure to clean it before changing from one oil to another, first with alcohol, then with water, and dry, so that you won't contaminate your valuable essential oils. It will take only a very small amount of oil to lend a wonderful aroma to the water, even if your spray bottle is large, so don't overdo it!

When your sniff test of the water in your spray bottle suits you, test it! Spray once into the air straight above you. As the mist wafts down around you, see how you feel. If you yearn for a bit more of a particular scent, add it a drop or two at a time and test. When you feel a lovely aura of peace and love, you are almost finished. You have created a magickal elixir that needs now only to be charged beneath that "starlight, star bright, first star" of Venus. If you are already beneath her, continue on with the charging of your Venus mist and the closing of your circle.

If you will be moving outdoors or waiting for another time to finish with the star, skip the charging and reserve it for then, and proceed right to the closing of your circle. If you are in some highly unusual situation where it will just not be possible to actually see Venus for some time to come, you could complete the ritual by visualizing her. Anything is possible with magick! Still, try if at all possible to complete your work with the "real thing."

Charging the Venus Mist

Beneath the light of Venus, take the spray cap off your bottle and place it carefully on the ground or altar. Look up and gaze at Venus, filling your heart with love for all things. Think of all the things you love and, with forgiveness and peace, for that which you do not love, for the Goddess dwells within all living things. Focus on the starlight and allow your feelings to build. Raise your hands up toward Venus, cupping them around her light. Most likely, your focus will create the optical illusion that Venus becomes two stars. At this moment, capture one of them in your cupped hands and bring it down over your open spray bottle, visualizing her light energy flowing into it. Concentrate on the energy for a few moments, and then replace the spray cap, waft some mist above your head, and relish it with joy as the wonderful aroma you have created flows down around you. Feel the Spirit of Venus, and silently thank her for her presence within you.

Closing

Beginning clockwise from Spirit, face toward the water point and, turning in place to each one, bow to the elemental and silently thank it for assisting in your rite. Then go stand before the white candle of Spirit. Bow down, kneeling, with your hands on the Earth, and then stretch high to the sky, as you once again thank

Venus for her love and her presence in your rite and in your soul. Extinguish the white candle.

Use your magickal mist whenever you feel the need.

The Magick of Mars
Most Ideal Timing

On Tuesday; in the hour of Mars; when the Moon is in Aries (or the exaltation sign, Capricorn); at the New Moon or Full Moon in Aries (or Capricorn). Also, when your natal Mars is receiving important aspects from other planets, or when transiting Mars is making significant aspects to your chart and you feel a special need to fire up your courage, will, or initiative. This ritual was created on a Tuesday, in the hour of Mars, with the Moon in Aries.

Preparation

In the center of your ritual area, place a source of fire, even if only a bright red candle. If you can arrange a place outdoors for a safely contained larger fire, so much the better. Burn dragon's blood resin for your incense, mixed with a pinch of each of the following crushed herbs: basil, cloves, and allspice. Use an oil mixed of two parts dragon's blood, and one and one-half parts each of frankincense and juniper berry. Play a tape or CD of drumming music in the background. Wear a red garment if you have one, or, if not, something red—perhaps a scarf or cord. Place a small altar table either in the center with your candle or other source of fire on it, or, if you are working with a bonfire at the center, place the altar in the south quarter of your area. Place candles (or torches, if outdoors) at each quarter. If possible, use a red altar cloth. On the altar, place your tools. You will need the following.

1. Incense and an incense burner.

2. A feather.

3. Anointing oil.

4. Small containers of water and salt.

5. Either a sword or an athame.

6. A small square of red cloth (three inches square is plenty).

7. One small Mars stone: a red jasper, bloodstone, or garnet.

8. About one yard of strong red string or cord.

The Ritual

Opening Meditation

Light your center fire and stare into its flame as you take three deep breaths and center yourself to begin. Hold your hands out as if embracing the aura of the fire and feel its warmth. Speak the following rhyme and, as you do, think of your most personal need and intent for invoking the energy of Mars. The general intent for which this ritual is created is to invoke the spiritual warrior within, so while your personal intent may be more specific, it should be compatible with the general intent.

> *By Fire's heat, by Fire's light*
> *Spirit of Mars shall be*
> *Charged within my will, my soul,*
> *As it harm none, so mote it be!*

Casting the Circle and Calling the Guardians

South and Fire: Walk clockwise to the south quarter and light the candle or torch. Say:

O mighty Guardians of the South, Powers of Fire, I do summon, stir, and call you up, to witness my rite and guard my circle.

Make a small bow to the Guardian, acknowledging the presence of the elemental.

Take up the sword or athame and hold it up high to the sky, visualizing the red point of light that is the planet Mars flowing down through the tip of your blade into your body. Say, *As above.* Thrust the blade downward, pointing to the Earth beneath your feet. Visualize the energy emitting from your body through the point of your blade, extending down deep into the Earth where it connects with the molten core of the Earth Mother. Say, *So below.* Bring your blade upward and rest it lightly against your chest, visualizing the red light energy of Mars and the red heat of the heart of the Earth's core blending with the energy of your body. Say, *As within.* Now thrust your blade straight out in front of you, pointing to the south quarter flame. Say, *So without.* Walk the entire circle clockwise, scribing it with your blade and visualizing red, hot energy emitting from the point. When you return to the south quarter, raise both arms to the sky and outward, still holding the blade in one hand. Say, *As the Universe.* Cross your arms over your chest, and finish by saying, *So the soul.* Kiss your blade and place it on the altar.

West and Water: Walk clockwise to the west quarter. Light the candle or torch and say:

O mighty Guardian of the West, Power of Water, I do summon, stir, and call you up, to witness my rite and guard my circle.

Make a small bow to the west and continue clockwise back to the altar in the south. Take up the container of water, continue clockwise to the west, and hold the water bowl up toward the west flame. Say, *May all fears and doubts be cleansed from this circle and from my soul. May the Powers of Water lend depth to my passion.*

Walk the entire circle, sprinkling water. As you do this, feel the cleansing power of the waters, and let go of any doubts you may have in regard to your ability to charge the Mars energy within you. Continue on past the west quarter and around again, returning to the south quarter. Return the water container to the altar.

North and Earth: Walk clockwise to the north quarter. Light the candle or torch and say:

O mighty Guardian of the North, Powers of Earth, I do summon, stir, and call you up, to witness my rite and guard my circle.

Make a small bow to the north and continue clockwise to the altar. Take up the container of salt and continue around to the north again, holding the salt up to the flame. Say, *May this circle and the intent charged within it be protected, and may my will and passion be grounded, strengthened, and structured with the Powers of Earth.*

Walk all around the circle, past north once again, and on around to the altar. As you go, sprinkle grains of salt, visualizing a shield of protection, and opening yourself to the strength of the Earth. Replace the salt container on the altar.

East and Air: Proceed around to the east. Light the east candle or torch and say:

O mighty Guardian of the East, Powers of Air, I do summon, stir, and call you up, to witness my rite and guard my circle.

Make a small bow to the east.

Move clockwise to your altar, pour incense on lighted charcoal in your burner, and taking it and the feather, walk clockwise to the east again. Hold the incense high toward the flame and say, *As with the Power of Fire, the essence of Air is sent aloft to charge and consecrate this circle, so may the Power of Air give clear and true direction to my will, passion, and intent, as it harm none and according to the free will of all concerned, so mote it be!*

Walk the circle, holding the incense burner outward. Direct the smoke toward the perimeter of the circle with the feather. Visualize blessing and charging the circle and also of your positive direction for your Mars energy. Return to the altar and replace the incense burner.

Invocation of Mars

Stand before your center fire, facing south (with the fire between you and the south altar). Stand firmly, with arms extended to the sky, and say:

Strong and vital Spirit of Mars. Send thy red light energy to charge the life blood racing through my veins. Charge me with the courage, passion, will, and conviction to dare and to do what I must do to grow and to serve my highest purpose. Show me my anger, but also show me the way to use its heat to destroy that which is out of harmony and forge that which will restore harmony. Burn out of my soul all fears, all doubts, and all that is unworthy. Infuse me with thy most sacred energy that I may become a spiritual warrior!

Hold your stance and feel the energy of Mars flowing into you.

The Working

Go clockwise to the altar, and take up your stone. Wash it in the water, saying, *With the Power of Water, this stone be cleansed of all impurities.*

Rub salt on it, and say, *By the Power of Earth, this stone be infused with protective power and grounding energy.*

Pass the stone through the incense smoke, saying, *By the Power of Air, may this stone remind me of this rite and of my commitment to direct my will and passions to constructive purposes and as a spiritual warrior.*

Anoint your forehead and the stone with the oil, saying, *By this oil of Fire, may the primary element of Mars energy infuse this stone and infuse my Spirit.*

Now hold the stone high toward the sky and then close to your heart, saying, *By the Powers of Fire and the Spirit of Mars, may this stone of Mars be a charm and token of the power of this rite and of the newfound understanding of the Power of Mars within my soul's purpose.*

Now carry the stone all around the circle, holding it toward the center flame. Walk the circle quickly eight more times, each time spiraling in closer to the fire. Dance if you wish, moving with the drumming rhythm. Finish close to the fire, facing into it and south. Say, *By the Power of Mars and three times three, warrior of Spirit I shall be!*

Return to the altar and place your stone in the center of the red square of fabric. Bring up the ends and firmly tie the string around them, enclosing the stone into a small pouch. Tie the ends of the string together and place your newly made amulet around your neck. Wear it or hang it where you can easily see it whenever you need an extra infusion and reminder of the Mars energy you have raised within.

Closing

Holding your hand over your amulet to your heart, and lifting your other hand toward the sky and Mars above you, say:

O mighty Spirit of Mars, my grateful thanks for the energy and the light within received from thee in this rite. Always shall I remember my commitment to be thy spiritual warrior as I share my energy within the world.

Now ground the energy by kneeling to place your hands on the Earth beneath you, allowing energy to flow back to the Mother, and also retain what you need for yourself.

Dance clockwise to each of the quarters, beginning with the west quarter. At each one, bow to the Guardian in thanksgiving and then snuff the flame. Finish at the south quarter, stretch high to the sky, and then bow deeply, once again touching the Earth. Snuff the flame.

If at all possible (and safe!), allow your center flame to burn itself out. Candles to be burned all the way down should be in metal holders or, if in glass, in a bowl of water deep enough to cover the glass. Do not leave the area while any fire is still burning. If you cannot attend to the fire, extinguish it with thanksgiving.

The Magick of Jupiter
Most Ideal Timing

On Thursday; in the hour of Jupiter; when the Moon is in Sagittarius (or the exaltation sign, Cancer); at the New Moon or Full Moon in Sagittarius (or Cancer). Also, when your natal Jupiter is receiving important aspect from other planets, or when transiting Jupiter is making significant aspects to your chart and you feel the need to grow in wisdom and spirituality, or to expand your horizons.

This ritual would best be done following the Jupiter meditation, in order to further charge the goal you chose then.

This ritual was written on a Thursday, in the hour of Jupiter, with the Moon in Aquarius, in the week following the Full Moon in Sagittarius.

Preparation

Before you begin, find or make a symbol that will remind you of your goal. This could be a picture, a talisman, a rock, a seed—anything that will easily trigger your thoughts of the goal you have chosen. Decorate your altar with whatever Jupiter-ruled items you may have, such as a purple altar cloth, an amethyst crystal, branches of juniper, gold or purple candles in gold or brass holders—or any other items that to you represent that which is regal and grand. Your tools will be dried sage leaves (white Indian sage, if possible) and an abalone shell or bowl in which to burn them, matches or a fire wand, your athame or sword, and a bell or chime. Place your chosen symbol in a prominent position. You may also mark the four quarters of your circle with candles or torches. Orient your altar to the east.

Light the candles on the altar.

The Ritual

Casting the Circle and Calling the Guardians

Take up your athame or sword and move clockwise to stand before the east quarter of your circle area. You will be using the blade to draw a banishing-earth pentagram in the air at each quarter, with a connecting line between them to scribe a circle. Begin by drawing a solar cross. Thrust the blade up toward the sky, saying, *In the name of the God* . . . Thrust the blade down to the Earth, saying, *and the Goddess* . . . Holding the blade upward, touch it to your right shoulder and then pass it across your body to touch your left shoulder. As you do this, say, . . . *who dwell within.* Now, thrust the blade skyward once more and then begin drawing the banishing pentagrams. Start the first pentagram at lower left (earth). In tracing your first stroke upward to the top point, you are banishing the mundane and reaching for Spirit. Complete the pentagram, and then thrust your blade into the center and scribe a small circle of Spirit. From that point, move clockwise to the next quarter, scribing a line in the air with your blade from one quarter to the next. Visualize luminous light energy emitting from the point of the blade. When you get to the south, repeat the pentagram, and so on around the entire circle, returning to the east. Kiss your blade, hold it across your heart, and return clockwise to your altar. (If you are familiar with the formal Kabbalistic Solar Cross and Lesser Banishing Ritual of the Pentagram, it is perfectly appropriate to do that instead.)

Hold the point of the blade into the leaves of sage and say, *By this sacred tool, by my will and intent, and in the sight of the Gods do I charge this herb of Jupiter to assist me in magickal rite.*

Light the sage leaves and blow out the flames gently so the smoke billows. Ring the chime three times. Take the smoking sage (and, if you have quarter candles, a tool to light them) to the east. Call the east as you hold the sage aloft, and then proceed clockwise to each quarter, calling them in turn and censing the entire circle with the sage smoke. Here are calls you can use.

East

> *Mind of Jupiter, hear my call*
> *Smoke of sage I offer thee*
> *Clear my vision, charge my thoughts*
> *Make magick here with me.*

South

> *Spirit of Jupiter, hear my call*
> *Smoke of sage I offer thee,*
> *Charge my courage, and by Jove,*
> *Make magick here with me.*

West

Joy of Jupiter, hear my call
Smoke of sage I offer thee,
Wash away all doubts and fears
Make magick here with me.

North

Giant Jupiter, hear my call
Smoke of sage I offer thee,
My goals are large, O help me grow
Make magick here with me.

Invocation of Jupiter

Returning to the altar, add fresh sage leaves and hold your symbol in the smoke, saying, *O herb of Jupiter, O great leader of the gods, O power of growth, beneficence, and expansion within, charge this symbol that it may serve as a talisman of my will and intent.*

Now, move the censer all around you—up, down, and all around—as you invoke the Spirit of Jupiter within. Do this silently by feeling, if that is your preferred style, or you could say these words:

O Spirit of Jupiter, I seek thy power within. Infuse me generously with vision, with just wisdom, and with openness to the growth that will fulfill my highest purpose. Charge me with confidence, and show me the rightful way that I may achieve my goal. Spirit be with me!

The Working

Replace the censer on the altar. Hold up your symbol and state this affirmation:

I see my goal; my path is clear. With every step, my goal draws near. Success is mine; success is here!

Repeat the affirmation, and as you do so, stre-e-e-tch! Jupiter is expansive. Feel that in your body. Hold your symbol up in the air, stretching up on your tiptoes and reaching as high as you can. Stretch to the right, to the left, down to touch the ground, and up again. Do it with exuberance, with confidence, and with joy. Visualize your goal as being accomplished. Stride confidently around the circle, taking large, grand steps, and repeat your affirmation like a chant. Reach your arms out wide and turn around in circles. Continue your expansive movements until you feel your energy peak, and then bow down before your altar, touching your hands and symbol to the Earth, saying, *Thanks be to Jupiter, that my goals be manifest.* Resolve in your heart and mind to do what you need to do in the world to attain your chosen goal.

Closing

Bow to each of the watchtowers, thanking the Guardian in your heart and mind, and extinguish its flame.

Place your symbol in a conspicuous place where you see it often as you move steadily toward your goal.

The Magick of Saturn

Most Ideal Timing

On Saturday; in the hour of Saturn; when the Moon is in Capricorn (or the exaltation sign, Libra); at the New Moon or Full Moon in Capricorn (or Libra). Also, when your natal Saturn is receiving important aspects from other planets, or when transiting Saturn is making significant aspects to your chart and you feel a special need to bring your goals into concrete manifestation, to become more self-disciplined, or to handle a burden or responsibility effectively.

This ritual was written on a Saturday, with the Moon in Capricorn applying to a trine with Saturn, and in the hour of Saturn.

Preparation

The working in this ritual will focus on the aspect of Saturn that involves awareness of the necessity for discipline, patience, and a solid foundation on which to build the structures of your life and bring them into manifestation.

You will need some modeling material to work with. Wet clay is great if you have a way to fire it after it is dry. It will be too fragile unfired, unless it is special craft clay that is meant to dry hard. If not, try Fimo clay or a similar-type product, which can be easily found in art and craft supply stores and can be fired in your home oven.

Set your ritual area in a place where you can work comfortably at a table or other hard surface. Assemble, as you choose, modeling or carving tools, a bowl of water (for cleaning your fingers and softening the clay), and a towel or paper towels. Also assemble symbols of each of the elements: salt for earth, a bowl of water, incense for air (I suggest a long-burning stick incense for this), and a red candle for fire. Place each of them at the corresponding quarter. If you like, select some good recorded meditation music and play it in the background.

The Ritual

Casting the Circle and Calling the Guardians

Relax, and ground and center yourself, breathing deeply. You might visualize a psychic root growing down out of your body deep into the Earth, where it is nourished by the power of the Earth Mother. Energy courses up through the root into your body, filling it and giving you strength.

Go to the east and light the incense. Hold it up to the east and say:

Guardian of the East, mighty Power of Air, I ask your aid in my rite, that my mind be clear, my thinking straight, and my ability to concentrate be focused. Be here now, and blessed be!

Now go completely around the circle clockwise, visualizing that all the air within it and within you be cleared. Return the incense to the east quarter and leave it there, safely in a holder, to continue burning. Continue clockwise to the south.

Light the red candle and hold it up to the south, saying:

Guardian of the South, Power of Fire, I ask your aid in my rite, that I have the courage to face the truth of what I have and what I must build, and that I may have the energy, faith, and Spirit that I need. Be here now, and blessed be!

Go completely around the circle clockwise, visualizing that the light of the candle is charging the area and you. Return the candle to the south quarter and leave it there, safely burning in its holder. Continue clockwise to the west.

Hold up the bowl of water to the west, saying:

Guardian of the West, Power of Water, I ask your aid in my rite, that any doubts or fears that I may not sustain my effort be washed away. Fill me with love and understanding of the lessons I must learn. Be here now, and blessed be!

Sprinkle yourself with water and wash away those doubts, then go completely around the circle clockwise, sprinkling water as you go, while visualizing the circle as being protected by the nurturing womb of the Mother.

Return to the west, leaving the bowl of water there, and continue on to the north.

Hold the container of salt up to the north, saying:

Guardian of the North, Power of Water, I ask your aid in my rite, that I may be firmly grounded as I approach my task, and have the discipline and patience to sustain it. Protect this sacred space and guide me in this sacred time of ritual. Be here now, and blessed be!

Go once more around the circle clockwise, sprinkling salt as a protective boundary around your circle. Return to the north, leaving the salt there, and go to your table where your modeling material awaits.

Standing at your table, draw a large, invoking-earth pentagram over the table, with all the modeling tools on it. Start at the top point and move your hand down to the lower left point, saying, *I now with the Power of Earth* (move your hand up to the upper right point), *the Power of Water* (move your hand across to the upper left point), *the Power of Air* (move down to the lower right point), *the Power of Fire* (return to the top point), *and in the name of our Lady and Lord, I do bless, consecrate, and charge you with this sign, that you be fitting tools for my magickal rite!*

Invocation of Saturn

In this sacred hour of Saturn, I do call thee, oh Great Sage and Father of Time, and I do call thee, oh Crone of wisdom. I respect thy boundaries and seek the lessons you shall teach me in this physical existence. Let this act of ritual be a new awareness of what I have, what I must build, and how I shall proceed to bring new growth into manifestation. Show me the way to grow in Spirit as I build my structures within this physical world. Descend within me, this your servant and priest/ess. I humbly seek thee, and I am filled. (Pause and feel the Saturnine energy fill you.)

The Working

It is now, quite literally, time to sit down and get to work.

Artistic talent is absolutely not necessary for this project. Build and model something that symbolizes to you what you are trying to build in your life. It could be represented by a complex art object, with colors and flair, or it could just as effectively be something as simple as a little tower built of clay "bricks." Whatever it is, it will take patience, and some aspects of it will probably be a bit challenging and need extra attention, but that's part of the point of all this, isn't it? Take your time—and don't give up! Everything has to be stuck together firmly in order to fire without coming apart. If you're adding one piece of clay to another, you'll have to score the pieces and press them together with a tool to make sure they are firmly joined. Toothpicks can make a handy tool for small things. (It wouldn't hurt to experiment a little before the ritual, if you're new to this. It's not difficult, but even a kid has to practice a little to learn how to make Playdough stick together. You can do this!)

If you're making a tower, you could carve a symbol or even a written word that represents your thoughts into each "brick." Carve lower bricks with the solid aspects of your "foundation" that you already have—traits, skills, and experiences that serve your current goals. As you move upward, carve symbols or words that stand for what you intend to build. If you build your tower up from a floor, the fired piece could perhaps become a small container for something on your altar. Hint: You can use a kitchen roller or a small, smooth bottle to roll out modeling materials into a thick smooth piece from which you can cut shapes. If you do this, a layer of vinyl covering or waxed paper for your table would be good, so you don't scar the table top.

Conclusion

When you have finished with your model, sit for a moment in silent meditation and thanks to Saturn, Sage, and Crone for what you have accomplished—and for what you have learned by thinking while you worked. (That still, small voice in your head that led you to the next step that felt "right" was surely their guidance.) Pledge that you will use the symbol you have made as a constant reminder of the intent you have set, that you may be assisted in your commitment to manifest it in your world.

Stand up, stretch, and then bow down to the ground, sharing your energy with the Earth.

Go to each of the four quarters and bow in meditative thanks for what they have contributed to your thinking (east), your courage and faith (south), your feelings (west), and your newly manifested symbol (north).

The circle is now open. Allow your model to dry hard, or fire it according to the instructions that came with the modeling product. Go forth to accomplish with disciplined intent what you have begun in this rite.

The Magick of Uranus
Most Ideal Timing

On Wednesday; in the hour of Mercury (Uranus is the higher octave of Mercury); when the Moon is in Gemini or Virgo (or the exaltation sign, Scorpio); at the New Moon or Full Moon in Gemini,
Virgo, or Scorpio. Also, when your natal Uranus is receiving important aspects from other planets, or when transiting Uranus is
making significant aspects to your chart and you feel a special
need to increase your freedom, reform something in your life, or
gain greater openness to change and adventure.

This ritual was written on a Wednesday, in the hour of Mercury, with the Moon in Leo, and within the period of a Gemini
New Moon.

Preparation

Choose a time period to begin when you can set aside several
hours of free time following the ritual—a whole day off, if at all
possible. Gather together a bunch of things you can easily stack
up around you. A big bag of children's blocks will do, or a bunch
of books, pots and pans, or whatever is handy (and not breakable).

The Ritual

Opening Meditation and Casting the Circle

Take a few moments to ground and center yourself, and then
begin building a wall around yourself with the things you have
gathered. Do this slowly and deliberately, and as you do so, meditate on the things in your life that limit your freedom. Let each
item that you add to your wall be a symbol of something that you
perceive as limiting, demanding of your time, draining, stifling,
preventing you from trying something new, or from feeling free to
make a change. Notice how physically piling these things up
around you makes you feel. By the time you finish this opening mediation, you're more likely to be feeling tense than relaxed! When

you feel you've piled enough up, sit quietly in the middle of your things for a few moments, thinking about the restrictions you have created within your life . . . yes, you. One way or another, your life and how you feel about it is your creation. Now, proceed to the invocation.

Invocation of Uranus

Oh, Uranian power of change, reform,
Send rays of light to me.
I must break through this heavy wall
To set my Spirit free!
Show me the Path that I should take,
Open my mind to see,
With harm to none, in love and trust
Come forth! So mote it be!

Chant

Set my Spirit free! Open my mind to see!

Continue chanting repeatedly, as you break through your barriers and boundaries. Do it impulsively. Don't think about where you're going to break through—just do it instinctively, and trust that Uranus is guiding you through it. Leave the wall in a pile for now. You are going on an adventure.

The Working: An Adventure of Discovery

Leave your ritual area and set off for your time of freedom. Don't do anything as you would normally do it. Take a different route. Go somewhere you've never been before. If you feel like eating, try something you've never tried before. Try not to think too much about what you're going to do. Don't plan ahead. Just follow the first thoughts that come into your mind . . . Well, let's keep one little restriction here, in that you avoid doing anything that is harmful to others or against the laws of the land. If your first thought falls in one of those categories, try another thought before you act! Silly, frivolous, eccentric . . . those thoughts are fine. Go for it!

Let this ritual be fun, though. Open yourself to surprise. Consider anything or anyone you encounter as an opportunity to discover something new. Follow your whims. If it's interesting and you want to explore it more, stick around. If it's not, and you want to move on, move on. This is your day, and you are free, free, free! Enjoy it!

After you've returned home, go back to your ritual area and contemplate your fallen wall. Notice which parts of it you broke through most forcefully, and if you can remember, notice what parts of your life they symbolized when you were building the wall.

Now, think back over your day. If you have a journal, write down the most notable experiences of your day, and what you've discovered about yourself in the process. (Journaling can be a very valuable tool. It's actually one of the best ways to learn how astrological transits work for you, for one thing; or how dreams can give you messages, for another. When you read back over a journal you've written, sequential entries will often show relationships you would have failed to notice otherwise.)

If your day has opened you to changes that you know you should make in your life, resolve to take appropriate steps to bring those changes about.

Closing

Thank Uranus:

Uranian power of change, reform,
Through rays of light I see
The Path I know that I must take.
To set my Spirit free!
Thank you for this blessed day,
Farewell and blessed be!

The Magick of Neptune

Most Ideal Timing

On Thursday; in the hour of Jupiter or Venus (Neptune is the higher octave of Venus; Jupiter is Neptune's ancient ruler); when the Moon is in Pisces (or the exaltation sign, Cancer); at the New Moon or Full Moon in Pisces (or Cancer). Also, when your natal Neptune is receiving important aspects from other planets, or when transiting Neptune is making significant aspects to your chart and you feel a special need to increase your imaginative or intuitive abilities, to divine the future, or to come into closer attunement with the spiritual and the divine.

This ritual was written on a Friday (Venus day) with the Moon in Pisces, in the hour of Venus.

The Ritual

Preparation

Although you will begin this ritual at an appropriately chosen time according to the planets, you will be continuing it over a considerably longer period of time. This ritual is intended to enhance your ability to remember and to benefit from dream messages. It will begin with your preparation of a dream pillow and a dream journal to use during at least a month of sleep times and meditation periods, before you have completed your working. Ideally, you should begin this ritual on an evening when, after you have completed the ritual preparation of your tools, you will be able to continue onward to your preparations to go to bed for the night.

Gather together the following tools:

1. A piece of fabric that is pleasing to you. The fabric should be longer than it is wide and big enough to fold in half and make a decent-sized little pillow, allowing a half-inch on three sides for the seam.

2. A needle and thread, or a sewing machine.

3. A pair of scissors.

4. Quantities of dried mugwort, lavender, and rose petals—enough to stuff your pillow.

5. A blank book. This you could purchase, hand decorate if you wish, or even make by stapling or stitching several pieces of blank paper together.

6. A pen or pencil.

7. A taper candle in a Neptune color (lavender, sea green, mauve, and opalescent hues), and a candle holder.

8. Anointing oil. Jasmine would be my first choice; other possibilities include rose, sandalwood, verbena, and ylang ylang.

9. Containers of salt and water.

10. Stick incense and an incense holder.

11. Matches or a fire wand.

12. An athame, if you wish.

Assemble your tools in a convenient place to work. If it is evening, an area of your bedroom would be good. It would be ideal if you could precede the ritual with a bath or shower. Make that part of the ritual, too. You might use the Neptune meditation from the previous chapter while you are bathing. Whether or not you do so, invoke the power of water as you enter it. Feel the water wash away your cares and cleanse both your body and soul. Take in its essence and feel relaxed and at peace.

Creating Sacred Space

Now go to your tools. Begin by lighting the incense, and then bless and consecrate the four elements: water, salt, and burning incense. Blend some of the salt into the water. Lightly sprinkle the candle and all your other previously unconsecrated tools (the herbs, fabric, book, etc.), saying, *With Earth and Water I cleanse thee that thee may aid me in this magickal rite.* Either pass your tools through the incense smoke or wave the stick of incense over them, saying, *With Fire and Air I cleanse thee that thee may aid me in this magickal rite.* Anoint the candle with the oil, and touch a bit of oil to all the other tools except for the herbs, saying, *I anoint thee with oil of magick, and consecrate thee to my purpose.* Then once more sprinkle the candle and each of the other tools, saying, *With Earth and Water I charge thee and arm thee with my will.*

Circle the room sprinkling salted water, saying, *With Earth and Water I do conjure this space to be sacred and protected, in the name of the great Goddess* (add the name of your favorite sea goddess here, such as Yemaya, Mary, or Morganna).

Circle the room again, waving the incense, saying, *With Fire and Air I do conjure this space to be sacred and protected, in the name of the great god Neptune.*

Invocation of Neptune and the Goddess of the Sea

Standing before your candle in its holder, light it and invoke:

O great Neptune and (insert your favorite sea goddess name here), I light this flame as a beacon to call thee within me. I seek the mysteries of thy depths, and the wisdom of deep insights through messages within my dreams. Be with me now, O Great Ones, and lend thy magick to my rite.

The Working

Now, sew the fabric together on three sides and turn it inside out, so the seam is inside. Mix the herbs together with your fingers, enchanting them as you do so, visualizing energy flowing into them and charging them with your intent. Add a few drops of the anointing oil to the mixture and say repeatedly as you work:

Herbs of magick, herbs of peace, bring dreams of mystic sight,
And when I wake, bring memory, wisdom, truth, and light.

Stuff the pillow with the herbal mixture, leaving at least a half inch of fabric, the raw edges of which can be turned inside. Sew the pillow shut, enclosing the herbal mixture neatly inside. On the first page of your blank book, write the date and the little verse that you said while you were enchanting the herbs.

Conclusion and Continuation

Complete this first stage of your ritual by thanking Neptune and the sea goddess for aiding you in your rite, and ask for their continued assistance and their messages in your dreams.

If it will be some time before you retire for the night, extinguish your candle and leave the pillow, the dream book, and the pen or pencil beside your bed. If you are almost ready for bed, leave the candle burning and complete your preparations to sleep. Just before sleeping, repeat the verse written on the first page of your book three times as you hold your dream pillow. Put the dream pillow under your regular pillow, or at least within the pillow case. (The herbs will work even through your regular pillow, but lying directly upon the dream pillow might allow more herbal fragrance than you'll be comfortable sleeping with, and could even become irritating—you'll have to judge. It depends partly on the strength of the herbs you use.) Allow yourself to drift peacefully off to sleep.

When you wake in the morning, try to wake slowly and stay in bed for a moment while you review what you were dreaming about. Write down whatever you can remember in your dream book, and date it. Sometimes only a small part of your dream will remain, but write it down anyway, whether it makes sense to you at the time or not. Often, more of your dream will come back to you as you write. Other times, you'll remember everything vividly. Don't get discouraged if you don't remember much at first. As you keep up this practice over a period of time, you'll remember more, and more often.

Keep up the dream journal for at least a month—one Moon cycle from when you began. Each night, light the candle for a few moments while you make your final preparations to sleep, then spend a quiet moment gazing into its flame in silent invocation for a message from Neptune and your sea goddess. Then repeat the little verse three times, position your dream pillow, extinguish the candle, and go to sleep. If your candle threatens to burn down before the month is over, prepare another one and light it from the flame of the one that is almost gone.

Once every week, take some time to read over what you have written. What did not make sense at first will often become quite clear in retrospect. Sometimes patterns will appear. Trust your own personal symbolism and interpretation, rather than looking to books that attempt to tell you what different things in your dreams mean.

Sometimes dreams will prove to be prophetic in some way, but more often they will give you helpful insight into things that are going on in your life, both your inner and outer life. Other people may be who they really are, or very often they are only in your dreams because they represent some aspect of yourself, so it is best not to take your dreams too literally. Look not so much for *who* that person in your dream is, but rather *why* he or she might be there. What does that person represent to you, in terms of characteristics, interests, and emotions? Could he or she be a symbol of something within yourself that needs your attention?

One bit of personal symbolism that has recurred for me at various times has involved traveling somewhere in a car. Over time, I've come to realize that when I feel reasonably in control of a situation, I am the driver. If, on the other hand, some aspect of concern in my life has seemed out of control, I am a passenger. This is a small thing that may or may not work for others.

The point is that things mean different things to different people. You are the best interpreter of your own dreams. Sometimes it can be worthwhile and interesting to talk them over with others, because something someone else says may trigger a thought that rings true for you. In the final analysis, though, your own meditation on your own dreams, journaled over a period of time, is most likely to yield the most profound messages.

The Magick of Pluto

Most Ideal Timing

On Tuesday; in the hour of Mars (Pluto is the higher octave of Mars); when the Moon is in Scorpio (or the exaltation sign, Aries); at the New Moon (for regeneration activities) or Full Moon (for power building) in Scorpio (or Aries); at the dark Moon for probing mysteries and letting go. Also, when your natal Pluto is receiving important aspects from other planets, or when transiting Pluto is making significant aspects to your chart and you feel a special need to let something go, to probe and purge old destructive patterns, to increase your inner powers of self-mastery, or to transform your life.

This ritual was written on a Tuesday in the hour of Mars, during the last-quarter lunar phase, with the Moon in Aries following a Full Moon in Sagittarius that was conjunct transiting Pluto.

Preparation

Often Pluto transits call for probing within to figure out why, one way or another, we keep falling into repetitive, destructive patterns, making the same mistakes in our lives and in our relationships with others. Often we are struggling to discover what is really significant in the midst of the clutter of competing demands. In order to discover our own inner truth and claim our power to follow it, we often have to experience the death of change and let something go. A first step can be to clear the mind, and this ritual is a physical exercise that may help you do that.

You will need a black candle in a metal candleholder. If you are working in a place that is not your normal ritual area, you will need to be sure the candle can burn safely. You can place the holder in the center of a pan of sand or water. You can also use a little banishing oil to anoint it, and a sage smudge stick or some house-blessing incense for a final blessing of the area after you've finished.[3] Wear work clothes, not ritual robes. With a grin of apology to those readers who may prefer that magick be elegantly structured, this ritual is "down and dirty"! I daresay most Witches will understand—with focused intent, any or no tools can serve magickal intent nicely.

Choose an area of your home or office that is the messiest, the most cluttered, the place you know you need to sort through and clear out, but have been avoiding and ignoring instead. We all have one—even if you are a super neatnik, you probably at least have one drawer full of junk. Be honest, now—pick a real challenge. Pluto is not easy, so you shouldn't try to make this ritual easy, either.

Your only other tools will be those that you need to clean your area: garbage bags, boxes, a broom, a mop, a pail of water, cleaning powder, dust cloths—whatever you need.

If what you are cleaning is a drawer, a trunk, or something you can haul into your normal ritual circle, fine. Otherwise, set your circle in the garage, attic, closet, office, or whatever other area you have chosen as your primary challenge.

Assemble your tools. Stand firmly in the center of your area and center yourself. Breathing deeply, visualize the energy of the cosmos flowing down through your crown, passing through each of your chakras and down into the Earth beneath you. Feel the flow. Now, visualize the upward flow of earth energy entering your body through your feet, flowing through each of your chakras, pouring out of your crown, and cascading down all around you. Conclude with *As above, so below; As within, so without, As the Universe, so the soul.*

The Ritual

Casting the Circle and Calling the Guardians

Mix cleaning powder into your pail of water and cleanse and consecrate it with the power of earth and water. Carry it clockwise around your room or area, sprinkling a little as you go, with the resolution that it be cleansed and consecrated to your work. Now, take up your broom and go to the east quarter. Knock the broom handle against the wall three times (if you have a wall there—make three short thrusts into the air if you don't), and say:

Mighty Guardian of the East, Powers of Air, I do summon, stir, and call you up to witness this rite, to clear my mind of clutter, to help me know what I must know, and to guard this circle. Hail, Sylphs, and blessings onto thee!

Repeat the same procedure at each succeeding quarter. Here are the calls:

Mighty Guardian of the South, Powers of Fire, I do summon, stir, and call you up to witness this rite, to charge me with the energy and courage I need to complete this task, to face the truth, and to guard this circle. Hail, Salamanders, and blessings onto thee!

Mighty Guardian of the West, Powers of Water, I do summon, stir, and call you up to witness this rite, to cleanse my mind that its mysteries may be revealed, to wash away my fears, to help me know what I must know, and to guard this circle. Hail, Undines, and blessings onto thee!

Mighty Guardians of the North, Powers of Earth, I do summon, stir, and call you up to witness this rite, to build my strength, to stabilize my purpose, to help me grow, and to guard this circle. Hail, Gnomes, and blessings onto thee!

Invocation and Magickal Working

Return to center. Light the black candle and, holding it, invoke the Dark Goddess and the Dark Lord, in your own words that most appropriately fit your specific intent, or with this more general call:

Persephone, Dark Queen of the Underworld, Lady of Wisdom, Pluto, Dark Lord of Shadows, be with me in the clutter of this place, in the dark shadows of my mind, and in the mysteries there that are not yet understood by my conscious self. Grant me guidance, growth in wisdom, and the power to make the changes that this rite will lead me to know I must make. Lead me back to the springtime of renewal. In perfect love and perfect trust, so mote it be.

Now, put the candle in the safe place you have prepared and let it burn all the way down. While it is burning, do your work! Do it with will, purpose, and intent. Sort out the clutter. Prepare the garbage for throwing out. Box up the good stuff that you haven't used for a long time and aren't likely to use (be honest), and mark it to give to charity (right after the ritual—don't procrastinate.) Put the stuff you really want to keep in its proper place. (In this case, it is okay to leave your circle area long enough to do so!) Don't stop until you have restored your designated area to order and cleanliness. Allow your mind to wander as it will, guided by the Dark Lady and Lord. Physical work can allow your mind the freedom to discover things you never might have thought of if you were merely sitting and trying to think. Within the context of the magick of this rite, each step you take in uncluttering that area has a corresponding effect on your mind—and on the power of Pluto within you.

Closing

When you have finished, light your incense and waft it all around the room in blessing and thanksgiving. Salute each direction, thanking the elementals who have assisted you, and spend a few final moments in silent thanksgiving to Persephone and Pluto for the wisdom you have received from this rite. Then pick up your tools, put them away, and take a nice, long shower!

---

1. The "angles" refers to the cusps (beginning degree) of the following houses of a horoscope: House 1 (Ascendant), House 4 (I.C., or *Imum Coeli*), House 7 (Descendant), and House 10 (Midheaven). Planets very close in degree to any of the four angles are especially strong. An angular planet's theme can dominate the personality, overshadowing even the Sun sign.

2. The five-pointed, eight-year orbital cycle of Venus was observed by various ancient cultures and incorporated into their religious practices. In the past decade, the late Neil F. Michelsen, founder of Astro Communications Services, Inc., programmed his computers to draw graphs of the orbital patterns of many planets and planetary combinations. The results of these precise calculations, based on the most accurate astronomy, are shown as mandalas in his book *Tables of Planetary Phenomena*. Two of his mandalas clearly demonstrate the five-pointed star formed by the eight-year cycle of Venus. The first mandala shows one eight-year cycle, and the second mandala shows that repeated eight-year cycles precisely duplicate the same pattern.

3. For the banishing oil you could use cloves, frankincense, lemon, myrrh, pine, or rosemary. For the house blessing, I particularly like dragon's blood resin mixed with lavender.

Appendix 1

Public Data Lists for Planetary Hour of Birth

In this section of the appendix, you'll find the lists of public people that I compiled in studying the planetary hour of birth. As I said before in the text, I actually based my interpretations more on the data of people I know personally and well, than on that of public figures. Still, the public list is interesting, if only for its variety. Some people seem to be listed right with the planet one would expect for them, while other listings are surprising or even baffling—which may simply be a demonstration that one's public persona can be quite different from who one is inside.

My choice of who to include in this sample is pretty random and hardly scientific. Here are my criteria:

1. People whose birth data can be considered very reliable.

2. People whose names should be easily recognizable to most readers.

In order to meet the first criterion, my final sample includes only data that has been graded AA by eminent researcher Lois Rodden, with just a few exceptions that are rated A. All the birth data was verified within AstroDatabank, a marvelous electronic database developed by Lois (an internationally recognized authority on accuracy in birth data), along with computer programmer Mark McDonough. AstroDatabank contains massive amounts of birth data, all rated as to its level of reliability. AA data must be based upon actual documentation of birth time; A data can be from the individual's own statement of reliable time (memory of family or official records) or on published birth announcements. Biographical information is given, along with a method of selecting many different criteria for filtering the selection, such as traits, attributes, occupations, interests, and so on. AstroDatabank is sure to become an indispensable program for anyone doing any type of astrological research.

The planetary hour of birth for each person was found by calculating the natal charts in Solar Fire, a popular, all-purpose chart calculation program distributed by Astrolabe. Once the chart is calculated, one only needs to click on "Reports," select "Horary," and the resulting screen shows the planetary hour of birth right in the middle of the top line. The use of these two fine programs made the prospect of compiling a decent-sized list of people infinitely easier than what I'd been doing before I got them. AstroDatabank is linked to Solar Fire such that you can export the data to be calculated, and also send personal charts you calculated in Solar Fire back into AstroDatabank.

It is interesting that at first, before I had my new computer programs and was compiling my initial, smaller sample of public data from various books, it seemed that it was a lot easier to find public people born under the hour of the Sun and Moon than the other planets. Conversely, my list of personally known people evened out fairly nicely among all seven planets. I was, at that time, admittedly, selecting mostly U.S. births to avoid the extra time needed to look up the right time zones and longitude/latitude to find the planetary hour in the Arlene Kramer's Sundial program. Arlene's program is by far the best for printing out an easy-to-use sheet of twelve-days worth of planetary hours to follow daily, but it does not lend itself well to finding the planetary hour of birth quickly for a lot of different charts. Also, it seems like there are a wealth of entertainers with easy-to-find, published birth times, but this is not so for people of other occupations, so I thought that might also be a factor in the preponderance of births in the hours of the Sun and Moon.

Once I was working with AstroDatabank, I was quickly able to more than double the size of my sample and include people from all over the world. I threw out anyone from the original list whose birth data couldn't be verified as AA, and added many more people, increasing my variety of occupations with the help of the biographical information. This time, I was surprised to find that the preponderance of public figures turned out to be born in the hour of Saturn! Actually, just like in my personal chart sample, the list of people evened out fairly well between all seven planets, but Saturn has the largest number. The wide variety of occupations includes several popular entertainers—and also a few notorious people. (The latter is represented in all the planets, too!)

What do I derive from this preponderance of people born in the hour of Saturn? Your guess is as good as mine. One way to look at it is that it verifies that Saturn has just as much or more to do with the discipline, organization, and persistence needed to become a public figure, than it does with limitation and all the various problems that tend to get associated with the old guy. Another way to see it, though, is just another factor of my own random choice of people selected—maybe Saturn subconsciously tends to choose more Saturn.

As for my inclusion of a few people with an A rating rather than AA, this was to enable me to include a few astrologers and Witches who would likely be known to readers of this book. The astrologers were easy—there are lots of them in the database, and I could have listed quite a few more. I had already randomly selected a few who are historically significant or are known well enough that they are most likely recognizable to lay readers (meaning those who are not professionals themselves or are serious students of astrology). I also did a search for all the authors of Llewellyn astrology books currently in the Llewellyn catalog. In order to list a few more of these, I included A data, as well as AA. (I should note that some professional astrologers decline to have their birth data published, so not being on the list may mean just that.)

Witches were another problem entirely! I did a search on Wicca and was shocked to find only myself plus thirteen anonymous listings for "Witch, American," along with their birth data. Now, I know there are a lot more of out of the broom closet than that! Those of you who are public and don't mind having researchers know about it, how about sending your data to AstroDatabank? Actually, in just scanning the list, fairly carefully, I did find Margot Adler, Sybil Leek, and Carl Weschcke—but that is all. The fact that those three didn't show up on the filtered search is probably an indication of the need to add "Wiccan" and "Witchcraft" to the word search, and I have reported that to the AstroDatabank people.

The following is my list of public figures, first by hour-of-birth planet, with one biographical line to identify those you may not recognize, and then again in alphabetical order with birth date and birthplace. Sorry, but it would be an infringement of copyright to give you the birth times derived from AstroDatabank. Though I could verify some of them from several other published sources, I thought it best to be consistent in presentation. I have used AstroDatabank to verify all data.

Born in the Hour of the Sun

Brigitte Bardot—Actress, sex kitten, animal activist.

Daniel Berrigan—Catholic priest, antiwar activist, arrested (with brother), author.

Marlon Brando—Oscar-winning movie actor, controversial political figure.

Helen Gurley Brown—Writer, editor of *Cosmopolitan* magazine.

Howard "Hopalong" Cassady—Football player at Ohio State, Associated Press Athlete of the Year, played for the Detroit Tigers.

David Copperfield—Celebrity magician and showman.

Claude Debussy—Composer and pianist, founder of impressionist school.

Jeanne Dixon—Psychic, newspaper Sun sign columnist, makes tabloid predictions.

Arthur Conan Doyle—Medical doctor best known as author of Sherlock Holmes stories.

Clint Eastwood—Movie star, "Dirty Harry" and many subsequent roles.

Alexander Fleming—Bacteriologist, discovered penicillin, won Nobel Prize for medicine.

Billy Graham—Celebrity evangelist, spiritual advisor to various U.S. presidents.

Carrie Fisher—Movie actress, writer, best known for *Star Wars* trilogy.

Harrison Ford—Movie star, "Indiana Jones" and many subsequent roles.

Whoopi Goldberg—Actress and comedienne who went from welfare to movie star.

Leona Helmsley—Real-estate millionaire, "Queen of Mean," imprisoned for tax evasion.

Charlton Heston—Movie actor famous for historical roles; head of the National Rifle Association.

Lena Horne—Glamorous and elegant stage and screen singer/actress.

Bruce Jenner—Olympic decathlon champion.

Janis Joplin—Singer, died of heroin overdose, known for her electric raw energy.

Edward Kennedy—Senator, liberal democrat, scandal over drowning of Mary Jo Kopechne.

Henry Kissinger—Former U.S. secretary of state, major figure in ending the Vietnam War.

J. Lee Lehman, Ph.D.—Astrologer, author, renowned expert in horary astrology who is cited in this book.

Charles Manson—Cult leader, ritualistic mass murderer.

Joseph McCarthy—The politician who ignited Communist paranoia, alcoholic.

Marquis de Sade—Writer of pornography, spent most of his life in prison for sado-masochistic violence.

Steven Spielberg—Director, producer, writer, Oscar winner.

John Travolta—Movie star, Scientologist.

Tammy Wynette—Country singer known for the song "Stand By Your Man," painkiller dependency.

Emile Zola—Famous French writer of fiction.

Born in the Hour of the Moon

Woody Allen—Actor, writer, comedian, compulsive worker, known for his depression.

Muhammad Ali—Boxing champ, Islam convert, lost boxing title for refusal to enlist in the military, won the title back.

Prince Andrew—British prince, Duke of York, married and divorced Sarah Ferguson.

Maya Angelou—Poet, writer, actress, sexual abuse at age six caused her to be mute for six years.

Neil Armstrong—American astronaut, first man on the Moon.

Warren Beatty—Movie star, considered running for the U.S. presidency in the year 2000.

Shirley Temple Black—Child star, United Nations representative.

George H. Bush—President of the United States from 1989–1993, father of current president.

Glenn Close—Popular actress on stage and screen.

Jean Cocteau—French artist, poet, novelist, critic, playwright, painter, and illustrator.

Ralph Waldo Emerson—Writer, essayist, and poet; Unitarian minister.

Aretha Franklin—The "Queen of Soul," recording star.

Sigmund Freud—Physician, developed psychoanalysis, pioneer in subconscious exploration.

Rob Hand—Widely respected astrologer, author, leader in the recovery of astrological history.

Ernest Hemingway—Great writer, committed suicide.

John Hinckley, Jr.—Attempted to assassinate Ronald Reagan, obsessed with Jodie Foster, imprisoned.

Dustin Hoffman—Oscar-winning movie actor.

Victor Hugo—Famous French writer.

Caroline Kennedy—Daughter of President Kennedy.

Grant Lewi—Astrologer, Llewellyn author, wrote *Heaven Knows What* and *Astrology for the Millions*.

Liberace—Flamboyant pianist, the world's highest paid entertainer in his time, died of AIDS.

Neil F. Michelsen—Pioneer of astrological computer technology, founded Astro Communications Services, published *American Ephemeris*.

Marilyn Monroe—Movie sex symbol, involved with the Kennedy brothers, apparent suicide questionable.

Jack Nicklaus—Golf champion.

Louis Pasteur—Scientist, biochemist, and bacteriologist, founder of preventive medicine.

Elvis Presley—Legendary singer, entertainer.

Roseanne—Superstar television comedienne.

Barbara Shafferman—Astrologer, Llewellyn author of *The President's Astrologer*.

Jimmy Swaggart—Television evangelist, involved in sex scandal.

Sharon Tate—Actress, one of the homicide victims in the Manson ritual murders.

Born in the Hour of Mercury

Loni Anderson—Actress, comic, married Burt Reynolds—ugly divorce.

Fred Astaire—World-renowned and much-loved dancer and movie star.

Joan Baez—Singer, spokeswoman of 1960s.

Jim Bakker—Evangelist, imprisoned for fraud.

Lucille Ball—Popular comedienne of *I Love Lucy* on television.

Drew Barrymore—Actress, wild child alcoholic, suicide attempt at age thirteen.

Kathleen Battle—Coloratura soprano with temperament to match talent.

Alexander Graham Bell—Teacher of deaf-mutes, inventor of the telephone.

Philip Berrigan—Catholic priest, antiwar activist, left the Catholic church, later married and had kids.

Tony Blair—British politician currently serving as prime minister.

Scott Carpenter—One of the seven original American astronauts.

Jimmy Carter—Thirty-ninth president of the United States, very active in charitable work as ex-president.

Coco Chanel—French fashion designer.

Charles, Prince of Wales—Heir to the British throne.

Xavier Cugat—Bandleader known as the "Rhumba King."

Edgar Degas—Painter and sculptor of the impressionist school.

Ariel Guttman—Astrologer, Llewellyn author, wrote *Mythic Astrology.*

Mata Hari—Spy, double agent during World War I, prostitute, executed.

Patty Hearst—Kidnap victim, brainwashed, fugitive.

Heinrich Himmler—Nazi, head of the Gestapo, committed suicide.

Rock Hudson—Double life: romantic movie star and closet gay, first noted celebrity to die of AIDS.

Charles Lindbergh—Famous pilot, won a Medal of Honor and Pulitzer Prize, his son was kidnapped and murdered.

Karl Marx—Communist philosopher.

Sydney Omarr—Author, syndicated columnist, featured on Llewellyn website, wrote several books.

Pablo Picasso—Highly prolific artist, ranked among the great masters.

Dan Rather—Emmy-winning television news correspondent.

Eleanor Roosevelt—First Lady, American icon.

Nicole Brown Simpson—The brutally murdered wife of O. J. Simpson.

Born in the Hour of Venus

Hans Christian Anderson—Writer of fairy tales and fables, translated into many languages.

Simone de Beauvoir—French writer, existentialist teacher in the early 1940s, feminist.

St. Bernadette of Lourdes—Peasant girl who saw fourteen visions of the Holy Mother.

Erma Bombeck—Humorist, author of books read by millions of people.

Johnny Carson—Popular host of the *Tonight* show on television for many years.

Enrico Caruso—Italian opera singer, considered one of greatest tenors in history.

Julia Child—Celebrity chef and writer of cookbooks.

Placido Domingo—Spanish opera star.

Adolph Eichmann—Nazi war criminal highly instrumental in the Holocaust, hanged in 1962.

Farrah Fawcett—Actress, one of *Charlie's Angels* on television, later made movies.

Jane Fonda—Actress, political activist, exercise leader.

King Henry VIII—Much married; split English church from Rome, fathered Elizabeth I.

Audrey Hepburn—Movie star, in later years was a goodwill ambassador for UNICEF.

Adolf Hitler—Charismatic Nazi leader, responsible for the Holocaust, committed suicide.

Jimmy Hoffa—Labor union leader, imprisoned until he was released by Nixon.

Erica Jong—Novelist, feminist.

Ursula LeGuin—Poet and science fiction writer.

Leonardo da Vinci—Renaissance artist, genius, inventor, engineer, sculptor, and painter.

Monica Lewinsky—Former White House intern involved in sex scandal with President Clinton.

Shirley MacLaine—Actress, Oscar winner, noted for metaphysical journeys.

Henri Matisse—French artist of the expressionist era.

Paul Newman—Movie star, Oscar winner, director.

George Patton—Famous World War II general and military commander; movie was made of his life.

Ross Perot—Industrialist and philanthropist, unsuccessful run for the U.S. presidency in 1992.

Sally Ride—Astronaut, America's first woman in space in 1983.

Gloria Steinem—Noted feminist crusader, writer.

Noel Tyl—Astrologer, international lecturer, editor, author of many Llewellyn books.

Born in the Hour of Mars

Paula Abdul—Pop singer, dancer, problem with binging and purging.

Spiro Agnew—Vice-president who resigned because of financial misconduct, lawyer, governor of Maryland.

Louisa May Alcott—Author, wrote *Little Women*, ardent feminist.

Alexander II—Russian czar who emancipated the serfs, assassinated in 1881 by a bomb.

Jim Bailey—Entertainer, female impersonator.

Tammy Faye Bakker—Television evangelist, married to Jim Bakker who was involved in a scandal.

Candice Bergen—Movie actress, "Murphy Brown" on television.

Carol Burnett—Comedienne on stage, in movies, and on television, won many Emmys.

Sean Connery—Actor, best known for "James Bond" character.

Jeffrey Dahmer—Serial killer.

Albert Einstein—Scientist, mathematician, physicist, genius, won Nobel Prize for physics.

Diane Feinstein—Politician, mayor of San Francisco, later a U.S. senator.

John Wayne Gacy—Sadistic murderer of thirty-two boys, buried them in his cellar, executed.

Al Gore—Vice-president, ran for U.S. presidency in the year 2000.

Lee Iacocca—Entrepreneur, tough talking, president of Ford Motor Company for eight years until fired. Also served as chairman of the Chrysler Corporation.

Sophia Loren—Glamorous and sexy movie star.

Martin Luther—Catholic priest who broke from the Catholic church, started the Protestant Reformation.

Christa McAuliffe—First teacher in space, died in the explosion of the space shuttle Challenger in 1986.

Jim Morrison—Lead singer of the Doors, songwriter, cult figure after his death.

Luciano Pavarotti—Leading operatic tenor.

Prince—Singer, songwriter, actor.

Carl Sagan—Celebrity astronomer, astrophysicist, educator, author.

John Paul Sartre—Writer, noted for his philosophy of existentialism.

Walter Schirra—One of the seven original American astronauts.

Barbra Streisand—Singer and actress; Tony, Emmy, and Oscar winner; director.

Mark Spitz—World-record holder, Olympic swimmer, won five gold medals in 1972.

Martha Stewart—Entrepreneur who's made millions as an icon of homemaking arts.

Linda Tripp—News figure in the Clinton scandal, taped phone calls between Bill Clinton and Monica Lewinsky.

Vincent van Gogh—Post-impressionist painter, suffered from madness, famous after his death.

Carl Llewellyn Weschcke—Owner of Llewellyn Publications, Wiccan High Priest.

Orson Welles—Writer, playwright celebrated for his wit and flamboyance.

Oscar Wilde—Writer, playwright celebrated for his wit and flamboyance.

Born in the Hour of Jupiter

Konrad Adenauer—Chancellor of West German Republic from 1949 to 1963.

Marshall Applewhite—Cult leader and guru of San Diego-area mass suicide group.

Pat Boone—Singer, actor, sold eighteen million records by age twenty-four.

Louis Braille—Blind organist who invented a transcription system for the blind in 1824.

William Buckley—Syndicated newspaper columnist, author, political conservative.

George W. Bush—Became president of the United States in 2001, former governor of Texas.

Paul Cezanne—One of the most significant impressionist painters.

Cher—Singer, first with Sonny Bono, later a movie star; style-setter.

Bill Clinton—Former U.S. president, scandal in 1998 and 1999, trial for impeachment, acquitted.

Chelsea Clinton—Daughter of former President Clinton.

Salvador Dali—Legendary painter of the surrealist school.

Christian Dior—Famous French fashion designer.

Shannen Doherty—Actress, one of the stars of the television show *Charmed*.

Elizabeth II—British royalty, queen since 1952.

Mia Farrow—Movie star.

Betty Friedan—Feminist pioneer and organizer, author of *The Feminine Mystique*.

Judy Garland—Singer and actress, top star from *The Wizard of Oz* at age thirteen.

Arthur Godfrey—Early prominent television personality, entertainer, businessman, ukulele player.

Marc Edmund Jones—Astrologer and popular author, active into his 90s.

J. Edgar Hoover—Former head of the FBI, revealed to be corrupt and a bigot; closet gay.

Madonna—Superstar singer and actress.

Maria Montessori—Italian doctor, internationally famous educator, founded the Montessori method.

Oliver North—Marine career officer involved in Iran-Contra scandal; later a politician.

Dolly Parton—Country singer and actress.

James Earl Ray—Assassinated Dr. Martin Luther King, Jr.

Robert Redford—Movie star, director.

Bil Tierney—Astrologer, Llewellyn author, author of the "Alive and Well" series, as well as *The Twelve Faces of Saturn*.

George Stephanopoulos—Political operative for Clinton, quit after scandal, wrote tell-all book.

Ted Turner—Entrepreneur, media mogul, billionaire, married and divorced Jane Fonda.

Born in the Hour of Saturn

Margot Adler—Witch, author of *Drawing Down the Moon*, radio correspondent.

Buzz Aldrin—Astronaut, second man on the Moon, war fighter pilot.

Czarina Alexandra—Married Nicholas of Russia in 1894; was assassinated with entire family.

John Belushi—Cult star of *Saturday Night Live*; died of drug overdose in 1982.

Sonny Bono—Trend-setting entertainer with Cher, later became a U.S. senator.

Johannes Brahms—Musician, composer, pianist, and conductor.

Willy Brandt—German chancellor, won a Nobel Prize for peace.

Lenny Bruce—Satirical nightclub comedian known for political commentary.

Anita Bryant—Entertainer, born-again Christian, anti-gay, sued in civil rights conspiracy case.

Nicolas Cage—Actor, won an Academy Award.

Billy Carter—Brother of former President Carter, managed peanut business, alcoholic.

Carol Channing—Movie star, singer.

Nicholas Copernicus—Astronomer and author who established that planets orbit the Sun.

Marie Curie—Physicist and chemist, winner of two Nobel Prizes.

Elizabeth I—The Virgin Queen, subject of recent popular movies, daughter of Henry VIII.

Betty Ford—Former First Lady, recovering alcoholic and addict, had a mastectomy.

Llewellyn George—Astrologer, Llewellyn founder, author of *The A–Z Horoscope Maker*.

Florence Griffith-Joyner—Olympic gold medal sprinter, was the fastest woman alive.

Basil T. Fearrington—Astrologer, Llewellyn author, wrote *The New Way to Learn Astrology*.

Jodie Foster—Oscar-winning movie star.

Goldie Hawn—Movie star, comedienne.

Hugh Hefner—Playboy publisher, hedonist.

Katharine Hepburn—Legendary movie star, won four Academy Awards for best actress.

Jim Jones—Cult leader, led mass suicide.

Grace Kelly—Actress, Princess of Monaco, died in a car crash.

Coretta Scott King—Civil rights activist.

Evel Knievel—Daredevil, beat a man and was imprisoned.

Karl Erst Kraft—Astrologer, Nazi, killed after falling from grace for predictions Hitler didn't like.

Timothy Leary—Professor, prominent in the 1960s psychedelic and acid movement.

Sybil Leek—Witch, writer, journalist, syndicated columnist.

Lucky Luciano—Gangster, leader of organized crime in eastern U.S.; deported in 1946.

Eric Menendez—Killed parents with brother Lyle, finally convicted after mistrials, got life in prison.

Giacomo Puccini—Composer of perenially popular romantic operas.

Dan Quayle—Vice-president under George H. Bush.

Franklin D. Roosevelt—U.S. president from 1933–1945, died during his fourth term.

Phyllis Schlafly—Politician, best known for being an antifeminist, ultraconservative Republican.

Philip Sedgwick—Astrologer, Llewellyn author, wrote *Sun at the Center*.

Maria Kay Simms—Author, astrologer, Wiccan High Priestess.

O. J. Simpson—Football star accused of murdering his wife; acquitted, but lost in civil trial.

Gloria Star—Astrologer, Llewellyn author, wrote *Astrology: Woman to Woman*, featured writer in Llewellyn annuals.

Meryl Streep—Movie star.

Toulouse-Lautrec—Artist of post-impressionist period, had a mental breakdown, alcoholic.

Rudolph Valentino—Actor, cult romantic figure.

Robin Williams—Comic actor.

Duke of Windsor—As King Edward VIII, he abdicated the British throne to marry Wallis Simpson, a divorcee.

Public Data List in Alphabetical Order with Birth Date, Place of Birth, and Hour-of-Birth Planet

Abdul, Paula	6-19-1962	Los Angeles, CA	Mars
Adenauer, Konrad	1-5-1876	Cologne, Germany	Jupiter
Adler, Margot	4-16-1946	Little Rock, AR	Saturn
Agnew, Spiro	11-9-1918	Forest Hill, MD	Mars
Alcott, Louisa May	11-29-1832	Germantown, PA	Mars
Aldrin, Buzz	1-20-1930	Glen Ridge, NJ	Saturn
Alexander II, Czar	4-29-1818	Moscow, Russia	Mars
Alexandra, Czarina	6-6-1872	Damstadt, Germany	Saturn
Allen, Woody	12-1-1935	Brooklyn, NH	Moon
Ali, Muhammad	1-17-1942	Louisville, KY	Moon
Anderson, Hans Christian	4-2-1805	Odense, Denmark	Venus
Anderson, Loni	8-5-1945	St. Paul, MN	Mercury
Andrew, Prince	2-19-1960	London, England	Moon
Angelou, Maya	4-4-1928	St. Louis, MO	Moon
Applewhite, Marshall	5-17-1931	Spur, TX	Jupiter
Armstrong, Neil	8-5-1930	Washington, OH	Moon
Astaire, Fred	5-10-1899	Omaha, NE	Mercury
Baez, Joan	1-9-1941	Staten Island, NY	Mercury
Bailey, Jim	1-10-1938	Philadelphia, PA	Mars
Bakker, Jim	1-2-1940	Muskegon Heights, MI	Mercury
Bakker, Tammy Faye	3-7-1942	International Falls, MN	Mars
Ball, Lucille	8-6-1911	Jamestown, NY	Mercury
Bardot, Brigitte	9-28-1934	Paris, France	Sun
Barrymore, Drew	2-22-1975	Culver City, CA	Mercury
Battle, Kathleen	8-13-1948	Portsmouth, OH	Mercury
Beatty, Warren	3-30-1937	Richmond, VA	Moon

Beauvoir, Simone de	1-9-1908	Paris, France	Venus
Bell, Alexander Graham	3-3-1847	Edinburgh, Scotland	Mercury
Belushi, John	1-23-1949	Chicago, IL	Saturn
Bergen, Candice	5-9-1946	Los Angeles, CA	Mars
Bernadette, St., of Lourdes	1-7-1844	Lourdes, France	Venus
Berrigan, Daniel	5-9-1921	Virginia, MN	Sun
Berrigan, Philip	10-5-1923	Two Harbors, MI	Mercury
Black, Shirley Temple	4-23-1928	Santa Monica, CA	Moon
Blair, Tony	5-6-1953	Edinburgh, Scotland	Mercury
Bombeck, Erma	2-21-1927	Dayton, OH	Venus
Bono, Sonny	2-16-1935	Detroit, MI	Saturn
Boone, Pat	6-1-1934	Jacksonville, FL	Jupiter
Brahms, Johannes	5-7-1833	Hamburg, Germany	Saturn
Braille, Louis	1-4-1809	Cupvray, France	Jupiter
Brando, Marlon	4-3-1924	Omaha, NE	Sun
Brandt, Willy	12-18-1913	Lubeck, Germany	Saturn
Brown, Helen Gurley	2-18-1922	Green Forrest, AR	Sun
Bruce, Lenny	10-13-1925	Mineola, NY	Saturn
Bryant, Anita	3-25-1940	Barnsdall, OK	Saturn
Buckley, William	11-24-1925	New York, NH	Jupiter
Burnett, Carol	4-26-1933	San Antonio, TX	Mars
Bush, George S.	6-12-1924	Milton, MA	Moon
Bush, George W.	7-6-1946	New Haven, CT	Jupiter
Cage, Nicolas	1-7-1964	Harbor City, CA	Saturn
Carpenter, Scott	5-1-1925	Boulder, CO	Mercury
Carson, Johnny	10-23-1925	Corning, IA	Venus
Carter, Billy	3-29-1937	Americus, GA	Saturn
Carter, Jimmy	10-1-1924	Plains, GA	Mercury
Caruso, Enrico	2-27-1873	Naples, Italy	Venus
Cassady, "Hopalong"	2-2-1934	Columbus, OH	Sun
Cezanne, Paul	1-19-1839	Aix-en-Provence, France	Jupiter
Chanel, Coco	8-19-1883	Saumur, France	Mercury
Channing, Carol	1-31-1921	Seattle, WA	Saturn
Charles, Prince of Wales	11-14-1948	London, England	Mercury
Cher	5-20-1946	El Centro, OK	Jupiter
Child, Julia	8-15-1912	Pasadena, CA	Venus
Clinton, Bill	8-19-1946	Hope, AR	Jupiter
Clinton, Chelsea	2-27-1980	Little Rock, AR	Jupiter
Close, Glenn	3-19-1947	Greenwich, CT	Moon
Cocteau, Jean	7-5-1889	Maisons Laffitte, France	Moon

Connery, Sean	8-25-1930	Edinburgh, Scotland	Mars
Copernicus, Nicholas	2-28-1473	Torun, Poland	Saturn
Copperfield, David	9-16-1956	Perth Amboy, NJ	Sun
Cugat, Xavier	1-1-1900	Gerona, Spain	Mercury
Curie, Marie	11-7-1867	Warsaw, Poland	Saturn
Dahmer, Jeffrey	5-21-1960	Milwaukee, WI	Mars
Dali, Salvador	5-11-1904	Figueras, Spain	Jupiter
Debussy, Claude	8-22-1862	St. Germain, France	Sun
Degas, Edgar	7-19-1834	Paris, France	Mercury
Dior, Christian	1-21-1905	Granville, France	Jupiter
Dixon, Jeanne	1-5-1904	Medford, WI	Sun
Doherty, Shannen	4-12-1971	Memphis, TN	Jupiter
Domingo, Placido	1-31-1941	Madrid, Spain	Venus
Doyle, Arthur Conan	5-22-1859	Edinburgh, Scotland	Sun
Eastwood, Clint	5-31-1930	San Francisco, CA	Sun
Eichmann, Adolph	3-19-1906	Solingen, Germany	Venus
Einstein, Albert	3-14-1879	Ulm, Germany	Mars
Elizabeth I	9-17-1533	Greenwich, England	Saturn
Elizabeth II	4-21-1926	London, England	Jupiter
Emerson, Ralph Waldo	5-25-1803	Boston, MA	Moon
Farrow, Mia	2-9-1945	Los Angeles, CA	Jupiter
Fawcett, Farrah	2-2-1947	Corpus Christi, TX	Venus
Fearrington, Basil T.	8-1-1954	Philadelphia, PA	Saturn
Feinstein, Diane	6-22-1933	San Francisco, CA	Mars
Fisher, Carrie	10-21-1956	Burbank, CA	Sun
Fleming, Alexander	8-6-1881	London, England	Sun
Fonda, Jane	12-21-1937	Manhattan, NY	Venus
Ford, Betty	4-8-1918	Chicago, IL	Saturn
Ford, Harrison	7-13-1942	Chicago, IL	Sun
Foster, Jodie	11-19-1962	Los Angeles, CA	Saturn
Franklin, Aretha	3-25-1942	Memphis, TN	Moon
Freud, Sigmund	5-6-1856	Freiberg, Czech Republic	Moon
Friedan, Betty	2-4-1921	Peoria, IL	Jupiter
Gacy, John Wayne	3-17-1942	Chicago, IL	Mars
Garland, Judy	6-10-1922	Grand Rapids, MI	Jupiter
George, Llewellyn	8-17-1876	St. Louis, MO	Saturn
Godfrey, Arthur	8-31-1903	New York, NY	Jupiter
Goldberg, Whoopi	11-13-1955	New York City, NY	Sun
Gore, Al	3-31-1948	Washington, DC	Mars
Graham, Billy	11-7-1918	Charlotte, NC	Sun

Griffith-Joyner, Florence	12–21–1959	Los Angeles, CA	Saturn
Guttman, Ariel	7–6–1949	St. Louis, MO	Mercury
Hand, Rob	12–5–1942	Plainfield, NJ	Moon
Hari, Mata	8–7–1876	Leeuwarden, Netherlands	Mercury
Hawn, Goldie	11–21–1945	Washington, DC	Saturn
Hearst, Patty	2–20–1954	San Francisco, CA	Mercury
Hefner, Hugh	4–9–1926	Chicago, IL	Saturn
Helmsley, Leona	7–4–1920	Marbletown, NY	Sun
Hemingway, Ernest	7–21–1899	Oak Park, IL	Moon
Henry VIII, King	7–7–1491	Greenwich, England	Venus
Hepburn, Audrey	5–4–1929	Ixellesi, Belgium	Venus
Hepburn, Katharine	5–12–1907	Hartford, CT	Saturn
Heston, Charlton	10–4–1923	Evanston, IL	Sun
Himmler, Heinrich	10–7–1900	Munich, Germany	Mercury
Hinckley, Jr., John	5–29–1955	Ardmore, OK	Moon
Hitler, Adolf	4–20–1889	Braunau am Inn, Austria	Venus
Hoffa, Jimmy	2–14–1913	Brazil, IN	Venus
Hoffman, Dustin	8–8–1937	Los Angeles, CA	Moon
Hoover, J. Edgar	1–1–1895	Washington, DC	Jupiter
Horne, Lena	6–30–1917	Brooklyn, NY	Sun
Hudson, Rock	11–17–1925	Winnetka, IL	Mercury
Hugo, Victor	2–26–1802	Besancon, France	Moon
Iacocca, Lee	10–15–1924	Allentown, PA	Mars
Jenner, Bruce	10–28–1949	Mount Kisco, NY	Sun
Jones, Jim	5–13–1931	Lynn, IN	Saturn
Jones, Marc Edmond	10–1–1888	St. Louis, MO	Jupiter
Jong, Erica	6–26–1942	Manhattan, NY	Venus
Joplin, Janis	1–19–1943	Port Arthur, TX	Sun
Kelly, Grace	11–12–1929	Philadelphia, PA	Saturn
Kennedy, Caroline	11–27–1957	New York City, NY	Moon
Kennedy, Edward	2–22–1932	Dorchester, MA	Sun
King, Coretta Scott	4–27–1927	Marion, AL	Saturn
Kissinger, Henry	5–27–1923	Furth, Germany	Sun
Knievel, Evel	10–17–1938	Butte, MT	Saturn
Kraft, Karl Erst	5–10–1900	Commugny, Switzerland	Saturn
Leary, Timothy	10–22–1920	Springfield, MA	Saturn
Leek, Sybil	2–22–1917	Staffordshire, England	Saturn
LeGuin, Ursula	10–21–1929	Berkeley, CA	Venus
Lehman, J. Lee	9–9–1953	Wakefield, NE	Sun
Lewi, Grant	6–8–1902	New York, NY	Moon

Lewinsky, Monica	7–23–1973	San Francisco, CA	Venus
Liberace	5–16–1919	West Allis, WI	Moon
Lindbergh, Charles	2–4–1902	Detroit, MI	Mercury
Loren, Sophia	9–20–1934	Rome, Italy	Mars
Lucky Luciano	11–25–1897	Lercara Friddi, Sicily	Saturn
Luther, Martin	11–19–1483	Eisleben, Germany	Mars
MacLaine, Shirley	4–24–1934	Richmond, VA	Venus
Madonna	8–16–1958	Bay City, MI	Jupiter
Manson, Charles	11–12–1934	Cincinnati, OH	Sun
Marx, Karl	5–5–1818	Trier, Germany	Mercury
Matisse, Henri	12–31–1869	LaCateau, France	Venus
McAuliffe, Christa	9–2–1948	Boston, MA	Mars
McCarthy, Joseph	11–14–1908	Grand Chute, WI	Sun
Menendez, Eric	11–27–1970	Livingston, NJ	Saturn
Michelsen, Neil	5–11–1931	Chicago, IL	Moon
Monroe, Marilyn	6–1–1926	Los Angeles, CA	Moon
Montessori, Maria	8–31–1870	Chiaravalle, Italy	Jupiter
Morrison, Jim	12–8–1943	Melbourne, FL	Mars
Newman, Paul	1–26–1925	Cleveland, OH	Venus
Nicklaus, Jack	1–21–1940	Columbus, OH	Moon
North, Oliver	10–7–1943	San Antonio, TX	Jupiter
Omarr, Sydney	8–5–1926	Philadelphia, PA	Mercury
Parton, Dolly	1–19–1946	Locust Ridge, TN	Jupiter
Pasteur, Louis	12–27–1822	Dole, France	Moon
Patton, George	11–11–1885	San Marino, CA	Venus
Pavarotti, Luciano	10–12–1935	Modena, Italy	Mars
Perot, Ross	1–27–1930	Texarkana, TX	Venus
Picasso, Pablo	10–25–1881	Malaga, Spain	Mercury
Presley, Elvis	1–8–1935	Tupelo, MS	Moon
Prince	6–7–1958	Minneapolis, MN	Mars
Puccini, Giacomo	12–22–1858	Lugues, Italy	Saturn
Quayle, Dan	2–4–1947	Indianapolis, IN	Saturn
Rather, Dan	10–31 1931	Wharton, TX	Mercury
Ray, James Earl	3–10–1928	Alton, IL	Jupiter
Redford, Robert	8–18–1936	Santa Monica, CA	Jupiter
Ride, Sally	5–26–1951	Los Angeles, CA	Venus
Roosevelt, Eleanor	10–11–1884	New York, NY	Mercury
Roosevelt, Franklin D.	1–30–1882	Hyde Park, NY	Saturn
Roseanne	11–3–1952	Salt Lake City, UT	Moon
Sade, Marquis de	6–2–1740	Paris, France	Sun

Sagan, Carl	11-9-1934	New York City, NY	Mars
Sartre, John Paul	6-21-1905	Paris, France	Mars
Schirra, Walter	3-12-1923	Hackensack, NJ	Mars
Schlafly, Phyllis	8-15-1924	St. Louis, MO	Saturn
Sedgwick, Philip	11-8-1950	Pittsfield, MA	Saturn
Shafferman, Barbara	8-24-1928	New York, NY	Moon
Simms, Maria Kay	11-18-1940	Princeton, IL	Saturn
Simpson, Nicole Brown	5-19-1959	Frankfurt am Main, Ger.	Mercury
Simpson, O. J.	7-9-1947	San Francisco, CA	Saturn
Spielberg, Steven	12-18-1946	Cincinnati, OH	Sun
Spitz, Mark	2-10-1950	Modesto, CA	Mars
Star, Gloria	9-6-1948	Abilene, TX	Saturn
Steinem, Gloria	3-25-1934	Toledo, OH	Venus
Stephanopoulos, George	2-10-1961	Fall River, MA	Jupiter
Stewart, Martha	8-3-1941	Jersey City, NJ	Mars
Streep, Meryl	6-22-1949	Summit, NJ	Saturn
Streisand, Barbra	4-24-1942	Summit, NJ	Mars
Swaggart, Jimmy	3-15-1935	Ferriday, LA	Moon
Tate, Sharon	1-24-1943	Dallas, TX	Moon
Tierney, Bil	11-4-1949	New York, NY	Jupiter
Toulouse-Lautrec, Henri	11-24-1864	Albi, France	Saturn
Travolta, John	2-18-1954	Englewood, NJ	Sun
Tripp, Linda	11-24-1949	Jersey City, NJ	Mars
Turner, Ted	11-19-1938	Cincinnati, OH	Jupiter
Tyl, Noel	12-31-1936	West Chester, PA	Venus
Valentino, Rudolph	5-6-1895	Castellaneta, Italy	Saturn
Van Gogh, Vincent	3-30-1853	Zundert, Netherlands	Mars
Vinci, Leonardo da	4-23-1452	Vinci, Italy	Venus
Welles, Orson	6-6-1915	Kenosha, WI	Mars
Weschcke, Carl	9-10-1930	St. Paul, MN	Mars
Wilde, Oscar	10-16-1854	Dublin, Ireland	Mars
Williams, Robin	7-21-1951	Milwaukee, WI	Saturn
Windsor, Duke of	6-23-1894	Richmond Surrey, Eng.	Saturn
Wynette, Tammy	5-5-1942	Red Bay, AL	Sun
Zola, Emile	4-2-1840	Paris, France	Sun

Appendix 2

Planetary and Elemental Correspondences

Planetary Correspondences

Sun ☉

Dignities
Rules Leo
Exalted: Aries
Detriment: Aquarius
Fall: Libra
Rules the fifth house

Element
fire

Classifications
hot and dry
masculine
positive polarity
active/kinetic
sustaining
diurnal, day

Direction
south

Other Deity Names
Helios, Apollo
Lucina, Brigid,
Aurora

Keywords
father
leader
dignity
status
vitality
creative
shining

will
purpose
life force
pride
self-esteem
ego
purpose
will
energy
honor

Body, Health
heart
upper spine
right eye of males
left eye of females

Metal
gold

Colors
yellow
orange
scarlet

Stones
topaz
amber
diamond

Herbs, Botanicals
cedar
cinnamon
frankincense
orange blossom
rosemary

Moon ☽

Dignities
Rules Cancer
Exalted: Taurus
Detriment: Capricorn
Fall: Scorpio
Rules the fourth house

Element
water

Classifications
cold and moist
feminine
negative polarity
passive/magnetic
changing
nocturnal, night

Direction
west

Other Deity Names
Selene, Diana
Sin, Nu'a/Noah*

Keywords
mother
the people
home/domesticity
roots
childbirth
nurturing
intuitive
feeling/emotion
mystery
memory
unconscious thought
receptivity
change
moodiness
instinct
sensitivity
habits

Body, Health
stomach
female organs
secretions
glands

Metal
silver

Colors
pale blue
iridescence

Stones
moonstone
pearl
opal

Herbs, Botanicals
white flowers
jasmine
eucalyptus
lotus
lemon balm
myrrh
sandalwood

*It's not easy finding any recognizable Moon gods! Sin is Babylonian; Nu'ah is the Babylonian Moon goddess reincarnated in The Book of Genesis as Noah.

Mercury ☿

Dignities
Rules Gemini and Virgo
Exalted: Aquarius
Detriment: Sagittarius and Pisces
Fall: Leo
Rules the third and sixth houses

Elements
air and earth

Classifications
cool; dry and moist
androgynous
positive (and negative)
active (and passive)
flexible
adaptable

Direction
east

Other Deity Names
Hermes, Woden
Minerva, Athena

Keywords
rational
the mind
the messenger
conscious thought
abstract thought
logic/reason
the intellect
communication
motion
indecisive
skill

clever
cunning
dexterity
writing, speech
adaptive
wit

Body, Health
hands
nervous system
thyroid
organs of speech
yellow

Metals
quicksilver
lodestones

Color
yellow

Stones
agate
adventurine
flourite

Herbs, Botanicals
lavender
marjoram
peppermint
lemon verbena
rosemary
bergamot

Venus ♀

Dignities
Rules Taurus and Libra
Exalted: Pisces
Detriment: Scorpio and Aries
Fall: Virgo
Rules the second and seventh houses

Elements
earth and air

Classifications
warm and moist
feminine
negative polarity
passive/magnetic
sustaining
nocturnal

Directions
north and east

Other Deity Names
Aphrodite, Freya
Cupid, Eros

Keywords
love, attraction
affinity
magnetism
aesthetic sense
comfort
sensuality
balance
fairness
diplomacy, tact
relating
money/finance
art
social graces
peace
pleasure

Body, Health
throat
kidneys
lower back
skin, sense of touch

Metal
copper

Colors
soft colors, tints

Stones
emerald
sapphire
rose quartz
turquoise
malachite

Herbs, Botanicals
balm of Gilead
catnip
geranium
mugwort
myrtle
rose
thyme
yarrow

Mars ♂

Dignities
Rules Aries (and Scorpio)
Exalted: Capricorn
Detriment: Libra (and Taurus)
Fall: Cancer
Rules the first house
(and eighth house)

Element
fire

Classifications
  hot and dry
  masculine
  positive polarity
  active/kinetic
  initiating
  diurnal

Direction
  south

Other Deity Names
  Ares, Tiw
  Athena, Artemis

Keywords
  action
  assertion
  competitive
  challenging
  war, aggression
  impulsive
  courageous
  overt sexuality
  passion
  ambitious/hard-driving
  passion
  strength
  haste
  impatience
  energy

Body, Health
  head, headache
  fever, infection
  burns, bites
  inflammation
  high blood pressure
  hemorrhage

Metals
  iron, steel

Color
  red

Stones
  diamond
  bloodstone
  garnet
  red jasper

Herbs, Botanicals
  allspice
  basil
  dragon's blood
  hops

  pennyroyal
  pine
  wormwood

Jupiter ♃

Dignities
  Rules Sagittarius (and Pisces)
  Exalted: Cancer
  Detriment: Gemini (and Virgo)
  Fall: Capricorn
  Rules the ninth house (and twelfth
    house)

Element
  fire

Classifications
  warm and moist
  masculine
  positive polarity
  active/kinetic
  expansive

Direction
  south

Other Deity Names
  Zeus, Thor
  Hera, Juno

Keywords
  wisdom
  growth
  faith
  jovial
  benevolent
  geniality
  idealistic
  confident
  judgment
  idealism
  grandeur
  optimistic
  enthusiastic
  generous
  lucky
  increase
  leaders, dignitaries
  overindulgence
  extravagance
  broadminded

Body, Health
  liver
  hips, thighs

pituitary gland
growth
cancer

Metal
tin

Colors
royal purple
deep blue

Stones
amethyst
turquoise

Herbs, Botanicals
cloves
juniper berry
sage
witch grass
wood betony

Saturn ♄

Dignities
Rules Capricorn (and Aquarius)
Exalted: Libra
Detriment: Cancer (and Leo)
Fall: Aries
Rules the tenth house (and eleventh
house)

Element
earth

Classifications
cold and dry
masculine/feminine
negative polarity
contracting

Direction
north

Other Deity Names
Kronos
Juno, Kali, the Fates

Keywords
limitations
boundaries
manifestation
crystallization
control
ambitious
serious
responsible
disciplined

traditional
conservative
realist
status-seeking
authority, elders
solid, stable

Body, Health
skin
hair
teeth
bones
spleen
sense of hearing

Metal
lead

Colors
black
brown
lead

Stones
hematite
jet-black tourmaline
Apache tears
onyx

Herbs, Botanicals
patchouli
rue
cypress
hemlock
holly
hemp

Uranus ♅

Dignities
Rules Aquarius (modern ruler)
Exalted: Scorpio
Detriment: Leo
Fall: Taurus
Rules the eleventh house
Higher octave of Mercury

Element
air

Classifications
cold and moist
masculine
positive polarity
active/kinetic
erratic

Direction
east

Other Deity Names
Loki
Urania

Keywords
intellectual
detached
humanitarian
innovative
inspiration
eccentric
iconoclastic
rebellious
upset
tension
anarchy
nonconforming
revolutionary
independent
sudden change
breaks boundaries
inventive
new technology
suddenness
surprise

Body, Health
ankles
parathyroid gland
aura
accidents

Metals
radium
uranium

Color
electric blue

Stones
lapis lazuli
amber
lodestone

Herbs, Botanicals
peppermint
pine
sage
wormwood

Neptune Ψ

Dignities
Rules Pisces (modern ruler)
Exalted: Cancer

Detriment: Virgo
Fall: Capricorn
Rules the twelfth house
Higher octave of Venus

Element
water

Classifications
warm and moist
masculine/feminine
negative polarity
passive/magnetic
flexible, malleable

Direction
west

Other Deity Names
Poseidon
Mary, Yemaya, Isis

Keywords
dreamer
art, music
idealist
compassionate
savior or victim
fantasy
psychic experience
psychic healing
high spirituality
substance abuse
secrecy, deception
karma
escape
vague
foggy
nebulous
trance
unreality

Body, Health
pineal gland
psychic centers
feet
lymphatic system

Metal
platinum

Colors
sea green
mauve
opalescent colors

Stones
coral
jade

aquamarine
ivory

Herbs, Botanicals
chamomile
coltsfoot
eucalyptus
rose geranium
thyme

Pluto ♇

Dignities
Rules Scorpio (modern ruler)
Exalted: Aries
Detriment: Taurus
Fall: Libra
Rules the eighth house
Higher octave of Mars

Element
water

Classifications
hot and moist
masculine/feminine
negative polarity
intensely magnetic
sustaining

Direction
west

Other Deity Names
Hades
Hecate, Persephone

Keywords
phoenix
control
repression
power
intensity
passion
confronts darkness
probing
penetrating
regeneration
transformative
death, rebirth
renewal
elimination
eruption
compulsion
recycling
the occult

Body, Health
pancreas
metabolism
organs of elimination
sexual organs

Metals
plutonium
tungsten

Colors
deep red, burgundy

Stones
beryl
obsidian
lava rock
topaz

Herbs, Botanicals
devil's shoestring
dragon's blood
galangal root
musk
pennyroyal
wormwood

Elemental Correspondences

Earth

Taurus
Virgo
Capricorn
Venus
Ceres
Saturn
north
winter
body
form
stable
green
sensation (Jung)
pentacle
pentacles (Tarot)
salt
sand
soil
north declination
cold and moist
the Ox (Taurus)
feminine
negative polarity
yin

magnetic
Gnomes

Air

Gemini
Libra
Aquarius
Mercury
Pallas
Uranus
east
spring
mind
consciousness
logical
yellow
thinking (Jung)
swords (Tarot)
athame
incense
sunrise
cool and dry
the Man (Aquarius)
masculine
positive polarity
yang
kinetic
Sylphs

Fire

Aries
Leo
Sagittarius
Mars
Sun
Jupiter
south
summer
spirit
energy
impulsive
red

intuitive (Jung)
wands (Tarot)
wand
staff
candle
south declination
hot and dry
the Lion (Leo)
masculine
positive polarity
yang
kinetic
Salamanders

Water

Cancer
Scorpio
Pisces
Moon
Pluto
Neptune
west
fall, autumn
soul
subconscious
intuitive
blue
feeling (Jung)
emotional
cups (Tarot)
chalice
cauldron
liquid
sunset
warm and moist
the Eagle (Scorpio)
feminine
negative polarity
yin
magnetic
Undines

$\mathscr{Bibliography}$

Books

Books on Planetary Rulerships

Bills, Rex E. *The Rulership Book: A Directory of Astrological Correspondences.* Richmond, Va.: Macoy Publishing & Masonic Supply Co., Inc., 1971. This book is one to which I've referred for many years—an extensive and useful list of astrological correspondences. It is currently available in a new paperback edition, published by the AFA (American Federation of Astrologers) in 1993.

Devore, Nicholas. *Encyclopedia of Astrology.* New York City, N.Y.: Philosophical Library, MCMXLVH. The publication date in Roman numerals indicates how old my copy of this book is! It's a useful, old favorite reference of many astrologers.

George, Llewellyn. *Improved Perpetual Planetary Hour Book.* St. Paul, Minn.: Llewellyn Publishing, 1975. Out-of-print; first edition was published in 1906.

Lehman, J. Lee, Ph.D. *The Book of Rulerships: Keywords from Classical Astrology.* Atglen, Pa.: Schiffer, 2000. This one has an expected publication date of January 2000, too late for me to have seen it before turning in this bibliography. Still, based upon this author's expertise, I'm sure *The Book of Rulerships* will be a valuable resource.

Books on Electional Astrology

March, Marion D. and Joan McEvers. *The Only Way to Learn Horary and Electional Astrology.* San Diego, Calif.: ACS Publications, 1994. This book takes a very basic instructional approach, taking you through the rules of horary and electional astrology step by step. A wealth of short case studies demonstrates the process. I find this book quite easy to use as a quick reference.

Scofield, Bruce. *The Timing of Events: Electional Astrology.* Orleans, Mass.: Astrolabe, 1985. This is the only book I know of that is totally devoted to electional astrology. The author, who specializes in electional work, summarizes traditional rules and gives case studies and tips based on his specific methodology and experience. His methods include 90° dial work.

Books on Astrological Timing for Your Natal Chart

Simms, Maria Kay. *Future Signs: How to Make Astrological Predictions.* San Diego, Calif.: ACS Publications, 1996. A beginner's guide to working with transits (where the planets are in the cosmos at any given time) in comparison with your birth chart. Introductory material includes a discussion on fate versus free will, how to find and anticipate your transits, how to evaluate the relative importance of transits, plus a few anecdotal stories. Following that are interpretations of all aspects of transiting planets to birth-chart planets, including New Moons, Full Moons, and eclipses. The emphasis is on taking charge of your transits and choosing how you will "do" them, rather than waiting for them to happen.

Books on Correlating Astrology with Craft and Magickal Work

Alexander, Skye. *Magickal Astrology.* Franklin Lakes, N.J.: New Page Books, 2000. This book is considerably less technical than *A Time for Magick*, but is an excellent overview of magickal methods and lore, and of astrology. Interested astrologers who are curious about magick, as well as interested Pagans who are completely new to astrology, will find this a welcoming, informative, and enjoyable introduction.

Daniels, Estelle. *Astrologickal Magick.* York, Maine: Samuel Weiser, Inc., 1995. This book is considerably more technical in its approach to astrology than *A Time for Magick*. It gives instruction in basic natal astrology and in timing for readers who are interested in Pagan and magickal practice. Included is information on how to set up an electional chart, and how to assess one's birth chart for an inclination toward psychic ability. This would be a good next step if you want to progress into working with astrological charts and more advanced electional astrology work, while continuing with a magickal emphasis.

Pottenger, Maritha. *Encounter Astrology.* Los Angeles, Calif.: TIA Publications, 1978. Experiential astrology, or astro-drama, are generic terms for an individual or a group acting out planets, signs, or more complex astrological configurations in order to understand them on a more intuitive level. This book is a forerunner, written before the term "experiential astrology" was publicly identified. It has lots of games and exercises that could trigger ideas for astrological rituals.

Schermer, Barbara. *Astrology Alive!* Freedom, Calif.: Crossing Press, 1988. This book is considered the definitive "how-to" on experiential astrology, and its author is one of the more well-known leaders in this astrological specialty. This is another good potential source of stimulation for ritual ideas based on astrology.

Simms, Maria Kay. *Circle of the Cosmic Muse.* St. Paul, Minn.: Llewellyn Publishing, 1994. Second edition published in 1996 as *The Witch's Circle: Rituals and Craft of the Cosmic Muse.* Though this book covers the history, worldview, ethics and practice, and various aspects of coven activity in eclectic Wicca, its unique emphasis is on the astrological basis for its rituals. You'll find complete rituals for each of the eight Sabbats based on the sequential eightfold cycle as defined by Dane Rudhyar, which is described in chapter 3 of *A Time for Magick*. The approach to the astrology is nontechnical, experiential, and intuitive. Complete rituals for each Full Moon of the year are based on the zodiacal sign of the Moon as the complementary opposite to the sign of the Sun, and each ritual includes a magickal working appropriate to the sign of the Moon.

Other Books Referenced in the Text

Cunningham, Scott. *Cunningham's Encyclopedia of Magical Herbs*. St. Paul, Minn.: Llewellyn Publishing, 1985. This is most valuable reference for astrological and magickal correspondences for herbs—a book I keep close at hand and consult often.

Michelsen, Neil F. *Tables of Planetary Phenomena*. San Diego, Calif.: ACS Publications, 1990. This final book by Michelsen offers easy look-ups for a great many astrological configurations and phenomena that were previously difficult to research. Interesting articles precede each computer-generated table. Includes computer-drawn mandalas of planetary orbital patterns, such as the pentagram pattern of Venus, which I cited in a footnote to my Venus ritual in chapter 7 of *A Time for Magick*.

Resources

Astrological Calendars

Llewellyn Publishing. *Llewellyn's Daily Planetary Guide* and *Llewellyn's Astrological Pocket Planner*. (800) THE-MOON, www.llewellyn.com. Either of these two Llewellyn annuals would be preferred for your use of the quick-timing techniques in chapter 4 of this book if you choose to work with the minor aspects and/or the four major asteroids in your timing. The spiral-bound *Daily Planetary Guide* is an engagement book with plenty of space to write in your appointments. Aspects and times are listed on each day-block in both Eastern and Pacific Standard Times. The *Astrological Pocket Planner*, which was used in this book to illustrate the quick-timing examples, is a smaller version of the *Daily Planetary Guide*. It covers the current year with space to write in appointments, and astrological calendar data for the following year, as well. For times of aspects, you need to turn to the aspectarian in the back pages.

Maynard, Jim. *Celestial Influences*. Quicksilver Productions, P.O. Box 340, Ashland, Oreg. 97520. This is the wall calendar I keep near my computer and phone, and is distributed by many astrological bookshops and businesses. It has all the information you need to do the quick-timing techniques from chapter 4 of this book at a quick glance, with no extraneous clutter to sort through and no other pages you have to check. There's still space to jot down your own daily reminders. A full ephemeris for the month appears on each facing page, along with some art. An ephemeris of the four major asteroids, as well as one for declinations, can be found in the back pages of the calendar. The same clarity of format is available in a spiral-bound engagement book, *Celestial Guide*, and the small, purse-size *Pocket Astrologer*. All of these calendar options are available in a choice of either Eastern or Pacific Standard Time.

Mother Tongue Ink. *We'Moon*. www.amazon.com. This spiral-bound engagement book features astrological information that would make it useful for the timing techniques given in this book. Each page is beautifully illustrated with goddess art from a variety of artists.

Computer Software for Finding Planetary Hours

CCRS, Mark Pottenger, Astro Communications Services, San Diego, Calif., (800) 888-9983, or sales@astrocom.com. This is a full-service astrological calculation program available in DOS and Macintosh formats. It does virtually every kind of calculation astrologers would want to do and probably a few many of them would never think of, including, of course, calculating planetary hours. Not recommended for computer beginners, but those with computer expertise will be able to customize many options.

Merlin's Calends, P.O. Box 473, 3700 AL ZEIST, The Netherlands. This DOS program may or may not still be available at the above address. I once heard it has been made available as shareware, although I have not been able to verify that through an Internet search. It is designed for Wiccan use, to find the exact time of the Sabbats and Moon phases, and to find planetary hours. It includes text about the Sabbats.

Solar Fire, Esoteric Technologies Pty. Ltd., of Australia. This highly popular, full-service astrological calculation program is distributed in the United States by Astrolabe (508-896-5081, www.alabe.com), and, through them, a number of other astrological businesses, including ACS. The chart entry system is easy enough for beginners. The full ACS atlas with coordinates and time changes for over 250,000 locations is included. When you have a chart up on your screen or call up a chart, you can get the planetary hour for it very quickly by clicking on "Reports," and then "Horary." This is how I checked the planetary hours of birth for the celebrity list in appendix 1 of *A Time for Magick*.

Sundial, Arlene Kramer, (818) 999-2389, arlenekramer.com, or ArleneKrmr@aol.com. This software, still in a DOS format at this writing, is soon to be released in an updated Windows version, which will include instant access to the ACS mini-atlas of about 9,000 locations. Even in the DOS version, this software is easy to use, but you do have to enter your location's longitude, latitude, and current time zone, according to whether it is standard time or daylight saving time. In the new Windows version, the coordinates and proper time zone and changes for the locations in the mini-atlas will be available instantly when you enter the city. For locations not in the atlas, the user will still be able to enter the coordinates and time zone, thus adding them to the database. This program prints out easy reference listings of the planetary hours—and the planetary minutes, if you wish—for each day in the clock time of the location. No interpolation needed—planetary hours are available at a glance!

Interpretive Computer Software for Astrology Beginners
The Electronic Astrologer Reveals Your Future.
The Electronic Astrologer Reveals Your Horoscope.
The Electronic Astrologer Reveals Your Love Life.

Rique Pottenger, computer programmer, ACS Publications, San Diego, Calif. (800) 888-9983, or sales@astrocom.com. Each of the above programs, or all three, can be obtained on a CD, including the indispensable ACS atlas. The entering of birth data to calculate a chart is the easiest to be found on any astrological software, and the amount of interpretive text is incredible—more than you'll find on much more expensive report-writing software intended for business purposes. Extensive, easy-to-use help functions provide entire teach-yourself textbooks on basic astrology. Charts come up in seconds after data is entered, and a click of the mouse on anything in the chart brings up an instant interpretation.

EA Horoscope contains interpretive text from *Easy Astrology Guide*, an excellent book on natal astrology by Maritha Pottenger.
EA Future contains the interpretive text from my book *Future Signs for Transits*, as well as information about secondary progressions from *Unveiling Your Future* by Maritha Pottenger and Zipporah Dobyns. EA Love Life contains the text and chart comparison method from Maritha Pottenger's book *A Starway to Love*.

Computer Software for Astrological Research
AstroDatabank, www.astrodatabank.com. Lois Rodden and Mark McDonough, AstroDataBank Company, 25 Raymond St., Manchester, Mass. 01944-1614, (978) 526-8864. A CD of the full research software, with its vast database and features, is available, or data selections can be ordered from the website. This program has become an indispensable aid to astrological research. For full information, check the website, which is worth a frequent look for its free features on people currently in the news. All those who own the software can subscribe to an e-mail service to receive interesting news about news making personalities.

Complete Astrology Services
Astro Communications Services, (ACS), 5521 Ruffin Road, San Diego, Calif. 92123, (800) 888-9983, (858) 492-9919, www.astrocom.com, or sales@astrocom. com. A huge product line of astrological calculations, interpreted reports, books, software, and gift items—everything for any level of astrological interest from beginner to professional. Order by phone or online. Very fast turn-around—orders normally go out the same day or next. All calculations and reports can be delivered in format by e-mail (though you won't get the reports bound with pretty color covers that way). Catalog available on request.

Additional Internet Websites

Starcrafts, www.starcraftsob.com. This is my daughter Molly Sullivan's store in Ocean Beach, Calif. You'll find the daily Moon phase on the main page. The website is updated prior to every Sabbat with seasonal lore, recipes, and a personal ritual. It's a pretty website, with a wealth of information about herbs and the Craft, including several articles by, of course, Molly's mom.

StarIQ, www.stariq.com. A treasure house of astrological information on all levels and all topics. The interpretations for each New Moon period by Jeff Jawer are excellent. Of particular interest to readers of this book is a series of articles by Rob Hand on astrology and magic.

Index